INTERNET OF THINGS

Technological Advances and New Applications

INTERNET OF THINGS

Technological Advances and New Applications

Edited by
Brojo Kishore Mishra
Amit Vishwasrao Salunkhe

APPLE
ACADEMIC
PRESS

First edition published 2024

Apple Academic Press Inc.
1265 Goldenrod Circle, NE,
Palm Bay, FL 32905 USA

760 Laurentian Drive, Unit 19,
Burlington, ON L7N 0A4, CANADA

CRC Press
2385 NW Executive Center Drive,
Suite 320, Boca Raton FL 33431

4 Park Square, Milton Park,
Abingdon, Oxon, OX14 4RN UK

© 2024 by Apple Academic Press, Inc.

Apple Academic Press exclusively co-publishes with CRC Press, an imprint of Taylor & Francis Group, LLC

Library and Archives Canada Cataloguing in Publication

Title: Internet of things : technological advances and new applications / edited by Brojo Kishore Mishra,
    Amit Vishwasrao Salunkhe.
Other titles: Internet of things (Apple Academic Press)
Names: Mishra, Brojo Kishore, 1979- editor. | Salunkhe, Amit Vishwasrao editor.
Description: First edition. | Includes bibliographical references and index.
Identifiers: Canadiana (print) 20220482012 | Canadiana (ebook) 20220482039 | ISBN 9781774911280 (hardcover) |
    ISBN 9781774911297 (softcover) | ISBN 9781003304609 (ebook)
Subjects: LCSH: Internet of things. | LCSH: Internet of things—Industrial applications.
Classification: LCC TK5105.8857 .I58 2023 | DDC 004.67/8—dc23

Library of Congress Cataloging-in-Publication Data

Names: Mishra, Brojo Kishore, 1979- editor. | Salunkhe, Amit Vishwasrao, editor.
Title: Internet of things : technological advances and new applications / edited by Brojo Kishore Mishra,
    Amit Vishwasrao Salunkhe.
Other titles: Internet of things (Apple Academic Press)
Description: First edition. | Palm Bay, FL, USA : Apple Academic Press Inc.; Boca Raton, FL, USA : CRC Press, 2023. |
    Includes bibliographical references and index. | Summary: "The Internet of Things has revolutionized many industries
    and sectors by connecting devices to the Internet with the use of smart sensors and actuators, resulting in many advantages
    to businesses and organizations, such as better information and resource sharing, better supply chain efficiency, among
    other benefits, resulting in better overall efficiency and cost savings. Internet of Things: Technological Advances and New
    Applications investigates the potential for initiating data-enabled and IoT-intensive applications to provide control and
    optimization of industrial operations and services. It presents an informative selection of quantitative research, case studies,
    conceptual chapters, model articles, theoretical backing, and more on many important technological advances, applications,
    and challenges in the current status of Internet of Things (IoT). The book features examples of IoT applications in such areas
    as food processing, automotive engineering, mental health, health tracking, security, and more. It discusses applying IoT in
    reverse logistics processes, developments in the Internet of Vehicles, the use of smart antennas, and machine learning in IoT.
    One chapter discusses a ground-breaking new device that uses IoT to convert audio recordings to Braille. Also discussed
    is the growing use of IoT in biometric technology (the use of technology to identify a person based on some aspect of their
    biology, such as fingerprint and eye unique pattern recognition). The enlightening information shared here offers state-
    of-the-art IoT solutions to many of today's challenges of improving efficiency and bringing important information to the
    surface more quickly than systems depending on human intervention. The volume will be of value for computer science
    engineers and researchers, instructors and students in the field, and professionals that are interested in exploring the areas
    of next-generations IoT"-- Provided by publisher.
Identifiers: LCCN 2022056129 (print) | LCCN 2022056130 (ebook) | ISBN 9781774911280 (hbk) | ISBN 9781774911297 (pbk) |
    ISBN 9781003304609 (ebk)
Subjects: LCSH: Internet of things.
Classification: LCC TK5105.8857 .I558 2023 (print) | LCC TK5105.8857 (ebook) | DDC 004.67/8--dc23/eng/20230106
LC record available at https://lccn.loc.gov/2022056129
LC ebook record available at https://lccn.loc.gov/2022056130

ISBN: 978-1-77491-128-0 (hbk)
ISBN: 978-1-77491-129-7 (pbk)
ISBN: 978-1-00330-460-9 (ebk)

About the Editors

Brojo Kishore Mishra, PhD, is Associate Dean (International Affairs) and Professor in the Computer Science and Engineering Department at the Gandhi Institute of Engineering and Technology University (GIET), Gunupur, Odisha, India. He has published more than 40 research papers in national and international conference proceedings, over 50 research papers in peer-reviewed and indexed journals, and over 37 book chapters. He has authored two books and edited eight books to date. His research interests include data mining and big data analysis, machine learning, soft computing, and evolutionary computation. He received his PhD degree in Computer Science from the Berhampur University, Brahmapur, Odisha, India.

Amit Vishwasrao Salunkhe, is currently working as Assistant Director of the Approval Bureau at the All India Council for Technical Education, New Delhi, India, and also as Additional Charge of the Regional Officer for the All India Council for Technical Education–Northern Regional Office, Kanpur. He received a best paper award on "Estimation of fat content in fresh milk using carbon rod." He has published more than 10 papers in SCI/SCIE and Scopus-indexed journals as well as more than 12 papers at international conferences. His research interests include neuro-fuzzy systems, artificial intelligence, and programming and coding.

Contents

Contributors .... *ix*

Abbreviations .... *xiii*

Preface .... *xvii*

1. **Compelling Forces and Challenges for the Food Processing Industry to Adopt Industry 4.0** 1
   S. Ranjith Kumar, N. Ramachandran, R. Sivasubramanian,
   J. Dhiyaneswaran, and Arun Kurien Reji

2. **Sensing Mental Health: A New Mileage to Mental Health Research** 17
   Sharmistha Dey

3. **How the IoT (Internet of Things) Is Poised to Jump-Start the Next Revolution** 37
   Aradhana Behura

4. **Implementation of the Industrial Internet of Things (IIoT) Is the Tool of Digital Transformation Technology** 61
   Kali Charan Rath, Raghvendra Kumar, and Brojo Kishore Mishra

5. **Opportunities for the Internet of Things in Automotives** 85
   R. B. Manoram, A. Sathishkumar, T. Devaarjun,
   Samson Jerold Samuel Chelladurai, and T. A. Selvan

6. **IoT Security** 101
   Nidhi Upadhyay

7. **Leveraging IIoT in Reverse Logistics: A WSN Approach** 119
   Vinod Kumar Shukla, Leena Wanganoo, Mohammed Yousuf, and Rajesh Tripathi

8. **A Pervasive Study on the Internet of Vehicles (IoVs)** 141
   Lopamudra Hota and Prasant Kumar Dash

9. **The Future Security Solution to the Internet of Things: Biometric Technology** 163
   Puja Agarwal, Anjana Mishra, and Brojo Kishore Mishra

10. Transforming Industries Using IoT...175
    Ritwik Raj, Tannu Kumari, and Amardeep Das

11. *Audio-to-Braille* Conversion Device (A.B.C.D): An IoT Application 187
    Subham Hati, Tulika Biswas, Suvam Saha, Sourabh Kr. Bania,
    Prafull Shyam, and Srijan Bhattacharya

12. Internet of Things: Applied Science and Technologies...........................201
    Deepti Mishra and Bhairvee Singh

13. Health Tracking System Using the Internet of Things 223
    Anshu Yadav, Tanisha Rastogi, and Deepak Kumar Sharma

14. Smart Antennas in IoT-Based Systems 269
    Shailesh and Garima Srivastava

15. Necessity of Time Synchronization for IoT-Based Applications............285
    Priyanka Singh and Manju Khari

16. A Review on Applications of Machine Learning in IoT:
    Challenges and Future Prospects 299
    Subrata Paul and Anirban Mitra

17. A Detailed Review of IoT with Various Applications
    Using Recent Research Directions...331
    A. Vidhyalakshmi and C. Priya

Index...*357*

Contributors

Puja Agarwal
C. V. Raman Global University, Bhubaneshwar, Odisha, India

Aradhana Behura
Gandhi Institute for Technological Advancement, Bhubaneswar, India

Sourabh Kr. Bania
Applied Electronics & Instrumentation Engineering Department, RCC Institute of Information Technology, Kolkata, India

Srijan Bhattacharya
Applied Electronics & Instrumentation Engineering Department, RCC Institute of Information Technology, Kolkata, India

Tulika Biswas
Applied Electronics & Instrumentation Engineering Department, RCC Institute of Information Technology, Kolkata, India

Samson Jerold Samuel Chelladurai
Senior Specialist, Accenture Technologies, Bengaluru, India

Amardeep Das
C. V. Raman Polytechnic, Bhubaneswar, Odisha, India

Prasant Kumar Dash
C. V. Raman Global University, Bhubaneswar, Odisha, India

T. Devaarjun
Senior Specialist, Accenture Technologies, Bengaluru, India

Sharmistha Dey
Brainware University, Kolkata, West Bengal, India

J. Dhiyaneswaran
Department of Mechanical Engineering, Sri Krishna College of Engineering and Technology, Coimbatore, India

Subham Hati
Applied Electronics & Instrumentation Engineering Department, RCC Institute of Information Technology, Kolkata, India

Lopamudra Hota
National Institute of Technology, Rourkela, Odisha, India

Manju Khari
School of Computer and System Sciences, Jawaharlal Nehru University, New Delhi, India

Raghvendra Kumar
GIET University, Odisha, India

S. Ranjith Kumar
Department of Mechanical Engineering, Sri Krishna College of Engineering and Technology, Coimbatore, India

Tannu Kumari
Department of Computer Science Engineering, C.V. Raman Global University, Bhubaneswar, Odisha, India

R. B. Manoram
Department of Mechanical Engineering, Sri Krishna College of Engineering and Technology, Coimbatore, India

Anjana Mishra
C. V. Raman Global University, Bhubaneshwar, Odisha, India

Brojo Kishore Mishra
GIET University, Odisha, India

Deepti Mishra
Department of CSE, G.L. Bajaj Institute of Technology and Management, Greater Noida, India

Anirban Mitra
Department of CSE, ASET, Amity University, Kolkata, West Bengal, India

Subrata Paul
Department of CSE, Brainware University, Barasat, West Bengal, India

C. Priya
Department Of Information Technology, Vels Institute of Science, Technology and Advanced Studies (VISTAS) Chennai, Tamil Nadu, India

Ritwik Raj
Department of Computer Science and Information Technology, C.V. Raman Global University, Bhubaneswar, Odisha, India

N. Ramachandran
Department of Mechanical Engineering, Sri Krishna College of Engineering and Technology, Coimbatore, India

Tanisha Rastogi
Department of Information Technology, Netaji Subhas University of Technology, (Formerly Netaji Subhas Institute of Technology), New Delhi, India

Kali Charan Rath
GIET University, Odisha, India

Arun Kurien Reji
Department of Mechanical Engineering, Sri Krishna College of Engineering and Technology, Coimbatore, India

Suvam Saha
Applied Electronics & Instrumentation Engineering Department, RCC Institute of Information Technology, Kolkata, India

Amit Vishwasrao Salunkhe
Approval Bureau, All India Council for Technical Education, New Delhi, India

A. Sathishkumar
Department of Mechanical Engineering, Sri Krishna College of Engineering and Technology, Coimbatore, India

T. A. Selvan
Department of Mechanical Engineering, Sri Krishna College of Engineering and Technology, Coimbatore, India

Shailesh
Guru Gobind Singh Indraprastha University, Sector 16 C, Dwarka, Delhi 110078, India

Deepak Kumar Sharma
Department of Information Technology, Netaji Subhas University of Technology, (Formerly Netaji Subhas Institute of Technology), New Delhi, India

Prafull Shyam
Applied Electronics & Instrumentation Engineering Department, RCC Institute of Information Technology, Kolkata, India

Vinod Kumar Shukla
Department of Engineering and Architecture, Amity University, Dubai, U.A.E.

Bhairvee Singh
Department of CSE, G.L. Bajaj Institute of Technology and Management, Greater Noida, India

Priyanka Singh
Department of Computer Science, NSUT, East Campus, New Delhi, India

R. Sivasubramanian
Department of Mechanical Engineering, Sri Krishna College of Engineering and Technology, Coimbatore, India
NSUT East Campus, Geeta Colony, New Delhi, Delhi, India

Garima Srivastava
NSUT East Campus, Geeta Colony, New Delhi, Delhi, India

Rajesh Tripathi
Department of General Management, University of petroleum and Energy Studies, Dehradun

Nidhi Upadhyay
Department of Computer Science and Engineering, Vivekananda College of Technology and Management, Aligarh, Uttar Pradesh, India

A. Vidhyalakshmi
Research Scholar, Department of Computer Science, Vels Institute of Science, Technology and Advanced Studies (VISTAS), Chennai, Tamil Nadu, India

Leena Wanganoo
Research Scholar, University of Petroleum and Energy Studies, Dehradun, India

Anshu Yadav
Department of Information Technology, Netaji Subhas University of Technology, (Formerly Netaji Subhas Institute of Technology), New Delhi, India

Mohammed Yousuf
Amity University Dubai, U.A.E.

Abbreviations

ABCD	Audio to Braille Conversion Device
ACO	multi-ant colony
AI	artificial intelligence
AM	additive manufacturing
AML	adversarial machine learning
API	application programming interface
App	application
ARC	automatic risk checker
AR/VR	augmented reality/virtual reality
BAN	body area network
BLE	Bluetooth low energy technology
CA	cloud application
CAD	computer-aided design
CAM	computer-aided manufacturing
CBM	condition-based maintenance
CBMF	cloud business model framework
CE	consumer electronics
CEP	complex event processing
CGM	continuous glucose monitoring
CI	cyber interface
CNC	computer numerical control
CoAP	constrained application protocol
COPD	chronic obstructive pulmonary disease
CPS	cyber physical systems
CVOs	composite virtual objects
CYCORE	cyber infrastructure for comparative effectiveness research
DCS	distributed control system
DDoS	distributed denial of service
DL	deep learning
DNC	direct numerical control
DoS	denial-of-service
DSMS	data stream management system
DSRC	dedicated short-range communication
DT	decision tree

D2D	device-to-device communication
EPC	electronic product code
EPCDS	EPC discovery service
EPCIS	EPC information services
EPCSS	EPC security services
ETC	electric toll collection
GAN	generative adversarial network
GDPR	general data protection regulation
HADS	hospital anxiety and depression scale
HMM	hidden markov method
HTTP	hypertext transfer protocol
IIoT	Industrial Internet of Things
IOE	Internet of Everything
IoT	Internet of Things
IoV	Internet of Vehicle
IP	internet protocol
ISM	industrial, scientific, and medical
IT	information technology
ITS	intelligent transport system
LoRaWAN	long-range wide area network
LoRaWANP	low-power wide area network protocol
LPWAN	low-power wide area network
LSI	local status indicator
MAE	mean absolute error
MAPE	mean absolute percentage error
MEMS	miniaturized scale electromechanical frameworks
MIMO	multiple-input and multi-output
ML	machine learning
MQTT	Message Queuing Telemetry Transport
MQTTP	messaging queuing telemetry transport protocol
MRP	material necessities arranging
M2M	machine-to-machine
NB-IoT	narrow-band IoT
NC	numerical control
NFC	near field communication
NSF	National Science Foundation
OEE	overall equipment effectiveness
ONS	Object Naming Service
OT	operating technologies

PAN	personal area networks
PIR	passive infrared
PLC	programmable logic control
PLM	product lifecycle control
ProSe	proximity service
PTSD	post-traumatic stress disorder
QOS	quality of service
QR	quick response
RBDS	Refreshable Braille Display System
RL	reverse logistics
RFID	radio frequency identification
ROI	return on investment
RUERC	rotational unique encrypted reference code
SoC	system-on-chip
SIM	subscriber identity module
STAI	state-trait anxiety inventory
SUDUN	suspected user data uploader node
SUMO	simulation of urban mobility
SVM	support vector machine
TCP/IP	Transmission Control Protocol/Internet Protocol
TMC	traffic management center
UERC	unique encrypted reference code
UI	user interface
UNS	ubiquitous networked society
URLLC	ultra-reliable and low latency communication
VMs	virtual machines
VOs	virtual objects
V2X	vehicle-to-everything
WAVE	wireless access in vehicular environment
Wi-Fi	wireless fidelity
Wi-SUN	wireless smart ubiquitous network
WLAN	wireless local area network
WSNs	wireless sensor networks
XMQP	extensible message and queuing protocol

Preface

The Internet of Things has revolutionized industries by connecting devices to the internet, which facilitated in the cumulative profit of the economy. This edited book contains quantitative research, case studies, conceptual chapters, model articles, review book chapters, theoretical backing, etc. This edited book will help to explore areas where intelligent Industrial Internet of Things (IIoT) could help other emerging technologies for delivering more efficient services. We believe our readers will be provided with the required information to manage current and future demand with the help of IIoT.

This book features 17 selected chapters with the current and highly relevant topics in the Industrial Internet of Things (IIoT).

Chapter 1 discusses the how the food processing industry is bound to adopt the latest trend as well as the challenges faced after adopting the new technology.

Chapter 2 discusses the state of the art of research on several mental health issues, their impact on human lives, and the approaches of their detection or prediction in coordination with machine learning and Internet of Things.

Chapter 3 describes the role of IoT in agriculture for the implementation of smart farming. It describes the various component of IoT, like network architecture, various applications, network topologies used and protocol. IoT-based smart farming includes cloud computing, big data, storage, and analysis of IoT sensor-based devices for better management of smart farming.

Chapter 4 explains the concept of IoT and IIoT with their application layout in digital manufacturing. The chapter also defines the application of IIoT in an assembling framework in association with computerized-assisted techniques.

Chapter 5 discusses the advancements of IoT in the automotive industry, like self-driving cars, intelligent transport system, predictive maintenance, electric toll collection, and smart parking.

Chapter 6 discusses IoT security, different types of attacks, its effect, and prevention. It explains the challenges of IoT security and also the application of it.

Chapter 7 proposes a real-time routing framework supported by new wireless sensor networks (WSNs) implementations. This WSNs-based real-time fault-tolerant system assists routing systems with a LSI on each sensor node to monitor and evaluate local node and channel conditions.

Chapter 8 provides an insight for researchers for pursing their research in this field and to enhance vehicular and traffic management. The basics related to applications and work done in IoV along with open challenges and future direction are provided in detail. Additionally, the work also provides several architectural sketches of IoV technology for better understanding of network structure of IoVs.

Chapter 9 talks about the Internet of Things and biometric security, the issues related to IoT devices, discussion on biometrics, need of enhanced security for the devices, use of IoT devices in different sectors, and the pros and cons of integrating biometric with IoT.

Chapter 10 tells about the discovery of Industrial IoT, its advancement in the modern time. This chapter helps in understanding the need of IoT in industries, its benefits, and the challenges faced by it. It also discusses the Industry 4.0 and the threats of Industrial IoT.

Chapter 11 talks about the Audio to Braille Conversion Device (A.B.C.D), designed to teach braille key by converting the speech from the user using an android application and sending the message to the NodeMcu, which converts each character to its corresponding braille key.

Chapter 12 focuses on the technologies meant and used for operating IoT. The chapter elaborates on the detailed specifications of enabling technologies utilized for the Internet of Things. It covers all security and integration related issues in detail. It also explores the relationship of IoT with other emerging technologies and their effect on each other.

Chapter 13 discuses the various health tracking devices using IoT and also summarizes that how health care systems using IoT are much beneficial.

Chapter 14 discusses the different sorts of MIMO antennas such as ultra wideband (UWB), single band, and multiband. The UWB MIMO antennas are utilized in flexible IoT wireless devices, lower 5G bands, and different wireless and IoT devices. The single band MIMO antenna discovers applications in 4G, 5G, and IoT devices. Multiband MIMO antenna is helpful in various wireless communication having frequency bands that are alluring for the IoT gadgets, 4G/5G for cell phones.

Chapter 15 discusses the basic concept of IoT, its related technologies, protocols, standards, and basic applications of IoT and the related issues that require precise time synchronization and the high connectivity technologies.

Chapter 16 presents a review on application of machine learning in IoT and discusses major issues and challenges faced during the application.

Chapter 17 presents the recent development of IoT technologies and discusses ThingSpeak and its connectivity with IoT.

Thanks to the contributors the authors, reviewers, and our family members for their support. Also editors are thankful to the members of Apple Academic Press for their constant support for completion of this project.

Brojo Kishoro Mishra
Amit Vishwasrao Salunkhe

CHAPTER 1

Compelling Forces and Challenges for the Food Processing Industry to Adopt Industry 4.0

S. RANJITH KUMAR, N. RAMACHANDRAN, R. SIVASUBRAMANIAN, J. DHIYANESWARAN, and ARUN KURIEN REJI

Department of Mechanical Engineering, Sri Krishna College of Engineering and Technology, Coimbatore, India

ABSTRACT

In today's competitive market, each and every industry or any business enterprises strive hard to sustain their position. As the technology gets upgraded at each and every phase, organizations and enterprises are forced to adopt the technologies. The technology that the industries and business enterprises want to embrace in the current scenario is Industry 4.0. German industrial giants in the year 2011 showcased Industry 4.0 at an Expo. Different companies like Cisco, GE called this technology with different names such as Internet of Services, Industrial Internet, etc., and at last this was named as a paradigm by the network specialists in the communication sector as Industry 4.0. The concepts and technological aspects caught the eyes of all industries across the globe. This technology later spread to other European continents and it is in the phase of introduction in Asian countries. Industrial Internet of Things are also an integrated component of Industry 4.0. Since it is the fourth technological advancement in the industry, it is named as Industry 4.0. The evolution starts from the first phase which is mechanization started in the beginning

Internet of Things: Technological Advances and New Applications. Brojo Kishore Mishra & Amit Vishwasrao Salunkhe (Eds.)

of the 18th century followed by the introduction of assembly lines in the verge of the 20th century. Examples are the Cincinnati slaughterhouse where a large volume of meat is sheared, cut packed into different parts and dispatched. The same methodology was reversed by employed by Henry Ford in the automobile assembly lines where smaller components are integrated together to formulate a car or any kind of automobile. The third industrial revolution started in the early 1970s with the introduction of internet and electronics followed by the Industrial revolution 4.0 which is the cyber-physical systems. This chapter focuses on how a food processing industry is compelled to adopt the latest trend as well as the challenges faced after adopting the new technology.

1.1   INTRODUCTION

1.1.1   COMPELLING FORCES FOR AN INDUSTRY TO ADOPT NEW TECHNOLOGY

The vision behind all the food processing industries is to deliver food products with utmost safety incorporating quality. And meeting the customers' demand is also a major goal. And this demand is regarding the identification of exotic products related to food and also researches to add fewer preservatives and additives. In the fourth phase of the Industrial Revolution, organizations and enterprises strive hard to book a place for themselves in the market. This might be either for the enhancement of their product, process, and service. Automation plays a major role in the food processing industry. The standards are also stringent for the products as well as for the processing methodology. The methodology devised for each and every industry will vary based upon their type of the product, capacity, specification, demand, etc., and other respective parameters. The implementation of the framework proposed by Industry 4.0 is a need for the industry in general, and for any food industry in particular, and should be seen as a great opportunity of progress for the sector.[1] Figure 1.1 depicts a generic information on the flow of a normal food processing industry. The layout looks simple but each and every step involves many intriguing steps to move on further to the next step. A common food processing industry runs with the following process controlling machineries, such as a drier, blower, filter, etc., and the energy supplying machineries include boiler, turbine, motor, gearboxes, etc.

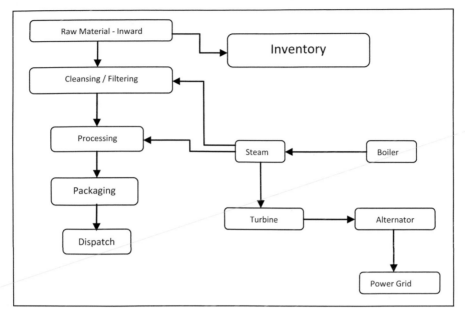

FIGURE 1.1   Generic representation of the flow of a food processing industry.

1.1.2   COST REDUCTION AND MINIATURIZATION OF SENSORS

Raw material purchases are to be done based upon the demand for the product in the market and supply chain analysis. Many industries face a lot of issues while purchasing raw materials and other inventory goods. Raw materials and few chemicals that are utilized in the food processing industry will have a shelf life. The prescribed shelf life is the maximum aging parameter of the product. The storage parameters are also to be well maintained in terms of humidity, temperature, air, etc. Normally a company which operates on a traditional management will not calculate the purchases of the demand and the supply. This attitude can be totally eradicated by means of any technological adoption such as Industry 4.0. By means of data analytics, forecasting can be done for a longer run and wastage incurring in the purchases and inventory goods can be reduced on higher rate. In the recent trends, sensors that are integrated to receive the input are overall miniaturized. Instead of having limit switches and relays, a proximity sensor or a signal deducer can be integrated in the component to reduce the overall cost in terms of sensory equipment. This becomes a basic reason for the compulsion force for an organization to adopt Industry 4.0.

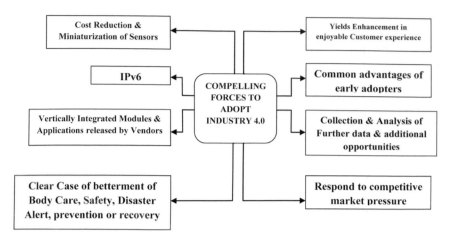

FIGURE 1.2   Compelling forces for an organization to adopt Industry 4.0.

1.1.3   IPV6 ADDRESSING

The internet protocol of version 6 has been introduced in the year 1999. Communications happen in a faster rate in terms of IPv6 rather than the previous version which is IPv4. The latter runs only on a 32 bit, whereas the former communicates with a unit of 128 bits. Moreover IPv4 consists only of numerical values to ascertain the interfaces and IPv6 consists of alphanumeric codes which engages the communication at a faster pace.[4] As the communication aspect has seen a global growth in terms of the interfaces organizations are more compelled to move on to the next technological phase. Intranet and extranet communications are an important communication aspect for an industry. A huge food processing industry must be comprised of both these facilities. Figure 1.3 depicts the block representation of a communication model in the food processing industry.

So interfaces and communications at a faster pace are possible only in IPv6, and this obviously becomes a compelling factor for organizations to adopt the recent trend.

1.1.4   VERTICALLY INTEGRATED MODULES AND APPLICATIONS RELEASED BY VENDORS

Vertical integration has become more popular after the introduction of internet. It became a mandatory concept in the field of manufacturing. The sole concept lies within the phrase "The owner becomes the seller." This is a common concept prevailing in the field of the food processing industry. The product is sold directly to the market by the manufacturer by transforming themselves as a retailer. Figure 1.4 represents the orientation of the respective processes by means of three types, namely, forward, backward, and balanced integration. When the processes lead on to packing, marketing, and selling in the markets, the wholesome dealership is taken by the organization itself. This is known as forward integration. When manufacturing a sole food product say for example a sugar manufacturing industry the final product is obviously sugar. When processing sugar, the reprocessing methodology delivers two other products such as molasses for the distillery plant which produces spirit which is widely used in the medical field. And the sugarcane, when it is crushed and fiberized we will get a final product at the end which is called as bagasse. This bagasse will be utilized internally as a fuel for the boiler. This process represents a backward integration methodology. And when both the forward and backward integrations are interfaced, then it will be called as balanced integration. As well as software applications development solely for the usage of suppliers and vendors such as supplier management system, vendor management system, dealer management systems, etc., force the organization to employ the new technological trend so as to pick a spot in the market.

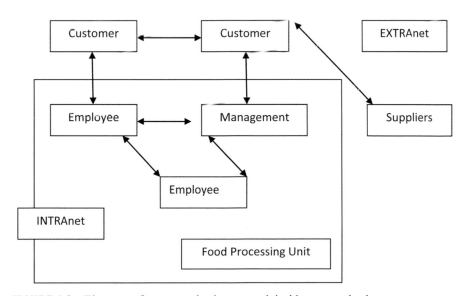

FIGURE 1.3   Elements of a communication network inside an organization.

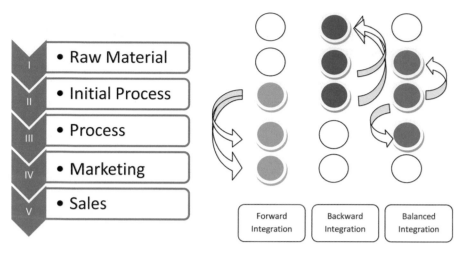

FIGURE 1.4   Types of integration methods in a manufacturing industry.

1.1.5   SAFETY

As the technological trend gets upgraded safety of the human being should also be considered. In the case of heavy food processing industries, safety is considered as a biggest challenge. This is because of the operating conditions of heavy machineries and equipment, such as boiler, turbine, steam lines, evaporators, heat exchangers, filters, large rotary equipment, etc. These types of industries always search for the betterment of safety of the employers. This can be totally rectified by employing Industry 4.0 technology in their plant. By adopting this technology, the machineries will be interfaced with other machineries, feedbacks will be continuously sent back and forth from the human–machine interface. Buzzers, sirens, signals will indicate anomalies in a machinery or process. Predictive analytics which is a subset of Industry 4.0 forecasts the processes and the trend of the market by means of the data stored through machine learning. By forecasting the machinery trend and the process alerts the employers can surely avoid accidents. By means of sensors measured, such as temperature, pressure, power, toxic gas anomalies, radiations, etc., it can be physically detected and converted into a digital format to give the alert to the user remotely. Even if the other forces do not compel the organization to adopt the new trend a clear case of the betterment of body care, safety, disaster alert, prevention or recovery will surely be a case of compulsion for the organization to adopt

Industry 4.0. As Industry 4.0 is upon us, it is time for Safety 4.0 to develop. The goal behind the latest trend is that to protect the industrial space which in turn increases productivity. Similarly, protection of the employer from occupational hazards plays a parallel role in the competitive advantage by reducing many safety management-related costs. The European Framework Directive on Safety and Health at Work (Directive 89/391 EEC) motivate the employers to be stringent in their working attitude and also to take up more preventive measures to enable the working culture healthier and a safer one with respect to the general management processes.[2] In this perspective, stringent regulations slated by the government and by the national bodies and international bodies play as a directive for the organizations in the light of safety awareness. And to avoid the hefty fines caused for violating the regulations and to protect the reputation of the industry, the management strive hard to protect the lines toward the protection of the occupational health and safety of the employee.

1.1.6 YIELDS ENHANCEMENT IN ENJOYABLE CUSTOMER EXPERIENCE

The rating given by the customers is based upon only by their experience with the respective product. This leads the management to put the customers in the first place in whatever they do. This in turn will increase the productivity and improve the satisfaction of the customers and simultaneously it will lead to an increase the profits. This will pave way for the organizations to walk along with the customer and the consumer to understand the nerve. The assessment can be made by taking online and live surveys, market analysis, feedbacks, etc. This will pave way for the manufacturer to identify the bottlenecks in the market and in turn strive to make the product and enjoyable experience for both the manufacturer and the consumer.

Customer experience is nothing but the experiences with the customer in parallel with the whole travel from the beginning of signing the contract of being your customer till now. This will transform the attitude of money-making and consuming into a loyal manufacturer and a happy customer.

Figure 1.5 represents the trend of all the relative business opportunities and in which customer experience stands a top with 20% of the overall statistics. Whereas in Figure 1.6, the loyalty of a customer experience is depicted. If a customer is not satisfied with the outcome, he is always willing to pay a better price to move on to your competitor. By employing Industry 4.0 as a forerunner, an organization will enhance in all its positive impacts which will have a mutual growth one being the customer and the other is the organization. So to walk hand-in-hand with the customer on a long run and to enhance the enjoyable experience an organization or an enterprise is compelled to adopt Industry 4.0 and to transform itself into a smart factory.

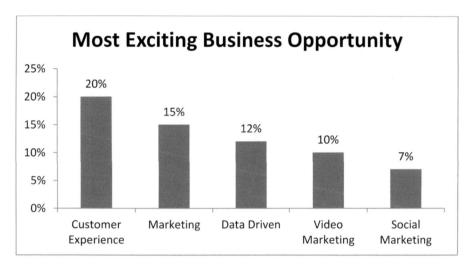

FIGURE 1.5   Trend of the business opportunities.

FIGURE 1.6   Customer loyalty & experience.

1.1.7 COMMON ADVANTAGES OF EARLY ADOPTERS

An early adopter is considered to be most experienced and the influential person in the market. They will in transform themselves as a leader when compared to the late adopters. These people who are considered as the early adopters generally have a higher level of socioeconomic status when compared with the other type of potential adopters. Accessibility to a newer tech and knowledge will not be far from them. Internet technology related teachers, trainers, and educators are the most important people in the market and are highly recommended early adopters, and it is a must for them to embrace the technology at a more initial pace.[9]

The best example is Nokia mobile phone manufacturer. When Google Co. introduced Android software for the smart phones all the mobile phone manufacturing companies went for the offer and incorporated the android software in their products. But Nokia wanted to follow the same old trend and did not succeed in the mobile phone market. Whereas other mobile phone manufacturers succeeded. The only reason is being the early adopters.

1.1.8 COLLECTION & ANALYSIS OF FURTHER DATA AND ADDITIONAL OPPORTUNITIES

Figure 1.7 depicts the usability of data in terms of risk prediction. By means of employing machine learning technology, the data collected is fed into the machine and a certain algorithm technique such as logistic regression, linear regression, and Gaussian distribution formulates an output program and delivers a risk prediction at the end to the user. The forecasted output will help the user to deduct errors or anomalies at the earlier stage. To know and analyze all the collected algorithms, an organization must adopt Industry 4.0.

1.1.9 RESPOND TO COMPETITIVE MARKET PRESSURE

This phase consolidates all the above compelling forces because in all the other parameters an organization's response to the competitive market pressure takes the center stage. Food companies always expect tough output with competition and price pressures in the food chain rising to the surface as the key issues.[10] Competition came out as the number one concern facing the food industry.

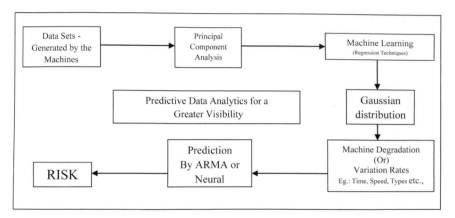

FIGURE 1.7   Predictive data analytics for a greater visibility.

1.2   CHALLENGES FOR AN INDUSTRY TO ADOPT INDUSTRY 4.0

An average technical expertise personal can name some challenges in terms of adopting Industry 4.0. So, the overall challenges are summarized within five types that are as follows:

1. Data.
2. Technology.
3. Skills and competencies.
4. Organization.
5. Environment.

1.2.1   DATA

Data are considered as the heart of an analysis process. Variability in the data and the heterogeneous characterization tends the machine to utilize an appropriate algorithm that provides the output program either for prediction or for the current operation. Figure 1.8 represents the challenges of adopting Industry 4.0 in terms of data. Data requirement, collection, communication, and analysis take three phases as represented in Figure 1.8. The first phase represents the format of the data that have to be collected. These data should be in the form of a pure and filtered format. The size of the data should also be clearly mentioned along with the proper depiction of time accuracy.[11] This represents the term volume–time accuracy. The second phase is the communication or the data passing phase.

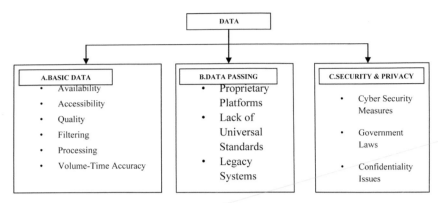

FIGURE 1.8 Data challenges.

Ownership of the software which could process the data should be identified and availing the accessibility is considered as a biggest challenge in terms of data. Lack of standards for employing Industry 4.0 is totally unavailable. This becomes a greatest challenge for the organization to set things in its place. The last challenge being the security and privacy of the data. To connect to a global enterprise, the data are to be communicated randomly to different machineries, computers, servers, clouds, etc. So security and privacy will remain a question mark for the organization to employ Industry 4.0.

1.2.2 TECHNOLOGY

Technology is the core for the upliftment of an industry. But sometimes availing this technology and incorporating it in the organization is a biggest challenge. This starts from the basic step of identifying the required technology to overcome the need. Figure 1.9 gives a representation of the challenges with respect to technology. It can be diversified into three phases. The first being the understandability of the respective software and the availability to employ in the industry. The second phase defines the collapsibility of the legacy of hierarchical structure.

The organizational culture gets totally ill-mannered and a greatest challenge that will lay in front of the industry to redevice the whole setup. Identifying the proprietary platforms for the ease of accessibility is also considered to be a greatest challenge for an industry.[12]

Example: A traditional technological process would run from the expert decision from the Manager–Engineering Division. But when the industry has incorporated the latest technology, a skill competent personal who is of less experience could be put in the place of the manager. So the overall culture gets collapsed and the manager should be redevised for another job. And also when robot does the work of an operator, rescheduling the position of the operator is a biggest challenge for an organization.

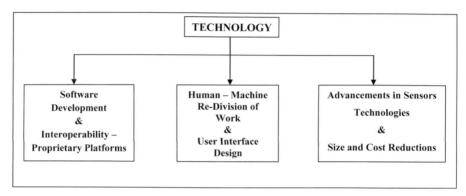

FIGURE 1.9   Challenges in technology.

1.2.3   SKILLS AND COMPETENCIES

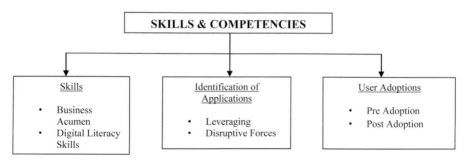

FIGURE 1.10   Skills and competency challenges.

A new technology implementation requires an advanced knowledge in the software as well as competent in the relevant field. Figure 1.10 specifies the skills that are required to overcome the challenges in an Industry 4.0 implemented organization. Business acumen is a skill of a personal who resolves issues within a short span of time. These kinds of reflex techno-logical skills are expected from an employee. All the digital literacy skills should be at the rate of proficiency level to attend and resolve an issue.[13]

Identification and elimination of disruptive forces are a biggest challenge in this level. And in the final phase, an analysis of how a user has adopted the technology has to be studied.

1.2.4 ORGANIZATION

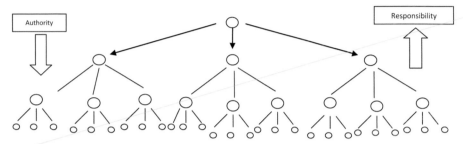

FIGURE 1.11 A typical hierarchy of a traditional organizational structure.

Figure 1.11 represents a typical hierarchical arrangement of a traditional organizational structure. As the flow goes to the lower level the authoritarian power minimizes for each ranking and as the hierarchy moves up the responsibility for each personal increases. The legacy system looks like an organized family.[14] But when the technology gets employed, the overall structure gets collapses. This is similar to the challenge as discussed in the redivisioning of work in technological challenges.

1.2.5 ENVIRONMENT

Environmental sustainability is defined as responsible interaction with the environment to avoid depletion or degradation of natural resources and allow for long-term environmental quality.[15] The practice of environmental sustainability helps to ensure that the needs of today's population are met without jeopardizing the ability of future generations to meet their needs. When we look at the natural environment, we see that it has a rather remarkable ability to rejuvenate itself and sustain its viability. For example, when a tree falls, it decomposes, adding nutrients to the soil. So taking care of the environment is a biggest challenge for an organization to adopt Industry 4.0.

Apart from the above-mentioned challenges, there are many other common challenges that can be quotes when implementing a new technology. This includes privacy issues, security, enterprise-related challenges, storage management, challenges related to emerging economy and development issues, server technologies, legal regulatory and rights issues, data center network identifications, energy demands, waste disposal, and many more.

KEYWORDS

- **Industry 4.0**
- **vertical integration**
- **food processing industry**
- **global enterprise**
- **automation**

REFERENCES

1. Luque, A.; Peralta, M. E.; De Las Heras, A.; Córdoba, A. State of the Industry 4.0 in the Andalusian Food Sector. *Procedia Manuf.* **2017** Jan 1, *13*, 1199–1205.
2. https://osha.europa.eu/en/legislation/directives/the-osh-framework-directive/the-osh-framework-directive-introduction.
3. Simon, J.; Trojanova, M.; Zbihlej, J.; Sarosi, J. Mass Customization Model in Food Industry Using Industry 4.0 Standard with Fuzzy-Based Multi-Criteria Decision Making Methodology. *Adv. Mech. Eng.* **2018,** *10* (3), 1687814018766776.
4. Hinden, R.; Deering, S. *Internet Protocol Version 6 (IPv6) Addressing Architecture*; RFC 3513, April, 2003.
5. Soosay, C.; Kannusamy, R. Scope for Industry 4.0 in Agri-Food Supply Chain. In *The Road to a Digitalized Supply Chain Management: Smart and Digital Solutions for Supply Chain Management. Proceedings of the Hamburg International Conference of Logistics (HICL)*, Vol. 25; epubli GmbH: Berlin, 2018; pp 37–56.
6. Caldwell, D. G., Ed. *Robotics and Automation in the Food Industry: Current and Future Technologies*; Elsevier, 2012.
7. McFarlane, I. *Automatic Control of Food Manufacturing Processes*; Springer Science & Business Media, 2012.
8. Seferlis, P. Measurement and Process Control for Water and Energy Use in the Food Industry. In *Handbook of Water and Energy Management in Food Processing*; Woodhead Publishing, 2008; pp 387–418.
9. Gillard, S.; Bailey, D.; Nolan, E. Ten Reasons for IT Educators to Be Early Adopters of IT Innovations. *J. Inform. Technol. Educ. Res.* **2008,** *7* (1), 21–33.
10. Schmitz, H. *Responding to Global Competitive Pressure: Local Co-Operation and Upgrading in the Sinos Valley*; Brazil, 1998.

11. Cai, H. et al. IoT-Based Big Data Storage Systems in Cloud Computing: Perspectives and Challenges. *IEEE Internet Things J.* **2016,** *4* (1), 75–87.

12. Madon, S.; Krishna, S., Eds. *The Digital Challenge: Information Technology in the Development Context: Information Technology in the Development Context*; Routledge, 2018.

13. Chryssolouris, G.; Mavrikios, D.; Mourtzis, D. Manufacturing Systems: Skills & Competencies for the Future. *Procedia CIRp* **2013,** *7* (2013), 17–24.

14. Ouchi, W. G.; Wilkins, A. L. Organizational Culture. *Annu. Rev. Sociol.* **1985,** *11* (1), 457–483.

15. Goodland, R. The Concept of Environmental Sustainability. *Annu. Rev. Ecol. Syst.* **1995,** *26* (1), 1–24.

CHAPTER 2

Sensing Mental Health: A New Mileage to Mental Health Research

SHARMISTHA DEY

Brainware University, Kolkata, West Bengal, India

ABSTRACT

Mental health, one of the burning issues of civilization, has raised the eyebrows of medical researchers with the rising curve of issues, especially during the recent pandemic situation. According to WHO, over 264 million of people is suffering from mental health disorder and more than 100 million of people are exaggerated by mental disorder related issues only in the western pacific region. According to another report, nearly 792 people suffer from several mental health related issues worldwide. Among several mental disorders, depression, anxiety issue, post-traumatic stress disorder, stress disorder, or bipolar disorders are certain problematic issues to be discussed in this chapter. It has been observed that with the evolution of technologies like the Internet of Things and machine learning, the researches in this area have witnessed a paradigm shift in mental health researches. This particular chapter explores the state-of-the-art of researches on various mental health issues, their impact on human lives, and the methods of their detection or prediction in coordination with machine learning and Internet of Things.

2.1 INTRODUCTION

Mental health related disorders are nowadays very common issue to discuss and it is spreading very fast among all age group or gender.[1,3] According to a

Internet of Things: Technological Advances and New Applications. Brojo Kishore Mishra & Amit Vishwasrao Salunkhe (Eds.)

recent statistics performed worldwide, it has been observed that because of mental health issues, a heavy amount of economic losses have to be bared by Government. According to a report by Lancet, by 2030 16 trillion of total economy will be cost by mental health disorders.[8]

Lancet collected 28 global experts' data in psychoanalysis, public health, advocacy, and cognitive science. The Commission's published report prepares a design and course of action to endorse mental comfort, avoid mental health disorders, and permit recovery from several mental health issues.

Mental disorders include emotional, social, and psychological well-being. It creates an impact on our thought process, or feelings, and our behavioral pattern as per those activities. It determines our approach to handle stress, controlling of thought process, belief systems, and choices. Mental health is important in our lives, from childhood to adulthood as it builds our thought and belief system.

Though we are not much aware or you can say not prefer much to say about mental health problems, but like other physical diseases mental health also creates some warning signs prior reaching to a severe level[6]:

- Eating or sleeping related issues.
- Going away from people and regular activities.
- Lack of energy or feeling tired is a sign of depression.
- Feeling dazed to a situation. The response to a situation may be very peculiar.
- Having unexplained pains in your joints.
- Feeling hopeless or not feeling enthusiasm may be a sign of depression.
- Unusual habit of smoking, drinking alcohol.
- Being confused, forgetful or being frustrated or bored easily.
- Screaming or fighting with family members and with your friends.
- Experiencing long-time mood swings which may even cause problems in relationships.
- Having tenacious thoughts and memories which you cannot remove from your memories.
- Believe in unbelievable things that do not exist or hearing uncanny voices.
- Thought of harming yourself or suicidal tendency or affecting others.
- Inability to complete daily tasks.

2.1.1 WHY MENTAL HEALTH ISSUES ARE REASON OF WORRY

Mental fitness is similarly important as physical fitness. In any condition, it should not be neglected, including mental adroitness, exercises into your daily routine help you to secure the benefits of a sharper mind and a healthy body. Always remember the famous proverb—"Health is wealth."

The world is showing an increasing trend on several mental health issues and which is not at all a good sign. In the next subsection, we shall discuss about the worldwide scenario of mental health issues and after the discussion, you will get a clear picture why the researchers should raise a concern about mental health issues and impacts.

2.1.2 WORLDWIDE STATISTICS OF COGNITIVE BEHAVIOR DISORDER

Mental health issues are becoming very serious in developed as well as developing countries. According to a recent report published by WHO, near around 264 million of people are affected by depression yearly and about 8 million people have a tendency to attempt suicide. The signs are very alarming.[3–5]

The population can be categorized according to different mental health issues. Figure 2.1 depicts the affect rate of male and female as per different mental health issues.

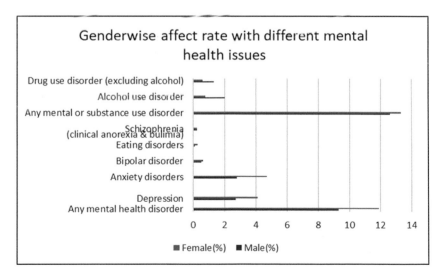

FIGURE 2.1 Rate of male and female affected by several mental health issues (shows the ratio of male and female as per various mental health categories).

The above diagram shows the ratio of male versus female affected by different mental disorder, such as eating disorder, sleep disorder, bipolar disorder, anxiety problem, depression, etc., and we can get a comparative analysis for worldwide population.

Now, we shall discuss the statistics of several mental health oriented statistics separately. In the next few figures, this scenario will be illustrated.

Figure 2.2 explains the rank of different countries having depression issues worldwide and in India also.

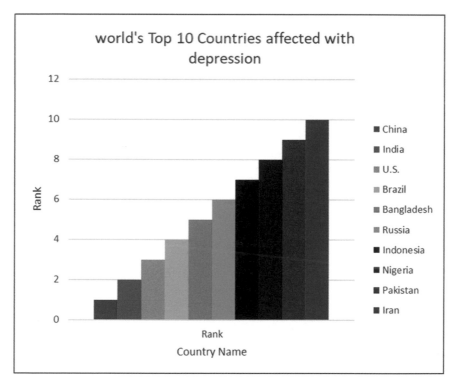

FIGURE 2.2   Top 10 countries in world showing the rate of depression.

Depression is one of the major concerns among all mental health issues. China is in Rank 1, having most of the mental issue cases, India holds rank 2 and mental health problem in India is increasing day by day. The above picture gives a worldwide scenario. The world population is suffering from depression and this problem has raised eye brows for the researchers.

We can focus more on depression issues. According to a survey done in 2017, the total world population of 10.7% is suffering with any kind of mental disorder.[9] This chapter discusses about mental health statistics worldwide. Figure 2.3 depicts gender-wise and age-wise statistics of depression rate.

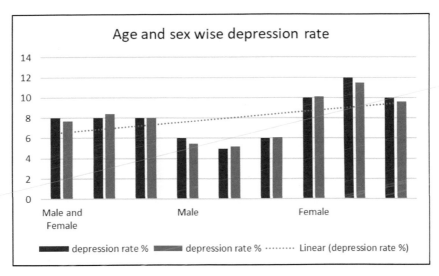

FIGURE 2.3 Age and gender wise mental health statistics.

Also, the tendency of mental health issues shows a steeper rising in the case of middle-aged persons more. The Depression rate is more in middle-aged women rather than the men. Figure 2.4 gives a clear idea about the distribution of the population having mental health issues according to the age range.

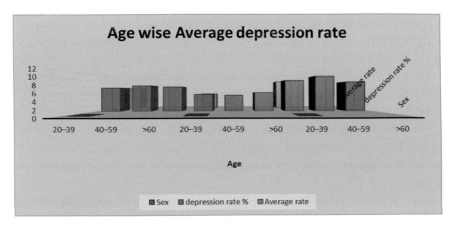

FIGURE 2.4 Age-wise average depression rate.

Along with the world population, now we can get the scenario in India, which is also facing an issue of increasing depression issue. Figure 2.5 is showing the increasing rate of depression issues in India.

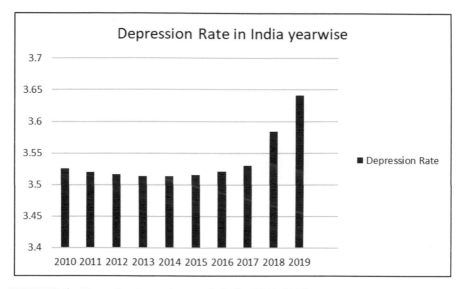

FIGURE 2.5   Year-wise depression rate in India (2010–2019).

From the above diagram, a sharp increase may be shown in 2019. Due to the pandemic situation of COVID 19 and hence the lockdown phase, people were compelled to stay in their house either alone or with someone or family. But more or less an impact can be observed in all the scenario. Figure 2.6 highlights this scenario.[15]

From the above diagram, the present scenario in the Indian context may be highlighted. It has been observed that during the pandemic phase, the mental issues have been increased.

Another issue of mental health is alcohol and drug abuse related issue. In many regions of world, this is a burning issue that even causes loss of life. Figure 2.7 shows the top 10 countries facing this issue.

The above diagram shows the rank of different countries and a worldwide scenario for drug and alcohol related issue. Not only this issue, but an anxiety disorder is also a very alarming issue worldwide and Figure 2.8 expresses the statistics about that.

From the above statistics, it can be understood why researches on mental health issues are important. In the next segment, we have discussed about different mental health disorders to be enclosed in this work.[7]

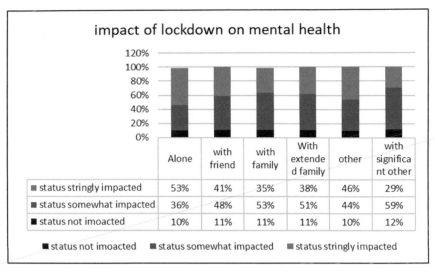

FIGURE 2.6 The impact of pandemic on mental health of people.

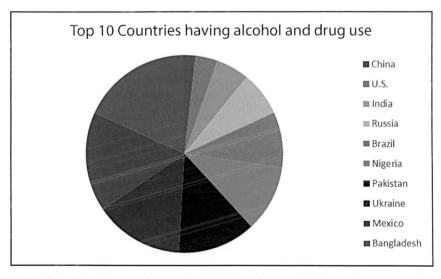

FIGURE 2.7 Top 10 countries worldwide facing drug and alcohol related abuse issues (Ranks 1–10 of different countries have been shown).

This present work has focused on several issues in this mental health research area such as:

- No specific roadmap on mental health related research.

- People should give more emphasizes on the use of hardware-based device, such as IoT-based device to track the behavioral disorder.
- Lack of direction about different tools, datasets, or libraries used for such type of researches.

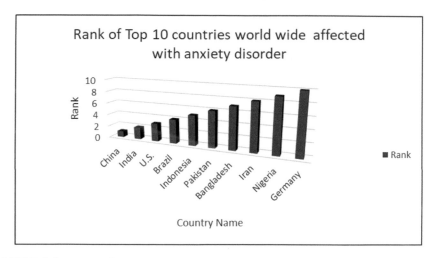

FIGURE 2.8   Rank of top 10 countries being affected with anxiety issue (2010–2019) [Ranks 1–10].

The major contribution of the present work in mental health related research may be outlined as follows:

- Stating about the state-of-the-art of researches in mental health researches.
- Finding out the research gap.
- Exploring several tools, dataset, libraries used for mental health related researches.
- Focusing on use of Internet of Things based devices and their impact in mental health related researches.

In Section 2.2, we shall briefly describe different types of mental health issues—their definition, symptoms, effects, etc. This will give the researches idea about the area of researches for mental health issue.

2.2   DIFFERENT TYPES OF MENTAL HEALTH ISSUES

Different mental well-being related issues are depression, anxiety attacks, post-traumatic stress disorder (PTSD), phobia, different eating or sleep pattern disorder, etc.

In this section, we shall discuss about each type of different mental health issue.

Depression—This is a very serious issue nowadays. It is a type of mood disorder continued for long term and thus it fluctuates from normal mood swing. Due to depression, people loss interest of doing anything, feeling fatigued, and unenthusiastic to do anything. Depression has different types and symptoms according to that. According to their severity, types, symptoms, and other side effects, depression is divided into several categories.[23]

2.2.1 MAJOR DEPRESSIVE DISORDER

It is a type of depression in which a person feels depressed for a maximum time in a day and this depression persists for long terms.[7] This leaves some physical or other signals like disinclination of doing something, loss of interest for any work, lack of energy, development of suicidal tendencies.

2.2.2 BIPOLAR DISORDER

In such type of disorder, the mood shifts between very high to very low, that is, being very energetic to totally depressed mood. Medication can be a resolution for this issue. With help of some mood stabilizer, temporary relief can be given to the person.[25]

2.2.3 PERSISTENT DEPRESSIVE DISORDER

Another name is dysthymia. It creates a long-term disorder. The main symptoms may be shown as a lack of interest in any work, feeling despairing, being low in self-esteem. The doggedness may prolong even years after years. This comes under clinical depression, consult with a clinical psychologist is mandatory for recovery from such disorder.[9]

2.2.4 PSYCHOTIC DEPRESSION

It is a major depressive disorder type and a type of psychosis. Person having such type of depression may have some illusions of listening to sound or seeing someone imaginary, unlike other clinical major depressive disorders.[23]

2.2.5   POSTPARTUM DEPRESSION

It is a special clinical depression generally developed after pregnancy. The main symptoms are anxiety, grief, sleep trouble, etc. Sometimes a suicidal tendency may develop for this. There are certain physical and emotional issues developed in this stage and this creates a severe depression

2.2.6   ANXIETY DISORDER

Anxiety disorder is a mental health problem where the person having such problem feels nervous, pains, sweating, trembling, or feeling tired. The feelings of anxiety inhibit with day-to-day activities, they are tough to control and are without proportion to the actual problem.[28]

- – The major symptoms of anxiety are as follows:
- – Feeling nervous or tensed.
- – Increased heart rate.
- – Perspiration.
- – Vibrating in several body parts.
- – Sleep disorder.
- – Being hopeless.
- – Avoiding the things which may cause worry.

There are different types of anxiety issues.

- ➢ **Agoraphobia**—People facing the problem of Agaro phobia dread and often dodge spaces or circumstances that might lead a person to panic, abandoned, or uncomfortable.
- ➢ **Anxiety disorder from certain medical conditions**—This includes indications of penetrating anxiety or fear that are stanchly produced due to a physical health issue.
- ➢ **Generalized anxiety disorder**—This is persistent and unnecessary anxiety and concern about activities or events—that may be ordinary, or normal routine issues. The worry is excessive and not as per the actual circumstance. It is really hard to control and changes your physical feelings. It frequently falls along with anxiety issues or depression.
- ➢ **Panic disorder**—It includes recurrent incidents of sudden feelings of penetrating anxiety and fear that may reach a highest level within a very short period of time. You may have the sensation of imminent

destiny, breathing issues, flapping, or thrashing heart. Such attacks may lead to perturbing about them and may happen recurrently.

➢ **Separation anxiety disorder**—It is a childhood disorder considered by anxiety that's unnecessary for the child's evolving level and relates the separation from parent or others parent-like figure.

➢ **Social anxiety disorder**—It is known as social phobia. This involves high levels of social anxiety, dread of avoiding from social situations for feelings of discomfort, uneasiness, and worry about being adjudicated or observed negatively by others.

2.2.7 SPECIFIC PHOBIAS

Specific phobias are characterized by major anxiety disorders when you are exposed to a specific object or situation and a desire to avoid it. Phobias provoke panic attacks in some people.

2.2.8 SUBSTANCE-ORIENTED ANXIETY DISORDER

It is considered by symptoms of penetrating anxiety disorder or panic attack. It is a direct result of drug abuse, alcohol abuse, or due to any medication.

2.2.9 POST-TRAUMATIC STRESS DISORDER (PTSD)

This is such a disorder where a person can experience deep fear, trembling who has faced any trauma or witnessed any trauma. Some personality changes like difficulty in controlling emotions, feeling of hopelessness, or unworthy may happen. Even for acute levels of PTSD suicidal thoughts may come.[29]

PTSD also has different types:

➢ **Normal or simple PTSD**—Where the symptoms are like being emotional or feeling pains and panic attacks but not very intense.

➢ **Complex PTSD**—It is an intense form of PTSD where the person having this disorder faces an intense panic or anxiety attack, unable to control responding to emotional events. People facing such problem may have a tendency to isolate themselves from others and may loss trust in people.

> ➤ **Comorbid PTSD**—It is a type of PTSD that may persists with other comorbid mental health issues like depression or anxiety disorder. Mostly women having PTSD are more prone to have depression.

In this section, we have discussed about several mental health issues. Now, in the next section, we shall discuss about detection or prediction of those issues using machine learning and shall also discuss the impact of Internet of Things technology for the detection of mental health problems.

2.3   RECENT WORKS IN MENTAL HEALTH DETECTION OR PREDICTION

In the previous section, several mental health issues have been discussed, which could help us to understand the possible areas of research in this field. This particular segment will explain several researches on machine learning and IoT to track mental health activities.

D'Mello et al. have published a detailed study on detection of several behavioral patterns using machine learning algorithms. They have primarily focused on three—learning-technical, episodic, and procedural learning.[38] This may be treated as a foundation of research in this area.

Ghosh and Dey have performed a review on different sensor devices used for mental health monitoring. They have discussed about several sensors used to detect mental health issues. Their survey has covered sensing technologies and too some extent IoT devices also.[25]

Tushar et al. have published on work as an exploratory study on sensing several mental health issues using smart technologies. In their work, they have discussed about several methods of sensing or tracking mental health issues. Along with that, they have presented a survey on therapeutic behavior and digital technologies used for that.[22]

Almeida et al. have developed an Arduino and Raspberry Pi based device to track and perform proper treatment of depression in elderly persons.[7] They have used color and humidity sensors to track the activity and body movements.

Buyn et al. have researched in determining depressive disorders by measuring heart bits with a low-cost heart rate sensor. Their study reveals the state of depression from their unusual heart bits.[40] The researchers mainly analyze using a support vector machine and by eliminating recursive features from an image.

Pandey has researched for stress determination using IoT-based devices. The researcher has adapted support vector machine and logistics regression.

They have used sensor for measuring pulse and heart bit rate. In the experiments, he has achieved 97% accuracy with logistics regression and 66% accuracy with support vector machine.[32]

Table 2.1 discusses about recent works in mental health research using IoT and sensor devices.

2.4   DISCUSSION

In the previous section, we have enclosed a study on recent works in the mental health recent area and specially focusing on IoT or sensor related researches. In this section, we shall extend our discussion regarding some popular questioners that are being used by mental health researchers. Though all questioners or dataset are not publicly available, but we have outlined some available questioners, so that the budding researchers can have an idea about the types of questioners may be prepared.

2.4.1   DIFFERENT QUESTIONERS AVAILABLE FOR MENTAL HEALTH AREA RESEARCHES

Different questioners are very popular for working in mental health related researches. Though all of them are not available publicly. But some can be downloaded and used in this regard. Following are some popular questioners used by mental health researchers:

- ❖ **PHQ-9: PHQ-9 Scale:** The Patient Health Questionnaire is a MCQ type question based self-reporting inventory that contains nine questions. It may be used as a broadcast and diagnostic tool for various mental health disorders, such as depression, alcohol abuse problem, anxiety attack, etc.
- ❖ **Hospital Anxiety and Depression Scale:** Hospital anxiety and depression scale in short, was planned by Zigmond and Snaith, in 1983. It contains a 14-item measure envisioned to measure symptoms of anxiety, depression, with importance on dropping the effect of physical illness over the whole score.[49]
- ❖ **State-Trait Anxiety Inventory:** It is a psychological record based on a four points Likert scale and contains 40 questions which is self-reporting. This considers two types of event—state (related to an event) or trait (related to a person). Higher the scores are high level of anxiety may be shown.[50]

TABLE 2.1 Comparative Study on Recent Works on Sensing Mental Health Problems Using IoT and Sensors.

Disorder type	Algorithm used	Tracking/sensing device used	Measuring process	Performance
Depression Almeida, Ferruzca and Tlapanco (2014)[7]	Marquardt back propagation	Arduino, color, and humidity sensor, Raspberry Pi	Body movement tracking	Not specified
Stress detection Pandey (2018)[32]	Logistics regression and support vector machine (SVM)	Node MCU pulse sensor	Heart rate	Accuracy (97%)- Logistics regression Accuracy(66%)- SVM
Major Depressive Disorder Byun et al. (2019)[30]	SVM, feature elimination	Heart rate sensor	Procomp infinity device for ECG heart rate variability	In total, 73% sensitivity, 74.4% result accuracy, and 75.6% specificity
Depression and Fall Detection Bai, Hibbing, Mantis and Welk (2018)[35]	Statistical analysis	Apple watch	Heart rate	Correlation-0.01
Cardiac defence Response to show negative emotion Gravina and Fortino (2016)[45]	Artificial neural network	ECG, Galvanic skin resistance	Cardiac defense response, ECG	In total, 10% improvement in sensitivity. Twenty-four percent in precision and 18% betterment in specificity from previous version
Stress Detection Salai, vassanyi, and Kosa (2016)[40]	Stress detection algorithm	Heart rate sensor, chest belt, MT-200 device	Through electro Mayogram or EMG, ECG	In total, 74.6% accuracy, 75.0% sensitivity, and 74.2% specificity

❖ **DASS 21 scale:** It is recognized as depression anxiety stress scales, ready using 42 questions and it is also self-reporting items. The total completion time may be required of 5–10 min. Each item reflects a set of negative emotion. It is also measured using the Likert scale.

❖ **DSM-5 scale:** It is a checklist with 11-item questionnaire which in turn measures the degree of mild, moderate, or severe scale of anxiety and depression. It is used to measure the diagnostic criteria. The score is determined with a yes or no in response. The overall experiment done by making the experiment over 12 months habit.[51]

The above questioners are being used for the mental health researches. In the next subsection, we shall discuss about several tools or libraries used for such research.

2.5   CURRENT ROADMAP AND FUTURE DIRECTION

Several researchers have worked for detection of mental health disorders. With the emergence of machine learning and data analytics technology, the detection of mental health problems has become easier. Machine learning algorithms can help to predict data in a better way. In the last few years, a sharp inclination can be observed in the case of mental health prediction. With IoT, the tracking of mental health has been accilarized. Nowadays, brain–computer interface plays an important role for tracking and monitoring of mental health disorders.

Present day, researchers are emphasizing on developing brain–computer interface for monitoring brain activity and mental health research. The associations like American Psychological Association and National Institute of Mental Health are doing researches on mental health area. The next move is going toward development of app-based mental health tracking device that will be ready to operate without any human intervention, performing remote counseling, or counseling with the help of an intelligent ChatBot. The future of psychiatry is showing an inclination toward personalized on-demand service.[54,55]

2.6   CONCLUSION

The present work performs a survey on existing works in the mental health area. In this work, we have explored existing work to identify the research scope in mental health area. The emphasize of the study has been given on Internet of Things based devices to monitor several mental health related issues. We have also given an idea about several questioners or dataset used for such type of research. The research trend shows a tendency toward service automation in this area also and the scope of remote counseling has been explored as a future prospect in this area. With the emergence of technology, the researches in mental health area leave an ample scope for the future researchers.

KEYWORDS

- **depression**
- **compulsive obsessive disorder**
- **bipolar disorder**
- **social anxiety disorder**
- **general anxiety disorder**
- **PTSD**

REFERENCES

1. Health in Western Pacific, WHO Report. https://www.who.in/westernpacific/mental-health (accessed Jan 25, 2021). Kolkata, India.
2. Depression Statistics Everyone Should Know [Online], 2019. www.verywellmind.com/depression-statistics-everyone-should-know-4159056
3. Reece, A. G.; Reagan, A. J.; Lix, K. L. M.; Dodds, P. S.; Danforth, C. M.; Langer, E. J. Forecasting the Onset and Course of Mental Illness with Twitter Data. 2016 arXiv:1608.07740.
4. Post-Traumatic Stress Disorder (PTSD). https://www.mayoclinic.org/disease-conditions/post-traumatic-stress-disorder/symptoms-causes/syc-20355967
5. Behavioral and Cognitive Psychology. https://www.apa.org/ed/graduate/specialize/behavioral-cognitive (accessed Sept 7, 2020). Kolkata, India.
6. What Is Mental Health?, 2020. https://www.mentalhealth.gov/basics/what-is-mental-health (accessed Jan 26, 2021). Kolkata, India.
7. Almeida, E.; Ferruzca, M.; Tlapanco, M. D. P. M. Design of a System for Early Detection and Treatment of Depression in Elderly Case Study. In *International Symposium on Pervasive Computing Paradigms for Mental Health*; Springer, Cham, 2014; pp 115–124.
8. Lancet Commission: Inaction on Mental Health Crisis Will Cost World $16 Trillion by 2030. https://globalmentalhealthcommission.org/wp-content/uploads/2018/10/Lancet-Commission-on-Global-Mental-Health-Press-Release.pdf

9. World Health Statistics, 2020. https://www.who.int/data/gho/whs-2020-visual-summary (accessed Sept 9, 2020). Kolkata, India.

10. Ali, S.; Kibria, M.G.; Jarwar, M.A.; Kumar, S. and Chong, I. Microservices Model in WoO Based IoT Platform for Depressive Disorder Assistance. In *2017 International Conference on Information and Communication Technology Convergence (ICTC)*; IEEE, Oct 2017; pp 864–866.

11. Deepika, M. P.; Suresh, V.; Pradeep, C. IoT Powered Wearable to Assist Individuals Facing Depression Symptoms. *IRJET* **2019**, *6* (1), 2019.

12. Vaseem, A.; Sharma, S. Depression: A Survey on the Indian Scenario and the Technological Work Done. In *International Journal of Engineering Research & Technology (IJERT)*, pp. 221–226.

13. de la Torre Díez, I.; Alonso, S. G.; Hamrioui, S.; Cruz, E. M.; Nozaleda, L. M.; Franco, M. A. IoT-Based Services and Applications for Mental Health in the Literature. *J. Med. Syst.* **2019**, *43* (1), 11–16.

14. Lakshmi, N. M. et al. IoT Based Smart Mirror Using Raspberry Pi. *IJERT* **2018**, *6* (13), 1–8.

15. Impact on Mental Health During the Coronavirus (COVID-19) Lockdown in India as of April 2020, by Companion, 2020. https://www.statista.com/statistics/1170404/india-impact-on-mental-health-covid-19-lockdown-by-companion/

16. Dey, S.; Chakraborty, C. Emotional Intelligence- Creating a New Roadmap for the Artificial Intelligence. *Int. J. of Engineering Systems Modelling and Simulation, Special Issue: Artificial Intelligence enabled Computing System Development*; Inderscience, 2020

17. Khoshemehry, Sh.; Bahram, M. E.; Pourvaghar, M. J. World Academy of Science, Engineering and Technology, The Effects of Physical Activity and Serotonin on Depression, Anxiety, Body Image and Mental Health. *Int J Sport Health Sci* **2018**, *12* (9).

18. Skinner, B. F. The Operational Analysis of Psychological Terms. *Behav Brain Sci* **1984**, *1984* (7), 547–581.

19. Contributions from Neuroscience to the Practice of Cognitive Behaviour Therapy: Translational Psychological Science in Service of Good Practice. *Behav. Res. Ther*. February **2020**, *125*, 103545.

20. Puengsungwan, S.; Jiraserccamomkul, K. IoT Based Stress Detection for Organic Lettuce Farms Using Chlorophyll Fluorescence (ChF). *2018 Global Wireless Summit (GWS)* **2018**, 354–357.

21. Uday, S.; Chandan, J.; Joseph, A. Detection of Stress Using Wearable Sensors in IoT Platform. *International Conference on Inventive Communication and Computational Technologies (ICICCT)*. DOI: 10.1109/ICICCT.2018.8473010

22. Tushar, A. K.; Kabir, M. A.; Ahmed, S. I. Mental Health and Sensing, Signal Processing Techniques for Computational Health Informatics. DOI: 10.1007/978-3-030-54932-9_11

23. Santos, A.; Macedo, J.; Costa, A.; Nicolau, M. J. Internet of Things and Smart Objects for M-Health Monitoring and Control. *Procedia Technol.* **2014**, *16*, 1351–1360.

24. Types of Depression [Online], 2020. https://www.webmd.com/depression/guide/depression-types#1 (accessed Aug 07, 2020).

25. Ghosh, A.; Dey, S. Sensing the Mind (2020) An Exploratory Study About Sensors used in E-Health and M-Health Applications for Diagnosis of Mental Health Condition, Accepted For :Efficient Data Handling for Massive Internet of Medical Things, Springer Nature, 2020.

26. Psychotic Depression [Online], 2019. https://www.webmd.com/depression/guide/psychotic-depression#1 (accessed Aug 5, 2020).

27. Ritchie, H.; Roser, M. Mental Health. https://ourworldindata.org/mental-health (accessed Sept 7, 2020), Kolkata, India.

28. Anxiety Disorder. https://www.mayoclinic.org/diseases-conditions/anxiety/symptoms-causes/syc-20350961

29. Types of Post-Traumatic Stress Disorder (PTSD). https://mentalhealth-uk.org/help-and-information/conditions/post-traumatic-stress-disorder-ptsd (accessed Jan 26, 2021), Kolkata, India.

30. Byun, S.; Kim, A. Y.; Jang, E. H.; Kim, S.; Choi, K. W.; Yu, H. Y.; Jeon, H. J. Detection of Major Depressive Disorder from Linear and Nonlinear Heart Rate Variability Features During Mental Task Protocol. *Comput. Biol. Med.* **2019**, *112*, 103381.

31. Boonstra, T. W.; Nicholas, J.; Wong, Q. J.; Shaw, F.; Townsend, S.; Christensen, H. Using Mobile Phone Sensor Technology for Mental Health Research: Integrated Analysis to Identify Hidden Challenges and Potential Solutions. *J. Med. Internet Res.* **2018**, *20* (7), e10131.

32. Pandey, P. S. Machine Learning and IoT for Prediction and Detection of Stress. *2017 17th International Conference on Computational Science and Its Applications (ICCSA)*; Trieste, 2017; pp 1–5. DOI: 10.1109/ICCSA.2017.8000018

33. Torous, J.; Onnela, J. P. High Potential But Limited Evidence: Using Voice Data from Smartphones to Monitor and Diagnose Mood Disorders. *Psych. Rehab. J.* **2017**, *40* (3), 320.

34. Quintana, D. S.; Westlye, L. T.; Kaufmann, T.; Rustan, Ø.; Brandt, C. L.; Haatveit, B.; Steen, N. E.; Andreassen, O. A. Reduced Heart Rate Variability in Schizophrenia and Bipolar Disorder Compared to Healthy Controls. *Acta Psych. Scand.* **2016**, *133* (1), 44–52.

35. Bai, Y.; Hibbing, P.; Mantis, C.; Welk, G. J. Comparative Evaluation of Heart Rate-Based Monitors: Apple Watch vs Fitbit Charge Hr. *J. Sports Sci.* **2018**, *36* (15), 1734–1741. https://doi.org/10.1080/02640414.2017.1412235

36. Canzian, L.; Musolesi, M. Trajectories of Depression: Unobtrusive Monitoring of Depressive States by Means of Smartphone Mobility Traces Analysis. In *Proceedings of the 2015 ACM International Joint Conference on Pervasive and Ubiquitous Computing*; ACM, 2015; pp 1293–1304.

37. Tushar, A. K. "We Need More Power to Stand Up": Designing to Combat Stigmatization of the Caregivers of Children with Autism in Urban Bangladesh. *Proceedings of the 11th International Conference on Information and Communication Technologies and Development P to Appear*, 2020.

38. Mello, S. D.; Franklin, S.; Ramamurthy, U.; Baars, B. A Cognitive Science Based Machine Learning Architecture.

39. Kaburagi, T.; Takenaka, M.; Kurihara, Y.; Matsumoto, T. A Linear Regression Model for Estimating Anxiety Index Using Wide Area Frontal Lobe Brain Blood Volume. *Int. J. Psychol. Behav. Sci.* **2017**, *11* (3), 115–118.

40. Salai, M.; Vassanyi, I.; Kosa, I. Stress Detection Using Low Cost Heart Rate Sensors. *J. Healthcare Eng* **2016**, 1–13. DOI: http://dx.doi.org/10.1155/2016/5136705

41. Oliver, N.; Pentland, A.; Bérard, F. LAFTER: A Real-Time Face and Lips Tracker with Facial Expression Recognition. *Pattern Recogn.* **2000**, *33* (8), 1369–1382.

42. McTeague, L. M.; Laplante, M.-C.; Bulls, H. W.; Shumen, J. R.; Lang, P. J.; Keil. A. Face Perception in Social Anxiety: Visuocortical Dynamics Reveal Propensities for Hypervigilance or Avoidance. *Biol. Psych.* DOI: 10.1016/j.biopsych.2017.10.004

43. Chakraborty, R.; Chattopadhyay, A. K.; Kairi, A.; Chakraborty, M. Brain–Computer Interface-Based Fear Detection: A Self-defense Mechanism. In *Proceedings of International Ethical Hacking Conference 2018. Advances in Intelligent Systems and Computing*; Chakraborty, M.; Chakrabarti, S.; Balas, V.; Mandal, J., Eds., Vol. 811; Springer: Singapore, 2019. https://doi.org/10.1007/978-981-13-1544-2_14

44. Gravania, R. et al. Multi-Sensor Fusion in Body Sensor Networks: State-of-the-Art and Research Challenges. *Inform. Fusion* **2017,** *35*, 68–80.

45. Gravina, R.; Fortino, G. Automatic Methods for the Detection of Accelerative Cardiac Defense Response. In *IEEE Trans. Affect. Comput.* **2016,** *7* (3), 286–298. DOI: 10.1109/TAFFC.2016.2515094.50

46. Lazar, S. W.; Bush, G.; Gollub, R. L.; Fricchione, G. L.; Khalsa, G.; Benson, H. Functional Brain Mapping of the Relaxation Response and Meditation. Neuroreport, 2000.

47. Hamilton, M. A Rating Scale for Depression. *J. Neurol. Neurosurg. Psych.* **1960,** *23*, 56–62.

48. Covello, R.; Fortino, G.; Gravina, R.; Aguilar, A.; Breslin, J. Novel Method and Real-Time System for Detecting the Cardiac Defense Response Based on the ECG. In *Proceedings of IEEE Symposium on Medical Measurements and Applications*, May 2013.

49. Edelstein, B. et al.. Assessment of Depression and Bereavement in Older Adults, 2015.

50. Lani, J. State-Trait Anxiety Inventory (STAI), 2010. http://www.statisticssolutions.com/state-trait-anxiety-inventory-stai/

51. DSM-5 checklist. https://dionysus.psych.wisc.edu:5001/sharing/hopaFRDVd (accessed Jan 27, 2021), Kolkata, India.

52. Wijsman, J.; Grundlehner, B.; Penders, J.; Hermens, H. Trapezius Muscle EMG as Predictor of Mental Stress. In *Proceedings of the 1st Wireless Health Conference (WH '10)*; ACM, Oct 2010; pp 155–163.

53. Lazar, S. W.; Bush, G.; Gollub, R. L.; Fricchione, G. L.; Khalsa, G.; Benson, H. Functional Brain Mapping of the Relaxation Response and Meditation. *NeuroReport* May 15, **2000,** *11* (7), 1581–1585.

54. Technology and the Future of Mental Health Treatment. https://www.nimh.nih.gov/health/topics/technology-and-the-future-of-mental-health-treatment/index.shtml

55. Reynolds, C. F.; Pilkonis, P. A.; Kupfer, D. J.; Dunn, L.; Pincus, H. A. Training Future Generations of Mental Health Researchers: Devising Strategies for Tough Times. *Acad. Psych.* **2007,** *31* (2), 152–159. https://doi.org/10.1176/appi.ap.31.2.152

CHAPTER 3

How the IoT (Internet of Things) Is Poised to Jump-Start the Next Revolution

ARADHANA BEHURA

Gandhi Institute for Technological Advancement, Bhubaneswar, India

ABSTRACT

The industrial Internet of Things (IIoT) refers to interconnected sensors, instruments, and other devices networked together with computers' industrial applications, including manufacturing and energy management. This connectivity allows for data collection, exchange, and analysis, potentially facilitating improvements in productivity and efficiency as well as other economic benefits. The IIoT is an evolution of a distributed control system that allows for a higher degree of automation by using cloud computing to refine and optimize the process controls. The IIoT is enabled by technologies such as cyber security, cloud computing, edge computing, mobile technologies, machine-to-machine, 3D printing, advanced robotics, big data, IoT, RFID technology,[1] and cognitive computing. In the era of technology, each and everything is going to be digital the device that we used nowadays is automatic means there is minimal involvement of human being because human being busy in their various field work so they are unable to monitor their things properly. In this era, IoT plays a vital role to develop a modern technology by providing sensor-based or automatic systems to provide proper monitor. The motive of this chapter is to present the role of IoT in agriculture for the implementation of smart farming, fundamental of IoT. This chapter presents the various component of IoT like network architecture, various application, network topologies used

Internet of Things: Technological Advances and New Applications. Brojo Kishore Mishra & Amit Vishwasrao Salunkhe (Eds.)

and protocol. IoT-based smart farming includes cloud computing, big data, storage, and analysis of whether through sensor also in IoT sensor based device developed for better management of smart farming rather than our country also other foreign country used this technology to better yield or monitoring.

3.1 INTRODUCTION

The concept of Internet of Things (IoT) firstly was given by Kevin Ashion of Procter and Gambel, later MIT Auto-ID center in 1999, then he prefer the phase IoT. Defining the term "IoT" simply the point in time when more and more things were connected to the Internet than people now IoT became the smarter technology by providing multiple application, such as smart health care, smart cities, security, traffic balance, and industrial control and also in one of the demanding sector in agriculture field. IoT is used in many field such as smart home, medical, transportation system, energy engagement, smart manufacturing, education system (in current time), and agriculture, which is shown in Table 3.2.

TABLE 3.1 Difference Between IoT and M2M.

	Machine-to-machine (M2M)	Internet of Things (IoT)
1	M2M means direct machine-to-machine communications	IoT means Internet of Things—a network of Internet-connected devices able to sensor, collect, and exchange information
2	Created for business to connect with machine	Evolved from M2M and created for both business and consumers
3	Hardware based	Hardware and software based
4	Usually wired connection	Wireless connection
5	Does not require Internet connection	Requires Internet connection
6	2 + machines communicating each other	Network with thousands of devices communicating each other.
7	It supports point-to-point communication	It supports cloud-based communication
8	Best for small-scale applications	Easy to large-scale applications
9	M2M application includes vending machines, ATMs, Smart meters	IoT applications include smart cities, offices and homes, telehealth, and connected cars

• *Security and surveillance*

WSNs are essential components of military command and power, message passing, computing, intellect power, monitoring, attacking systems, and observations. The sensor nodes and devices guarantee observation of enemy, battleground monitoring, conflict destruction evaluation, attacking, nuclear, botanical, and enzymatic blast discovery techniques.[1]

• *Environmental monitoring*

Several WSN implementations in earth science research are covered by environmental sensor networks, associating sensing volcanoes, glaciers, forests, and oceans. To recognize slight soil movements and modifications, a landslide detection system utilizes WSN in several parameters that happen before or during landslides. Before it truly happens through data accumulated through sensors, it may be the same to check for landslides.[16]

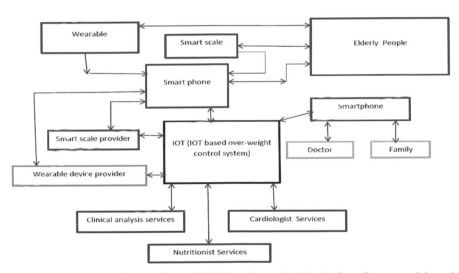

FIGURE 3.1   A machine learning and IoT-based smart health platform for overweight and obesity control.

• *Health applications*

To observe patients' physiological data and to trace and detect patients to manage drug administration and doctor's sensor networks are associated in modern health care centers. Different uses are glucose level detectors, organ scanning, general health monitoring, and cancer detection. Inside a human body implanting wireless biomedical sensors is promising though great challenges such as ultra-safety, security, and minimal maintainability of the system is associated.

• *Industrial applications*

For machinery condition-based maintenance, WSNs are enlarged as they guarantee high-cost savings and allow new works. Through wireless sensors, earlier inaccessible locality, rotating machinery, dangerous, or regulated regions, and mobile assets are reached.

• *Structural monitoring*

Wireless sensors monitor moves inside premises, framework such as flyovers, cross-over, tunnels and hills, monitor assets remotely, permitting engineering works without expensive site visits.

TABLE 3.2   The Internet Of Things: From Connecting Devices to Human Value.

1	Device connection and connectivity	IoT devices, IoT connectivity, embedded intelligence
2	Data sensing and collecting	Capture information, sensors, and tags storage
3	Communication	Focus on access network, cloud, edge data transport
4	Data analytics	Big data analysis, AI, and cognitive analysis at the edge
5	Data value	Analysis to action, APIs, and processes, actionable intelligence
6	Human value, apps, and experience	Smart applications, stakeholder benefits, and tangible benefits

Smart school transportation and office, smart building management and classes, smart cafeteria, and student activity tracking are the important aspect of the 21st-century education system.

In field of agriculture, IoT technology finding the solution that the farmer faces nowadays, such as suddenly shortage of water, climate condition, soil condition, and many more. By using the technology IoT in smart farming, we can monitor the thing that is happened in the field by using a sensor. It provides information about the condition in the field to the hub through the Internet by doing this, we can properly monitor the field to better yield with minimal involvement of human being by using IoT, it enhanced the productivity also it can use the resource in limited quantity that is not going to waste in agriculture field through secure connectivity.[57]

- Now different uses of IoT and relevant devices also sensor-based application have been discussed.
- Now lot of industry invests in IoT-based smart farming. The policy of IoT-based smart farming made by different countries for the standardization also have been discussed
- Then the challenges that comes to improve the IoT-based smart farming.

TABLE 3.3 Difference Between IIoT and IoT.

Concentration	IIoT (Industrial Internet of Things)	IoT (Internet Of Things)
1. Area of focus	Industrial application	General applications
2. Focus on development	Industrial systems	Smart devices
3. Security and risk measures	Advanced and robust	Utility centric
4. Interoperability	CPS integrated	Autonomous
5. Scalability	Large-scale network	Low-scale network
6. Precision and accuracy	Synchronized with milliseconds	Critically monitored
7. Programmability	Remote on-site programming	Easy off-site programming
8. Output	Operational efficiency	Convenience and utilization
9. Resilience	High fault tolerance required	Not required
10. Maintenance	Scheduled and planned	Consumer preferred
11. Impact	Revolution	Evolution
12. Current status	New devices and standard	Existing devices and standard
13. Connectivity	Ad-hoc	Structured
14. Criticality	Important but not critical	Mission critical: analytics, security, data integrity, response time
15. Data volume	Medium to high	Very high (ex. Big Data)
16. Servicing	User	User, vendor

3.2 IOT ROLE IN APPLICATION

For observing various environmental situations, a WSN includes numerous distributed sensors like motion, sound, pressure, temperature, and images. For further mandatory measures in WSNs, the data sensation by this sensor is forwarded to the fusion center.[8–10,56] The communication of data are endangered to various critical situation to the base station. Such as, when

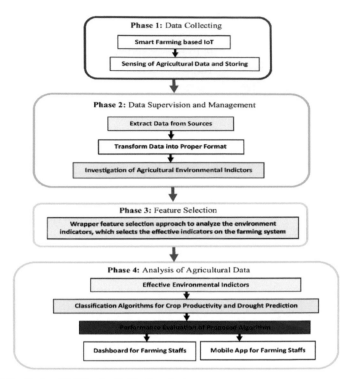

FIGURE 3.2   Role of IoT in the field of agriculture.

TABLE 3.4   Differences Between IoT and IOE.

	Internet of Things (IoT)	Internet of Everything (IOE)
1	Network of physical devices and items embedded with electronics to enable connectivity and to exchange information	Border concept than IoTs which defines as the intelligent connection of people, processes, data, and things
2	Communication occurs between machine-to-machine	Communication occurs between machine-to-machine (M2M), machine-to-people, and technology-assisted people-to-people
3	IoT is less complex than IOE	IOE is more advanced than IoT

sender transmits the data from source node to the destination node to a hacker it would not be difficult to change the original message which sensor node received thus WSN is not a closed system where there are rare reliability considerations, such as wires configuration. The judgment considered in the ground of the message is not accurate when the fusion center gets in current data. Toward terrible destruction, the incorrect conclusion shows a law enforcement power. So, to keep safety and reliability in WSN is more essential.[12–20] As many researches are going on the terrible restriction to the wireless sensor network, such as energy usage, frequency range and storage restriction, and processing capacity. Since the reliability of wireless sensor networks are a great challenging task that requires to be marked mainly in active sensor operators in defense and rule implementation society. In various active hypermedia uses of WSNs are very much essential and challenging tasks that need emergency solutions are placement of detectors according to the pictures, assembling of images in sensor nodes, object tracing using sensor image processing, image processing to deduct the computations, description to the entity outlook by utilizing optical detector operators, power and bandwidth limitations, image processing in WSN for network security,[21–24] reliable and successful capturing of images and video, and preprocessing inside WSN like image compression. Based on environmental situations, such as pressure, temperature, sound, and other characteristics offer in wireless sensors networks, these are geographically saturated self-governing sensors, with comparatively move their data all over the network transmission exist in the process of all network identification process. According to the military, implementations exist in the real-time implementations development process in battlefield and wireless sensors networks are viable. For retrieving services from process implementation in recognizing different permitted users got into implementations development. Nowadays, WSN is utilized as the process in the business and industrial implementations.[51–55]

S. No	Parameter	MANETs	VANETs
1	Cost of production	Cheap	Expensive
2	Change in network topology	slow	Frequent and very fast
3	Mobility	low	High
4	Node Density	Sparse	Dense and frequently variable
5	Bandwidth	Hundred Kps	Thousand Kps
6	Range	Up to 100 m	Up to 500 m
7	Node Lifetime	Depends on power resource	Depend on lifetime of vehicle
8	Multihop routing	available	Weakly available
9	Reliability	medium	High
10	Moving pattern of nodes	random	regular
11	Addressing scheme	Attribute based	Location based
12	Position Acquisition	Using ultrasonic	Using GPS, RADAR

Wireless sensor network is a cluster node with collective transmission between consistent data communication. In this transmission, all node must link with different nodes and also attach with one sensor, each sensor network joins with faithful communication with different ports situated in the network. It includes radio transceiver and intent antenna operations situated in the process application and this antenna managed by the process microcontroller that inserted to that specific process transmission in wireless sensor network application process. Basically, there are four main features and some optional elements in a wireless sensor node.

- Specific detecting part is inhabited by each sensor node that accommodates an A/D converter and one and various sensors are employed for data acquisition.
- Memory is used for storing output where for another information every sensor node has a processor, more storage capacity, and a microcontroller.
- For transmission of data using wireless medium an RF unit is utilized.
- A particular unit for supplying energy to detectors.
- Technique to locate the position conviction.
- For location and position changing a unit is called as a mobilizer.

In various fields such as cultivating in modern technique to observe the surroundings for productive utilization of land and water resources, prediction of underwater, target tracking, traffic observing and implementation, multiscale monitoring, medical diagnosis, image change sensation, networked gaming, smart parking, habitat monitoring, vineyard monitoring, smart video and audio monitoring, and remote sensing, WSNs can be utilized for various implementations.[25,50]

- *Wireless Architecture*

This architecture contains five layers which are described below.

Physical layer: By decreasing the path loss consequence and shading an enlarged authenticity is the goal of this layer. This layer set up link, bit transmission channel, encoding, frequency sensing, signal creation, and inflation.

Data link layer: This layer guarantees interoperability in internode connection. It can manage error recognition, multiplexing, continuous data delivery, and avoidance of packet loss.

Network layer: The finest route for secure routing is established by this layer. This is in control of forwarding message from a particular point to base station, point-to-point, point to the cluster head, point-to-sink, and in reverse. LEACH and PEGASIS protocols relate the techniques to consume power and to increase sensor life. WSNs utilize identity-related protocols for routing, LEACH offers cluster-based data delivery, and PEGASIS is a chain protocol. To generate an efficient routing protocol, in WSN, a network node performs as a router and they utilize transmission mechanism. By encryption and decryption techniques, efficient routing is secured.

Transport layer: This layer links data transmission with outer networks that are interrelation of sensor network to the Internet. It is the one of the challenging tasks in WSN.

Application layer: By securing data transmission to lower layers, this layer offers complete output. Through application software to receive efficient results, it is responsible for management, data cluster, and transmission. Security protocols in sensor networks give data integrity, replay conservation, low cost, and semantic security.

There are four layers used in industrial IoT (IIoT). The layers are device layer, content layer, network layer, and service layer. Various implementations are encouraged by WSNs such as few are revolutionary whereas various are virtually necessary. The latter's application diversity is unbelievable target tracking, environment monitoring, oil, water and gas monitoring, accurate farming, provide chain management, systematic health monitoring, transport facility, active volcano monitoring, health care center,[39,40] below ground mining, and human job monitoring are some of them.

3.3 CLOUD AND FOG INFRASTRUCTURE FOR DATA SECURITY

Cloud computing infrastructure is composed up of many components, such as storage, hardware, networking, and virtualization, each integrated with one another into a single architecture supporting various types of important operations. Proper security mechanism is required so that intruder cannot alter any sensitive information.[2] As cloud computing in agriculture continues to increase, so too will the number of questions about it. It describes a secure steganography-based fog as well as mobile edge computing environment. Basically, steganography is consisted of two main processes, namely embedding process and extracting process. At some point of the embedding method, watermark is embedded into the multimedia records (virtual records). The original digital data (multimedia content) will slightly modified after embedding the watermark, this modified data are called as watermarked data. At the same time as in extraction manner, this embedded watermark is extracted from the watermarked facts and recovers the original multimedia information. The extracted watermark is then compared with the authentic watermark; if the watermark is identical it effects in authenticated data. During the transmission of the watermarked data over the public network through cloud or fog, attacker may tamper the data, and if any, modification in the data can be detected by comparing the extracted watermark with the original watermark. The proposed quantum steganography system ensures the authentication and security for fog cloud IoT users.

In this chapter, we discussed the role of IoT in smart health care through a wireless body area network. There are many existing algorithms are proving the better performance. Sensors (retina artificial arm chips)[6-8] inside retina can be embed for helping one blind human being for seeing once more. By using WBAN, the sufferers accompanied by heart disease,[9] asthma, diabetes, Alzheimer's problem, Parkinson's problem, and so on can be performed.[10] Inside conventional wellness programs, there is a necessity for sufferers for staying inside hospital, yet WBAN confesses these sufferers for continuing through usual everyday schedule of them. It mitigates pharmaceutical work cost and also foundation cost. Biosensor nodes choose one route that has smallest distance toward sink node as well as absorbs small energy. The WBANs policies found at cloud technique possesses more edges like improved efficiency, larger performances, as well as utilities as well as greater reliability and so on, even so this will quiet inside its advance phase as well as might possess various oppositions as well as practical problems.[22] Thus, here we study dual sink technique utilizing clustering inside body area network. This is very important at improving duration of network with effectively using nodes battery time duration. Here, we can get optimized result in terms of less collision, faster packet delivery rate, and less sensor node failure rate by using nature-inspired algorithm. In future, we can optimize[42,43] by selecting efficient cluster head through taking the help of machine learning and IoT efficiently.

- Efficient saturated information storing and retrieving: Concentrating in achieving message during data transmission, achieving the message in storage is not appropriately labeled in this dissertation. WSNs are visualized to give global sensation of data, reserve, and satisfy supplying facility in context with global computing. A growing saturated network saving information as well as recovery technique has presented newly for the reason of secure data management. This

TABLE 3.5   Difference Between IoT Security and IoT Forensics.

IoT Security	IoT Forensics
Provides security insurance for both physical and logical security issues	Determines and reconstructs the chain of events by analyzing physical evidence and electronic data
Applies diverse security techniques to minimize the scope of the attack and prevent further damage	Applies investigative techniques to identify, extract, preserve, and analyze digital information
Real-time response: implements different techniques in order to confront the threats during a live incident	Post-mortem investigation: identifies deficits after the incident occurred or while the system is inactive (however, when applying live forensics techniques, forensics professionals acquire digital evidence during a real-time incident)
Generalized: looking for any possible harmful behavior	Case-centered: reconstructing a given criminal scenario
Continuous process: keeps alert 24 hours a day	Time-restricted process: after a crime is alleged to have occurred (notitia criminis)
Security training and awareness: applies a set of security procedures, processes and standards, in order to have a securely-ready system, and prevent future cyber-threats from happening	Forensics Readiness: meets the forensics requirements and applies forensics standards, in order to be ready to undertake an investigation; takes measurements to maximize the forensic value of the potential evidence, and minimize the amount of resources spent on the investigation
Specifies the judicial region and legal aspects in service legal agreements regarding the security	Specify the judicial region and legal aspects in service legal agreements regarding the forensics issues
Well-established computer science field	Young and unexplored branch of the Digital Forensics

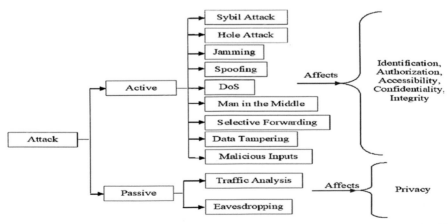

FIGURE 3.3   Various types of attack. (a) Denial of service attack, (b) spoofing and sybil attacks, (c) jamming attack, (d) man in the middle attack, (e) selective forwarding attack, and (f) malicious input attack.

creates the vacant of mechanisms for achieving stored data to become a bigger problem. Therefore, large experimental attempts have been given in such problem.

- Secure data aggregation: In various applications, for the reason of deducting the transmission cost and efficiency expenditure in data collection, the raw data felt by each and every sensor should be combined. In this dissertation, we learn event boundary detection which is an important form of data collection. Therefore, as required by the given applications data aggregation in WSNs can be of different forms. Each different type of data collection may need personalized efficient communication techniques. So, to deduct the complexity of the protocol stack general techniques should also be grown. Various researches should be created in this area.

- Privacy-aware security services: Recent security research in WSNs seldom judge privacy problem. Therefore, in various applications, information and network transmission confidentiality can be a large problem. Privacy-aware security services should be again enlarged as WSNs are visualized to become more and more extensive.

Wireless sensor network is endangered varieties of anomalies. That can be elaborately classified in below:

- Attacks on confidentiality and legitimacy: Confidentiality and legitimacy of transmission paths should be secured by decryption methods from packet replay anomalies, eavesdropping, and changes of data packets.

- Attacks on network availability: Denial-of-service (DoS) attacks are called attacks on availability. This chooses all layers of a sensor network.

- Stealthy attack against service integrity: the aim of the attacker in a stealthy attack is to create the network to receive an incorrect data value. Such as, through the sensor node a hacker encompasses detector point and inserts an incorrect message.

Having the detector network accessible for its deliberately working is necessary in these attacks. Denial of service against wireless sensor networks should allow day today actual problem to our body and security of human being. An effort to dispose, disturb, and ruin the networking system is generally known as denial of service. Moreover, incident which eradicates system strength to carry out the involvement can be a DoS attack. The network layer of WSNs is unsafe because of various types of attacks.

- *Transport layer attacks*

The transport layer attacks which can be launched in a wireless sensor network are desynchronization and flooding attack.

- *Node replication attack*

A hacker tries for appending its connecting points with a survived wireless network in this type of attack by replicating the identification number with existing survived point in networking. Likewise, in WSN point copied, connected with network will create critical disturbance for information transmission which damage the data by passing data through inaccurate paths. It causes separating network transmission incorrectly. On behalf, it can be feasible to replicate decipher keys to utilize as information transmission to duplicated point, if hacker obtains physical access to the whole network. The attacker could very comfortably access a particular part of network like that he assigns duplicated points through networking system, perhaps it creates division of network.[3]

- *Attacks on privacy*

As spontaneous data assembling through the systematic and deliberate deployment of sensors are feasible for WSNs, it is at risk to the abundant resources. In a WSN secrecy maintenance of delicate data is especially very tough challenge. However, to obtain sensitive data, a challenger may collect apparently safe data and finds for combining information gathered through various detector points. In comparison to the *panda hunter problem*, by comprehensively observing the network traffic where the hunter can exactly calculate the situation of the panda.

- In mobile computing and wireless research methodology, WSN is fascinating more interest over last decade. The uses of the wireless network are abundant which increasing a lot such as strategic battlefield. Anyhow, these networks are unsafe to various security threats because of saturated nature and their implement in rural areas that can directly influence their result.
- In wireless multimedia sensor networks (WMSNs), various components are responsible for the outlined in networking system. It is permitted for the transmission of many streams of theory. The pattern of a WMSN is basically affected by various constituents that are described in this[55] part.

- There are various necessities to the large area of implementations predicted on WMSNs. For that in data transmission systems, multimedia data comprise snapshot and flowing content. In very few moment, a very short data hold event-triggered monitoring can be acquired. With a very lengthy periods of time flowing, these data are created and need assisted message forwarding. Therefore, a powerful base is needed to carry out QoS and evaluate application-specific needs. Concerning a union of bounds on power utilization, accuracy, authenticity, delay, tampering, or network lifetime, these demands may exist to more domains and can be demonstrated with others.
- Large data flow rate: Generally video data need a data flow rate which is the magnitude greater and carried out with presently obtainable detector. Data rates such as one order of magnitude greater may be needed for high-end multimedia sensors, with equivalent energy consumption. So, it requires to be supported large amount of data with less energy utilization method. With regard to ultra-wide band, delivery mechanism appears especially favorable for WMSNs.
- Power consumption: In WMSNs, power consumption is a basic involve in traditional wireless sensor networks. Where multimedia applications generate large amount of information, which need efficient data delivery powers with large computing.
- Multiple media coverage: In specific video sensors, various multiple media detector has greater sense power. Moreover, if a clear mark resides in middle of the play with detector video where sensors can retrieve images. Therefore, a model is enlarged in WSN, which is insufficient for multiple media detector.
- Connecting other wireless technologies: By correlating regional "islands" of sensors through different Wi-Fi schemes, sensor networks must be added. Without giving up on the reliability of the performance, this is necessary to be secured within each and every individual technology. When the network is used for various mission-critical applications, this problem is very danger like that in a strategic battlefield. In real-life deployment, scenarios accidental collapse of nodes is also very often. Traditional security mechanisms with a large overhead of computation and transmission are impossible in WSNs due to resource constraints in the sensor nodes.

TABLE 3.6 Comparisons Between Cloud Computing, Edge Computing, Fog Computing, and Mist Computing.

	Cloud Computing	Fog Computing	Edge Computing	Mist Computing
Architecture	❖ Central processing based model. ❖ Fulfils the need for large amounts of data to be accessed more quickly, this demand is ever-growing due to cloud agility. ❖ Accessed through internet.	❖ Coined by CISCO ❖ Extending cloud to the edge of the network ❖ Decentralized computing ❖ Any device with computing, storage, and network connectivity can be a fog node, can be put on railwy track or oil rig. ❖ Fog computing shoves intelligence down to the local area network level of network architecture, processing data in a fog node or IoT gateway	❖ Fog computing usually work with cloud and Edge can work without cloud or fog. ❖ Edge is limited to smaller number of peripheral layers ❖ Edge computing pushes the intelligence, processing power and communication of an edge gateway or appliance directly into devices like programmable automation controllers (PACs)	❖ Middle ground between cloud and edge/fog ❖ Lightweight computing residing in the network fabric using micro-controllers and microchips ❖ Not a mandatory layer of fog computing
Pros	❖ Easy to scale ❖ Low cost storage ❖ Based on Internet driven global network on robust TCP/IP protocol	❖ Real time data analysis ❖ Take quick actions ❖ Sensitive data remains inside the network ❖ Cost saving on storage and network ❖ More scalable than edge computing ❖ Operations can be managed by IT/OT team	❖ Edge computing simplifies internal communication by means of physically wiring physical assets to intelligent PAC to collect, analysis and process data. ❖ PACs then use edge computing capabilities to determine what data should be stored locally or sent to the cloud for further analysis	❖ Local decision making data ❖ Works with fog computing and cloud platform

TABLE 3.6 *(Continued)*

	Cloud Computing	Fog Computing	Edge Computing	Mist Computing
Cons	❖ Latency/Response time ❖ Bandwidth cost ❖ Security ❖ Power consumption ❖ No offline-mode ❖ Sending raw data over internet to the cloud could have privacy, security and legal issues	❖ Fog computing relies on many links to move data from physical asset chain to digital layer and this is a potential point of failure	❖ Less scalable than fog computing ❖ Interconnected through proprietary networks with custom security and little interoperability ❖ No cloud-aware ❖ Cannot do resource pooling ❖ Operations cannot be extended to IT/OT team	
Misc.		❖ Less sensitive and non-real-time data is sent to the cloud for further processing ❖ Fog node can be deployed in private, community, public or hybrid mode	❖ PACs (programmable automation controllers) then use edge computing capabilities to determine what data should be stored locally or sent to the cloud for further analysis ❖ Intelligence is literally pushed to the network edge, where our physical assets are first connected together and where IoT data originates ❖ The current Edge Computing domain is a sub-set of Fog Computing domain	❖ Architecture may not require Cloud

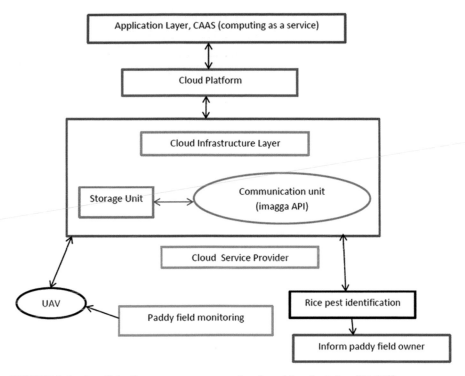

FIGURE 3.4　Possible disease symptoms on plant by taking the help of UAV.[59]

3.4　COVID HANDLING USING IOT

To minimize the spread rate of fatal COVID disease, scientists are trying and doing research to identify disease-affected person. From Figures 3.5 and 3.6, we came to know about the architecture of the process, fog computing framework, and customer registration process. The number of infected as well as suspected people can be found by using this method nationwide.[58,59] There are many terminologies used here, which we will discuss below:

- ARC: Automatic risk checker.
- CA: Cloud application.
- SUDUN: Suspected user data uploader node.
- UERC: Unique encrypted reference code.
- RUERC: Rotational unique encrypted reference code.
- BLE : Bluetooth low energy technology.

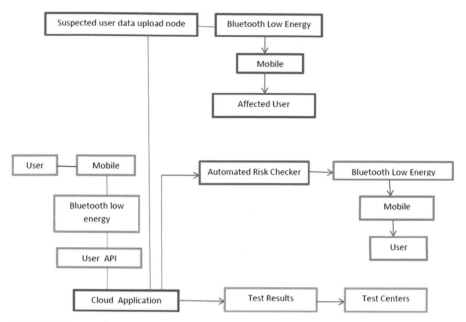

FIGURE 3.5   Application of COVID system overview.

3.5   CONCLUSION

IoT is a technology that provides a platform where network of devices can communicate, explore data, and practice information manually to cater to the needs of individuals or organizations. Enabling autonomous interaction between the interconnected devices and objects gives rise behavior to another emerging interdisciplinary area as well as influencing new paradigm of Internet. Among the other extension of IoT, Internet of behavior is the recent one and can be compiled under the fields like technology, data analytics, and behavioral science.

This chapter's objective is to explore the concepts and applications related to IoT with the vision to identify and address its behavioral applications focusing into decisions, intensifications, and companionship while using the technology in healthcare solutions, agriculture and supply chain, industry, and in other smart applications. Due to this, all-in-one embedded nature of IoT and its behavioral applications, its architectural design, implementation, operational manageability, and maintenance are raising numerous prevalent concerns that are the challenges for researchers and academicians.

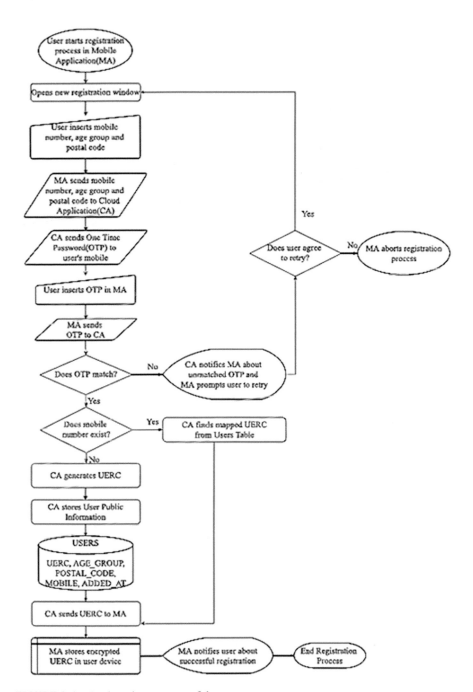

FIGURE 3.6   Registration process of the user.

KEYWORDS

- **IoT**
- **smart environment**
- **security**
- **challenges**

REFERENCES

1. Escamilla-Ambrosio, P. J.; Rodríguez-Mota A.; Aguirre-Anaya E.; Acosta-Bermejo R.; Salinas-Rosales M. Distributing Computing in the Internet of Things: Cloud, Fog and Edge Computing Overview. In *NEO 2016. Studies in Computational Intelligence*; Maldonado, Y., Trujillo, L., Schütze, O., Riccardi, A., Vasile, M.; Eds.; Vol. 731; Springer: Cham, 2018. https://doi.org/10.1007/978-3-319-64063-1_4.

2. Abd El-Latif, A. A.; Abd-El-Atty, B.; Hossain, M. S.; Elmougy, S.; Ghoneim, A. Secure Quantum Steganography Protocol for Fog Cloud Internet of Things. *IEEE Access* **2018,** *6,* 10332–10340.

3. https://www.designworldonline.com/part-1-connectivity-and-iot-in-motion-and-general-automation/

4. Behura, A.; Priyadarshini, S. B. B. Assessment of Load in Cloud Computing Environment Using C-means Clustering Algorithm. In *Intelligent and Cloud Computing*; Springer: Singapore, 2019; pp 207–215.

5. Behura, A.; Kabat, M. R. Energy-Efficient Optimization-Based Routing Technique for Wireless Sensor Network Using Machine Learning. In *Progress in Computing, Analytics and Networking*; Springer: Singapore, 2020; pp 555–565.

6. Buvana, M.; Loheswaran, K.; Madhavi, K.; Ponnusamy, S.; Behura, A.; Jayavadivel, R. Improved Resource Management and Utilization Based on a Fog-Cloud Computing System with IoT Incorporated with Classifier Systems. *Microprocessors Microsyst,* 103815.

7. Sahoo, S.; Halder, R. Blockchain-Based Forward and Reverse Supply Chains for E-waste Management. In *International Conference on Future Data and Security Engineering*; Springer: Cham, 2020; pp 201–220.

8. Stoyanova, M.; Nikoloudakis, Y.; Panagiotakis, S.; Pallis, E.; Markakis, E. K. A Survey on the Internet of Things (IoT) Forensics: Challenges, Approaches, and Open Issues. *IEEE Commun. Surv. Tutor* **2020,** *22* (2), 1191–1221.

9. Alenezi, A.; Zulkipli, N. H. N.; Atlam, H. F.; Walters, R. J.; Wills, G. B. The Impact of Cloud Forensic Readiness on Security. In *Proceedings of the 7th International Conference on Cloud Computer Services and Science* 2017; pp 539–545.

10. Cook, A. et al. *Internet of Cloud: Security and Privacy Issues*; Springer: Cham, Switzerland, 2018; pp 271–301.

11. Ramachandra, G.; Iftikhar, M.; Khan, F. A. A Comprehensive Survey on Security in Cloud Computing. *Procedia Comput. Sci* **2017,** *110* (2012), 465–472.

12. Hossain, M.; Hasan, R.; Skjellum, A. Securing the Internet of Things: A Meta-Study of Challenges, Approaches, and Open Problems. *Proc. IEEE 37th Int. Conf. Distrib. Comput. Syst. Workshop (ICDCSW)* **2017**, 220–225.

13. Khan, A.M. and Salah, K. IoT Security: Review, Blockchain Solutions, and Open Issues. *Future Gener. Comput. Syst.* **2018**, *82*, 395–411.

14. Ammar, M.; Russello, G.; Crispo, B. Internet of Things: A Survey on the Security of IoT Frameworks. *J. Inf. Security Appl.* **2018**, *38*, 8–27.

15. Aly, M.; Khomh, F.; Haoues, M.; Quintero, A.; Yacout, S. Enforcing Security in Internet of Things Frameworks: A Systematic Literature Review. *Internet Things* Jun. **2019**, *6*, Art. no. 100050.

16. Machorro-Cano, I.; Alor-Hernández, G.; Paredes-Valverde, M. A.; Ramos-Deonati, U.; Sánchez-Cervantes, J. L.; Rodríguez-Mazahua, L. PISIoT: A Machine Learning and IoT-Based Smart Health Platform for Overweight and Obesity Control. *Appl. Sci.* **2019**, *9* (15), 3037.

17. Lu, Y.; Xu, D. L. Internet of Things (IoT) Cyber Security Research: A Review of Current Research Topics. *IEEE Internet Things J.* **2019**, *6* (2), 2103–2115.

18. Balaji, S.; Nathani, K.; Santhakumar, R. IoT Technology, Applications and Challenges: A Contemporary Survey. *Wireless Pers. Commun.* **2019**, *108*, 363–388.

19. Ćolaković, A.; Hadžialić, M. Internet of Things (IoT): A Review of Enabling Technologies, Challenges, and Open Research Issues. *Comput. Netw.* **2018**, *144*, 17–39.

20. Hasan, Z. M.; Al-Rizzo, H.; Al-Turjman, F. A Survey on Multipath Routing Protocols for QoS Assurances in Real-Time Wireless Multimedia Sensor Networks. *IEEE Commun. Surveys Tuts.* **2017**, *19* (3), 1424–1456, 3rd Quart.

21. Adeel, A. et al. *A Survey on the Role of Wireless Sensor Networks and IoT in Disaster Management*; Springer: Singapore, 2019; pp 57–66.

22. Ahmed, R.; Malviya, K. A.; Kaur, J. M.; Mishra, P. V. Comprehensive Survey of Key Technologies Enabling 5G-IoT. *SSRN Electron. J.* Apr. **2019**, 488–492.

23. Yin, J.; Yang, Z.; Cao, H.; Liu, T.; Zhou, Z.; Wu, C. A Survey on Bluetooth 5.0 and Mesh. *ACM Trans. Sens. Netw.* **2019**, *15* (3), 1–29.

24. Bembe, M.; Abu-Mahfouz, A.; Masonta, M.; Ngqondi, T. A Survey on Low-Power Wide Area Networks for IoT Applications. *Telecommun. Syst.* **2019**, *71* (2), 249–274.

25. Al-Turjman, F.; Ever, E.; Zahmatkesh, H. Small Cells in the Forthcoming 5G/IoT: Traffic Modelling and Deployment Overview. *IEEE Commun. Surveys Tuts.* **2019**, *21* (1), 28–65.

26. Andrews, G. J. et al. What Will 5G Be?" *IEEE J. Sel. Areas Commun.* **2014**, *32* (6), 1065–1082.

27. Agiwal, M.; Saxena, N.; Roy, A. Towards Connected Living: 5G Enabled Internet of Things (IoT). *IETE Tech. Rev.* **2019**, *36* (2), 190–202.

28. Ullah, H.; Nair, G. N.; Moore, A.; Nugent, C.; Mus-champ, P.; Cuevas, M. 5G Communication: An Overview of Vehicle-to Everything, Drones, and Healthcare Use-Cases. *IEEE Access* **2019**, *7*, 37251–37268.

29. Conti, M.; Dehghantanha, A.; Franke, K.; Watson, S. Internet of Things Security and Forensics: Challenges and Opportunities. *Future Gener. Comput. Syst.* **2018**, *78*, 544–546.

30. MacDermott, Á.; Baker, T.; Shi, Q. IoT Forensics: Challenges for the Ioa Era. *Proc. 9th IFIP Int. Conf. New Technol. Mobile Security (NTMS)*, Jan. **2018**, 1–5.

31. Alenezi, A.; Atlam, F. H.; Alsagri, R.; Alassafi, O. M.; Wills, B. G. IoT Forensics: A State-of-the-Art Review, Challenges and Future Directions. *Proc. 4th Int. Conf. Complexity Future Inf. Syst. Risk (COMPLEXIS)*, May **2019**, 106–115.

32. Lillis, D.; Becker, B.; O'Sullivan, T.; Scanlon, M. Current Challenges and Future Research Areas for Digital Forensic Investigation. In *Proc. 11th ADFSL Conf. Digit. Forensics Security Law (CDFSL)*; Daytona Beach, FL, USA, May 2016.

33. Arafat, Y. M.; Mondal, B.; Rani, S. Technical Challenges of Cloud Forensics and Suggested Solutions. *Int. J. Sci. Eng. Res*. **2017**, *8* (8), 1142–1149.

34. Zawoad, S.; Hasan, R. Digital Forensics in the Age of Big Data: Challenges, Approaches, and Opportunities. *Proc. IEEE 17th Int. Conf. High Perform. Comput. Commun. IEEE 7th Int. Symp. Cyberspace Safty Security IEEE 12th Int. Conf. Embedded Softw. Syst.*, Aug. **2015**, 1320–1325.

35. Yaqoob, I.; Hashem, T. A. I.; Ahmed, A.; Kazmi, A. M. S.; Hong, S. C. Internet of Things forensics: Recent Advances, Taxonomy, Requirements, and Open Challenges. *Future Gener. Comput. Syst*. **2019**, *92*, 265–275.

36. Sadineni, L.; Pilli, E.; Battula, B. R. *A Holistic Forensic Model for the Internet of Things*; Springer International: Cham, Switzerland, 2019.

37. Hossain, M. Towards a Holistic Framework for Secure, Privacy-Aware, and Trustworthy Internet of Things Using Resource Efficient Cryptographic Schemes; Ph.D. Dissertation, Apr. 2018. DOI: 10.13140/RG.2.2.33117.72165.

38. Chung, H.; Park, J.; Lee, S. Digital Forensic Approaches for Amazon Alexa Ecosystem. *Proc. 17th Annu. DFRWS USA*, **2017**, S15–S25.

39. Al-Sharrah, M.; Salman, A.; Ahmad, I. Watch Your Smart Watch. *Proc. Int. Conf. Comput. Sci. Eng. (ICCSE)*, **2018**, 1–5.

40. Rondeau, M. C.; Temple, A. M.; Lopez, J. Industrial IoT Cross-Layer Forensic Investigation. *Wiley Interdiscip. Rev. Forensic Sci*. **2019**, *1* (1), Art. no. e1322.

41. Wang, K.; Du, M.; Sun, Y.; Vinel, A.; Zhang, Y. Attack Detection and Distributed Forensics in Machine-to-Machine Networks. *IEEE Netw*. **2016**, *30* (6), 49–55.

42. Tekeoglu, A.; Tosun, A. Investigating Security and Privacy of a Cloud-Based Wireless IP Camera: NetCam. *Proc. 24th Int. Conf. Comput. Commun. Netw. (ICCCN)*, Oct. **2015**, 1–6.

43. Knight, E.; Lord, S.; Arief, B. Lock Picking in the Era of Internet of Things. *Proc. IEEE CPS Workshop Data Security Privacy Forensics Trust (DSPFT)*, **2019**, 835–842.

44. Al-Turjman, F.; Abujubbeh, M. IoT-Enabled Smart Grid via SM: An Overview. *Future Gener. Comput. Syst*. **2019**, *96*, 579–590.

45. Bhoopathy, V.; Behura, A.; Reddy, V. L.; Abidin, S.; Babu, D. V.; Albert, A. J. IoT-Harpseca: A Secure Design and Development System of Roadmap for Devices and Technologies in IoT Space. *Microprocess. Microsyst.* **2021**, 104044.

46. Abassi, R. VANET Security and Forensics: Challenges and Opportunities. *Wiley Interdiscip. Rev. Forensics Sci*. **2019**, *1* (2), Art. no. e1324.

47. Hossain, M.; Hasan, R.; Zawoad, S. Trust-IoV: A Trustworthy Forensic Investigation Framework for the Internet of Vehicles (IoV). *Proc. IEEE 2nd Int. Congr. Internet Things (ICIoT)*, Oct. **2017**, 25–32.

48. Lee, K. E.; Gerla, M.; Pau, G.; Lee, U.; Lim, H. J. Internet of Vehicles: From Intelligent Grid to Autonomous Cars and Vehicular Fogs. *Int. J. Distrib. Sens. Netw*. **2016**, *12* (9), 1–14.

49. Al-Turjman, F.; Lemayian, P. J.; Alturjman, S.; Mostarda, L. Enhanced Deployment Strategy for the 5G Drone-BS Using Artificial Intelligence. *IEEE Access* **2019**, *7*, 75999–76008.

50. Renduchintala, A.; Jahan, F.; Khanna, R.; Javaid, Y. A. A Comprehensive Micro Unmanned Aerial Vehicle (UAV/Drone) Forensic Framework. *Digit. Invest.* **2019,** *30,* 52–72.
51. Jain, U.; Rogers, M.; Matson, T. E. Drone Forensic Framework: Sensor and Data Identification and Verification. *Proc. IEEE Sensors Appl. Symp. (SAS),* **2017,** 1–6.
52. Ferrag, A. M.; Maglaras, L. Delivery Coin: An IDS and Block Chain Based Delivery Framework for Drone-Delivered Services. *Computers* **2019,** *8* (3), 58.
53. Karie, M. N.; Kebande, R. V.; Venter, S. H.; Choo, K.-K. R. On the Importance of Standardising the Process of Generating Digital Forensic Reports. *Forensics Sci. Int. Rep.* Apr. **2019,** *1,* Art. no. 100008.
54. Oriwoh, E.; Jazani, D.; Epiphaniou, G.; Sant, P. Internet of Things Forensics: Challenges and Approaches. *Proc. 9th IEEE Int. Conf. Collaborative Comput. Netw. Appl. Worksharing,* Oct. **2013,** 608–615.
55. Hasan, K.; Biswas, K.; Ahmed, K.; Nafi, N. S.; Islam, M. S. A Comprehensive Review of Wireless Body Area Network. *J. Netw. Comput. App.* **2019,** *143,* 178–198.
56. Nieto, A.; Rios, R.; Lopez, J. A Methodology for Privacy-Aware IoT-Forensics. *Proc. 16th IEEE Int. Conf. Trust Security Privacy Comput. Commun. 11th IEEE Int. Conf Big Data Sci. Eng. 14th IEEE Int. Conf. Embedded Softw. Syst.* **2017,** 626–633.
57. Tahsien, S. M.; Karimipour, H.; Spachos, P. Machine Learning Based Solutions for Security of Internet of Things (IoT): A Survey. *J. Netw. Comput. App.* **2020,** *161,* 102630.
58. Whaiduzzaman, M.; Hossain, M. R.; Shovon, A. R.; Roy, S.; Laszka, A.; Buyya, R.; Barros, A. A Privacy-Preserving Mobile and Fog Computing Framework to Trace and Prevent Covid-19 Community Transmission. *IEEE J. Biomed. Health Inform.* **2020,** *24* (12), 3564–3575.
59. Bhoi, S. K.; Jena, K. K.; Panda, S. K.; Long, H. V.; Kumar, R.; Subbulakshmi, P.; Jebreen, H. B. An Internet of Things Assisted Unmanned Aerial Vehicle Based Artificial Intelligence Model for Rice Pest Detection. *Microprocess. Microsyst, 80,* 103607.

CHAPTER 4

Implementation of the Industrial Internet of Things (IIoT) Is the Tool of Digital Transformation Technology

KALI CHARAN RATH, RAGHVENDRA KUMAR, and
BROJO KISHORE MISHRA

GIET University, Odisha, India

ABSTRACT

In the present digital competitive worldwide market, fabricating businesses are occupied looking for groundbreaking plans to decrease lead time, customization of new item advancements that meet all client assumptions like tasteful, cost, nature of items, and so on. Nowadays different assembling areas embraced computer-aided design, computer-aided manufacturing, computer-aided engineering, rapid prototyping, additive manufacturing, digital manufacturing, etc., give business benefits in lessening the item advancement cycle. This chapter briefly described the concept of Internet-of-Things and industrial Internet of Things (IIoT) with their application layout in digital manufacturing. Along with this, the chapter also defines the application of IIoT in assembling frameworks in association with computerized assisted techniques.

4.1 INTRODUCTION

Current assembling is at the center of modern creation from base materials to semicompleted merchandise and end results. Introduced in three sections, modern manufacturing processes begins by covering progressed fabricating.[1]

Internet of Things: Technological Advances and New Applications. Brojo Kishore Mishra &
Amit Vishwasrao Salunkhe (Eds.)

Current manufacturing is focused on being an industry chief by giving the best arrangement-based items.

The first industrial revolution was set apart by progress from hand creation strategies to machines using steam force and water power. The usage of new innovations took quite a while, so the period which this alludes to it is somewhere in the range of 1760 and 1820, or 1840 in Europe and the United States. The second industrial revolution, otherwise called the technological revolution, is the period somewhere in the range of 1871 and 1914 that came about because of the establishments of the broad railroad and transmit networks, which took into consideration quicker exchange of individuals and thoughts, just as powerful. Expanding jolt permitted plants to build up the advanced creation line. The third industrial revolution, otherwise called the digital revolution, happened in the late 20th century.[2,3]

The fourth industrial revolution comprises of a huge number when looking carefully into our general public and current computerized patterns. To see how broad these parts are, here are some contributing advanced advances as examples.[4,5]

Industrial Internet of Things (IIoT) is the utilization of data and correspondence innovation in the computerized fabricating field to reshape the cutting-edge producing framework. The digitalization of assembling is pointed toward the better improvement in component manufacturing plan, plant capacity, and administration as needed in changing the activities, cycle, and energy impression of industrial facilities w.r.t. the executives of assembling supply chains.

Computerized production is being driven by the appearance and development of numerous advances, including superior registering, computer-aided design (CAD), and computer-aided engineering programming, distributed computing, Internet of Things (IoT), IIoT, progressed sensor innovation, 3D printing, modern robot, information investigation, artificial intelligence, machine learning, and remote availability that better empowers machine-to-machine correspondence.

The IIoT underpins producing observing, controlling, and execution framework. It coordinate the data for different machines on the plant floor in the inventory network framework. The IIoT supports to expand industrial facility effectiveness and improve profitability. The prescient and preventive support can be all around taken consideration because of the usage of IIoT in the assembling unit.

Computerized fabricating is a greater area of cutting-edge innovation in the assembling field. Through this innovation, the assembling units can be ready to make their item according to the wanted style and amount in time scales that is be superior to the customary strategies.[6] It includes representation, fabricating recreation, machine factor investigation, comprehensive perspective on item, and cycle plan according to requirements and capacities.

Progressions in innovation and serious rivalry, both at home and abroad, will consistently push associations to enhance new cycles for item advancement. By adopting a coordinated strategy to get the product from plan to assembling, associations can without much of a stretch quicken their improvement cycle.

In the present worldwide assembling digital system, the market is changing essentially and recharacterizing contract producing. To help fashioners and manufacturers to these changes, some incorporated plan through-assembling devices empower information catch for extraordinary robotization, computer numerical control (CNC) for assembling and part manufacturing, respectively. It empowers them to all the more cautiously consider fabricating strategies during the plan stage.

4.2 COMPARISON BETWEEN IOT AND IIOT

The parameters that differentiate IoT from industrial IoT include security, interoperability, scalability, precision and accuracy, programmability, low latency, reliability, resilience, automation, and serviceability.

Modern cycles force grave prerequisites on IoT arrangements. Item administrators should represent these extra necessities in the plan and designing. They should comprehend the particular use cases, just as the conditions the arrangements will be put into. IoT focuses on basic technology such as IP-based connectivity, interoperability, software suits, analytics, etc.

IoT and IIoT subsequently frequently need to satisfy totally various assignments notwithstanding the authoritative system. They focus on a automization and in this manner at a further proficiency increment in the processes.[7] It is in this way to be expected that successive utilize cases incorporate preventive upkeep, quality affirmation, or postfiguring of requests, for example, those territories which frequently have high data necessities and which recently needed to give moderately intricate and hence costly help measures in modern creation because of an absence of data.

In the event that frameworks are conveyed to clients, who at that point keep on being worked to various degrees, for example, through support contracts with the client, distant checking has gotten practically unavoidable to try not to need to continually complete costly help visits nearby. To a limited degree, this as of now incorporates parts of the item situated IoT frameworks.

IIoT is the branch of IoT and is specifically used in the manufacturing industry. Various industrial devices are connected through IIoT and making them more intelligent. The ultimate result of this is to increase the manufacturing process and safety to run the production very smoothly with lower costs. That is, the use of IIoT gives a quicker manufacturing at lower costs with minimum resources.

The intelligent devices of the manufacturing industries now play a vital role in IIoT and help in communicating various important information in a superior manner. These data can further will be well analyzed through the analysis system for various decisions. Business decisions can be taken care in a faster rate with accuracy.

TABLE 4.1   Comparision between IoT and IIoT.

Sl. So.	IoT	IIoT
1	General applications, like retail, health care, insurance, connected car, smart cities and energy, etc.	Industrial applications, like heavy industries, such as manufacturing, energy, oil and gas, and agriculture where industrial assets are connected to the Internet
2	Smart devices	Industrial systems
3	Utility-centric	Advanced and robust
4	Autonomous	Integrated system
5	Off-site programming	On-site programming
6	Convenience and utilization	Operational efficiency
7	Consumer preferred maintenance	Industrial process schedule and maintenance
8	Human centric	Machine centric
9	Basically wireless	Both wireless and wired
10	Lighter communication standards	A high number of connectivity standards and technology machines, sensors, software, hardware, and integration system
11	Important but not critical	A critical connection
12	Low scale network	Large-scale network

4.3   INTERNET OF THINGS AND INDUSTRY 4.0

In the area of assembling, computers have consistently assumed an imperative job in taking item thoughts from idea to the real world. The capacity of

PC-supported assembling (CAM) to diminish the time needed to plan and model without reconfiguring or retooling the assembling line has inserted computer-aided manufacturing (CAM) arrangements in numerous industry verticals.

CAM is currently taking on a more extensive part in all activities of an assembling plant, including arranging, the board, transportation, and capacity. Innovation improvements are making this conceivable by mixing information catch, CAD, CAM, computer integrated manufacture, and item conveyance.

The applied popularity of the Internet innovations-related exercises, for example, the accompanying: showcasing, plan, and process arranging, manufacturing, and client support at various areas into an incorporated climate.[8,9] This has now been broadly acknowledged that the future examples of assembling associations will be data arranged and information-driven, and a large number of their day-by-day activities will be robotized around a worldwide data network that interfaces everybody together.[10–12]

Different strategies have been engaged with assembling measures and now the trend-setting innovation utilizes advanced qualities with its assistance to dispose of the uncertainty of got information and to change the substantial information through mathematical qualities or conditions into computerized values.[13,14] As more mechanized devices have gotten utilized in assembling plants, it has gotten important to show, mimic, and dissect the entirety of the machines, tooling, and input materials to improve the assembling process.

The Internet-of-Things (IoT), reality catch increase, computerized reasoning (AI), blockchain, and distributed computing are totally ready to upset the assembling business not long from now. These advancements are uniting and taking into consideration totally new PC-supported assembling models to be made—known as Industry 4.0.

Predicated on IoT, IIoT goes about as an impetus for the upset in Industry 4.0. At a time, when IoT altogether effects and impacts the worldwide shopper conduct,[15,16] the IIoT changes the manner in which ventures work. Albeit both IoT and IIoT are conceived of a similar mother, they are bound to assume different jobs in this digitized world.

The force behind the IoT environment is practical and interesting. The impending correspondence scene in the midst of continuous remote sensors, GPS, and control frameworks is upsetting the worldwide customer conduct just as enterprises across the world.

Digital manufacturing is an advancement that permits the get-together and examination of information across machines, empowering quicker, more adaptable, and more effective cycles to deliver more excellent merchandise at decreased expenses. Thus, basic Industry 4.0 is tied in with associating machines, cycles, and frameworks to consider the making of keen organizations self-sufficiently controlling one another. Models incorporate machines foreseeing their own disappointment and setting off support cycles or self-coordinated machine coordinations which respond to sudden changes underway interest.

The qualities given for Industry 4.0 can be considered as:

a)   Customization of items with exceptionally adaptable creation.
b)   Self-upgrading, self-designing, self-indicative, comprehension, and canny help of progressively complex work.

The Internet-supported assembling will profit by this sort of insightful framework advancement, conveying more effectively. Yet, CAM has its own advantage as a component of the more extensive, incorporated item, and administration conveyance measure. Maximum organizations and manufacturing processes have been restricted to one industrial facility. In Industry 4.0, limits of individual processing plants are changing and in all probability going to replace by advanced technology. CAM assembling will turn out to be increasingly more organized until everything is interlinked with all the other things. This causes the unpredictability of creation and provider organizations to develop hugely.

Digital manufacturing system backings following significant principles of operational for execution:

a)   Interoperability.
b)   Information transparency.
c)   Actionable insights.
c)   Automation.

CAM and IIoT coordination are used across the entire worth chain for product development, assembling, and data information to computerized administrations arrangement monitored by executives.[17,18] The requirement of coordination reflects new innovations for the target vision of the industry.

IoT empowers buyers to receive the benefit; the IIoT encourages machine-to-machine (M2M) correspondence profiting businesses across areas. Henceforth, IIoT is a conventional term alluding to another and creating manufacturing environment. Here, machines, devices, and manufacturing processes are interconnected and monitored by software programming, gathering enormous measures of information to upgrade the work after some time just as to maintain a strategic distance from framework disappointments.

4.4 INDUSTRIAL INTERNET OF THINGS (IIOT) PLATFORM

The technological elements that are necessary to connect and analyze various data from machines and equipment include (1) hardware, such as chips, sensors, or gateways, (2) connectivity protocols and services, (3) software components, including infrastructure, IoT platforms, and analytics, (4) applications that are built on top of the software layer, etc.

IIoT is a standards technology, low-cost innovation, and ease of use. It integrate a cooperative environment in synchronize manner with various protocols, datasets, ERP systems, and operating technologies by including SCADA, M2M, and others. IIoT network involves controllers, robots, machinery, sensors, and some non-IoT devices also. Such a network operates and executes various scheduling, data collection, analysis, interoperability, workflow integration, decision-making, and integration of manufacturing unit with business-oriented systems.

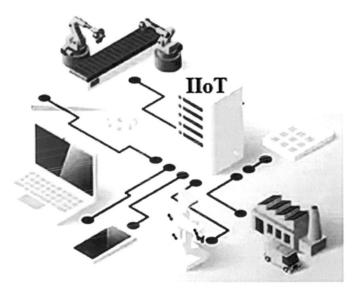

FIGURE 4.1   Basic layout of IIoT in manufacturing industry.

The viewpoints of IIoT in industrial application are tied into systems and classified into five functional domains:

a)   Information domain
b)   Operations domain
c)   Control domain

d) Application domain

e) Business domain

In recent times, product lifecycle control (PLM) system changed the classical manufacturing system for product development, technique layout, and development facts. The maximum of these facts remains with manufacturers. As huge information get stored in the database and the analytics carried out to those repositories make it possible to statistically correlate format to ordinary performance, an outstanding deal of these records will start to accompany the product to the marketplace. Corporations will ought to make difficult alternatives, just as they did while software-enabled merchandise hit the market.

The mix of digitization advancements[19] and fabricating framework empowered the producer to react to client's necessity, quickly, by gathering data, rebuilding the data, and to execute the recreation and prototyping of the capacity and configuration; to submit the assembling mission of the ideal item.

CAD is a contemporary format and recreation device. It has high criticalness of time, cash, and endeavors by guaranteeing the accuracy and revision of the favored drawing and plans. Not handiest will it improve the item improvement way through top-notch mechanization, anyway it will likewise impact the high-caliber of the end result going to fabricate.

CAD programming is likewise changing at an improved speed to adjust to the always changing over the universe of virtual time. Various organizations worldwide have delivered cutting perspective collective and cloud essentially based answers which offer a whole new assortment of functionalities. Organizations and associations of all sizes are enjoying enhancing and permitting computer-aided designing with new capacities which might be utilized for better planning of product, machines, and various substances.

Computer-aided designing has progressed as outstanding amongst other modernized planning systems and empowers a wide exhibit of delivering procedures with the guide of moving the exhaustive outlines without issues to a creation and planning for manufacturing of various products. With its assistance, both 2D and 3D diagrams can be created, and these are easily turned around at any disposition to see the information from a particular demeanor.

Algorithm of a specialized drawing for CNC machining:

Stage 1: Define and spot the main perspectives on the part.

Stage 2: Consider adding area sees if the part has hidden geometry.

Stage 3: Add development lines (center lines, center marks, and center mark patterns).

Stage 4: Add measurements, beginning with the main first.

Stage 5: Specify the specific area and measurements, all things considered.

Stage 6: Add tolerances as required but it must be as per design standard.

Stage 7: Fill the product design name in title box and add notes for the manufacturer.

4.4.1 DEPENDENT OF IIOT ON SOME FEATURES OF IOT

The IoT is changing the mechanical way of life. It is a tool for new modern change and key in the computerized change of associations.

Modern IoT (IIoT) brings machines, distributed computing, examination, and individuals together to improve the presentation and efficiency of industrial processes. With IIoT, modern organizations can digitize measures, change plans of action, and improve execution and efficiency, while diminishing waste. These resource serious organizations working in a scope of ventures, for example, producing, energy, agribusiness, transportation, and utilities, are chipping away at IoT projects that interface billions of gadgets and convey an incentive across an assortment of utilization cases including prescient quality and upkeep examination, resource condition checking, and measure improvement in the manufacturing process.

Assembling control is an idea from information assortment to regulator determination; at that point distinguishing proof of a control framework for information preparing and creation controlling, from a solitary control highlight station connect and the cooperation interface between the administrator and a framework. Assembling gadgets and related examinations can be connected to each other by means of the web to work next to each other.

An average industrial facilities have a great many sensors creating information. With IIoT, manufacturers can consolidate machine information from a solitary line, plant, or an organization of destinations, for example, fabricating plants, assembly facilities along with treatment facilities, to proactively improve execution by distinguishing possible bottlenecks, disappointments, production process gaps, and quality issues before they occur. Consolidating information from manufacturing units through network can likewise bring about a more proficient control of material stream, supply bottlenecks, and the enhanced activity of hardware and software used for machine operations through the IIoT facility (Figure 4.2).

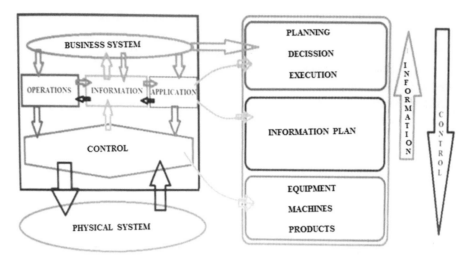

FIGURE 4.2   Integrated manufacturing system through IIoT domain.

4.4.2   INDUSTRIAL IOT APPLICATIONS

(a) Boeing: using IoT to drive manufacturing efficiency

Aviation pioneer William Boeing jested that it "benefits nobody to excuse any original thought with the assertion, 'It isn't possible.'" The worldwide avionics organization established in Boeing's name clearly still buys in to that ethos. It is currently running after the drawn-out objective of making its administration contributions more significant than its items while being the most important data supplier in flight. The organization has just made huge walks in changing its business. Boeing and its Tapestry Solutions auxiliary have forcefully sent IoT innovation to drive proficiency all through manufacturing plants and supply chains. The organization is likewise consistently expanding the volumes of associated sensors implanted into its planes.

(b) ABB: smart robotics

Force and mechanical technology firm ABB is quite possibly the most obvious to grasp the idea of prescient support, utilizing-associated sensors to screen its robots' upkeep needs—across five main locations—and trigger repair before parts break. Additionally identified with IoT is the organization's shared advanced mechanics. Its YuMi model, which was intended to team up close by people, can acknowledge input by means of Ethernet and modern conventions like Profibus and DeviceNet.

(c) Airbus: factory of the future

To state that collecting a business jetliner is an intricate undertaking would be putting it mildly. Such arts have a huge number of segments and a huge number of gathering steps, and the expense of missteps during the cycle can be colossal. To handle the difficulty, airbus has dispatched a computerized fabricating activity known as factory of the future to smooth out tasks and support creation limit. The organization has incorporated sensors to apparatuses and machines on the shop floor and given laborers wearable innovation—including mechanical shrewd glasses—intended to decrease blunders and reinforce security in the working environment.

(d) Amazon: reinventing warehousing

Amazon is "testing the limitation of computerization and human–machine joint effort." While the organization's desire to utilize drones for conveyance has won extensive media consideration, the association's satisfaction stockrooms utilize multitudes of WiFi-associated Kiva robots. The fundamental thought behind the Kiva innovation, which Amazon procured for $775 million in 2012, is that it bodes well to have robots find racks of items and carry them to laborers instead of have workers go to the racks to chase for items. In 2014, the robots helped the organization cut its working expenses by 20%, as indicated by Dave Clark, a senior VP at Amazon.

(e) Caterpillar: an IIoT pioneer

Weighty hardware creator caterpillar has for quite some time been an IoT projects pioneer. As of late, the organization, which presently frequently passes by "Cat" has been magnificent the products of its interests in IoT innovation.

4.4.3   ADVANTAGES, CHALLENGES, AND RISKS OF IIOT

(a) Advantages of IIoT Integration

The IIoT has numerous prompt, direct advantages to the assembling business in manufacturing industries and its labor force. Albeit a portion of these enhancements is more evident than others, a portion of the essential selling purposes of the IIoT include:

(b) Improved working environment security

Automated machines and shared robots—otherwise called robots—use the IIoT to perform a large number of similar errands as their human partners. They are additionally consistently allotted to the more hazardous and unsafe positions in the manufacturing plant. However, makers will likewise acquire expanded quality and consistency through robotized creation lines.

(c) Greater customization and on-demand production

Manufacturers are as of now utilizing the IIoT to improve correspondences with their clients and make hand-crafted or on-request items. Activities likewise advantage from new, rapid machines, and admittance to more materials than any time in recent memory.

(d) Upgraded production network and enhanced supply chain functionality

The IIoT additionally improves usefulness all through the inventory network. Interconnected frameworks furnish key workforce with admittance to stock records and item data from almost any gadget that has web access. Transported merchandise is handily followed—continuously—through sensors that show data on their present area, their current circumstance, and even their state of being.

(e) Challenges of manufacturer to adopt IIoT

As innovation proceeds to progress and a greater amount of the world, including fabricating plants and items themselves, becomes associated, understanding the threats related to IIoT arrangements is progressively significant.

IT associations considering dispatching an assembling or modern IoT activity, or interfacing existing innovation for automation and far off observing or access, should consider the total of the possible intimidation and attack vectors related to choices.

The critical difficulties of actualizing IIoT may appear to be overwhelming. Nevertheless, the issues related to gadget abilities, production network concerns, security, splits among individuals, and wellbeing all eventually show the degree to which offices, whole ventures, and makers should cooperate to explore this new pattern in innovation going ahead.

IIoT-associated industries have some interesting traps because of digital society. All in all, when something turns out badly in the advanced world, the outcomes can happen in reality.

For instance, ill-advised combinations figure flawed calculations or errors could make harm the autonomous system, finished result, or unfinished materials. Devices may overheat, detonate, or breakdown such that harms items, hardware, or even harms laborers.

Additionally, adding of more networks in manufacturing industries call for more risk. This makes more open doors for cybercriminals to hack the framework whether as a demonstration of treachery, an endeavor to gather emancipate, or a political assault. Some of the time, programmers even access hardware by some coincidence.

In any case, keeping programmers out of the keen manufacturing plant framework is not the solitary thing that needs to stress over. Network, perceivability, the abilities hole, and guaranteeing that inheritance process works with incorporated devices, all current interesting difficulties that could represent the deciding moment an IT association's change endeavors.

Given the degree of security that IIoT innovations request, IT links should think of an arrangement for smoothing out information checking, the executives, and capacity, taking into consideration quick reaction times to approaching threats. This implies relation should get ready for secure, transient stockpiling arrangements (like edge figuring), just as a drawn-out arrangement (cloud or server farms) for long-haul stockpiling.

Furthermore, constant experiences are fundamental for acknowledging cost-investment funds and forestalling personal time. For instance, an association may utilize sensors to screen the presentation of key hardware. For this situation, the framework ought to have the option to identify mileage as it occurs, empowering clients to fix issues before they lead to interruptions underway, which could cost the association lost time and cash.

It is additionally significant that using advanced sensors, various electronics devices, and softwares may likewise present various kinds of design and manufacturing information along with business data. For instance, an assembling organization may utilize a venture asset arranging (ERP) or material necessities arranging (MRP) framework that utilizes a social information base to monitor stock, unfinished materials, and approaching requests.

The issue is that IoT sensors may produce heterogeneous information, that is, overseen through nonsocial datasets. This is enough for hackers to know about the organizations for their benefit from an associated framework, ERP information, client records, and IoT bits of knowledge need to meet up in one, coupled see.

Another key IIoT challenge is that regardless of whether an Internet connection can execute the whole of the correct sensors, programming, and mechanism, its return on investment must be acknowledged.

(c) Risks of IIoT

Some of the dangers related to industrial IoT are:

a) Device seizing.
b) Data siphoning.
c) Denial of administration assaults.
d) Data breaks.
e) Device burglary.
f) Man-in-the-middle or device "satirizing."

Coming up next are some security chances in IoT gadgets from producers:

a) Weak, guessable, or hard-coded passwords.
b) Hardware issues.
c) Lack of a protected update component.
d) Old and unpatched implanted working frameworks and programming.
e) Insecure information move and capacity.

Through IoT, individuals actually do not think a lot about it. While the greater part of the dangers of IoT security issues is as yet on the assembling side, clients, and business plans can make bigger dangers. One of the furthermost IoT security issues and difficulties is the client's obliviousness and absence of familiarity with the IoT usefulness.

The absence of actual solidifying can likewise cause IoT security issues. Even though some IoT devices ought to have the option to work independently with no intercession from a client, they should be actually made sure about from external threats. Here and there, these devices can be situated in distant areas for extended lengths of time, and they could be genuinely altered, for instance, utilizing a USB streak drive with Malware.

Guaranteeing the actual security of an IoT connections starts from the maker. Be that as it may, building secure sensors and transmitters in the generally ease device is a difficult assignment for makers regardless.

Clients are additionally answerable for keeping IoT devices truly made sure about. A keen movement sensor or a camcorder that sits outside a house could be messed with if not satisfactorily secured.

4.5   IIOT AND DIGITAL MANUFACTURING

Digitization has totally changed the client experience across most of retail subsectors. Monetary services, professional services, transportation, technology, telecommunications and media, and publishing.

The IoT is one of the key computerized change advances. IIoT innovation begins with availability; however, it is digitization where things get intriguing. All organizations, of all shapes and sizes, can change into computerized organizations by utilizing an IoT stage ready to digitize their actual items. The digitalization of assembling is changing how items are planned, created, utilized, and adjusted, similarly as its changing the tasks, cycles, and energy impression of production lines and supply chains.

The IoT can drive change in an association and giving information into a wide scope of operational exercises. The IIoT depicts the organization of actual items—"things"—that are installed with sensors, programming, and different advances to interface and trading information with different devices and frameworks over the Internet.

Advanced assembling can be characterized as a coordinated way to deal with assembling that is based on a CIM framework. A machine can peruse a CAD (PC helped configuration) document to convey it in a couple of hours. Computerized fabricating increases profitability and is quicker at producing excellent models.

Normal assembling innovations include software–CAD, CAM, CNC, direct numerical control, programmable logic control, numerical control, program enhancement programming, and frameworks coordination programming.

Each advanced assembling measure includes the utilization of modernized mathematical controlled machines (CNC), robots, RP machines, etc. This is essential in computerized fabricating as it empowers large-scale manufacturing and adaptability; however, it likewise gives a connection between a CAD model and manufacturing.

CNC represents CNC, as a difference to traditional processing machines where the shaper's developments can be constrained by turning a hand-wheel. The unpredictability of the manufacturing process relies upon the product that is utilized: for CNC machining just as for 3D printing. Where conventional CAM programming (the product to compute the CNC tool paths) was intended to be utilized by gifted CNC-trained professionals, these days additionally another sort of CAM programming is accessible, intended to be utilized by clients without CNC skill and experience.

4.5.1　DIGITAL FABRICATION

The advanced age empowered a direct computerized connection between what can be spoken to and what can be worked through "record to-manufacturing plant" cycles of PC mathematically controlled (CNC) creation. There is an uncommon explicitness with which advanced plan data can be utilized in the development of structures. The result is that planners are getting significantly more straightforwardly associated with the manufacture, as they can productively make the data that are made an interpretation of straightforwardly into the control information that drives the advanced creation hardware.

IIoT Improves CNC Operations

The IIoT permits the utilization of recognizable devices, for example, PDAs and tablets, to associate with CNC machines advantageously, a good ways off, and in an assortment of ways.

For instance, mechanical engineers can plan support for their things utilizing cell phones or, then again, choose to get warnings when the machines themselves "notice" they are expected for a checkup. Enhancements in power sensors and burden cells to execute precustomized undertakings and reacting to the progressing needs of CNC machines on shop floors. Since CNC machines will in general utilize drills, machines, switches, factories and processors, wellbeing boosting robots could end up being perhaps the most mainstream sorts of IIoT organizations in the coming years. Machines that speak with each other can organize their endeavors in a way that is better than independent machines. In a plant setting, get-together and item dealing with equipment downstream can caution upstream hardware of breakdowns and bottlenecks. This makes tightening the speed of creation up or down a lot simpler and may mechanize it totally as expected.

CNC machines coordinated with sensors and machine regulators can help in removing valuable information: When CNC machines utilized for aluminum machining parts then they are incorporated with different significant sensors like, pressure, temperature, etcetera, and afterward associated with a machine regulator—this machine regulator can help in assortment information and furthermore control the machine also, with an activity rationale. At that point with the assistance of a GPRS empowered passage, IoT can help in accepting the machine information and putting away the significant information on a cloud or nearby worker.

The sending of associated sensors across a progression of machines achieved in the shrewd assembling industry with colossal sensors all at once and makes it straightforward for human administrators to get information on deformities just as item quality continuously. Creation and gathering offices that depend on CNC machines would do well to consider the IIoT a dynamic resource, as well.

Since, the information is getting to put away in a worker, locally, or cloud based—the information can be gotten to and afterward dissected from anyplace asper innovation received by the business (IIoT, IoT, or both). The machine limits boundaries, just as continuous observing of the machines, can help in truly improving the proficiency of the said machine, and even lessen wastage too. This will likewise help in lessening vacation and consequently expanding yield as well.

A similar information can be utilized by the R&D division and CEOs of the assembling business, and hence get an away from about the operability of the CNC machines followed by needs for the development of theory.

Nowadays greatest assembling organizations have either a keen processing plant activity that is continuous or they are chipping away at creating one. CNC machines are now PC subordinate, making them an alluring spot to start such endeavors.

4.6 INDUSTRIAL IOT IN MONITORING PROCESS

The hardware associated with an IIoT framework can move data identified with activities to the plant the board framework and to handle engineers. This way cycle robotization and enhancement is made beneficial by empowering activity directors and processing plant heads to distantly deal with the plant units.

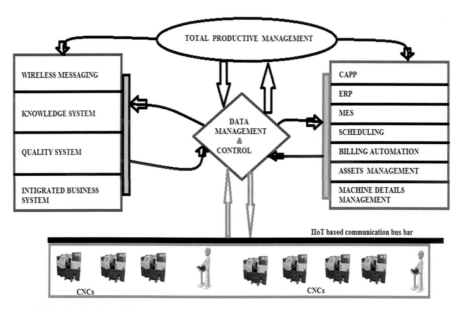

FIGURE 4.3   CNC and data management system.

4.6.1 EQUIPMENT MONITORING

In assembling ventures, the manufacturing process assumes an essential job in keeping the endeavor business pushing ahead. In relationship with the production cycle, the device/resources utilized in the manufacturing process are critical to speculations, safe assembling, and enhancing creation proficiency, keeping up booked personal time, and lower unprepared vacations/machine breakdowns.

Sensor-based observation: IIoT fortifies your gear condition checking by transforming it into "Keen hardware." Every equipment is observed with every development continuously with the assistance of industry hardware explicit sensors (pressure, temperature, vicinity, vibration, development discovery sensors, etc.).

In an industry that includes hardware, software, and machine equipment for cutting and embellishment of metal, vibration, or development identification sensors can be fastened to the device. These sensors handle information with each development of the machine and keep a steady watch on execution measurements, in this way helping screen the state of the electronics devices. Any fault will be accounted for to the chiefs through cautions.

Predictive maintenance: IIoT enables network with machine and devices condition checking in ventures with the instrument of preventive maintenance. When continuous information is caught and shipped off a cloud, information is separated and changed over from cutting edge calculations to intelligible, fundamental mechanism condition data to chiefs. Predictive maintenance is accomplished with customary updates and alarms (feedback) that help plan and timetable support personal times, rework/divert changes in the arrangement of strategies.

Let us take an example of the chemical plant where stockpiling of synthetic substances and checking holders are vital to forestalling blasts and guaranteeing a protected workplace. Steady temperature checks, nearness checks, holder/equipment condition, booked support, and creation advancement are made a reality with the examination and expectation that IIoT gives. Directors can likewise know about mechanism needs occasionally and practice safeguard as opposed to handling inconspicuous misfortunes.

Connected equipment and units: IIoT innovation weaves together AI instruments, robots, CNC, and different other automation devices inside the computer-integrated manufacturing industry. Thus, the whole working of the endeavor becomes mechanized ruling out manual upkeep blunders that might actually build dangers and end measures in different spaces of the undertaking.

In any industrial facility, production lines breakdown, and resource the board is a bad dream. Selecting IIoT arrangements will transform resources and hardware into a confidence manner and activity. Order highlight accessible as a feature of some IIoT arrangements will empower automation work process in the region. Computerized stock refilling and the board combined with AI robots to play out a fundamental capacity in the event that need emerges, does not put in onus on manual reliance, making it viable. Manufacturing unit in-charges and administrators along with management of the plant are solid equipped with information, investigation, and execution measurements that help keep a watch on frameworks and hardware condition.

Digital twin: Another preferred position of IIoT is the computerized twin. Advanced twin for all intents and purposes repeats actual process that can be utilized for reenactments before genuine process and cycles are constructed and changed. This clears route for better arranging, observing, and upkeep system of ventures. Along these lines, hardware work productivity and upkeep plans are graphed before any adjustment in the manufacturing arrangement through the production plan.

Managers presently do not need to execute change with the dread of losing hardware condition possibilities. Condition checking is underpins with highlights like that of the computerized twin working out of sight.

Sensors set in the assembling line triggers alarms dependent on condition-based support. The vast majorities of the machine apparatuses are basic and are intended to work between a particular temperature, vibration ranges, and other desired variables as fit in the system. At whatever point a device goes wrong from its endorsed boundaries, IoT sensors can effectively screen machines and send an alarm. Producers in this manner can monitor energy, lessen costs, wipe out machine rest, and increment operational productivity, by guaranteeing the endorsed working climate for apparatus.

4.6.2   PRODUCTION LINE MONITORING

IoT in assembling is equipped for observing a whole creation line be it from the refining process totally down to the bundling of end results. Since this total observing of the cycle happens progressively. It gives the extension to suggest any changes in activities for better administration of the business as well as manufacturing process. Since the checking is done closely, it slacks in the genuine manufacture in this manner wiping out squanders and point-less work.

Inventory monitoring: This is the best modern IoT application, through IoT frameworks checking of events across a production network is refined. These frameworks permit one to follow the stock and follow it worldwide on a detail level. This way the clients are informed if there are any critical deviations from the strategy. Accordingly, this gives an expansive and cross-channel perceivability into inventories, and that helps chiefs in getting practical assessments of the accessible material, the work in advancement and the assessed appearance season of new materials. At last this makes supply more ideal and diminishes extra and shared costs that emerge in the worth chain.

Safety and security monitoring: A laborers' wellbeing and security in the plant improve by IIoT joined with huge information investigation. The IIoT framework screens some key performance indicators of safety and security, for example, the quantity of wounds, successive paces of sickness, vehicle occurrences, and property harm or any sort of misfortune caused during everyday tasks. Accordingly, a practical observing framework guarantees better and compelling welfare. On the off chance that there are a few pointers that are slacking, they tended to, in this manner guarantee better wellbeing, security, and climate issues. That is nobody can ignore modern IIoT applications.

Quality control and monitoring: The manufacturing plant has different process planning stages. IIoT as associated with IoT sensors gathers a combination of item information and other outsider synchronized information from the phases of the process cycle. This information contains data on the synthesis of unfinished materials utilized in the manufacturing of products or components, the temperature and workplace, various squanders, the significance of transportation, and so forth during the last creation of the items. Additionally, the IoT gadget can likewise give information about the client estimations while he/she utilizes the item. These contributions from various sources and through IoT frameworks can break down to distinguish and address likely quality issues.

Packaging and monitoring: Manufacturers can acquire experiences into the utilization examples and treatment of the item from various clients by utilizing IoT sensors inserted in products as well as packaging. There are brilliant following components that can follow item deterioration during item travel. Different factors, for example, climate sway, the state of streets, and other natural factors on the item. Through these bits of knowledge, one can re-engineer items and their bundling for conveying better execution in the two expenses of packaging and client experience.

4.6.3 SUPPLY CHAIN MONITORING WITH THE HELP OF IOT

In this mechanical, IIoT is associated with IoT applications, it gives admittance to continuous store network data by following materials on the way, items, and hardware as they travel through the plant and manufacturing network. Through workable detailing, producers can gather and take care of the conveyance data into frameworks like ERP, PLM, etc. On the off chance that the plants will associate with the providers, all the concerned gatherings in the store network can follow interdependencies, producing process durations, and material stream. Accordingly, this information will assist makers with decreasing stock, anticipate expected issues, and furthermore lessens capital prerequisites.

4.7   SOFTWARE SOLUTIONS FOR MANUFACTURING FLOOR

Digitalization is not only for huge, money-rich organizations. What's more, it is not only for innovative ventures. Digitalization-connecting virtual and genuine universes to make business esteem rapidly is being grasped by all scope of organizations, all scope of ventures.

Computerized fabricating advancements connect frameworks and cycles across all territories of creation to make an incorporated way to deal with assembling, from plan to creation and on to the adjusting of the end results.

A computerized methodology, at times called an advanced media technique, is an arrangement for expanding the business advantages of information resources and innovation-centered activities. An effective advanced system requires a cross-practical group with chief initiative, showcasing, and data innovation (IT) individuals.

Each progression in the execution of the IIoT must be assessed as far as the choices it impacts. Connecting each progression to the estimation of better choices that outcome should be the reason for organizing them and advocating for them financially.

a)   The best test for shop floor administrators will decide.
b)   The right information assortment.
c)   Who will get the data as received from the network information?
d)   How this data will be utilized?
e)   Taking the correct choices according to the necessary examination.

Different sorts of programming are utilized by assembling ventures, for example, item advancement measure programming, item information the executives programming, item life-cycle the board programming, endeavor asset arranging (ERP) programming, CAD programming, CIM supported assembling, and so forth.

4.8   CONCLUSION

The digital revolution is the progressing computerization of conventional assembling and mechanical works, utilizing current shrewd innovation. Enormous scope M2M correspondence and the web of things (IoT) are incorporated for expanded robotization, improved correspondence, and self-checking, and the manufacturing of sense machines that can dissect and analyze issues without the requirement for human mediation. Deploying current innovation instruments offered in assembling designing is to streamline execution while decreasing time leads and work escalated assets. The data flow in the digital manufacturing system get accessed by each and individual unit of the plant. The associated person will access the information for better monitoring and helps to take appropriate action against the error, problem, maintenance of machine, process modification, etc. The paper overall focused on the application of IIoT and IoT in the manufacturing system to decrease the lead time.

KEYWORDS

- **IoT**
- **IIoT**
- **digital technology**
- **manufacturing system**
- **system monitoring**

REFERENCES

1. Buckholtz, B.; Ragai, I.; Wang, L. H. Cloud Manufacturing: Current Trends and Future Implementations. *J. Manuf. Sci. Eng.* **2015,** *137* (4), 040902-1-9.
2. Cheng, M.; Zhong, R. Y.; Li, Y. Y.; Luo, H.; Lan, S. L.; Huang, G. Q. Cloud-Based Auction Tower for Perishable Supply Chain Trading. *Procedia CIRP* **2014,** *25*, 329–336.
3. Davis, J.; Edgar, T.; Porter, J.; Bernaden, J.; Sarli, M. Smart Manufacturing, Manufacturing Intelligence and Demand-Dynamic Performance. *Comput. Chem. Eng.* **2012,** *47*, 145–156.
4. Feeney, A. B.; Frechette, S. P.; Srinivasan, V. A. Portrait of an ISO STEP Tolerancing Standard as an Enabler of Smart Manufacturing Systems. *J. Comput. Inf. Sci. Eng.* **2015,** *15* (2), 021001.
5. Ferreira, L.; Putnik, G.; Cunha, M.; Putnik, Z.; Castro, H.; Alves, C.; Shah, V.; Varela, M. L. R. Cloudlet Architecture for Dashboard in Cloud and Ubiquitous Manufacturing. *Procedia CIRP* **2013,** *12*, 366–371.
6. Ansari, F.; Erol, S.; Sihn, W. Rethinking Human-Machine Learning in Industry 4.0: How Does the Paradigm Shift Treat the Role of Human Learning? *Procedia Manuf.* **2018,** *23C*, 117–122.
7. Jang, Y. J.; Yosephine, V. Teaching Stochastic Systems Modeling Using Lego Robotics Based Manufacturing Systems. In *Proceedings of the 11th Conference on Stochastic Models of Manufacturing and Service Operations*; ITIA-CNR: Milano, Italy, 2017; pp 293–300.

8. Koren, Y.; Wang, W.; Gu, X. Value Creation Through Design for Scalability of Recon-Figurable Manufacturing Systems. *Int. J. Prod. Res.* **2017,** *55* (5), 1227–1242.

9. Li, B.; Hou, B.; Yu, W.; Lu, X.; Yang, C. Applications of Artificial Intelligence in Intelligent Manufacturing: A Review. *Front. Inform. Tech. El.* **2017,** *18* (1), 86–96.

10. Ragaglia, M.; Zanchettin, A. M.; Rocco, P. Safety-Aware Trajectory Scaling for Human-Robot Collaboration with Prediction of Human Occupancy. *Int. Conf. Adv. Robot.* 2015.

11. Rojas, R.; Rauch, E.; Dallasega, P.; Matt, D. T. Safe Human-Machine Centered Design of an Assembly Station in a Learning Factory Environment. *Proceedings of the International Conference on Industrial Engineering and Operations Management, Bandung*; Indonesia, March 6–8, 2018; pp 403–411.

12. Syberfeldt, A. A Lego Factory for Teaching Simulation-Based Production Optimization, In *Proceedings of the 2010 Industrial Simulation Conference*; EUROSIS-ETI: Ostend, Belgium, 2010; pp 89–94.

13. Schuh, G.; Prote, J. P.; Dany, S.; Cremer, S.; Molitor, M. Classification of a Hybrid Production Infrastructure in a Learning Factory Morphology. *Procedia Manuf.* **2017,** *9*, 17–24.

14. Tisch, M.; Ranz, F.; Abele, E.; Metternich, J.; Hummel, V. Learning Factory Morphology-Study of Form and Structure of an Innovative Learning Approach in the Manufacturing Domain. *Turk. Online J. Educ. Technol.* Special Issue 2 for INTE **2015,** 356–363.

15. Tao, F.; Cheng, Y.; Xu, L. D.; Zhang, L.; Li, B. H. CCIoT-CMfg: Cloud Computing and Internet of Things-Based Cloud Manufacturing Service System. IEEE Trans. Ind. Inform. **2014,** *10* (2), 1435–1442.

16. Wang, X. V.; Xu, X. A Collaborative Product Data Exchange Environment Based on STEP. *Int. J. Comput. Integr. Manuf.* **2015,** *28* (1), 75–86.

17. Wang, M. L.; Zhong, R. Y.; Dai, Q. Y.; Huang, G. Q. A MPN-Based Scheduling Model for IoT-Enabled Hybrid Flow Shop Manufacturing. *Adv. Eng. Inform.* **2016,** *30* (4), 728–736.

18. Xu, X. From Cloud Computing to Cloud Manufacturing. *Robot. Comput. Integr. Manuf.* **2012,** *28* (1), 75–86.

19. Zhong, R. Y.; Dai, Q. Y.; Qu, T.; Hu, G. J.; Huang, G. Q. RFID-Enabled Real-Time Manufacturing Execution System for Mass-Customization Production. *Robot. Comput. Integr. Manuf.* **2013,** *29* (2), 283–292.

CHAPTER 5

Opportunities for the Internet of Things in Automotives

R. B. MANORAM[1], A. SATHISHKUMAR[1], T. DEVAARJUN[2], SAMSON JEROLD SAMUEL CHELLADURAI[2], and T. A. SELVAN[1]

[1]*Department of Mechanical Engineering, Sri Krishna College of Engineering and Technology, Coimbatore, India*

[2]*Senior Specialist, Accenture Technologies, Bengaluru, India*

ABSTRACT

Being core technology of digital transformation, Internet of Things has become an inevitable part in the automotive sectors. Starting from autonomous cars to electric toll collection, IoT has brought in lot of advancements to all the applications involved in and out of automotive industry. These advancements are all supported by the sensor technology, big data analytics, cloud computing, improved communication systems and embedded systems. This chapter briefly explains the technology involved in implementing IoT in automotive industry viz autonomous cars, Intelligent Transport System, electric toll collection, predictive maintenance and smart parking. This chapter gives a brief introduction about the various technologies involved in the applications and processes and challenges involved in implementing. This chapter also gives the glimpse on future possible advancements on these applications with advancements in Artificial Intelligence and Machine Learning.

5.1 INTRODUCTION

Internet of Things (IoT) is the technology that interconnects the things attached with sensors, computing, and mechanical devices, that enables to exchange

Internet of Things: Technological Advances and New Applications. Brojo Kishore Mishra & Amit Vishwasrao Salunkhe (Eds.)

data from one thing to other and also to automate the machines with the help of actuators using the processed information. This growing IoT technology has brought several advancements in all realms including transportation, manufacturing, and automotive. This chapter explains the advancements of IoT in the automotive industry like self-driving cars, Intelligent Transport System (ITS), predictive maintenance, electric toll collection, and smart parking. Since it is a booming area, the literatures pertaining to the application of IoT in automotive industry is limited. QaziEjaz Ali et al. discussed the concerns, challenges, and research prospects in ITS in the perception of security. Barabas et al. discussed the challenges faced by autonomous driving. He expressed that current traffic regulations do not go hand on hand with the technologies. Keshav Bimbraw gave a vast review about the latest developments pertaining to autonomous vehicle. Sabbir Ahmed et al. focused on an automated toll collection system using RFID tags. They articulated that transparency in toll payment with reduced human effort and error will be ensured by using RFID technology. Yang Li implemented an Electronic toll collection system with RFID technology in open road. Subhankar et al. implemented low-cost electronic toll collection system in India using RFID technology. Paul George Parakkal used GPS-based navigation system for autonomous cars. Filip Majer et al. presented a universal visual navigation method, which enables vehicle to repeat paths without any human intervention. Qian Luo et al. discussed about counter measures for the threats and challenges imposed by the autonomous cars. Lucas de Paula Veronese et al. used low weight and precise localization method for driverless cars.

5.2   SELF-DRIVING AND AUTONOMOUS CARS

The self-driving cars are called with different terms like Autonomous cars, driverless car, and robot car around the globe. With the exceptional technical advancements in the recent years in areas like Information Technology, Communication, Data Analysis, Cloud Storage, and Actuation, these autonomous cars have moved from "may be possible" to "definitely possible." Autonomous cars that are nothing less than traditional cars and has the ability to move anywhere without or with very less human intervention and moves as if an experienced driver is operating the vehicle. Autonomous cars senses the local environment, detects the object around them, and interprets the sensory information to recognize the relevant navigation path without violating the traffic rules. The first Invention of vision guided Mercede -Benz in the year 1980s turned the interest of automobile companies towards autonomous vehicle. Since then, with the advancements in sensors and cameras, the automation levels in the autonomous cars started increasing. There are various technologies like sensors, actuators, machine learning, and network infrastructure, which aids the evolvement of Autonomous vehicle. The outfit of the car is attached with high-resolution cameras and sensors like Radar, Lidar/Laser light Radar, which helps to detect the objects around. Radar uses radio wave to determine the proximity of the object while Lidar/ Laser light Radar measures the proximity of the object by illuminating the target object with laser light and measure the reflection with a sensor. Apart from these sensors some of the high-resolution cameras are also used to detect the presence of object. The data generated by the high-resolution cameras and sensors are raw and need to be processed to obtain information. Technologies like Artificial Intelligence and Deep learning plays a significant role in image recognition, processing, motion detection, and data analysis. These functions collectively help the vehicles to detect other vehicles, pedestrians, and traffic signals. To ensure the safety of the passengers, pedestrians, and other vehicles, Intel and Mobileye has developed a safety standard –Responsibility-Sensitivity Safety framework. According to Intel, Responsibility-Sensitivity Safety framework is defined as a mathematical model that defines "safe state" to autonomous vehicle by providing specific and measurable parameter of human concept of responsibility and caution. The network infrastructure is a technology that ensures uninterrupted connectivity between autonomous vehicle and external sources. The advancement in 5G technology ensures high-speed connections that enables a wide range of services from infrastructure communication to in-vehicle infotainment. The network infrastructure uses two different communication protocol namely V2X and V2V. V2X helps to communicate with nearby infrastructure while V2V helps to communicate with other vehicle to prevent collision and to operate within the speed limit. Advancements in these technologies not only improve the autonomous capability of the vehicle but also the safety and security. Society of Automotive Engineers defines the stages of autonomous in six levels starting from fully manual (level 0) to fully automate (level 6). These levels have been approved by the U.S. Department of Transportation.

- ➢ **Level 0:** No Automation. Human is liable for all the chores pertaining to the operation of vehicle
- ➢ **Level 1:** Driver Assistance. Truck assists the human driven in minor steering and acceleration task
- ➢ **Level 2:** Partial Automation. Truck performs some driving task like advanced cruise control, parking assist while driver have look at the environment and perform rest of the required task

> **Level 3:** Conditional Automation. Truck accomplishing driving task and environmental monitoring while the driver take control when required by the system
> **Level 4:** High Automation. Truck accomplishing driving task and environmental monitoring without the need of driver to take control. Operation is limited to certain environmental conditions.
> **Level 5:** Full Automation. The truck accomplishes all chores under all conditions. No need of any human intrusion.

The autonomous vehicle provides numerous advantages. They help in reducing the traffic collisions and traffic congestion. Due to reduction in traffic collisions and accidents, the vehicle insurance also will decrease. Scarcity of the parking slot will reduce as autonomous cars has the ability to park itself anywhere after dropping off the passengers. People who find driving as a difficult task will feel relieved. The travel time will also decrease as autonomous vehicle can travel at higher speeds at very less chance of errors. Although the idea of autonomous cars may sound simple but it poses as much challenges as advantages. Driving is considered as one of the most complicated task that not only need certain traffic rules to be encoded into the Machine learning system but also the decision taken by the human making an eye contact with the other driver to ensure the right way, react to environment conditions, and making judgment calls that are difficult to encode. The implementation of legal framework and establishment of government regulation for who is liable to the cars' damage is one of the serious challenge need to be accounted. Since all the operations are cloud based, the potential risk of criminal and terrorist intrusion is also higher. These autonomous vehicles will act as a gateway of various terrorist activity.

5.3   INTELLIGENT TRANSPORT SYSTEM (ITS)

People in the urban areas travel to schools, colleges, offices, malls, and other places for several purposes. Owing to population explosion and lack of seriousness during driving, road accidents, traffic congestion, and excessive travel delays result. ITS is an advanced application that aims to leverage the traffic problems and improve safety, efficiency, and sustainability of transportation networks by providing innovative services pertaining to different mode of transport and traffic management. This advanced technology enables user to be more informed about real time running information on traffic, local convenience, and seat availability. ITS is not only just limited to manage the traffic-related problems but also lends hand in road safety, environment impact, and effective usage of transport infrastructure.

ITS is made possible by the combined application of information, computers, electronics, and communication technology integrated with management techniques in the field of transport system management. To operate these technologies, people from different streams like Civil, Mechanical, Electrical, and Computer Science are required. With the help of these technologies, people using the transport system will be given appropriate and accurate information at the right time. Technologies that enable ITS are listed in Table 5.1.

TABLE 5.1 Enabling Technology of ITS.

Communication technology	Information technology
Fiber optics	Data acquisition
Electromagnetic compasses	Data transmission
GPS	Data analysis
Digital map databases	Information utilization

Data Acquisition is the most important part in enabling technology of ITS. This technology helps in getting precise and accurate information related to traffic and road conditions using sensors, radar, video image detector and visual image from CCTV. These sensors and video cameras records data like vehicle count in traffic lane, location and delay of public transport, travel time and speed, change in routes, diversions, work zone conditions, and accidents on roads. The CCTV footages are widely used in surveillance monitor and keep track of activities at locations. Apart from CCTV footages and sensor data, smart cameras are also used. These smart cameras can carry out tasks beyond capturing photo and recording footages. With the inbuilt image processing and pattern recognition algorithm, smart cameras can identify movement of the object and read vehicle number plates. The data generated by these hardware devices are shared to the local servers, which has the capability to store large amount of data for analysis. The data acquired from these sensors are raw and needs to be analyzed to convert into a useful information. For the passenger, the analyzed data give information about where the traffic is high, what is the alternate route to the destination and availability of public transport to the destiny. From the vehicle side, this processed information gives information about navigation (i.e) possibly easiest way to reach the destiny. The data can be processed either in local server or by cloud computing. The next important technology in enabling ITS is data communication. The raw data from the sensor has to reach the server or cloud for further processing while the processed information from the server has to reach the passenger. Bandwidth plays a huge role in opting between wired or wireless technology for communication. The sensor information is normally small and requires low bandwidth while the data generated by the video cameras are relatively large and need many bits of information to be shared per unit time that required broad bandwidth of communication technology. On the vehicle side, wireless communication is much preferred than the wired communication technology as the vehicle keep on moving. With the information acquired, the passenger will be able to plan their travel schedule, vehicles could navigate based on the traffic congestion and adaptive cruise control helps in reducing the vehicle speed.

The architecture of ITS has four layers namely ITS access technologies, ITS network and transport, ITS facilities, and ITS applications. This architecture provides a standard architecture for technology preparation, description, and integration that enables ITS, which is depicted in Figure 5.1. The ITS access technologies include the technologies that generate data using the hardware devices, while the network and transport layer communicates the generated data. Bandwidth and data rate play a huge role in transferring data. The network layer is responsible for telling which data to be shared to which device. This layer takes care of naming the device and ensure the data have been transferred correctly. The ITS plays a domineering role in most of the applications pertaining to traffic and transport management. Some of the applications include:

➢ Travel and traffic administration
➢ Public transport operations
➢ E-payment
➢ Private/heavy vehicle operations
➢ Emergency management
➢ Maintenance and construction management

Although there are numerous advantages that can be listed with the implementation of ITS technology, it also faces certain challenges.

1. Limited resource for maintenance and operation.
2. The data generated is huge in volume and it is difficult to analyze.
3. Limited awareness of ITS among public reduces the utility of the end product.

4. The technologies used in the ITS are being updated, which makes the implementation tough and obsolete.

FIGURE 5.1 ITS architecture.

5.4 ELECTRIC TOLL COLLECTION (ETC)

With the improving People's living standards, private vehicles keeps on swelling in numbers. Also, the vehicles passing the toll collection centers seem to be significantly greater than before, which in turn makes the vehicles wait in line. The automobile exhaust during the waiting period in the toll line causes more pollution than running on the road and fuel consumption also increases because of this waiting time. So it is crucial to promote a fully free-flow tolling system suitable for the toll road.

ETC is a technology that is generally used in open road tolling or free-flow tolling. Electronic Toll Collection system can gather the information from the vehicles passing the toll gate, recognize the number plate, truck model, and RFID tag attached to the vehicle and recover the associated registration data from the record, match registration data with the information ETC system and deduct the amount automatically from the linked bank account without requiring the truck/car to slow down to remit the cash. It is also possible to diminish the necessity for vehicle owners and toll collection authorities to issue receipts and collect tolls manually.

1. Vehicle Identification

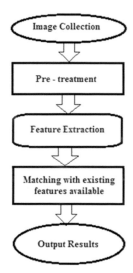

FIGURE 5.2   Steps involved in vehicle identification.

2. License Plate Recognition

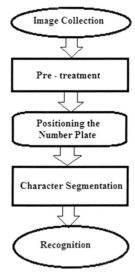

FIGURE 5.3   Steps involved in license plate recognition.

In an automatic electronic toll collection architecture, information pertaining to the toll payment can be effectively conveyed between the vehicle owners and toll/government authorities. Therefore, transparency on toll payment can be guaranteed with diminished human effort and error. Building a smart toll collection framework by this way will make the toll collection much simpler. The point behind developing an electric/smart toll payment is to make an advanced toll collection framework that can reduce the delay on toll roads, collecting money digitally, and without making vehicles to stop. As there is no requirement for vehicles to stop or for authorities to manually collect the tolls, this framework eradicates traffic congestion and plausible human mistakes that regularly happen in a toll collection system making it an increasingly productive method. Steps engaged with Electronic toll collection are as follows.

RFID-based technology is used in Automated Toll Collection System to answer the traffic issues and to keep up transparency in the toll collection system. RFID is the radio frequency identification technology that uses the road-side reader (RFID reader) to classify on-vehicle electronic tags. The e-tag contain information about the vehicle namely Vehicle number, owner's name, owner's bank account details, etc., Innovation in RFID is extended to different areas, without direct communication with the objects detected, or even fully unidentifiable objects can also be identified using electromagnetic waves to transmit information, fast, precise and exceptionally helpful. RFID technology comprises of three components namely antenna, transceiver, and transponder. The scanning antenna and transceiver combined are called as reader. The antenna transmits the radiofrequency waves to trigger the RFID tag while transponder communicates the information again to the antenna in the form of radiowave.

FIGURE 5.4 Working of electric toll collection.

The optical character recognition system has also been used as a key monitoring system that plays a vital role in assisting the concerned department in vehicle license plate recognition. A vehicle like a car, bus, or any other commercial vehicle doesn't have a similar weight. Utilization of strain gauge load cell enables to assess the vehicle's load and load cell embedded with microcontroller will predict the toll amount of the commercial truck accordingly and the required amount will be automatically detected from the client's account using the information from the database. This ETC framework is completely automated and cost-effective. On execution of this framework, the income gained will be more compared with the conventionally used system, which reduces the cost incurred for involving of labor for toll collection. The application of ETS also helps in reducing the traffic congestion at toll plaza. Quicker and secure transaction draws in more clients and with the utilization of prepaid smart card augments on the advantage of electrical cash transaction.

5.5   PREDICTIVE MAINTENANCE

We depend on a wide variety of machines every day, the fact is that each machine inevitably breaks down, unless it is properly maintained. In order to improve operational reliability and minimize costs, individual companies follow various maintenance programs. One approach is "Reactive Maintenance," where the machine/device is used to its complete ability and repairs are carried out only after the event of malfunction. For example, reactive maintenance can be used for tube bulb but for a complex system with very expensive parts following reactive maintenance won't work. For a complex system, it is always advisable to go for "Predictive Maintenance." Predictive maintenance – as the name implies, the failure in the machine is predicted by frequent maintenance.

One major problem with preventive maintenance is deciding when to conduct maintenance, because we do not know when failure is going to happen and we need to be doubly cautious in preparing for critical equipment to run safely. But by scheduling maintenance early, there are chances that the machine's lifetime may affect and it also adds on your cost. However if we could predict the machine's failure and if we could schedule maintenance right before the failure way we can minimize the downtime and maximize the equipment lifetime. To achieve above implementation with help of some sensors, we are able to build an algorithm or application that give dashboard of time window that will be showing with "Within how many "X" days device will have an event of malfunction and when it needs maintenance?"

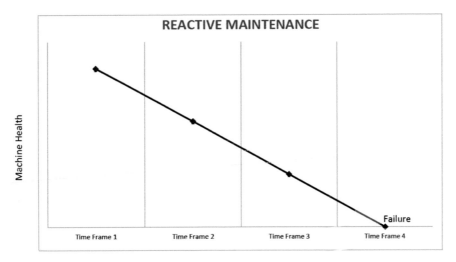

FIGURE 5.5 Reactive maintenance.

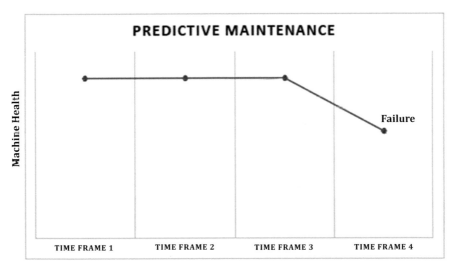

FIGURE 5.6 Predictive maintenance.

1. Acquire data:

The first move is to gather a wide number of sensor data reflecting safe and defective operations, under different operating conditions. Some machines may fail early based on the operating condition. Collecting all the sensor data pertaining to machine would help you to build a robust algorithm that can better recognize faults such as seal leakage, block inlets, and component wear.

2. Preprocess Data:

Once you have data, you have to delete the abnormal data raised because of the noise in the environment. In order to disclose additional details that may not be evident in the original type of data, further preprocessing is often needed.

3. Identify indicators:

Convert Time domain data to frequency domain that helps to distinguish healthy and faulty condition. The data will allow you to understand the stable and defective function of the system when converting it. This stage will not define parts need to repair and time left until failure

4. Machine Learning:

Using data model/machine learning stage we can extract the feature to train the machine learning models to act accordingly. By determining anomalies, we can write algorithm to identify variety of faults, so that once can have better insights into which parts of machine failure needs observation and when you should schedule maintenance.

5. Deploy & Integration:

After detecting the data, the algorithm will articulate and shows in application or dashboard when the machine needs maintenance and which parts need to changes

FIGURE 5.7   Steps involved in predictive maintenance.

5.6   SMART PARKING

In recent days, rapid increase in usage of vehicles along with the mis-management of parking slots arises parking related issue and congestion in public places. It's been a habitual traffic issue confronted as there is insufficient parking space in these heavily populated urban areas. Developing the smart parking system with IoT system of communicative devices is considered as a significant aid to relieve from this issue. This technology helps drivers to find a suitable parking slot in real time for their car, providing information about empty parking spaces in the garage and reserves the parking space accordingly.

In smart parking, a method in which authentication is done using the RFID tag has been preferred. Cloud-based storage is preferred for the application. Digital application that give information pertaining to available parking slot is made to fit at the entrance of the parking. With the use of the following technological elements, the system improves parking approachability:

> Ultrasonic Sensors: The sensors placed at the entrance of each parking slots to monitor the parking spaces, the ultrasonic wave detects for any physical intrusion and bounce back to the sensor when they hit any obstacle.
> Infrared: Tracks changes in the temperature of the atmosphere and senses motion.
> Application Systems: Based on the response from the sensors the algorithm helps to identify whether vehicle is present in the slot. The collected data provide a pictorial view of the whole parking area that gives the information about the occupancy and parking time of the vehicles inside the slot.
> RFID tag is provided to authorize a person entry to the parking place.
> Cloud Storage: These data are being shared to the cloud server frequently by wireless communication technology. The cloud server stores and process the data about all parking slots. Pictorial overview of the slot can be seen on the Mobile/website application or Display screen placed in front of the slots so that the users can effortlessly find the slot and Reserve.

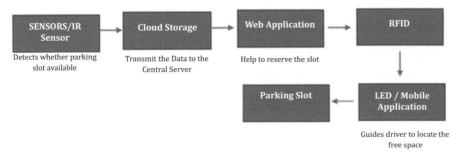

FIGURE 5.8 Steps involved in smart parking.

How to detect the space:

➢ Unavailable Space: The ultrasonic wave detects the presence of vehicle, if the wave return back to the sensor after hitting the vehicle at the distance within the range 10–50 cm from the sensor.

➢ Available Space: If the wave does not return back to the sensor, then the slot is free for having some other vehicle.

➢ Space is Dirty: If the wave return back after hitting any obstacle within 10 cm, then the system identifies it as dirt and informs that system need to be checked.

➢ Though Smart Parking system has so many advantages like reduced traffic, enhanced user application, new revenue streams, improved safety and real-time data insight, it also faces some challenges to be addressed like upfront cost and interoperability issue.

KEYWORDS

- **Autonomous Cars**
- **Intelligent Transport systems**
- **Electronic toll collection**
- **predictive maintenance**
- **smart parking**

REFERENCES

1. Ali, Q. E.; Ahmad, N.; Malik, A. H.; Ali, G.; ur Rehman, W. Issues, Challenges, and Research Opportunities in Intelligent Transport System for Security and Privacy. *Appl. Sci.* **2018,** *8,* 1–24. DOI: 10.3390/app8101964.
2. Barabás, I.; Todoruţ, A.; Cordoş, N.; Molea, A. Current Challenges in Autonomous Driving. *IOP Conf. Ser. Mater. Sci. Eng.* **2017,** 252. DOI: 10.1088/1757-899X/252/1/012096.
3. Bimbraw, K. Autonomous Cars: Past, Present and Future: A Review of the Developments in the Last Century, the Present Scenario and the Expected Future of Autonomous Vehicle Technology. *ICINCO 2015—12th Int. Conf. Informatics Control. Autom. Robot. Proc.* **2015,** *1,* 191–198. DOI: 10.5220/0005540501910198.
4. Ahmed, S.; Tan, T. M.; Mondol, A. M.; Alam, Z.; Nawal, N.; Uddin, J. Automated Toll Collection System Based on RFID Sensor. *Proc. - Int. Carnahan Conf. Secur. Technol.* **2019,** *2019,* 1–3. DOI: 10.1109/CCST.2019.8888429.

5. Li, Y.; Zhuang, P. RFID Based Electronic Toll Collection System Design and Implementation. *Lect. Notes Inst. Comput. Sci. Soc. Telecommun. Eng. LNICST.* **2018,** *226,* 635–640. DOI: 10.1007/978-3-319-73564-1_64.
6. Chattoraj, S.; Bhowmik, S.; Vishwakarma, K.; Roy, P. Design and Implementation of Low Cost Electronic Toll Collection System in India. *Proc. 2017 2nd IEEE Int. Conf. Electr. Comput. Commun. Technol. ICECCT* **2017,** *2017.* DOI: 10.1109/ICECCT.2017.8117934.
7. Parakkal, P. G.; Sajith Variyar, V. V. GPS Based Navigation System for Autonomous Car. *2017 Int. Conf. Adv. Comput. Commun. Informatics, ICACCI 2017* **2017,** *2017,* 1888–1893. DOI: 10.1109/ICACCI.2017.8126120.
8. Majer, F.; Halodov, L. For Autonomous Vehicles **2019,** 90–110. DOI: 10.1007/978-3-030-14984-0.
9. Luo, Q.; Cao, Y.; Liu, J.; Benslimane, A.; Localization and Navigation in Autonomous Driving: Threats and Countermeasures. *IEEE Wirel. Commun.* **2019,** *26,* 38–45. DOI: 10.1109/MWC.2019.1800533.
10. De Paula Veronese, L.; Guivant, J.; Auat Cheein, F. A.; Oliveira-Santos, T.; Mutz, F.; De Aguiar, E.; Badue, C.; De Souza, A. F. A Light-Weight Yet Accurate Localization System for Autonomous Cars in Large-Scale and Complex Environments. *IEEE Conf. Intell. Transp. Syst. Proceedings, ITSC* **2016,** 520–525. DOI: 10.1109/ITSC.2016.7795604.

CHAPTER 6

IoT Security

NIDHI UPADHYAY*

Department of Computer Science and Engineering, Vivekananda College of Technology and Management, Aligarh, Uttar Pradesh, India

ABSTRACT

IoT security is the newness district stressed over protecting related devices and associations in the snare of things (IoT). IoT incorporates adding web organization to a game plan of interrelated figuring contraptions, mechanical and progressed machines, articles, animals or possibly people. Every "thing" is given an interesting identifier and the capacity to consequently move information over an organization.Allowing devices to interface with the web lets loose them to different real shortcomings in case they are not suitably made sure about.

IoT security is the newness district stressed over protecting related devices and associations in the snare of things (IoT). IoT incorporates adding web organization to a game plan of interrelated figuring contraptions, mechanical and progressed machines, articles, animals, or possibly people. Every "thing" is given an interesting identifier and the capacity to consequently move information over an organization. Allowing devices to interface with the web lets lose them to different real shortcomings in case they are not suitably made sure about.

Executing security endeavors is essential to ensuring the prosperity of associations with IoT devices related with them. The IoT energizes the blend between the genuine world and PC correspondence associations, and (applications, for instance, establishment the board and common noticing make assurance and security methodology fundamental for upcoming IoT systems.[4-6]

Internet of Things: Technological Advances and New Applications. Brojo Kishore Mishra & Amit Vishwasrao Salunkhe (Eds.)

IoT systems need to guarantee data assurance and address security issues, for instance, mocking attacks, interferences, DoS attacks, scattered DoS (DDoS) attacks, staying, tuning in, and malware. We examine IoT confirmation, access control, secure offloading, and malware location.

6.1   IOT ATTACK MODEL

Comprising of things, administrations, and organizations, IoT frameworks are defenseless against network, physical, and programming assaults just as protection spillage. We center around the IoT security dangers as follows:

6.1.1   DOS ATTACKER

The aggressors flood the objective worker with pointless solicitations to keep IoT gadgets from getting administrations. Perhaps the most perilous kinds of a DoS assault are when DDoS assailants use a great many Internet convention delivers to demand IoT administrations, making it hard for the worker to recognize the authentic IoT gadgets from aggressors. Disseminated IoT gadgets with lightweight Learning-Based Authentication Learning-Based Access Control Learning security conventions are particularly defenseless against DDoS assaults.

6.1.2   JAMMING

Aggressors impart counterfeit signs to intrude on the continuous radio transmissions of IoT gadgets and further drain the data transfer capacity, energy, focal preparing units (CPUs), and memory assets of IoT gadgets or sensors during their bombed correspondence endeavors.

6.1.3   SPOOFING

A satirizing hub imitates a legitimate IoT gadget with its personality, for example, the medium access control address and RFID tag to pick up unlawful admittance to the IoT framework and can additionally dispatch assaults, for example, DoS and man-in-the-center assaults.

6.1.4 *MAN-IN-THE-MIDDLE ATTACK*

A man-in-the-center assailant imparts sticking and caricaturing signs with the objective of subtly checking, listening in, and modifying the private correspondence between IoT gadgets.

6.1.5 *SOFTWARE ATTACKS*

Portable malware, for example, Trojans, worms, and infections can bring about security spillage, monetary misfortune, influence exhaustion, and organization execution corruption of IoT frameworks.

6.2 A SYSTEMIC APPROACH FOR IOT SECURITY

A remarkable meaning for IoT does not exist yet. Most importantly, the association among individuals and objects to send shrewd applications in savvy conditions. The principal plan of Internet was human-driven. In this methodology, information was made by individuals.

Distinctive "items" or "things" can be associated as well. In this way, human-driven methodology can not be applied any longer. IoT worldview is perhaps the most exciting developments of the new years. When each item has correspondence abilities, the quantity of potential applications turns out to be possibly boundless. This uplifting news is balanced by the thought that additionally the quantity of potential assaults to people and items security will develop dramatically. Subsequently, another worldview of trust, security, and protection is needed to confront these future issues in the IoT. In creators portray, a foundational and intellectual methodology for IoT security. In their work, they think about three primary tomahawks: compelling security for small implanted organizations, setting mindful and user centric protection, and the foundational and psychological methodology for IoT security.

In reality, creators avow that the IoT is an unpredictable framework in which individuals' interface with the innovative biological system dependent on shrewd articles through complex cycles as appeared. In this methodology, associations between various hubs have a particular character contingent upon complex climate of the IoT. In this work, we will present our perspective in respect of the rule parts laid out in Figure 6.1 and that we will call "centers" and "strains." To feature the distinction among hub and pressure, we can utilize the case of patients trading clinical information with their primary care physicians by utilizing the accessible mechanical biological system. In this model, patients and specialists allude to hub "individual", clinical exercises allude to "measure," correspondence frameworks allude to "mechanical biological system" and clinical hardware (model: X-beam machine) allude to "astute item." Right off the bat, the specialist should have the option to correctly distinguish the patients, and afterward recover their clinical records

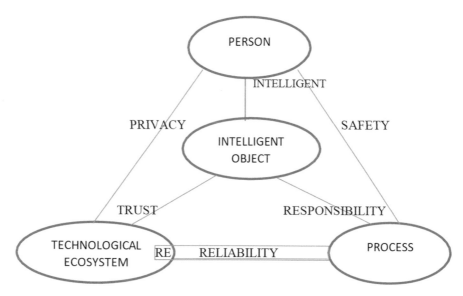

FIGURE 6.1   Approach for IoT security.

This model is comprised of four hubs collaborating in the IoT climate and speaking to the essential entertainers of the security framework. We can identify three traditional hubs in particular individual, measure, and mechanical biological system.

6.2.1   *PERSON*

Principal hub assuming an essential job in the IoT security structure. The HR is answerable for security rules the executives, which incorporates:

- Characterizing security practices and protocols.
- Examining practices and rules proficiency.

6.2.2   PROCESS

The subsequent hub alludes to a way to achieving errands in the IoT climate as per some security prerequisites. The cycle is needed to be consistent with the security strategies to keep the climate secure at various levels. Besides, because of the intricacy of the model and the presence of various communications starting from this hub, security measures are hard to execute.

6.2.3   INTELLIGENT OBJECT

This hub is the core of the new methodology. It alludes to an "object" expanded by the electronic highlights expected to allow it to speak with different articles in the general climate. These items will become dynamic members in business, data, and social cycles.[2] Indeed, objects in the IoT system will have the option to participate, offer and trade data about the climate, and react to occasions occurred in the climate by achieving sufficient tasks. Because of their normal pervasively, the right plan and improvement of security rehearses inside the origination of canny articles is crucial to guarantee the correct degree of security to the entire climate encompassing them.

6.2.4   TECHNOLOGICAL ECOSYSTEM

This hub alludes to mechanical decisions made to guarantee IoT security. As indicated by data security innovation falls into a few general classes:

- Security Design and Configuration
- I&A: Identification and Authorization
- Enclave inner
- Enclave limit
- Physical and natural

The judgment identifies with every one of these components may incorporate framework design, correspondences conventions, actualized calculations, access control techniques, execution, and so on. It is apparent that a compromise among security necessities, practicality, and innovation advancement should be found to guarantee the proper degree of security without debasing the presentation of the framework.

6.3 TENSION

Fundamental and intellectual methodology for IoT security of Figure 6.1, the hubs are the beginning and objective entertainers of a strain that speaks to their cooperation, and mulls over the intricacy of the climate. Thus, security practices might be more muddled, however, more viable. It will be simpler to characterize the satisfactory answer for a given security issue in a framework that regards this model. Accordingly, extraordinary interest should be consented to comprehend these pressures and their security prerequisites. In particular, the pressures that we will consider are distinguishing proof/confirmation, trust, dependability, auto-invulnerability, protection, obligation, and security. To more readily clarify our foundational approach, these strains should be profoundly broke down, estimated, and examined.

6.3.1 IDENTIFICATION AND AUTHENTICATION

1. "Distinguishing proof and validation" is the strain that attaches the clever item with the individual. In the IoT setting, objects are spread around the world. An effective goal plot should be set to recognize various elements. Protection and other security issues should be contemplated just as the particular capacity of the item, which can change throughout the time. Besides, an article can have one center personality and a few transitory characters; a medical clinic can turn into a gathering place for a wellbeing meeting or an asylum after a fire. A ton of exploration has just been proposed on this pivot. We will restrict our examination to the introduction of some significant tasks of this space.
2. Different undertakings could be recorded here, for example, Smart Product 4, QR-Code 6. Open examination issues: In, many exploration given have been represented. For instance, worldwide ID plans should be viewed as when savvy items and people interface. In addition, a proficient character of the board approach should be characterized. Portability, protection, pseudonymity, and namelessness angles need further examination and exploration. For instance, when we limit our degree to the RFID structure, we can undoubtedly individuate halfway contemplated research points identified with the meaning of conveyed coherent per users or the investigation of a RFID networks where the two labels and per users are portable.

6.3.2 TRUST

"Trust" is pressure that attaches the wise item with the mechanical environment. Fundamentally, it speaks to the degree of certainty that the climate can concede to the keen article. The IoT climate can be pervaded with extremely heterogeneous items, which may contrast for both their capacities and their abilities. In a particularly heterogeneous climate, when characterizing trust, the board, we should consider additionally the serious asset limitations to which the articles are oppressed, and which will requirement the decisions of the innovative biological system. Consequently, trust the executives' tasks, for example, setting up, refreshing, and renouncing keys and authentications are significant examination points in the IoT structure.

An absence of an immediate connection between these two hubs can be seen here. Moreover, in IoT structure, trust the executives may include irregular and nonhuman substances. Along these lines, trust between interfacing substances is irreplaceable and trust-pertinent tasks and applications should be created to be reliable. This worry directly affects specialized decisions, techniques, originations, and usage. A significant undertaking that manages the referenced issues for IoT is you TRUST it. Its goal is to show and execute an instrument for building and testing trust. In another specific situation, Gligor and Wing present "a hypothesis of trust in organizations of people and PCs that comprises of components of computational trust and social trust." Creators propose an abstract conduct trust model for Social IoT, which abuses the "social" bound existing among objects (proprietorship, parental, co-area, and so on). This model has been additionally definite in. Open exploration issues: The primary targets of trust research in IoT structure are the accompanying. Second, the execution of trust components for the distributed computing. Third, the improvement of uses is dependent on hub trust (ex. directing, information collection, and so on).

As indicated by an intriguing issue is to build up a hypothesis for computational trust. Thus, this way to manage connections between computational trust and conduct trust, to make new convention zones, and to keep up strength trust properties. Practically speaking, creators propose an organization foundation to oversee trust ideas. On another hand, when overseeing trust, angles, for example, geography of the items, inclusion sending, target following, confinement, and IoT applications should be thought of.

6.3.3   PRIVACY

Protection is a significant pressure in the foundational model for IoT security due to the universal character of the climate. Notwithstanding, the presence of sufficient examination exercises in security of the executives systems by and large, there is as yet a rundown of destinations to be satisfied. To make things more clear, in, creators partition security into three fundamental tomahawks:

1. Privacy in information assortment,
2. Privacy in Data Sharing and Management, and
3. Data security issues.

In the accompanying, we will refer to the main examination exercises for every one of these headings. Regarding the primary examination hub, "protection in information assortment," we can make reference to the cryptographic arrangements and the obstructing approaches definite in and. For the subsequent hub, we can list total of information gathered by sensors, the Platform for Privacy Preferences 9, semantic web, and other security conservation instruments, for example, k-namelessness, l-variety, and t-closeness. At long last, in the information security issues, we can name secret word assurance, cryptographic arrangements, and web elements with a semantic approach language. Open examination issues: Even, however, a ton of exploration has just been proposed for this pressure, still numerous points should be additionally researched. Here we can propose a rundown of fascinating themes. Above all else, the computerized key administration conspires. This activity is delicate on account of IoT. It might incorporate key provisioning, refreshing, renouncement, moving and key understanding. In addition, noncryptographic activities like enlistment, reinforcement, and recuperation should be routed to ensure an elevated level of security. Another issue is to build up another plan for unbalanced key administration including age, approval, and conveyance.

6.3.4   RESPONSIBILITY

Sharing assets and other added values, which are helpful for various cycles, advantages, and access rights should be obviously characterized by protection requirements. Moreover, duties and liabilities rules of every element should be considered to stay away from risks when the article manages a cycle. In writing, two fundamental access control models have been created: Role-based admittance control and Attribute-based access control.

6.3.5 AUTOIMMUNITY

"Autoimmunity" ties the keen article in self-circle. The target of this pressure is to propose a fake resistant framework answer for IoT. In this pattern, two principal research exercises can be evoked here. To start with, creators in portray a reproduction and invulnerability trial of a remote sensor to keep away from electromagnetic aggravation in substation. Secondly, insusceptibility-based plans can be utilized to identify interruptions in the IoT. For instance, the creators of recreate self and nonself antigen in IoT, just as youthful, develop and memory identifier, to identify assaults in the IoT. Open examination issues.

6.3.6 SAFETY

"Wellbeing" is a strain that attaches the individual with the cycle. A climate penetrated with shrewd items should adapt to numerous security challenges. At the point when considered as an exploration hub for the IoT, security purposes have been broadly examined. We could illustrations as drivers for mechanical and logical developments along this examination pivot. For instance, we can zero in on the climate perception: contamination impacts, timberland fires contemplate, and so on; the actual security of building: VMC, spills, gatecrashers, and so forth; and furthermore, the business field: assurance of items against fake.

6.3.7 RELIABILITY

"Unwavering quality" is the pressure that attaches the cycle with the innovative environment. The dependability manages information and correspondences the executives. The unwavering quality targets ensuring accessibility of data after some time through proficient methods of overseeing information archives. Dependability of correspondence connections can be guaranteed through the repetition gave by various ways. Open exploration issues: An open examination issue is connected with the advancement of bunching correspondence procedures to guarantee joins unwavering quality. Another issue will zero in on making a mechanized answer for IoT administration the executives to improve their dependability.

6.4   IOT SECURITY CHALLENGES

6.4.1   *OBJECT IDENTIFICATION*

The fundamental test of item ID is to guarantee the uprightness of records utilized in the naming design. Regardless of the fact that the Domain Name System gives name interpretation administrations to Internet clients, it is a shaky naming framework.

6.4.2   *AUTHENTICATION AND AUTHORIZATION*

Albeit public-key cryptosystems have advantage for building confirmation plans or approval frameworks, the absence of a worldwide root testament authority (worldwide root CA) prevents numerous hypothetically achievable plans from really being sent. Without the worldwide root CA, finish up exceptionally testing to plan a verification framework for IoT. Moreover, it very well might be infeasible to give an endorsement to an item in IoT since the all-out number of articles is regularly tremendous.

6.4.3   *PRIVACY*

In this part, we will portray the difficulties to IoT sending on protecting security. The difficulties could be isolating into two classifications: information assortment strategy and information anonymization. Information assortment strategy depicts the approach during information assortment where it upholds the kind of collectable information and the entrance control of a "Thing" to the information.

6.4.4   *LIGHTWEIGHT CRYPTOSYSTEMS AND SECURITY PROTOCOLS*

Contrasted and symmetric-key cryptosystems, public key cryptosystems by and large give greater security includes yet endure high computational overhead. Be that as it may, public key cryptosystems are frequently attractive when information respectability and genuineness are required. In this manner, calculation overhead decrease for public-key cryptosystems just as unpredictable security conventions remains a significant test for IoT security.

6.4.5 SECURITY ISSUES FROM ANDROID

On the off chance that heterogeneous gadgets associate with the Android framework shaping individual zone organization (PAN), the security issues explicitly for Android will be brought into IoT. The fundamental concern is touchy information spillage. The current authorization security just gives course-grain the board, in particular win or bust decision, to confine the sort of associated gadgets and handicap the runtime control. Convoluted conditions and application situations should be considered to incorporate more conceivable conceded consents. Google coincidentally delivered runtime consent control, AppOps, in Android 4.3, yet before long eliminated in 4.4. AppOps shows that dynamic administration is possible. Then again, Android malware is another major issue when IoT meets Android. Dissimilar to iOS, Android is publicly released. That makes it simple to find weaknesses of the framework.

6.5 THE SYSTEMIC APPROACH FOR APPLICATION OF THE IOT

The incorporation of a clever article inside the IoT suggests the making of new applications just as the expansion of existing ones. In this section, we need to detail the connection between a part of traditional application areas and the strain of our fundamental methodology, to feature limitations and prerequisites forced by the security. Solidly, in Table I, we pick transportation and coordination, medical care, and brilliant climate as areas of use, and we portray every pressure of the proposed conspire by the methods for a model with regards to that space. To give a few insights concerning this table, we think about the upper piece of the table for instance. It centers around the impact of our foundational approach on the transportation and coordination space.

To satisfy IoT necessities, the entirety of the pressures clarified above should be thought of. To start with, proper ID should be performed between people (buyers and suppliers) on one side: and insightful articles (items) on the opposite side. Second, touchy information might be traded among network private/public assets including connections and applications; and afterward, their security should be ensured. Third, an inventory network may include various people and different articles. To ensure that every one of them have completely achieved their errands in this chain, a believed relationship should be set up, kept up, and continually assessed. Fourth, during the transportation cycle, security of people and vehicles should be an early stage worry to dodge street mishaps. Fifth, when controlling and GPS beacons, obligations of mediating substances should be handily recognized. This is useful when an exceptional intercession or cross examination is needed if there should arise an matter of a given episode or only for straightforward logging activity. Sixth, having a dependable biological system is a solid condition to set up acts of examining and staying away from abnormalities, for example, robbery, misfortune, or mechanical breakdown. At last, stop strategies might be applied at the end of interruption recognition to guarantee autoimmunity of the wise article, for example, items or money box when conveyed or put away.

6.6   SECURITY CRITICAL APPLICATION AREAS OF IOT

Security is exceptionally basic in practically all IoT applications that have just been sent or are presently arranged. The uses of IoT are expanding quickly and infiltrating the vast majority of the current enterprises. In spite of the fact that administrators uphold these IoT applications through existing systems administration advancements, a few of these applications need more severe security uphold from advances they use. In this segment different security basic IoT applications are talked about.

6.6.1   SMART CITIES

Shrewd urban areas include broad utilization of arising calculation and correspondence assets for expanding the general personal satisfaction of the people. It incorporates brilliant homes, keen traffic the board, savvy calamity the executives, savvy utilities, and so forth. In spite of the fact that the utilization of brilliant applications is planned to improve the general personal satisfaction of the residents, it accompanies a danger to the protection of the

TABLE 6.1 IoT Application Domains-Tension Examples.

Tension/ Application	Identification	Privacy	Trust	Safety	Responsibility	Reliability	Auto-immunity
Transportation on and logistics domain	RFID-based identification management of consumers, providers, and products	A customer can provide private data to benefit from some advantages or reductions	Objects that perfectly accomplished their previous tasks in a supplychain	Increasing safety of consumers and vehicles during transportation process	Traffic monitoring and control devices	Detection, analysis, and avoidance of anomalies	Stop techniques in case of intrusion detection
	Identificationof staff, patients, and medical equipment	Data, including clinical diagnosis and treatment,must be kept private	Patients should trustmedical institutions in terms of reliability and privacy	Setting up procedure s to ensurethe patient safety during health-care activities	Parameters setting of health-care objects	Reliability of the link incase of remote diagnosis	An object that provides alertin case of accident
Smart environment domain	Identification of the employees in the same enterprise and access control to network resources	Financial details of a given project (domestic or professionall) should be confidentiall	Newly bought objects belonging to the sameowner	Locating lost thingslike domestic animals orminor/old people	Control devices for personal environment	For the continuity ofservices assurance, an electric power supply reliability should be guaranteed	Disaster prediction and alerting

residents. Keen card administrations will in general put the card subtleties and buy conduct of the residents in danger. Smart portability applications may release the area hints of the clients. There are applications utilizing, which guardians can monitor their youngster.

6.6.2 SMART ENVIRONMENT

Keen climate incorporates different IoT applications, for example, fire identification in backwoods, checking the degree of snow in high height districts, forestalling avalanches, early recognition of seismic tremors, contamination observing, and so forth. All these IoT applications are firmly identified with the life of individuals and creatures in those territories. In this unique situation, both bogus negatives and bogus positives can prompt sad outcomes for such IoT applications. Accordingly, brilliant climate applications must be profoundly exact, and security penetrates and information altering should be kept away from.

6.6.3 SMART METERING AND SMART GRIDS

Brilliant metering incorporates applications identified with different estimations, checking, and the executives. There likewise exist some IoT applications that utilization keen meters to gauge the water pressure in water transport frameworks or to quantify the heaviness of merchandise. In a brilliant home zone network, all electric hardware at home are associated with keen meters and the data gathered from these types of gear can be utilized for burden and cost the board. Purposeful interruption in such corre-spondence frameworks by the shopper or an enemy may adjust the gathered data, prompting money-related misfortune for the specialist organizations or purchasers.

6.6.4 SECURITY AND EMERGENCIES

There are different structures whose frameworks have delicate information or that house touchy merchandise. Security applications can be sent to ensure touchy information and goods. IoT applications that identify different fluids can likewise be utilized to forestall consumption and break downs in such delicate structures. Security breaks in such applications can likewise have different genuine results. Likewise, bogus radiation level caution check has genuine prompt and long-haul impacts.

6.6.5   SMART RETAIL

IoT applications are as a rule broadly utilized in there tail sector. Various applications have been created to screen the capacity states of the products as they move along the inventory network. IoT is additionally being utilized to control the following of items in the stockrooms so that restocking should be possible ideally. Different insightful shopping applications are likewise being created for helping the clients dependent on their inclinations, propensities, hypersensitivities to specific segments, and so forth. Components to give the experience of web-based shopping to offline retailers utilizing increased reality strategies have additionally been created. Different organizations in retail have confronted security issues in conveying and utilizing different IoT applications.

6.6.6   SMART AGRICULTURE AND ANIMAL FARMING

Savvy farming incorporates checking soil dampness, controlling miniature atmosphere conditions, particular water system in dry zones, and controlling mugginess and temperature. Use of such progressed highlights in agribusiness can help in accomplishing exceptional returns and can save ranchers from financial misfortunes. Control of temperature and dampness levels in different grain and vegetable creation can help in forestalling parasite and other micro-bial foreign substances. Controlling the atmosphere conditions can likewise help in expanding the vegetable and harvest yield and quality. Much the same as harvest checking, there are IoT applications to screen the exercises and the ailment of livestock by appending sensors to the creatures. In the event that such applications are undermined, at that point it might prompt the burglary of animals from the homestead and enemies may likewise harm the harvests.

6.6.7   HOME AUTOMATION

Home computerization is perhaps the most generally utilized and conveyed IoT applications. This incorporates applications, for example, those for distantly controlling electrical apparatuses to save energy, frameworks sent on windows and ways to identify gatecrashers, and so on observing frameworks are being applied to follow energy and water supply utilization. Interruptions are distinguished by looking at the client activities at key areas of the home with typical conduct of the client in these areas. Nonetheless, assailants may pick up unapproved access of the IoT gadgets in the home and attempt to hurt the clients.

6.7 ALLIED SURVEYS ON IOT SECURITY

TABLE 6.2 Related Surveys on IoT Security.

Year	Author	Contributions
2016	Arsalan Mosenia et al..	A brief discussion of vulnerabilities faced by the edge side layer of IoT
2017	Yu wei et al.	Survey on using Edge Computing to secure IoT
2017	Jie Lin ea al.	Discussion on relationship between IoT andFog computing
2017	Y yang et al.	A brief discussion on most relevant limitationsof IoT devices
2017	L chen, S. Thombre et al.	Security issues specific to location-basedservices in IoT
2018	A H Ngu, V. Metsis et al	Security issues related to the IoT middle ware
2018	I Farris, T Taleb et al	Security mechanism for IoT security like SDNand NFB
2019	Ikram Ud din, M. Guizani et al.	Trust Management techniques for internet ofthings

KEYWORDS

- **IoT**
- **IoT Security**
- **Sensor**
- **DoS Attack**
- **Malware**

REFERENCES

1. Yang, Z.; Yang, M.; Zhang, Y.; Gu, G.; Ning, P.; Wang, X. S. Appintent: Analyzing Sensitive Data Transmission in Android for Privacy Leakage Detection. In *Proceedings of the 2013 ACM SIGSAC Conference on Computer & Communications Security*, 2013; pp 1043–1054.
2. Conti, M.; Nguyen, V. T. N.; Crispo, B. Crepe: Context-Related Policy Enforcement for Android. In *Information Security*; Springer, 2011; pp 331–345.
3. Chen, K. Z.; Johnson, N. M.; D'Silva, V.; Dai, S.; MacNamara, K.; Magrino, T. R.; Wu, E. X.; Rinard, M.; Song, D. X. Contextual Policy Enforcement in Android Applications with Permission Event Graphs. In *NDSS*, 2013.
4. Li, X.; Lu, R.; Liang, X.; Shen, X. Smart Community: An Internet of Things Application. *IEEE Commun. Mag.* **2011,** *49* (11), 68–75.
5. Firner, B.; Moore, R. S.; Howard, R.; Martin, R. P.; Zhang, Y.; Poster: Smart Buildings, Sensor Networks, and the Internet of Things. In *Proceedings of the ACM Conference on Embedded Networked Sensor Systems*, Nov. 2011; pp 337–338.
6. Sheng, Z.; Yang, S.; Yu, Y.; Vasilakos, A. A Survey on the IETF Protocol Suite for the Internet of Things: Standards, Challenges, and Opportunities. *IEEE Wirel. Commun.* **2013,** *20* (6), 91–98.
7. Andrea, I.; Chrysostomou, C.; Hadjichristofi, G. Internet of Things: Security Vulnerabilities and Challenges. In *Proceedings of the IEEE Symposium on Computers and Communication*, Larnaca, Cyprus, Feb. 2015; pp 180–187.
8. Roman, R.; Zhou, J.; Lopez, J. On the Features and Challenges of Security and Privacy in Distributed Internet of Things. Comput. Netw. **2013,** *57* (10), 2266–2279.
9. Chen, S.; Xu, H.; Liu, D.; Hu, B. A Vision of IoT: Applications, Challenges, and Opportunities with China Perspective. *IEEE Internet Things J.* **2014,** *1* (4), 349–359.
10. Zhou, J.; Cao, Z.; Dong, X.; Vasilakos, A. V. Security and Privacy for Cloud-Based IoT: Challenges. *IEEE Commun. Mag.* **2017,** *55* (1), 26–33.
11. Xiao, L.; Li, Y.; Han, G.; Liu, G.; Zhuang, W. PHY-Layer Spoofing Detection with Reinforcement Learning in Wireless Networks. *IEEE Trans. Veh. Technol.* **2016,** *65* (12), 10037–10047.
12. Abu Alsheikh, M.; Lin, S.; Niyato, D.; Tan, H. P. Machine Learning in Wireless Sensor Networks: Algorithms, Strategies, and Applications. *IEEE Commun. Surv. Tutor.* **2014,** *16* (4), 1996–2018.
13. Xiao, L.; Xie, C.; Chen, T.; Dai, H. A Mobile Offloading Game Against Smart Attacks. *IEEE Access* **2016,** *4*, 2281–2291.
14. Xiao, L.; Li, Y.; Huang, X.; Du, X. J. Cloud-Based Malware Detection Game for Mobile Devices with Offloading. *IEEE Trans. Mobile Comput.* **2017,** *16* (10), 2742–2750.

CHAPTER 7

Leveraging IIoT in Reverse Logistics: A WSN Approach

VINOD KUMAR SHUKLA[1], LEENA WANGANOO[2], MOHAMMED YOUSUF[3], and RAJESH TRIPATHI[4]

[1]Department of Engineering and Architecture, Amity University, Dubai, UAE

[2]Research Scholar, University of Petroleum and Energy Studies, Dehradun, India

[3]Amity University Dubai, UAE.

[4]Department of General Management, University of petroleum and Energy Studies, Dehradun

ABSTRACT

During the pandemic lockdown, e-commerce sales spiked with the change in consumer shopping habits. Thee-trailer develops strategies for faster last-mile delivery, neglecting the return of goods process. In a highly competitive environment, the e-trailer must provide consistently high reverse logistics (RL) services, including quick, efficient collection, sorting, and reprocessing. In this process, the transportation and warehouse operations play a critical role. The supply chain's service quality has evolved over the period, that is, and digitization technology deployed in the tracking. Internet of Things (IoT) has enhanced transparency in the process through collaboration among the intermediaries and material handling equipment. The IoT has given a promising chance to create robust industrial systems and apps by leveraging the increasing ubiquity of RFID (Radio Frequency Identification) and

Internet of Things: Technological Advances and New Applications. Brojo Kishore Mishra & Amit Vishwasrao Salunkhe (Eds.)
© 2024 Apple Academic Press, Inc. Co-published with CRC Press (Taylor & Francis)

wireless, mobile, and sensor devices. But still unable to provide real-time visibility due to lack of integration. Hence, to improve interoperability, transparency, real-time visibility, an economical and straight forward solution to tracking and to monitor the entire supply chain and physical conditions is the Wireless Sensor Network (WSN). Such sensors assist in data collection, analysis, and wireless communication.

WSN Technology offers the versatility of small and low-cost sensors and is very useful for analyzing data in different applications. This article reviews IIoT (Industrial Internet of Things), which consists of web-connected machines and state-of-the-art analytical tools to process data. IIoT devices are ranging from small sensors to large robots. In recent years, a wide variety of IIoT apps have been created and implemented. Specifically, in RL management, the application IIoT in the Storage facilities, fleet tracking. The current routing structures for meeting the quality of service (QoS) specifications of limited QoS applications, with the inherent weakness of sensor network and wireless communication reliability. It will ensure easy and effective collection, data transfer, processing, energy management, and data routing through WSNs, which ensures more efficient implementation of reserve logistics. The research proposes a real-time routing framework supported by new WSNs implementations. This WSNs based real-time fault-tolerant system assists routing systems with a local status indicator on each sensor node to monitor and evaluate local node and channel conditions. The node dynamically modifies the transmission capacity by using this fault-tolerant framework to reduce the performance loss of the real-time service induced by network failures and preserve the required quality and timeliness.

7.1   INTRODUCTION

The year 2020 transformed consumer lives to a greater extent. The consumer adopted digital technology in all the spheres of life, specifically in the retail sector. During the lockdown in many countries and online buying surged, leading to exponential growth in the e-commerce sector.[1] this behavior is likely to last postpandemic. The data indicates that online shopping has not been limited to only food and essentials, but it has gone beyond. Figure 7.1 shows the change witnessed in online shopping increase in all categories, food, and essential items top on the list. The primary reasons to shop online are the price, convenience, and contactless delivery. In the long term, the retailer should focus on the supply chain to provide a value proposition to the customer and sustain in the competitive environment.

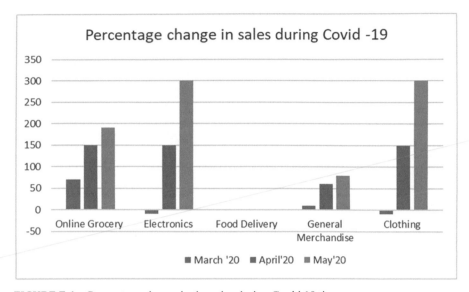

FIGURE 7.1 Percentage change in the sales during Covid 19 times.
Source: Earnest Research/NYTimes, 2020 Oliver Wyman COVID-19 Customer Survey on Retail Impact.

The e-trailer ensures an agile and flexible last-mile delivery rather than a robust return process to attain a competitive advantage. As along with the growth of online purchases, the return of goods is an ugly reality. To meet this daunting challenge, the retailer needs a strategy and a laser-focused on rapid execution process. The return supply chain needs an accelerated transformation with technology, people, and methods to rapidly execute and satisfy the customer.

Return of goods returned by the customer holds significant importance in e-commerce from a customer service perspective. The return management (Reverse Logistics (RL)) operation is complex and cost-inefficient because it is paid twice. RL focuses on the process of a product return from the customer to the manufacturer. RL is defined as a process of planning, implementing, and controlling the efficient, cost-effective flow of raw materials, in-process inventory, finished goods, and related information from the point of consumption to the end of origin to recapture value or proper disposal. Figure 7.2 shows all the activities involved in the RL process.

Customer's collection are the first and critical stage in the recovery process. At each customer location, the products are located, collected, and, if required, transported to facilities for rework and remanufacturing. The local logistics provider undertakes this activity.

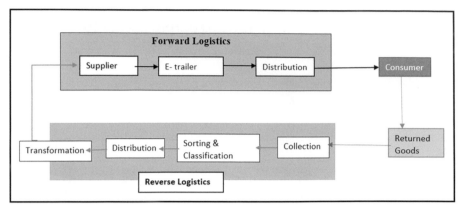

FIGURE 7.2   Forward supply chain and reverse logistics.

Source: Reprinted from Nicolau, J. J. N. (2016) Impact of RFID information-sharing coordination over a supply chain with reverse logistics. Open access.

- Sorting/Inspection—All the collected items need to be sorted and inspected; this activity is completed either at the collection point, local centralized warehouse, or at the retailer rework site.
- Preprocessing Inspection/Sorting may be carried out either at the point/time of collection itself or afterward (at collection points or rework facilities). Collected items generally need sorting.
- Redistribution—Based on the product decision on recycling, reuse, remarketing, or refurbishing the product. The redistribution logistics network, which is often intertwined with the existing logistics network.
- Transformation—Transformation in the case of returned products means disposal of the products, remanufacturing the product, the act of moving the product, and resale of the product in the second-hand market.

High operation and challenges are associated with each other. Labor cost, traffic, shipping cost, receiving and warehousing cost, counterfeit items, lack of visibility across the supply chain, inability to forecast, credit reconciliation documents laden, and insufficient response time are major challenges in RL. The organizational perspective is the most neglected activity because the expenses in recovery are higher than its investment. For a seamless operation, integrating emerging technology and information flow among the intermediaries is critical. Information system and flow are essential components in the return process. Figure 7.3 explains the various participating entities' information and the product flow in the entire flow.

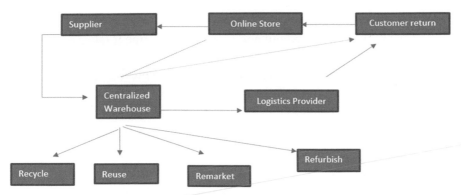

FIGURE 7.3 Information flow in the reverse logistics process.

The flow becomes more complicated in the global supply chain, with additional challenges in cross-border return entities. The information system capabilities in RL are usually not available in their RL networks since RL is of secondary importance. Due to the unavailability of critical information and transparency in product returns, such as the number of in-transit returns or the number of in-store returns, operational planning becomes very difficult in the RL network. An effective information technology (IT) infrastructure is necessary for an RL system, considering the need for accurate time projection and the number of returned products.

7.1.1 CHALLENGES IN RL

Following are the challenges in the RL management:

a) Tracking of the goods
b) Uncertainty of the returned goods
c) Data and process transparency among intermediaries

However, with the advancement in digitization, the integration among the various participants has improved but still visibility. Traceability, forecasting, and data security across the supply chain need attention. Deployment of emerging technologies will enhance the trust among the various intermediaries and guarantee data integration, traceability, and security of valuable data across the supply chain.

Companies thereby benefit from accurate, timely information on returned products, enabling them to:

• Intelligently track products through the return process

- Share status updates with consumers
- Streamline returns overall and accelerate the time it takes consumers to get their money back
- Reconcile returned products with current inventories
- Proactively determine the next best action for an item
- Maintain records of any items in need of repair or refurbishment

7.1.2   NEED FOR IIOT IN RL

Enhanced visibility and transparency can significantly benefit RL services where provenance tracking is required. The interoperability and transparency influence the service performance and cost in Reverse Logistics. For a performance-driven RL, the e-tailer needs to focus and deploy the technologies for communication, monitoring (Inventory and Vehicle), and transparency. Figure 7.4.

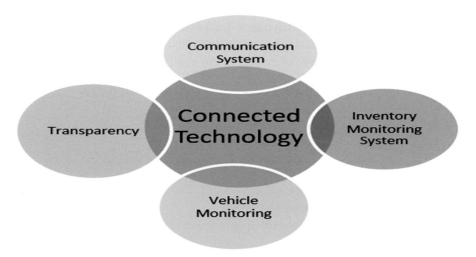

FIGURE 7.4   Integrated technology drivers.

The Industrial Internet of things (IIoT), composed of a proliferation of connected sensors and smart devices, can increase the supply chain's real-time visibility through advanced sensor networks.

The IIoT can put the power to make data-driven decisions firmly in an operations manager's hand, reducing the number of errors in operation. The study's objective is to analyze the IIoT tool, reduce the performance loss of the real-time service, and preserve the quality and timeliness required in the RL.

7.2 IIOT—AN INTRODUCTION

IIoT reflects a range of Internet of Things (IoT) technologies, smart product design concepts, and data-driven automation activities in the economy industry. Current sensor technology is commonly used to enhance different equipment types with capabilities for remote monitoring and maintenance. Increased use of existing data sources and incorporation of new generation points provide greater visibility of device users' industrial processes. Such transparency is used to recognize inefficiencies and to fix them. Sources include the elimination of waste materials and energy consumption in the sense of discrete production. IIoT would revolutionize manufacturing by allowing much greater data volumes to be collected and accessed at far higher speeds and much more effectively than before.

By incorporating smart, connected devices in their factories, various innovative companies have begun implementing the IIoT. IIoT is one of the primary trends affecting industrial businesses today and in the future. Industries call for the modernization of processes and facilities to comply with new regulations, keep up with the market's increasing pace and complexity, and cope with disruptive technologies. Companies that have implemented the IIoT have seen significant performance improvements. This trend is expected to continue with more adoption of IIoT technologies.

The ignition IIoT solution for industrial organizations greatly enhances communication, performance, scalability, time savings, and cost savings. It can unite the people and structures on the plant's floor with those on the business's top. It can also allow companies to make the most of their process without being limited by technological and economic constraints. Enhanced use of existing data sources and incorporation of new generation points provide greater visibility of system users' industrial processes. Such transparency is used to recognize inefficiencies and to fix them. Sources include the elimination of waste materials and energy consumption in the sense of discrete production.

The IIoT history begins with Dick Morley's 1968 invention of the programmable logic controller (PLC), which General Motors used in its production division for an automatic transmission. The PLCs enabled the regulation of each part in the production chain to be perfect. The globe's first Distributed Control System (DCS) in 1975, the TDC 2000, and a CENTUM model were introduced by Honeywell and Yokogawa, respectively. These DCSs were the step toward flexible management of processes across a plant, with the added value of backup inefficiencies/redundancies by extending control across the whole network and eliminating a security issue in a centralized room.

7.2.1 GROWTH OF IIOT SENSORS

The rising commercial recognition of IIoT sensors is a crucial driver of market growth. The necessity of cost reduction primarily increases the use of IIoT sensors. The IIoT sensors market is developing as a core element in all areas, as IIoT sensors speak of a possible future response to evaluate and convert objects into a quantum value, that is, used later by some other client or gadget.[5]

7.2.2 IMPACT ON BUSINESS DUE TO LACK OF IIOT SENSOR

In the RL process, due to a lack of system integration between process and resource, there are several challenges such multisource data, time-consuming collection phenomena, severe delay, vulnerability to error, etc. The information is received from several. Constant urgent tasks and regular plan adjustments during actual production contribute to severe problems, such as the implementing program's low operational effectiveness, lack of adequate job management, and over-control of goods.

Suppose the relationships between multisource information and key operational processes monitoring have not been multilayer with interactions and an integrated model. In that case, it is not easy to present any key direction and connections in the process promptly and exactly.[6]

7.2.3 HOW THE IIOT WORKS IN RL

An increasing number of companies are using the power of the IIoT. Through computer vision, big data, and automation, we hope to improve productivity, efficiency, and quality management around the supply chain. The technology establishes a system that can capture, analyze, and transfer data correctly, reliably, and precisely. The IIoT will be the next huge performance and operational growth, utilizing existing systems like digital computing, advanced sensors, mobile software, cloud services, etc., to make information available.

This approach's key components can be defined as intelligent cooperative, Predictive analysis, data management and on-site monitoring, and projective analytics.

An active IIoT strategy is based on consolidating data from multiple systems in the cloud, applying higher-level analytics, and exploiting specialists who are often physically remote from the factory site. Predictive analytical approaches can turn work processes from manual, reactive to mechanical, and constructive, helping prevent unplanned downtime and improving performance and security. They allow companies to keep a better track of everything that happens at the factory, remote locations, subcontractors and supplier facilities, and all over the world on goods in transit.

7.3   STATE OF THE ART TECHNOLOGY: CYBER-PHYSICAL SYSTEM

This is why an established IoT application demonstrates how real industrial data to big industrialized data can be produced. CPS (Cyber-Physical System) seamlessly links the physical world with IT and software's virtual world, using various types of data, digital communications techniques, and amenities available. Nevertheless, using IoT, particularly in industry, the use of CPS leads to the development of large quantities of information that require manipulation and analysis for practical thinking and actual value extraction. Big data analytics encourage the overcoming of the bottlenecks created to meet this challenge generated by IoT. The definition of the IoT adopted is "Anytime, Anyplace, Everything, and Anyway links people and things through the IoT, preferably with any path/network and every service.".[7]

This includes IoT applications in the industry by using sensors and electric motors, control systems, machine-to-machine, data analysis, and industrial safety mechanisms. Numerous important IIoT applications have emerged. With three pillars, that is, optimizing the operation, optimizing resource use, and creating a dynamic independent system, IIoT will integrate traditional industries. The IoT is a sector of multidisciplinary activity.

The IoT paradigm is due to the convergence of internet-oriented, interpret, and embedded visions. The CPS model advocates the use of IoT-philosophized monitoring devices, which go beyond the conventional on-site data collection, storage, and visualization approaches. Robustness, reconfiguration capacity, reliability, intelligence, and cost efficiency constitute the key criteria for monitoring systems in production. Specific topologies can be used to link screens.

7.3.1   IIOT AND WIRELESS SENSOR NETWORK (WSN)

The most qualifying applicants are in the manufacture of the network wireless sensor topologies, which deliver mobility and scalability in dynamic environments such as shop floors. There are a large number of WSNs that work together to achieve a common purpose The sensors which monitor production can compose a WSN in the context of manufacturing systems in order to increase or reduce production KPIs. The sensors that track operation may make up a WSN in the sense of manufacturing systems to improve or increase output KPIs.

Some of the most important results of IoT emergence is the production of massive volumed statistics with more than 40 trillion gigabytes before 2020 and the need for precise exploitation in order to provide useful information.

Emerging technologies, such as IoT/cloud computing, technically allow large data analysis via the Internet to provide data accessibility.[8] Cloud technology and in general the cloud creation patterns serve as a way to facilitate universal access to information and the interaction between various IT resources. A detailed literature review has been conducted on cloud production.[9,10] The researchers discuss the emerging use of cloud in development phases and conclude the literature review with a conceptual framework with critical elements such as cyber-physically active systems, intelligent sensor networks, large data processing, and cloud computing. Cloud manufacturing can embrace the concept of designing anywhere, offering scalability access to all sorts of network and modeling for company sizes and needs.[11]

7.3.2   I-IOT AND BIG DATA

In order to implement this concept of digital production, big data analytics often play a very significant role by catalyzing technologies like additive manufacturing.[12] Big data analytics are also the basis for modern mass customization, implying customer-specific requirements.[11] The acquired data has to be tested until considered valid for applications like prognostics and health management for production systems.[13] Large data sets can be analyzed to improve the information depots and to enhance decision-making at various stages, including assembly operations.[14] Intelligent products are other sources of information that must be taken into account. The product contains information regarding their life cycle using embedded information devices (PED) such as RIFD.

A new McKinsey Global Inc. study says that the importance of Big Data for manufacturing reveals that large-scale manufacturing operations can clash product designing and production costs by up to 50% and minimize working capital by 7%.[15] In this context, CPS can also be built to manage large data to achieve the objective of smart, resilient, and automated machines by using machine interconnectivity. Industrial companies need to be digitalized to improve their performance and competitiveness. Connectivity, communication and being agreed for standard are the main challenges. However, the handling of large data produced from a diverse manufacturing process origin using large data techniques is another main challenge. Data visualization from many different sources and managing that data is also one of the crucial issue to address, especially when everything needs to connected/displayed in one platform.

7.4 THE IMPLEMENTATION OF INDUSTRIAL BIG DATA IN PRODUCTION BY IIOT

Data are generated by various sensors, which may be integrated in different platform like machine tools, cloud-based services, and in various business management-based solutions. As per Batty et Al., over a total volume of over 1000 Exabyte per year is estimated to be in the industrial data.[15] IoT adoption in production aims mainly to develop smart factories that communicate and link machines' resources in a network.

To that end, an organization has to connect Internet to industrial tools, resources, and existing tools explicitly or via outside interfaces. Various machines and machine tools need to learn how to communicate with cyber world, in order to behave like "Cyber machine tool," which can help for data transmission and data analysis. To turn operators into "cyber operators," portable devices to the Internet network will also link services that include human input.

Finally, the network will be connected to existing IT tools and management tools that capture heterogeneous data from various sources. Such a smart company produces smart products knowing how they have been produced, collecting, and transmitting data as they are used will collecting and analyzing these huge amounts of data. It is of the highest importance that the information produced by a firm's lowest level, directly through the machinery and from human workers, is used and analyzed to make such data flexible and sensitive to provide meaningful information to a company's highest levels. As a result the base of the production system with a special focus. It is of the highest importance that the information produced by a firm's lowest level, directly through the machinery and from human workers, is used and analyzed to make such data flexible and sensitive to provide meaningful information to a company's highest levels. The design and implementation of common and reliable communication protocols that can link existing systems and collect the share production data is the major challenge for this transition.

7.4.1   THE IMPLEMENTATION OF IIOT IN RL MANAGEMENT

Using the IIoT, the logistics provider can monitor real-time the truck carrying the returned goods from each customer point, improving supply chains' reliability and effectiveness. The deployment of WSN offers technical capabilities for continuous sense and response capabilities. From each collection point, the DAQ system (Data acquisition) unit can be used for the acquisition and monitoring, such sensors are chosen so that the application for control of machine tools are nonintrusive and installable easily.

DAQ help to identify and provide the current state with maximum or configured observation, which can help to find the related with various other parameter like power consumption and status and correlation with other sensors/machine tools.[16]

7.4.1.1   MONITORING SYSTEM VIA WSN

Old machines, therefore, often lack the necessary connectivity capabilities. Therefore, the legacy controller must be converted into an IoT device with special effort. This research introduces a wireless network sensor (WSN) monitoring system, Consensus Time Synchronization, as existing sensors, a hall-effect sensor, and a screen are part of the monitoring tool.

WSN offers complementary advantages over the use of Radio Frequency Identification (RFID) in supply chains. Through the WSN, wirelessly reporting the collected measurements, supervisors can communicate in-transit problems, correct it before it reaches the destination. In-transit communication and monitoring help the company consolidate, merge, and convert the less than truckload to full truckload. The WSN speed up the transmission of the information with real-time connectivity.

After the collection from the supplier (Figure 7.5), the goods reaches the warehouse. With the implementation of IIoT, the communication between the logistics provider, e-trailer will be more reliable and dependable. The WSN is used as a create active tracking device as the nodes can be attached to SKU (stock-keeping units), roll containers, pallets, and shipping containers.[17]. The warehouse can detect damage, theft, and sorting the product as per the final treatment required due to sudden shocks or containers' opening. This also results in significant quality of service improvements and greater efficiency, leading to lower transport costs.[18]

Along with the tracking and monitoring of the returned goods, the IIoT also collaborates with the warehouse's material handling equipment in the warehouse. The preload sensors capture and rely on the data to each node. With the IIoT-driven tracking in the returned warehouse, tons of data can be generated that will help forecast the return demand.

The fully connected IIoT helps the e-trailer acquire real-time visibility and transparency across the supply chain, communicate with the logistics provider, and take a real-time decision for scheduling and operational planning. Similarly, with the help of real-time data, the supplier can make a well-informed decision and collaborate with the other intermediaries to reduce the errors and transfer credit for the damage goods faster.

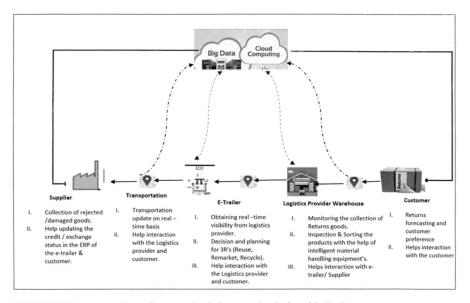

FIGURE 7.5 Integration of reverse logistics supply chain with IIoT.

7.4.2　*RADIO FREQUENCY TECHNOLOGIES FOR WSN'S*

The widespread adoption of hand-held scanner and item-level tagging, using low-cost device like RFID. The wireless reader captures data from pallet and eliminates the time-consuming task of manual counting and volume scanning. Table 7.1 shows the benefits of WSN as compared with RFID.

TABLE 7.1　Benefits of WSN compared with RFID.

Radio Frequency technologies	Standards	Unfavoured facts
Bluetooth Technology	IEEE 802.15.2	• When in active mode it drains a lot of battery
		• Lacks security
		• Short range
Wi-Fi Technology	IEEE 802.11.a/b/h/g	• Interference
		• Short range
		• Security risk
Ultra Wide Band Technology	IEEE 802.15.2	• high energy needed
		• no proper frequency sharing
WAVENIS Technology	EN 300-220 And FCC (coronis system)	Possible risk of data collision
Wibree Technology	IEEE 802.15.5	Not really suitable for high bandwidth required applications.

Though RFID technology has overcome the shortcoming of barcode, however, with automation evolving in the logistics area, the need is for a high-speed noncontact identification device such as WSN for speedy management of reverse supply chain.[19] The WSN links each activity. Each link in the reverse supply chain is connected with the node that transmits the information to the next level in the supply chain. The sensors in the WSN monitor and the condition of the goods and alert the warehouse manager.

NODE: There are hundreds of dozens of smaller transmitters/devices called nodes in WSNs. The sensor device is often shortened as a node. A Sensor is an input sensor, which transmits the data to a node Figure 7.6.[20] Sensors are being used to assess psychical environment alterations such as pressure, moisture, sound, vibration, etc.

A Node contains a transmitter, storage/memory, battery, A/D to attach to that of a sensor, as well as an ad hoc network emitter. A note and sensor create a Sensor Node combined. The sensor node configuration is multiple;

sensors may be installed on a node for various purposes. Occasionally motes are often called smart dust. A sensor node constitutes a fundamental sensor network unit. The nodes that are basically used within sensor networks are small and also have substantial energy restrictions.

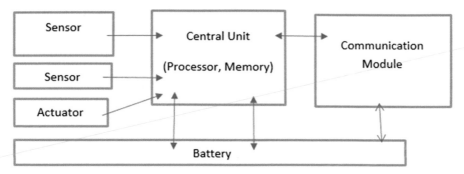

FIGURE 7.6   Structure of a sensor node.

Sensor location is a basic and critical problem for network monitoring and activity. The nodes used by the sensor networks remain small and have large energy restraints. The sensors are installed in many modern world situations without understanding their locations at once and no supporting infrastructure can be identified and controlled when they are deployed.

7.4.3   WSN FUNCTIONALITIES

Following are the functions of WSN and the significant role it will play to enhance the real-time visibility and overall performance in the effective management of RL operations.

Fault Diagnosis: Since the WSN has continuous changes, strict registration for fault prevention maybe 100% unprotected. To identify and diagnose the failures caused, a primary fault diagnostic system is often needed. In either of the following three ways these techniques may be conducted: (i) self, (ii) group, and (iii) hierarchical treatment at centralized or decentralized networks. Each fault must be identified and the features and actions of the fault are examined after identifying fault and isolation techniques.

Fault recovery needs to be optimized to minimize/eliminate the impact following a thorough analysis of observed faults. The primary task is to prevent the effects of defects during all stages.[21] Fault repair process. It can be achieved with correct techniques for redundancy. The data, time, and code are some of the normal inefficiencies implemented on several levels. The inefficiency of information provides FT through active/passive duplication of the information needed.

WSN hardware faults classes: Hardware defects can be categorized under several criteria but, as far as their length is concerned, open WSN research problems should be resolved following three defects. Such defects are temporary, sporadic, enduring, and future.

Transient defects: Transient error factors, such as temperature, earthquakes, and cosmic radiation, are responsible for environmental conditions. The experiences of this sort of fault are usually much less pronounced because it happens occasionally. For instance, a signal from the origin end system might not reach the target but could reach once the source end system is retransmitted. So it was also called soft defects.

Intermittent defects: This sort of defect follows a loops' mannerism that the defect then disappears and then pops up. Un-environmental conditions like loose ties, dormant materials etc cause occasional failures. Intermittent failure causes great bafflement since it is hard to diagnose. For example, the unstable recurring wrong condition of any system illustrates this form of fault.

Permanent defects: The permanent defect effect stays stable and persists until the failed part has been repaired or replaced.[22] Permanent defects include chips with factory defects, burnt-out lights, and so forth. Possible failures reduced hardware nodes generally leads to possible faults such as battery power. Depleting the power from the battery removes the entire WSN system feature.

Fault Prevention: Fault detection is an act to detect an unusual fault that usually involves operations in WSN applications. Prevention function along with key phases of the development of applications for WSN can be integrated they are:

- Describing phase
- Stage of development and design
- Observing phase

It avoids incomplete specifications and inaccurate specifications during the specified phase. Through implementing acceptable hardware quality standards and identifying those flows along with controlled structures at network coverage and connection level, preventive acts can be taken into account when designing and developing. Bad use/handling of resources/ events or operational deterioration caused by multiple factors can lead to fault generation. This is why it is also important to track the status of the node, the reliability of the connection and the congestions.

7.4.4 IIOT A WAY FORWARD WITH RL

IIoT provides an opportunity to add value to the return management by tracking and tracing the product beyond the warehouse and improving the operation's efficiency. The cloud-based services and big data optimize the performance by monitoring the fleets, taking real-time decisions by reacting quicker to any error or changes required. Figure 7.7 shows the benefits of IIoT offers to supply chain management. It not only increases efficiency but also enhances the performance of the operation. The adoption of IIoT will also monitor the fleet drivers' safety and provide real-time feedback on the changing customer demand to the e-trailer. All this helps the e-trailer develop a customer-centric strategy.

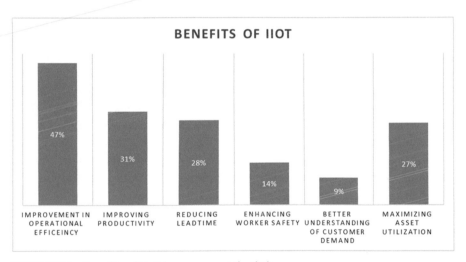

FIGURE 7.7   Benefits of IIoT in reverse supply chain.

Sensor nodes should be organized and cooperated in order to perform a dynamic sensing function such as data fusion. Data fusion is a significant result that aggregates data gathered from various nodes. Unless the sensor nodes are not aligned, the data estimate is unreliable.

There are at least three major reasons why this would not necessarily imply an extraordinarily stable device interface for sensor nodes.

- Firstly, sensor nodes are extremely expensive and therefore, cannot always be equipped with the finest quality components.
- Secondly, strict energy limitations mean that recurrent and computing solutions are often impractical.

- Thirdly, these devices are implemented in tougher conditions than modern computers. Even though programming and versatility in sensor networks are highly important, stringent energy constraints can lead to excessive use of application-related designs that can use up to two orders lesser energy for the same usability. We assume that some subsystems can achieve the targeted degree of failure tolerance while at the same time low energy usage through heterogeneous BISR tolerant technologies.

7.5   IIOT—CHALLENGES

Security: IIoT systems pose security issues, as offenses impact people and organizations prone to financial and organizational failure. In their position as manufacturing companies that used a variety of IIoT technologies, they expose to security issues, visibility shortfalls, hack vulnerabilities, IT/OT convergence-related risks, and intruder threats. The biggest challenge is to lack extensive cybersecurity solutions as the selection process includes safety capabilities. Unless it has a strong security feature, the introduction of IIoT technology would be resisted hype. That's why IT firms are so vigilant about IIoT technology.

 Connectivity and Visibility: There is a shortage of access to the crucial IIoT deployment challenges. The management of IIoT machines is crucial, but it is essential to track devices in real-time and ensure optimum output efficiency. Improved visibility and deeper insights into machine safety are also important if irregularities are to be identified and problems to be solved before they happen. IIoT devices are connected to various components, but as a result of internet faults, electrical outages, or mechanical/technical errors, synchronizations are often difficult.[23] The effect of this is the elimination of smart devices from the networks, which can harm millions of people during the entire production cycle. If you scale it internationally, IIoT will bring more challenges.

7.6   CONCLUSION

WSNs have created a number of obstacles to tackle. The impacts day-to-day lives of WSNs are more likely than Internet. This sector would definitely provide a great chance to change the way we see the world today. To enhance the service quality of RL, the return logistics network and intermediaries must be integrated. IIoT integrates the organization involved in collecting and transporting with sensors' help and transmits real-time information back to the origin for reuse. In the RL network, logistics providers play a significant role and add value to the entire operation using sensors, and WSN provides real-time monitoring of returned shipments. Decisions like in-transit consolidation, cross-docking, and providing customized service to the customer with IIoT technology help. The deployment of technology to improve the internal process also.

We can also see the various defects in WSN as a whole and the node's physical layer. To provide an effective management system, we have seen the basic tenet of self-managed solutions. Nevertheless, there is a balance between sensor networks' difficulty and resource use to architectural design for failure management for WSNs. We have established that perhaps the basic functioning of the modules of the WSN protocol stack, including sensor nodes, ensures that any WSN application has a high "performance" rate when each layer and component contributes its work to WSN. We also see how to improve the efficiency level in IIot as a whole, both security-wise and connection-wise.

KEYWORDS

- **WSN**
- **reverse logistics**
- **QoS (quality of service)**
- **IIoT**
- **IoT**
- **sensors**

REFERENCES

1. Fabius, V.; Kohli, S.; Timelin, B.; Veranen, S. M. *How COVID-19 is Changing Consumer Behavior—Now and Forever*; October 21, 2020. Retrieved from https://www.mckinsey.com/industries/retail/our-insights/how-covid-19-is-changing-consumer-behavior-now-and-forever.

2. Degbotse, A.; Ang, A. K.; Vuong, N. Q.; Tan, J. S. K. Predictive Analytics in Reverse Supply Chain Management Commodity Life Expectancy for Quality Engineering. In

2017 IEEE 19th Electronics Packaging Technology Conference (EPTC), Singapore, 2017; pp 1–7. DOI: 10.1109/EPTC.2017.8277546.

3. Nativi, J. J.; Lee, S. Impact of RFID Information-Sharing Strategies on a Decentralized Supply Chain with Reverse Logistics Operations. *Int. J. Prod. Econ.* **2012,** *136* (2), 366–377. https://doi.org/10.1016/j.ijpe.2011.12.024.

4. Krafft, M.; Goetz, O.; Mantrala, M.; Sotgiu, F.; Tillmanns, S. The Evolution of Marketing Channel Research Domains and Methodologies: An Integrative Review and Future Directions. *J. Retail.* **2015,** *91* (4), 569–585. https://doi.org/10.1016/j.jretai.2015.05.001.

5. Mikusz, M. Towards an Understanding of Cyber-Physical Systems as Industrial Software-Product-Service systems. *Procedia CIRP* **2014,** *16*, 385–389

6. https://www.forbes.com/sites/insights-hitachi/2017/12/18/5-areas-where-the-iot-is-having-the-most-business-impact/#1646a4da4396

7. Hashem, I. A. T.; Yaqoob, I., Anuar, N. B.; Mokhtar, S.; Gani, A.; Khan, S. U. The Rise of "Big Data" on Cloud Computing: Review and Open Research Issues. *Inf. Syst.* **2015,** *47*, 98–115.

8. Wanganoo, L.; Shukla, V. K. Real-Time Data Monitoring in Cold Supply Chain Through NB-IoT. In *2020 11th International Conference on Computing, Communication and Networking Technologies (ICCCNT)*, Kharagpur, India, 2020; pp 1–6. DOI: 10.1109/ICCCNT49239.2020.9225360.

9. Mourtzis, D.; Vlachou, E. Cloud-Based Cyber-Physical Systems and Quality of Services. *TQM Emerald J.* **2016,** *28* (6)

10. Xu, X. From Cloud Computing to Cloud Manufacturing. *Robot. Comput. Integr. Manuf.* **2012,** *28* (1), 75–86.

11. Tien, J. M. Big Data: Unleashing Information. *J. Syst. Sci. Syst. Eng.* **2013,** *22*, 127–151.

12. Chen, X.; Cheng, K.; Wang, C. Design of a Smart Turning Tool with Application to In-Process Cutting Force Measurement in Ultraprecision and Micro Cutting. *Manuf. Lett.* **2014,** *2*, 112–117.

13. Renu, R. S.; Mocko, G.; Koneru, A. Use of Big Data and Knowledge Discovery to Create Data Backbones for Decision Support Systems. *Procedia Comput. Sci.* **2013,** *20*, 446–453

14. McKinsey Global Institute. Big Data: *The Next Frontier for Innovation, Competition, and Productivity Report*, January, 2011. [33] IBM. *The Rise of Machine Data: Are You Prepared?* 2014. Available online: http://www-01.ibm.com/common/ssi/cgibin/ssialias?subtype=BK&infotype=PM&appname=SWGE_IM_EZ_USEN &htmlfid=IMM1414 2USEN&attachment=IMM14142USEN

15. Tien, J. M. The Next Industrial Revolution: Integrated Services and Goods. *J. Syst. Sci. Syst. Eng.* **2012,** *21*, 257–296.

16. Mourtzis, D.; Vlachou, E.; Doukas, M.; Kanakis, N.; Xanthopoulos, N.; Koutoupes, A. Cloud-Based Adaptive Shop-Floor Scheduling Considering Machine Tool Availability. In *ASME*, Houston, Texas, 2015.

17. Wireless Sensor Network for Intelligent Supply Chain Management. Science & Engineering Research Support Society, 2016. https://doi.org/10.14257/astl.2016.139.42

18. Evers, L.; Havinga, P. J. M.; Kuper, J.; Lijding, M. E. M.; Meratnia, N. SensorScheme: Supply chain management automation using Wireless Sensor Networks. In *2007 IEEE Conference on Emerging Technologies and Factory Automation*, Patras, 2007; pp 448–455. DOI: 10.1109/EFTA.2007.4416802.

19. Tao Xua; Lina Gong; Wei Zhang; Xuhong Li; Xia Wang; Wenwen Pan. *Application of Wireless Sensor Network Technology in Logistics Information System*, 2017. https://doi.org/10.1063/1.4981549

20. Vieira, M.; et.al. Survey on Wireless sensor Network Devices. In *Proceedings of Emerging Technologies and Factory Automation, 2003 IEEE Conference*, Vol. 1, 16–19 September, 2003; pp 537–544.

21. https://search.proquest.com/openview/5537d2ee60ee6de592a6eff444f93c8f/1?pq-origsite=gscholar&cbl=1626343

22. Koren, D.Sc.; Krishna Ph.D.; Mani, C. Fault-Tolerant Systems, 1st ed.; Morgan Kaufmann, 2007.

23. Jae Min Lee; Wook Hyun Kwon; Young Shin Kim; Hong-Ju Moon. Physical Layer Redundancy Method for Fault Tolerant Networks. In *Proceedings of International Workshop on Factory Communication Systems*.

CHAPTER 8

A Pervasive Study on the Internet of Vehicles (IoVs)

LOPAMUDRA HOTA[1] and PRASANT KUMAR DASH[2]

[1]*National Institute of Technology, Rourkela, Odisha, India*

[2]*C.V. Raman Global University, Bhubaneswar, Odisha, India*

ABSTRACT

The era of 5G with Internet of Things (IoT) has led off future Internet providing faster and reliable communication by revolutionizing the present Internet scenario. Thereby attracting researchers and educationalist to this field directing toward smart city, smart home, smart health monitoring, and smart vehicles leading to Intelligent Transportation System. For efficient and faster vehicular communication, IoT has proved to be one of the best technologies providing real-time management of data processing dealing with vehicular control on road and traffic management. IoT merged with vehicular communication is Internet of Vehicle (IoV); it provides services for accident detection and avoidance, minimizes traffic congestion, and various application-oriented information transmission services. This work provides an insight to researchers for pursing their research in this field and enhances the vehicular and traffic management, the basics related to applications and work done in IoV along with open challenges and future direction are provided in details. Furthermore, the work also provides several architectural sketches of IoV technology for better understanding of network structure of IoVs.

Internet of Things: Technological Advances and New Applications. Brojo Kishore Mishra & Amit Vishwasrao Salunkhe (Eds.)

8.1   INTRODUCTION

Internet of Things (IoT) is a revolutionary communication paradigm that aims to bring forth an invisible and innovative framework to connect a plethora of digital devices with Internet. Automotive industries are in the pace of growing providing an expansive number of applications and opportunities for drivers and also passengers due to the emanation of the blooming IoT. Since years there has been ceaseless development in technology with advancement in information and network technology as development in software and hardware preceded the promotion of incredible connectivity between humans and everything else in the universe. IoT basically comprises of embedded systems providing connectivity for infrastructure and with end-users to process, store, access, and compute through Internet. IoT is used in various applications like health centers, libraries, homes, city centers, agriculture, weather forecasting, manufacturing, smart grids for providing smart services, and developing smart cities, automotive industries are no exceptions. For providing smart driving with safety and comfort, providing real-time updates, making travel cost efficient and providing infotainment, IoT is infused in vehicles called Internet of Vehicles (IoVs). According to a survey[26] more than 30 billion things have been referred to as IoT-enabled devices associated with the Internet and by the end of 2020 it is estimated to increase to 75.44 billion by 2025.

A better and efficient connectivity of Vehicle-to-Everything (V2X) communication is the major goal of IoT in vehicular technology. IoT allows faster and efficient data dissemination for safety such as accident alerts as well as nonsafety messages such as infotainment. Deployment of sensors for controlling speed, direction, and acceleration of vehicles, an adaptive cruise control based on artificial intelligence (AI) is presented in Ref. [19]. IoT is paving path for the development of IoV by traffic flow management and control, diverting vehicles to a different route in case of congestion or accidents on road, automatic application of brake if there is chance of accident and platooning of vehicles to faster and efficient vehicle's movement on road. IoV provides applications and various services by intravehicular (within vehicle via its components) as well as intervehicular (between two different vehicles and other units) communication, a type of intravehicular communication is shown in Ref. [42] that provides interaction between "vehicle" and "thing," and "vehicle" and "human".

The high speed cellular 5G network implemented in IoVs has advantage for fast and reliable communication transmitting volumes of data with low latency. Similarly, by evolution of Multiple-Input and Multi-Output (MIMO), the V2X communications on autonomous vehicles is supported by Third-Generation Partnership Project (3GPP)[1] providing network reliability and scalability. Furthermore, V2X communication is advanced with embedding more capabilities of AI, machine learning (ML), and Big Data technologies for future 6G network enhancement. Road safety and safety message dissemination is also a prime concern to be handled by the upcoming technological advancements for causality reduction on road. The Block-Chain technology with distributed ledgers is implemented in IoVs or V2X communication for privacy preserving, secure, trustworthy service initiation; by incorporating the crypto-currency mechanism cooperation of vehicles and incentive mechanism for data dissemination can be implemented.[27] IoV in a summarized form eliminates the limitations of vehicular communication such as providing QoS in terms of latency, end-to-end delay, packet delivery rate and throughput, scalability, data processing, interoperability, and safe reliable data transmission.

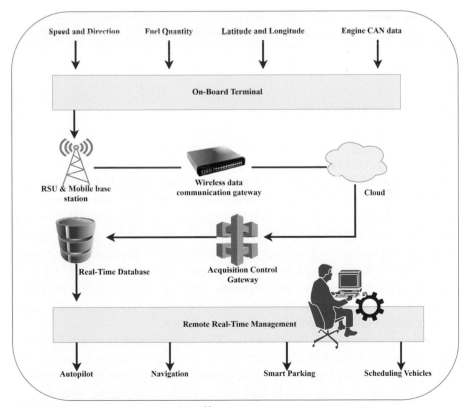

FIGURE 8.1 System structure of IoV.[14]

Applications of IoV include: traffic management, allocation of parking slots, personal assistance (maps, navigation system, infotainment, advertisement services), road safety warning message transmission, health monitoring on road for passengers as well as driver and providing immediate service in case of emergency, congestion and collision detection and redirecting vehicles to different path in case of any road mishaps and crowd scenario, detecting quantity of fuel present and alerting driver beforehand, and auto-braking in case of a predicted accident.

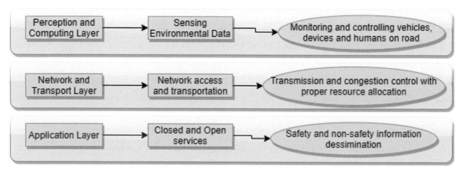

FIGURE 8.2   Layered architecture of IoVs.

8.2   IOV ARCHITECTURE

Basically, the IoV architecture is divided into three layers network and transport layer, computing and perception layer and application layer. The application layer deals with safety and nonsafety application services for better transportation efficiency by mobile communication via 5G network for Vehicle-to-Vehicle, Vehicle-to-Infrastructure, and Vehicle-to-Pedestrian by packet-switching concept. The application layer provides services in two forms: closed and open. The closed services include industrial applications such as traffic management, whereas the open services deal with business services such as real-time applications. The computing layer provides cooperative communication and computing including vehicles, humans and devices with cognitive capabilities for computation.

Further the perception layer contains the devices such as cameras, radio frequency identification (RFID) for mining environmental data. Lastly, the network and transport layer mostly support data transmission via network communication by intra-vehicle and inter-vehicle connection. The data is further processed for decision-making, analysis, and storage for traffic congestion detection, smart applications, safety and nonsafety application, weather analysis, and road analysis for smooth transportation. Overall, these layers deal with data processing, analysis and transmission, and network access for monitoring and management of traffic in real-time. The major capability of the IoV architecture is to provide dynamic inter- as well as inter-vehicular mobile communication in heterogeneous environment. Similarly, work has been done in where an IoV architecture is divided into four layers: Vehicle Network Environment Sensing and Control layer; Network Access and Transport layer; Co-ordinative Computing Control layer; and Application layer.[42]

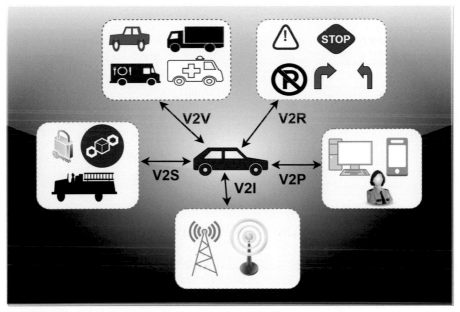

FIGURE 8.3   Generic communication model in IoVs.[14]

8.2.1   5G IMPLEMENTATION FOR V2X COMMUNICATION

5G improves network capabilities and provides faster connection. The services work on Internet Protocol (IPv4 or Ipv6) and interoperability between wireless and mobile networks for control data and packet routing in a better way. Users are connected to the base station via virtual cells[31] which are further researched for reliable communication. V2X communication is a part of concern of 5G network for reduced latency of safety message delivery, high throughput, handling mobile and diverse environment thereby providing Intelligent Transportation in autonomous vehicles.

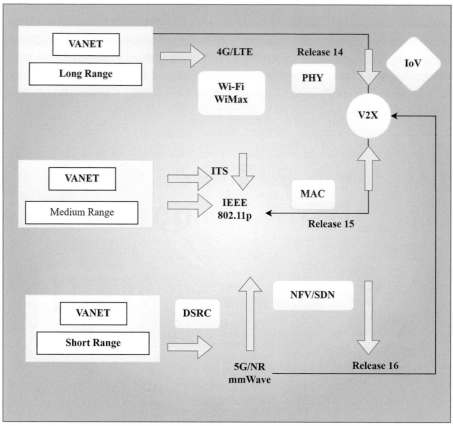

FIGURE 8.4   Communication ranges for V2X.[33]

5G technology uses the OFDM orthogonal code mechanism of high-level packet processing for reliability and flexibility.[29] The most talked about and researched problem of spectrum usage is also minimized to a good extent as in 5G technology there opens up a possibility for a single device having multiple smart antennas and short wavelength for diverse and dense network reducing the cell size. Till now, the development of VANET is such that, for long range communication 4G is implemented along with Wi-Fi or Wi-MAX, for medium-range communication IEEE 802.11p, and advancement in Intelligent Transportation whereas for short range 5G or radio communication is implemented.[33]

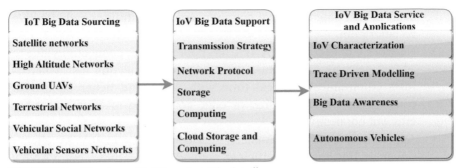

FIGURE 8.5   Structure of IoV based on Big data.[41]

Implementation of IoV with Big data technology is an important research direction. To store the massive amount of data generated and transmitted by IoT-based devices Big data plays a major role. Not only data source, that is, the units that generates data but also channel or link that transmit data has to be concern about the authentication and integrity of data along with less packet loss and delay prioritizing emergency and infotainment data or other nonsafety-oriented data. Cloud-based IoV is yet another technological advancement providing feasibility, less latency, high transmission throughput, and on-demand services for vehicular communication, further enhanced with Mobile Edge Computing for better services and communication efficiency.

8.3   COMPARATIVE ANALYSIS OF VANET VS IOV

- Goal: VANET only provides effective traffic management avoiding road accidents or causalities, whereas IoV apart from traffic management also enhance road safety, provides real-time emergency service as well as infotainment for smooth and efficient driving experience.
- Communication Categories: VANET communications are confined on Vehicle-to-Vehicle and Vehicle-to-Infrastructure, whereas IoV provides Vehicle-to-Pedestrian, Vehicle-to-Cellular network, Vehicle-to-Sensors, Vehicle-to RSUs apart from V2V and V2I; thus overall IoV provides Vehicle-to Everything (V2X) communication.
- Scope of Usage: VANET provides a local and discrete scope with limited applications, whereas IoT provides a global scope with varied applications by incorporating intelligent vehicular communication.
- Size of Data: VANET can handle only limited amount of data due to localized control, whereas IoV handles enormous amount of data (Big

data) in real time by global communication capabilities and effective collaboration.

- Network Connectivity: VANET has poor network connectivity due to ad-hoc network architecture with frequent connection lost, whereas IoVs communicate in real time with faster and better bandwidth connectivity via cloud, fog, or edge computing in 4G/5G or other efficient connectivity.
- Application Utility: Guaranteed service delivery in IoV by client–server architecture and efficient network connectivity, but VANET does not provide guaranteed services due to poor network connectivity and disconnection issues.
- Internet Facility for Connectivity: Due to dependency on RSUs in VANET, Internet connectivity is not always available for reliable communication, whereas IoV imparts reliable communication as IoT has the capability to connect to anything, everything, everywhere on demand with faster Internet services.
- Computational capabilities: Due to the lack of data mining and Big-data-driven computation because of less storage and computational capabilities, VANET lacks decision-making where, implementation of AI over Big-data and data mining computation provides efficient decision-making capabilities to IoVs.

Thus, we can conclude IoV has gained much attention in research as well as commercial applications due to its real-time execution capabilities and ability to handle global data with faster data processing rate.

8.4   RESEARCH PROPOSALS IN IOVS

Development of Intelligent Transportation systems based on IoT incorporated in vehicles has shown rapid maturing of smart vehicles not only in terms of providing efficient and reliable transportation but also avoiding accidental loss to vehicles as well as road-side infrastructures; paving the right path for vehicles without traffic congestion, providing proper parking lot and many more. IoT-based VANET is mostly used for smart city, to make efficient use of resources, provides better transportation facilities, minimized energy consumption and improvise the quality and performance of service. Many researches have already been done with reference to IoV, a review of inter-vehicular communication,[3] smart parking system in car,[11] self-driven shared vehicles,[10] vehicular LTE communication,[34] safety application research such as accident position detection,[24] vehicle tracking,[29] vehicle management in smart cities,[35] collision and accident avoidance,[7] traffic congestion avoidance alert,[40] pedestrian safety alert from vehicles,[46] and nonsafety based application research such as, real-time vehicle navigation system,[4] data streaming with wireless connection in vehicles,[25] and speech recognition technology in cars.[45]

8.4.1 REAL-TIME VEHICLE NAVIGATION

For smart driving facilities with safety, real-time navigation plays a major contribution. The applicability of real-time navigation includes providing live maps to drivers, tracking of school buses and other emergency vehicles like ambulance, providing accidental alerts and many more. Navigation system mostly utilizes the best routing mechanism with single cost function and the shortest navigation path. This application of IoV focuses on designing optimal navigation model for crowded vehicular scenario analyzing the traffic load and interval of transmission. Mostly real-time navigations are used for crowd awareness and management with less latency with efficient data processing and storage. Many works are done in literature for real-time navigation services in IoV described below.

Elbery et al.[8] proposed a smart navigation application based on evacuation of people after a special event or during emergency situation avoiding crowd and accidents. An optimization-based navigation model for system optimization is proposed based on vehicular crowd. This work implements an optimization technique for computation of vehicle assignment in traffic scenario fully utilizing the available resources, taking condition of traffic and capacity of road link as constraints. The routes are periodically updated based on recent optimization of vehicle route assignments. Linear programming model with stochastic routing for emergency evacuation was used. Traffic management system is proposed for vehicle routing in proper direction. The system provides efficient evacuation mechanism for crowd avoiding congestion, yet performance analysis based on network overload and resource utilization is not considered.

The same work has been extended by Elbery et al.[9] for smart navigation of vehicular crowd in FIFA 2022, vehicular optimal stochastic routing mechanism is used for crowd management. An optimization problem based on a linear model is computed to reduce the travel time network-wide by computation of assignment parameter of link flow. In both Elbery et al.[8,9] vehicles are used as sensors that communicates in real time with their state information to Traffic Management Center (TMC). Linear programming model with TMC is designed for proper vehicle routing in crowded event scenario with optimum stochastic routing based on link capacity and traffic condition. Minimize network wide time for evacuation of vehicles in crowd, performance based on network load, and reliability of communication is not analyzed. Many vehicle navigation systems have been developed in the last decade to make the vehicle move in a sequential path to evacuate the space. Nahar et al.[23] proposed a congestion control method in traffic scenario to estimate the optimal path and reduce the travel time with Ant-Colony algorithm. Automotive Navigation System is used to find the fittest path based on distance factor, ACO algorithm is used to determine the best path depending on time factor. The system provides a better way for traffic congestion management with the shortest travel time, still the system performance can be improved by better resource utilization and better network condition.

To compute and minimize the total evacuation time and traffic load management a multiagent evacuation model was proposed by Zong et al.[47] with multi-Ant Colony (ACO) strategy. Multi-ACO for routing problem minimizes evacuation time and balances the traffic load. It provides evacuation in stipulated time frame eliminating the congestion problem of single ACO providing better routing plan still performance of system can be improved by proper resource allocation. Vehicle's own speed can be used to determine traffic condition and divert the vehicles to less congested path[27] selects the best path by random selection and comparison.

Koh et al.[15] proposed a deep learning-based concept for vehicle navigation implementing Reinforcement Learning. A real-time routing and navigation system are proposed by computing task as sequence of decision. The main aim is to minimize traffic congestion thereby reducing energy consumption and travel time in urban traffic scenario.

8.4.2 SECURITY AND ANTI-THEFT SYSTEM

Security and Privacy are prime concerns in Internet-based applications as data is communicated via insecure means. Pertaining to the requirement of a greater number of devices for communication and information exchange the need of security of data has become a challenge. There are various malicious and illegal attacks done by injecting and modifying data then relaying it that hampers and also is a threat to user's personal details. Authentication is one of the most critically handled applications in IoV for user security and privacy in handling sensitive personal information. Some work or research progressed in this area is demonstrated below.

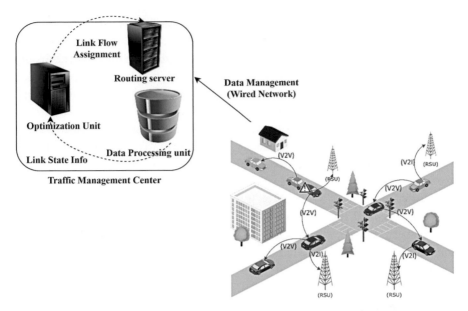

FIGURE 8.6   Traffic Management Architecture for real-time scenario.[9]

Chen et al.[5] proposed an authentication scheme for detecting offline attacks, replay, and spoofing attacks reducing the time consumption in detection of the attack. The vehicles are registered for authorization, in case of detection of an unauthorized user the report is send to the vehicle assistance. Cognitive IoV enables safety and security by data mining from network data space, IoV provides stable service modeling based on group cognitive; optimization of 5G network slicing and resource distribution is done on demand; cognition is implemented for inter-vehicle, intra-vehicle, and beyond-vehicle communication. The protocol provides safety transportation, efficiency resource sharing, security of cyberspace; network slicing should have been analyzed more efficient driving.

Chen's protocol is a modification of the proposed work by Ying et al.[44] with a patched protocol to improve the efficiency and reliability. Ying's protocol works on three phases: the registration phase for vehicle registration with the Trust Authority, login phase for vehicle to login with smart card, and authentication phase here vehicle communicates with trust authority in a secure manner. Smart card protocol is used to address anonymity and authentication of legitimate users employing low-cost cryptographic operations, a login identity-based algorithm is proposed to prevent attackers, the off-line password guessing attack is eliminated by

ASC protocol; Diffie–Hellman problem is computed by security model. It provides efficiency and confidentiality with low-cost communication and computation with less latency and packet loss ratio, but the major demerits of this protocol are lack of scalability, attacks like linking attack, replay attack, offline detection attack, identity guessing attack, attack due to misplaced smart cards still exist which is overcome by Chen et al.

Tapia et al.[36] proposed a trustworthy message-exchange mechanism based on virtualization and blockchain concept. The virtualization layer on TCP/IP protocol stack is incorporated to make responsible for ensuring secure dissemination of message from vehicles to RSUs merging with blockchain technology for providing reliability, integrity, and traceability. Virtualization layer on top of TCP/IP stack for efficient message delivery implemented with blockchain to provide data security and integrity, for smart contract Ethereum is implemented. This work has been implemented on the VaNetChain[38] Architecture that has blockchain on top of TCP/UDP layer, which has been extended by virtual nodes. Grid VANET layout by Torres et al.[38] is used to eliminate obstacles, leader is elected from a group of vehicles for request and response of content delivery; backup nodes are designed with synchronization to provide service in case of failure; the web content within VANET is accessed via http and virtualization layer on top of TCP for routing. It provides a reliable, trustworthy, robust, and traceable communication, for better spectral allocation, reliability and wide range communication IEEE 802.11bd can be adopted.

Many of secure authentication mechanisms[22] and privacy preserving[21] techniques in IoV applications are implemented in the past literature.

8.4.3   TRAFFIC MANAGEMENT

Traffic management has a remarkable role in the stability of the vigorous country's economy. Due to rapid urbanization and expanding cities, vehicles on road are also increase so as the demand for traffic management for accident control, road condition monitoring, and congestion detection and control. Devices such as CCTV, speed video cameras, traffic lights, sensing devices, and trackers are installed in vehicular scenario for detection and monitoring of real-time traffic. Traffic monitoring mostly applied for accident avoidance, emergency message dissemination, traffic detection and control, human proximity analysis and detection, and autonomous vehicle management. There are many prevailing problems in real-time scenario to be overcome by traffic management such as congestion, accidents, road clogging caused by the drastic growth in the number of vehicles on the road.

To overcome this problem, many researchers are still working on; some of the works related to traffic management are described below.

Javaid et al.[13] have proposed a scheme based on centralized as well as distributed approach to manage the flow of road traffic and avoid congestion. AI-based algorithm is designed to predict the future traffic condition and manage congestion. Smart Traffic Management System with hybrid approach for traffic flow optimization is designed; another algorithm based on AI for future prediction of traffic density is designed; RFIDs are implemented to prioritize emergency services in traffic jams; smoke sensors are embedded to detect fire emergency on road. A proper road planning is laid out handling congestion in traffic scenario; real-time delay constraint modeling can be implemented with the module for fast and reliable communication. The protocol tracks the traffic condition and in case of emergency situation redirect to the rescue team to avoid any mishaps.

Wan et al.[39] have proposed a crowd-sensing mechanism for congestion control, a novel cloud assisted mobile crowd sensing is used to detect the traffic. This protocol provides dynamic choice of routes to drivers in real-time basis prediction of traffic thereby avoiding road congestion. Mobile crowd sensing mechanism is implemented for dynamic route choice for drivers handling congestion, Cloud-Assisted IoV provides traffic density analysis in present and future scenarios; a spatiotemporal correlation for traffic prediction is designed. It provides reliable traffic prediction thereby avoiding congestion, Cloud-assistant IoV can be further improved by imple-mentation on high density urban scenario in real time

Traffic management at the toll and parking lots is also an important scenario to be dealt with, Roy et al.[32] provide a less traffic congestion and tranquil payment at the parking lot. An algorithm for smart traffic handling and smart parking is designed based on Dijkstra's shortest path algorithm; smart toll collection is also implemented using IoT to save time a toll gates by automated number plate recognition technique. It provides an insight to research moving toward the field of designing smart city with smart parking and smart traffic monitoring in real time without latency. Similarly, type of vehicle detection[17] before the toll charged is imposed to save time and avoid congestion at the toll gates with the help of database or web query mechanism. Tesseract OCR and Raspberry Pi are used for the detection and charging storing the data in the database and web server with automatic deduction of price from user's account and alert message is sent after deduction; OpenCV for vehicle detection. It provides a practical and effective way of toll charge collection without delay and efficient cost; the performance can still be improved by implementation of AI and real-time monitoring systems to improve the latency factor.

8.4.4   EMERGENCY VEHICLES MANAGEMENT

Emergency vehicles like ambulance, fire brigade, police vans, need to be dislocated to alternate shortest path in case of fatal emergency like in the case of cardiac arrest by minimizing the time to some minutes to reach the hospital. Prioritizing emergency vehicles is essential to avoid and mishap that may occur due to some millisecond delay in providing such services. Traffic signal controller with sensors can be used to detect emergency vehicles on road via siren or signal generated from vehicle to provide priority to such vehicles for road crossing or moving ahead or other vehicles. Machine learning concepts such as reinforcement learning, deep learning, AI, and blockchain technology play a major role for providing emergency message and security. Work on this area is listed below with brief description.

Sumia et al.[35] proposed an intelligent traffic management scheme for prioritizing vehicles depending on emergency services they are providing and relocate them to the shortest path. An Intelligent Traffic Management System is designed to handle emergency vehicles and navigates them to the shortest path; the vehicles are handled based on determination of priority levels; hacking is also detected and overcome to provide security. The proposed system eliminates the problem of time delay in case of emergency scenario such as medical cases; different priority level can be assigned to the vehicle for better efficiency in management of traffic; security can also be enhanced by use of blockchain.

Lai et al.[18] proposed an intelligent traffic management scheme based on warning signal generation by RFID and wireless mechanism for emergency medical services to avoid collision between medical service providing vehicles and public vehicles. The intelligent warning system for emergency vehicle is developed by IoT providing a real-time visual warning with RFID for emergency vehicle warning and Wi-Fi technologies. The system provides an efficient real-time visual and emergency warning to beware of approaching vehicles; other updated AI/ML mechanism can be used for better performance in stipulated time. Similar work has been proposed by Reeta et al.[30] for traffic control of emergency vehicles by capturing and processing the sound of ambulance by placing sensors in the lanes. Sound detector with auto-recording mechanism is implemented for distinguishing ambulance siren and clearing traffic; the traffic controller takes decision when the vehicle passes the road. It provides a sufficient traffic management for ambulance that succeeds in paving the quickest and safest path to destination; the work is implemented for single lane which can be enhanced to provide services in multiple lane scenario within time constraint.

Hooda et al.[12] proposed a traffic management scheme by the implementation of image processing and synchronizing the vehicle's connected to each other with real-time processing capabilities. Traffic system management is designed based on existing infrastructure such as CCTV, area traffic control; dynamic timing approach is implemented for traffic signals for release of traffic depending on load capacity and congestion along with emergency vehicle preemption technique; a system recovery is proposed for power failure resistance of traffic lights. The proposed work provides a smooth traffic scenario with congestion control, less delay, cost efficient and emergency vehicle pre-emption in urban scenario; a better traffic management can be implemented by using recent technologies such as AI/ML and blockchain for security.

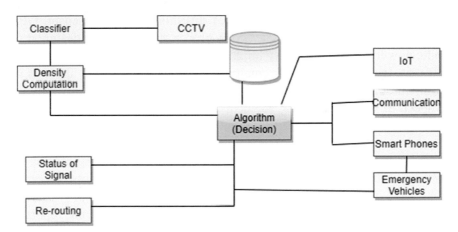

FIGURE 8.7   System architecture of emergency vehicle management.[12]

8.4.5   *MONITORING OF DRIVER HEALTH ON ROAD*

During travel, driver health and alertness is a very important factor as the responsibility of a safe ride is dependent on the driver; he has to ensure the safety of himself, passengers, other vehicles, pedestrian, and other units nearby. This is basically done by incorporating sensors in suitable position near the driver; body sensors can also be placed to keep a check on abnormal behavior of the driver while driving. In long distance driving, the driver may get drowsy and tired which need to be monitored and alert message to be provided for making the driver conscious. Some of the proposed work for health monitoring on road is discussed below.

In long distance driving the driver may get drowsy and tired, Ahmed et al.[2] proposed a system to detect the drowsiness and tiredness of the drivers modeled by Raspberry Pi that detects the blinking of eyes of the driver and sensors to detect the body temperature, heartbeat, etc. The system detects the health parameter and drowsiness of driver with Pi-Camera and Raspberry Pi model integrated with wearable sensors; a buzzer will be activated on eye-blink and abnormal behavior of driver. It reduces the accident risk, monitoring each and every aspect of road condition that enables to take fast decision; some of the new technologies such as AI and ML can be used for future traffic prediction along with tracking of driver's activity for safe travel.

Similarly, Petkar et al.[28] used AI to detect the physical health parameters of the driver. Sensors detect the driver drowsiness and other behavior avoiding road accidents with a range of threshold value for sensor, GPS detects the location and sent via GSM; power supply unit is designed to handle power consumption, eye blink, and heart beat sensors provide alert messages. It effectively handles major road accidents posed by driver's ill health; automatic braking system rather than alarms automatically reduces the speed of vehicle avoiding accidents and also an automatic system can be designed to move vehicle to a proper location if stopped in middle of the road.

Cherif et al.[6] proposed a model for real-time telemonitoring of driver's health, with the collaboration of hardware and software devices to keep a track on the driver and steering wheel with the help of sensors or Bluetooth connected to the smart phones. In case of any abnormality, the report is forwarded to the tele-vigilance center by TCP/IP over 4G/3G connectivity. Telemonitoring for driver's health in realtime; driver communicates with intelligent steering wheel through Bluetooth link and monitor for safety driving; electrocardiographic signal for heart rate monitoring, photoplethysmographic technique for blood oxygen saturation monitoring is used; the data collected is sent to tele-vigilance centers in case of abnormalities involving 4G/3G connections. The application triggers alarm in case of tachycardia, bradycardia, or cardiac arrhythmia, and respiratory decomposition. Practical system for health monitoring in real time is implemented. Additional biomedical sensors can be used for better health analysis, in driving environment visual and nonvisual information can be combine. These can be integrated with smart phones, GPS, automatic brake application and speed limiter for emergency services.

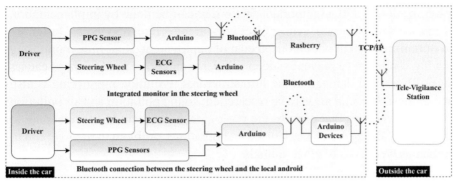

FIGURE 8.8   Model of Smart Steering Wheel to detect health condition.[27]

Zhenyu et al. have proposed a model for accident prevention caused due to consumption of alcohol by the driver and tracks the Royal Society for the Prevention of Accidents and drowsiness of the driver done with the help of camera implemented for monitoring of eye-blink, health monitoring by wearable sensor devices, and alcohol sensor for alcohol consumption detection. USB Camera used for Eye-Blink Monitoring provides alarm to driver during the drowsy condition. GPS is used to track driver's location; web application is designed where admin will be controlling the parameters of the system and forward message to the fellow beings. Wearable heart beat sensor, temperature sensor, and alcohol sensor take care of driver's health. Monitoring and tracking driver's health for safety driving in the case of emergency message is sent to doctor with proper location via GPS for providing emergency service. Automatic braking system can be implemented instead of speed limiter for better efficiency in travel avoiding accidents.

8.5   OPEN CHALLENGES AND FUTURE DIRECTIONS

In ubiquitous computing such as IoV, the major threat is privacy, as the detailed information is passed over Internet that opens up the route for malicious and security hampering intrusions. A robust security strategy must be implemented to safeguard the privacy of the driver and passengers. As a lot of computing activities are going on with communication from V2V, V2I, V2P, and V2X, power consumption and maintenance is also a major challenge, implementing an energy-efficient protocol with reliable connectivity is a need of future. Power supply without any disruption to the communication mechanism of the entire system can be done by taking solar energy and efficient battery consumption taking into consideration. Accuracy of shared data without any error is to be maintained to hold on to the trust and dependability of interested users. Cost minimization is still an important factor that can be done by implementation of low-cost machineries, sensors, network architecture, and tools. Designing an optimized system with reduced cost of deployment. Real-time monitoring is a big challenge to prevent sudden accidents and other road mishaps causes loss of lives and damage to the infrastructures. Pollution monitoring is also one of most essential areas to be researched; sound pollution and air pollution caused by vehicles that disturbs the ecological balance and have a tending to cause many diseases such as nausea and breathing problem in the long run to human as well lives of other animals.

8.6 CONCLUSION

Due to the growing demand for autonomous driving, IoV has become one of prime researched technologies. IoV technology interconnects not only vehicles to vehicles, but vehicles to pedestrians, vehicles to road-side units, and vehicles to other trust authorities for security purpose. In this work, we focused on the application of IoV and its advantages over VANET, by the study of work proposed by researchers related to various applications and services provided IoV such as theft management, traffic management, emergency vehicle management, and health monitoring on road. A comparative anlaysis of VANET vs IoV is presented to depict a clear picture of need of IoV in vehicular communication. Finally, we have presented the open challenges and research directions for further enhancement of IoV based on various factors such as privacy, location management, operational management, enabling robust communication, promoting autonomous driving, and efficient communication capabilities.

KEYWORDS

- **IoV**
- **5G**
- **V2X**
- **Autonomous**
- **Traffic management**
- **Security**
- **Big data**

REFERENCES

1. 5G-PPP Automotive Working Group. 2018. A Study 5G V2X Deployment. [Online]. Available: https://5g-ppp.eu/wp-content/uploads/2018/02/5G-PPP-AutomotiveWG-White-Paper.
2. Ahmed, F.; Singh, Y.; Yadav, V.; Bhattacharya, S. IoT Based Driver Drowsiness Detection and Health Monitoring System. *J. Xi'an Univ. Archit. Technol.* **2020,** *1006–7930, XII* (IV), 3276.
3. Bajaj, R.; Rao, M.; Agrawal, H. Internet of Things (IoT) in the Smart Automotive Sector: A Review. *IOSR J. Comput. Eng.* **2018,** 36–44.
4. Chadil, N.; Russameesawang, A.; Keeratiwintakorn, P. Real-Time Tracking Management System using GPS, GPRS and Google Earth. In *2008 5th International Conference on Electrical Engineering, Computer Telecommunication and Information Technology*; IEEE, 2008; pp 393–396.
5. Chen, M. C.; Xiang, B.; Liu, Y.; Wang, H. K. A Secure Authentication Protocol for Internet of Vehicles. *Spl. Sect. Secur. Priv. Cloud IoT* **2019,** *7*, 2169–3536.
6. Cherif, H. F.; Cherif, H. L.; Benabdellah, M.; Nassar, G. Monitoring Driver Health Status in Real-Time. Rev. Sci. Instrum. **2020,** *91*, 035110. DOI: 10.1063/1.5098308.
7. Diewald, S.; Möller, A.; Roalter, L.; Kranz, M. Drive Assist-a V2X-Based Driver Assistance System for Android, Mensch and Computer. 2012—Workshopband: Interaktiv Informiert—allgegenwärtig und allumfassend!'/ Oldenbourg Verlag: Munchen; 2012, (S. 373–380). 14.
8. Elbery, A.; Hassanein, S. H.; Zorba, N.; Rakha, A. H. VANET-Based Smart Navigation for Emergency Evacuation and Special Events. *IEEE* **2019.** DOI: 978-1-7281-1016-5.
9. Elbery, A.; Hassanein, S. H.; Zorba, N.; Rakha, A. H. VANET-Based Smart Navigation for Vehicle Crowds: FIFA World Cup 2022 Case Study. *IEEE* **2020.** DOI: 978-1-7281-0962-6.
10. Gurumurthy, K.; Kockelman, K.; Loeb, B.; Sharing Vehicles and Sharing Rides in Real-Time: Opportunities for Self-Driving Fleets. *Adv. Transp. Policy Plan* **2019.**
11. Hassoune, K.; Dachry, W.; Moutaouakkil, F.; Medromi, H. Smart Parking Systems: A Survey. In *2016 11th International Conference on Intelligent System and Theoritical Applications*; IEEE, 2016; pp 1–6.
12. Hooda, W.; Bhole, A.; Yadav K. P.; Chaudhari, D. D. *An Image Processing Approach to Intelligent Traffic Management System*; International Institute of Information Technology, ACM, 2016.
13. Javaid, S.; Sufian, A.; Pervaiz, S.; Tanvee, M. Smart Traffic Management System Using Internet of Things. In *2018 20th International Conference on Advanced Communication Technology*; IEEE, 2018; pp 393–398.
14. Ji, B.; Zhang, X.; Mumtaz, S.; Han, C.; Li, C.; Wen, H.; Wang, D. Survey on the Internet of Vehicles: Network Architectures and Applications. *IEEE Commun. Standards Mag.* **2020.** DOI: 10.1109/MCOMSTD.001.1900053.
15. Koh, S.; Zhou, B.; Fang, H.; Yang, P.; Yang, Z.; Yang, Q.; Guan, L. Zhigang Ji, Real-Time Deep Reinforcement Learning Based Vehicle Navigation. *Appl. Soft Comput. J.* **2020,** *96*, 106694. https://doi.org/10.1016/j.asoc.2020.106694
16. Kponyo, J. J.; Kuang, Y.; Li, Z. Real-Time Status Collection and Dynamic Vehicular Traffic Control Using Ant Colony Optimization. In *2012 International Conference on Computational Problem-Solving, ICCP*; IEEE, 2012; pp 69–72.

17. Krishna, A.; Naseera, S. Vehicle Detection and Categorization for a Toll Charging System Based on Tesseract OCR Using the IoT. In *International Conference on Communications and Cyber Physical Engineering 2018*; Springer, 2019; pp 193–202.

18. Lai, L. Y.; Chou H. Y.; Chang, C. L. An Intelligent IoT Emergency Vehicle Warning System Using RFID and Wi-Fi Technologies for Emergency Medical Services. *Technol. Health Care.* **2018,** *26,* 43–55.

19. Liang, L.; Ye, H.; Li, Y. G. Toward Intelligent Vehicular Networks: A Machine Learning Framework. *IEEE Int. Things J.* **2019,** *6* (1), 124–135.

20. Ma, S. H.; Zhang, E.; Li, S.; Lv, Z.; Hu, J. A V2X Design for 5G Network Based on Requirements of Autonomous Driving. *SAE Tech. Paper* **2016**. DOI: 10.4271/2016-01-1887.

21. Manivannan, D.; Moni, S. S.; Zeadally, S. Secure Authentication and Privacy-Preserving Techniques in Vehicular Ad-Hoc NETworks (VANETs). *Veh. Commun.* **2020,** *25,* 100247.

22. Manvi, S. S.; Tangade, S. A Survey on Authentication Schemes in VANETs for Secured Communication. *Veh. Commun.* **2017,** *9,* 19–30.

23. Nahar, A. A. S.; Hashim, H. F. Modelling and Analysis of an Efficient Traffic Network using Ant Colony Optimization Algorithm. In *2011 Third International Conference on Computational Intelligence, Communication Systems and Networks*; IEEE, 2011; pp 32–36.

24. Nasr, E.; Kfoury, E.; Khoury, D. An IoT Approach to Vehicle Accident Detection, Reporting, and Navigation. In *2016 IEEE International Multidiscipline Conference on Engineering Technology*; IMCET, 2016.

25. Ninan, S.; Gangula, B.; Alten, V. M.; Sniderman, B. *Who Owns the Road? The IoT Connected Car of Today—and Tomorrow*; Deloitte University Press, 2015; p 18.

26. Oza, S.; Ambre, A.; Kanole, S.; Dhabekar, K. N. P.; Paliwal, K.; Hendre, V. *IoT, The Future for Quality of Services*; Lecture Notes Electrical Engineering, 2020; pp 291–301.

27. Park, Y.; Sur, C.; Kim, H.; Rhee, H. K. A Reliable Incentive Scheme Using Bitcoin on Cooperative Vehicular Ad Hoc Networks. *IT Converg. Pract.* **2017,** *5,* 34–41.

28. Petkar, T. B.; Bhagya, C.; Gagan T. K.; Lokesha, K. Automatic Driver Drowsiness Alert and Health Monitoring System using GSM. *IJERT* **2018**. ISSN: 2278-0181. NCESC-2018 Conference Proceedings.

29. Raj, J.; Sankar, J. IoT Based Smart School Bus Monitoring and Notification System. *IEEE* **2017,** 89–92.

30. Reeta, R.; Kirithiga, R.; Kavitha V. K.; Jaishree M. IoT-Based Traffic Signal Control for Ambulance. *IJEAT* **2020,** *9* (3). DOI: 10.35940/ijeat.C6331.029320, ISSN: 2249-8958.

31. Riggio, R.; Gomez, F.; Goratti, L.; Fedrizzi, R.; Rasheed, T. V-cell: Going Beyond the Cell Abstraction in 5G Mobile Networks. In *Proceedings of IEEE Network Operations and Management Symposium (NOMS)*, Krakow, Poland; 2014; pp 1–5.

32. Roy, A.; Siddiquee, J.; Datta, A.; Poddar, P.; Ganguly G.; Bhattacharjee, A. Smart Traffic and Parking Management Using IoT, In *2016 IEEE 7th Annual Information Technology and Electronics Mobile Communication Conference*; IEEE, 2016; pp 1–3.

33. Storck, R. C.; Figueiredo, D. F. A Survey of 5G Technology Evolution, Standards, and Infrastructure Associated with Vehicle-to-Everything Communications by Internet of Vehicles. *IEEE* **2020,** *8*. DOI: 10.1109/ACCESS.2020.3004779.

34. Srivastava, A.; Prakash, A.; Tripathi, R. Location Based Routing Protocols in VANET: Issues and Existing Solutions. *Veh. Commun.* **2020,** *23,* 100231.

35. Sumia, L.; Ranga, V. Intelligent Traffic Management System for Prioritizing Emergency Vehicles in a Smart City. *Int. J. Eng.* **2018,** 278–283.
36. Tapia, V. P.; Torres, B. J.; Nores, L. M.; Segovia, G. P.; Morales, O. E.; Cabrer, R. M. VaNetChain: A Framework for Trustworthy Exchanges of Information in VANETs Based on Blockchain and a Virtualization Layer. *Appl. Sci.* **2020,** *10,* 7930. DOI: 10.3390/app10217930.
37. Tiwari, K. S.; Bhagat, S.; Patil, N.; Nagare, P. IoT Based Driver Drowsiness Detection and Health Monitoring System. *IJRAR* **2019,** *6* (2). ISSN: 2348-1269.
38. Torres, F. B. J.; Nores, L. M.; Fernández, B. Y.; PazosArias, J. J.; Morales, O. F. E. VaNet-Layer: A Virtualization Layer Supporting Access to Web Contents from Within Vehicular Networks. *J. Comput. Sci.* **2015,** *11,* 185–195.
39. Wan, J.; Liu, J.; Shao, Z.; Vasilakos, V. A.; Imran M.; Zhou, K. Mobile Crowd Sensing for Traffic Prediction in Internet of Vehicles. *Sensors* **2016,** *16,* 88. DOI: 10.3390/s16010088.
40. Wedel, J.; Schünemann, B.; Radusch, I.; V2X-Based Traffic Congestion Recognition and Avoidance. In *2009 10th International Symposium on Pervasive System Algorithms, Networks*; IEEE, 2009; pp 637–641.
41. Xu, W.; Zhou, H.; Cheng, N.; Lyu, F.; Shi, W.; Chen, J.; Shen, S. X. Internet of Vehicles in Big Data Era. *IEEE/CAA J. Autom. Sin.* **2018,** *5* (1).
42. Yang, F.; Li, J.; Lei, T.; Wang, S. Architecture and Key Technologies for Internet of Vehicles: A Survey. *J. Commun. Inf. Netw.* **2017,** *2* (2), 1–17.
43. Yang, F.; Wang, S.; Li, J.; Liu, Z.; Sun, Q. An Overview of Internet of Vehicles. *China Commun.* **2014,** *11* (10), 1–15.
44. Ying B.; Nayak, A. Anonymous and Lightweight Authentication for Secure Vehicular Networks. *IEEE Trans. Veh. Technol.* **2017,** *66* (12), 10626–10636.
45. Zhang, Y.; Faneuff, J.; Hidden, W.; Hotary, J.; Lee, S.; Iyengar, V. Automobile Speech Recognition Interface, 2010.
46. Zhenyu, L.; Lin, P.; Konglin, Z.; Lin, Z. Design and Evaluation of V2X Communication System for Vehicle and Pedestrian Safety. *J. China Univ. Post Telecommun.* **2015,** *22,* 18–26.
47. Zong, X.; Xiong, S.; Fang, Z.; Li, Q. Multi-Ant Colony System for Evacuation Routing Problem with Mixed Traffic Flow. In *IEEE Congress on Evolutionary Computation*; IEEE, 2010, pp 1–6.

CHAPTER 9

The Future Security Solution to the Internet of Things: Biometric Technology

PUJA AGARWAL[1], ANJANA MISHRA[1], and BROJO KISHORE MISHRA[2]

[1]*C. V. Raman Global University, Bhubaneshwar, Odisha, India*

[2]*GIET University, Gunupur, Odisha, India*

ABSTRACT

The interconnection of devices of our everyday use like vehicles, coolers, cell phones, brilliant entryways, gadgets for checking, or monitoring devices is basically Internet of Things. As web clients are expanding so is innovation and in this manner security has become a significant concern. The devices attached with smart sensor, internet connectivity empowers the devices to gather and send information. IoT is served by the set of secure data points. It focuses on data integrity that is generally received and sent. The data points share valuable information that makes important connections, which are required for the functioning of IoT devices. The devices often share sensitive user data and thus it becomes important to secure the data that is transmitted or received and their security using biometrics comes into role. Biometrics generally deals with recognition using biological characteristics like scanning fingerprints retina or sometimes the whole body. It can also be used to verify using gestures or body movements.

9.1 INTRODUCTION

Nowadays devices are connected to each other with connection to the Internet and sensors embedded in them, which helps to send and receive important data.

Internet of Things: Technological Advances and New Applications. Brojo Kishore Mishra & Amit Vishwasrao Salunkhe (Eds.)

IoT contributes in many domains. It has been exploited for the improvement of new applications to assist society. IoT can help in boosting the quality of lives in the ICT mainly known as information and communications technology. Smart objects represent a context recognized from the surroundings and communicate with each other. It can very well be utilized to screen traffic in cities or expressways and redirect traffic thus to stay away from congestion.

Based on the reading of a temperature, smoke detector sensor, or even a fire alarm can be set automatically. Some appliances like lights can be turned on at current space. Water faucets will be open at the kitchen, doors in room can be opened, such kind of applications are helpful for elderly people who stay alone at home. This is based on the movement of occupants residing at home.[14]

It can be actualized in plant, buildings, homes, and office via sensors that can be appended with household requirements like air conditioners, lights, refrigerator. It can screen environment inside the house, office, and even a plant.[17] The lighting arrangement of a house can be modified as per the time, most of the lights in the evening are going to be switched on, whereas they are going to be switched off once it's nighttime.

Safety as well as security of pharmaceutical product are of importance. Directly patients are benefitted from the smart labels on every medicine by knowing expiry, dosages of medicines. This view helps smart labels that are hooked up to drugs for the observance and monitoring the status, while being stored and transported. There are many sectors where IoT is already executed like healthcare, transport, monitoring homes, and offices.[7]

Security plays a major role when using the IoT devices because as a user we expect our data to be protected and not being modified by someone else. So it ought to follow the objectives of Internet security. These are commonly known as confidentiality, integrity, and availability. (Figure 9.1).

9.1.1   CONFIDENTIALITY

It is the significant objective of Internet security. Main purpose of confidentiality is in guarding individual information from an unapproved individual. Confidentiality ensure that data are available only to the intended, approved, authorized person.[6]

9.1.2   INTEGRITY

It is the second objective of Internet security. Sole usage of integrity is to keep up precision and consistency of information. Integrity mainly assures that data are exact, trustworthy, and not changed by unauthorized person or hacker. The data sent should be same as the data received by the recipient. There is an assurance that even a single bit of data is not changed.[8]

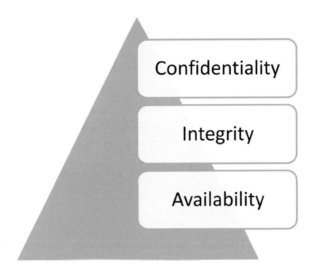

FIGURE 9.1   CIA triangle.

9.1.3   AVAILABILITY

It is the third objective of Internet security. Fundamental reason is to ensure that all the organization assets and data for transmission should be ceaselessly accessible to the verified clients, at whatever point they need it.[8]

9.2   SECURITY ISSUES IN IOT DEVICES

Security is the main challenge in IoT. Application information of IoT can be consumer, industrial, personal, or enterprise organization. This data ought to be secured and should be confidential against theft and altering. For instance, the IoT applications store the results of a patient's health or shopping store. IoT assists in improving communication between many devices but still, there is variety of problems mainly related to the response time, scalability, accessibility, and availability. Security is an important factor wherein data needs to be safely transmitted over the internet.[13]

9.2.1   DATA PRIVACY

It is very vital and essential. As with every single IoT device lot of customer data will be associated with that device of customer. In this context, information should be kept hidden so that clients' data stays protected constantly.

9.2.2   DATA SECURITY

Protection of data is likewise a notable challenge. While transmitting information, it is essential for the devices data to be hidden from gazing on the internet. It is critical to shield our information from unapproved access and information defilement.

9.2.3   SPECIALIZED CONCERNS

There are many technical issues. Due to the expanded use of IoT devices, there is a great deal of traffic created by devices. In this context, there is a need to inflate network limit, and subsequently, it has become a challenge to store that much measure of information for investigation, analysis, and exploration.

9.2.4   SYSTEM VULNERABILITIES AND SECURITY ATTACKS

IoT devices face specific types of assaults that include active assaults and passive assaults, which could disturb the working of the devices and might lessen the advantages of its services. In active assault, the attacker gets the records and attempts to do malicious wok. Moreover, In a passive assault, an outsider can simply sense the node or might also additionally even steal the records however in no way physical attack can be done. These vulnerable attacks can prevent the devices from vulnerable attacks and consequently protection constraints have to be implemented in an effort to save devices from malicious assaults.[10]

9.2.5   INSUFFICIENT TESTING AND LACK OF UPDATES

Regular updates are crucial for heading off IoT security problems as with old software program gadgets can be uncovered to countless malware and hacker assaults and different breaches of protection. Therefore, it is the manufacturer's duty to offer normal updates to the device's software program as quickly as vulnerabilities are uncovered and certain malware assaults turn out to be widespread.

9.2.6 HOME INVASIONS

Use of IoT is growing at homes as they supply delivery to "agile homes," and protections of those gadgets are important situation as they're at threat. The Shodan searches make feasible for hackers to discover the Ip cope of the gadgets. We can save our devices from breach via way of means of connecting through VPNs and securing the login credentials.[16]

9.3 BIOMETRICS

Biometrics assists us with offering an explanation to a principal security question–how to check a client who says who they are?

As many users rely on textual passwords that is very easy to guess and is vulnerable to attacks. The users generally have simple default password that increase the vulnerability of their device and moreover they leave their IoT-connected devices with simple passwords only.

With the help of biometric, the security system of device's can identify personal characteristics that are unique for the user, which are hard for hackers to replicate.

Biometric security provides solutions that include scanning of body parts like either through fingerprint or facial recognition Iris scanning and voice recognition or even using gestures and body movements.[19]

RFID badges, keys, and passwords can be lost but there is no chance of losing biometric password. While no measure of security can be safe completely from hackers. In fact biometrics can offer a security layer that will be difficult to exploit by hackers and also convenient for the end-user (Figure 9.2).

9.4 BIOMETRIC SECURITY FOR IOT CONNECTED DEVICES

Recently, the most common biometric identification techniques that are currently used in many IoT-connected devices are basically fingerprint as well as voice recognition.

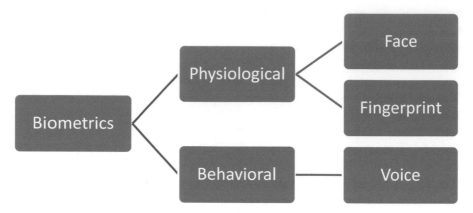

FIGURE 9.2   Common Biometric techniques used in IoT devices.

Voice recognition is basically the most popular as now many people have a home assistant. It is there either in their own home or at the office. The assistants mostly rely on voice commands for them to function. They generally use voice recognition as core functionality.[5]

Most of these devices, such as Google Home, Siri, and Alexa now support the use of voice recognition so as to access features, like multiuser profiles.

Recognition using fingerprint is perhaps most common technique in the market. It is also familiar to users. In today's date many smartphone devices mainly use fingerprint recognition as a security feature to unlock the phone as well as for other applications. However, fingerprint recognition is being widely utilized in IoT-connected devices.[18]

As there are many complicated methods for biometric identification and there is already a wide adoption of use of facial recognition, that it is expected that the use of facial recognition in IoT-connected devices will increase. Facial recognition can be used in wide range in many different sectors although it is a controversial biometric. The technique of facial recognition can be considered as the most accurate and fastest biometric system if it is used ethically (Figure 9.3).

9.5   BIOMETRIC SECURITY FOR IOT DEVICES IN THE MEDICAL SECTOR

In medical field use of IoT is growing exponentially. It is mainly referred to as Internet of Medical Things. The sector focuses at utilizing IoT technology for the improvement of healthcare quality in health sectors and to provide an extra layer of security (Boi, 2011).

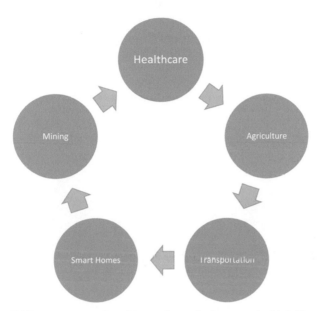

FIGURE 9.3 Different sectors where biometric can be integrated with IoT.

Technology has enabled doctors to use IoMT devices in order to keep the track of its patient's health, after they have already been discharged, without even the need of patient for regular visits. There is a range of many IoT-connected smart devices such as watches and other wearables that keep a track of information like heart rate and blood pressure.[12] The access to these data via the secure biometric identification can help the doctors to manage their patient's health without even needing then to be in the same physical place.[5]

This technology has really helped doctors and patients in the current COVID-19 crisis. As there is complete lockdown and COVID-19 cases are increasing around the world but with technology it becomes easy at this time for patients to consult their doctors from the safety of their own house, without even putting their life at risk.[9]

A new App was recently invented by NEC along with a team of Kiwi developers. The App is capable of monitoring the health of the patients who all are showing the symptoms of Corona Virus. The NEC iQuarantine application prompts check-in up to three times daily to patients and also permitting the healthcare professionals to monitor and track their health directly using the app. If any changes happen to their health then the app immediately shows notifications and then the patient can be suggested to take the, further steps. The NEC iQuarantine application mostly uses the facial recognition technique in order to correctly identify the patient (Figure 9.4).

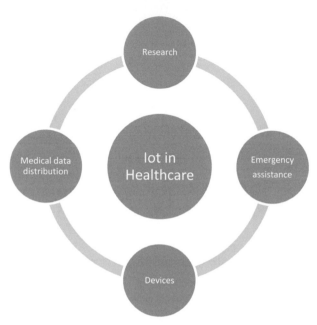

FIGURE 9.4   Healthcare sector where biometric can be integrated with IoT.

9.6   IOT FOR SAFER MINING PRODUCTION

IoT can contribute a lot in mining. It is significant concern in countries where workers need to work in mines. Mishaps happen a lot and are critical to pause and diminish mishaps inside the mines, and there comes the utilization of IoT technologies so as to detect the mining signal. It can help in giving warning, detect disaster forecasting, and can help in safety of underground production. Wi-Fi technologies, RFID, and many other devices enable us to communicate effectively in underground mines.[11] Many mining companies are able to track the situation of underground mines. Critical data can be collected via sensors to reinforce different safety measures. Therefore to secure the critical data we can implement biometric technology.

IoT can help in detecting diseases and can even help in diagnosis. As workers need to work in hazardous environment their safety is important. For that we can use biological and chemical sensors that are accustomed to detect dust. Even harmful gases and various environmental hazards can be sensed. They can sense data from biological organs and even stoma. The wireless devices would need power and in turn they will detonate gas. This is a challenging task to handle. Further research is in progress regarding the protection characteristics of devices employed in production (Figure 9.5).

FIGURE 9.5 Mining sectors where biometric can be integrated with IoT.

9.7 ADVANTAGES

These systems offer more accuracy as compared to normal techniques as individual's data need to be matched with his or her stored data in the database.

Biometrics systems have low processing time as compared to the other systems of authentication.

Biometric affords extra stage of protection and has supplied a complicated degree of protection in comparison to the conventional authentication methods. It is preferred over different authentication strategies because of the reality that bodily presence of the legal individual is must on the factor of identity this means that only that the legal individual have the entry to the particular resource.

No need for users to type the passwords again and again and neither remembering of passwords is required. Device updates can be done with the help of fingerprint. Nowadays, the tools are made so as to recognize voice and retina as just when we look at screen, or say hello, the phone opens (Figure 9.6).[15]

FIGURE 9.6   Advantage of using biometric technology.

9.8   DISADVANTAGES

If the biometrics is compromised then it can not be reset again.

If the authenticating device does not function properly or there is software corruption then it can make open path for attacks and breaches.

If there is not adequate knowledge of the proper functioning of that IoT-based biometric systems then it can cause potential risk for essential data.

9.9   CONCLUSIONS

Biometric integration with IoT devices will enhance security and will be a boon to technology as it ensures high security than normal authentication techniques. The devices often share sensitive user data and thus it becomes important to secure the data that is transmitted or received. Biometrics will allow users to use their devices without remembering the passwords.

Devices need to be protected from major security threats and intruders. The passwords that come default with the devices should be changed for better surveillance.

The challenge for biometric system is the huge cost for the biometric technology, the marketing cost, training of employees, hardware maintenance, processing power, infrastructure, system maintenance, real-time implementation, salary of employees, and others.[3]

Biometrics in many IoT devices have already been implemented and it is predictable that the latest security measures maintained by biometric technology will set out to the next level with different application being used in different sectors.[2]

As internet users are increasing so is technology and therefore security has become a major concern. So as to preserve vital and confidential data the integration of biometrics along with IoT can be trusted to ease user's ways of managing and storing confidential data.

KEYWORDS

- **Security**
- **Biometrics**
- **IOT Devices**
- **Sensors**

REFERENCES

1. Security Related Challenges Of Internet Of Things (IoT). *J. Crit. Rev.* **2020,** *7* (14), 222–288.
2. Abdur, M.; Habib, S.; Ali, M.; Ullah, S. Security Issues in the Internet of Things (IoT): A Comprehensive Study. *Int. J. Adv. Comput. Sci. Appl.* **2017,** *8* (6), 50.
3. Kumar, J. S.; Patel, D. R. A Survey on Internet of Things: Security and Privacy Issues. *Int. J. Comput. Appl.* **2014,** *90* (11).
4. Xu, L. D.; He, W.; Li, S. Internet of Things in Industries: A Survey. *IEEE Trans. Industr. Inform.* **2014,** *10* (4), 2233–2243.
5. Pawar, S.; Deshmukh, H. R. Monitoring of Smart Systems Using Internet of Things in Healthcare. *Indian J. Public Health Res. Dev.* **2019,** *10* (6), 1461.
6. Bisoy, S.; Mishra, A. Understanding the Aspect of Cryptography and Internet Security: A Practical Approach, 2018.
7. Hossain, M. M.; Fotouhi, M.; Hasan, R. Towards an Analysis of Security Issues, Challenges, and Open Problems in the Internet of Things. In *2015 IEEE World Congress on Services*; IEEE, 2015; pp 21–28.
8. Forouzan, A. B. *Cryptography and Network Security*, 2nd ed.; Tata McGraw-Hill Publishing Company Limited: New Delhi, 2010.
9. Jha, V.; Bassi, A.; Arfin, S.; John, O. An Overview of Mobile Applications (Apps) to Support the Coronavirus Disease 2019 Response in India. *Indian J. Med. Res.* **2020,** *151* (5), 468.
10. Stallings, W. *Cryptography and Network Security Principles and Practice*, 5th ed.; Pearson Education: USA, 2011.
11. Rghioui, A.; Oumnad, A. Internet of Things: Visions, Technologies, and Areas of Application. *Autom. Control Intell. Syst.* **2017,** *5* (6), 83–91. DOI: 10.11648/j.acis.20170506.11

12. Faundez-Zanuy, M. Biometric Security Technology. *IEEE Aerosp. Electron. Syst. Mag.* **2006,** *21* (6), 15–26.

13. Ning, H.; Liu, H.; Yang, L. T. Cyberentity Security in the Internet of Things. *Computer* **2013,** *46* (4), 46–53.

14. Abomhara, M.; Køien, G. M. Security and Privacy in the Internet of Things: Current Status and Open Issues. In *Privacy and Security in Mobile Systems, International Conference on*; IEEE, 2014; pp 1–8.

15. Jain, A. K.; Bolle, R.; Pankanti, S.; Eds. *Biometrics: Personal Identification in Networked Security*; Kluwer Academic Publishers: Dordrecht, 1999.

16. Yoon, S.; Park, H.; Yoo, H. S. Security Issues on Smarthome in IoT Environment. In *Computer Science and Its Applications*; Springer, 2015; pp 691–696.

17. Atzori, L.; Iera, A.; Morabito, G. The Internet of Things: A Survey. *Comput. Netw.* **2010,** *54* (15), 2787–2805.

18. van Kranenburg, R.; Anzelmo, E.; Bassi, A.; Caprio, D.; Dodson, S.; Ratto, M. The Internet of Things. In *Proceedings of the 1st Berlin Symposium on Internet Society*, Berlin, Germany, 2011; pp 25–27.

19. Wickes, J. Facial Recognition: Designing 21st Century Rules. *Biometric Technology Today*, **2018,** *2018* (10), 7–10.

CHAPTER 10

Transforming Industries Using IoT

RITWIK RAJ[1], TANNU KUMARI[2], and AMARDEEP DAS[3*]

[1]*Department Of Computer Science and Information Technology, C.V. Raman Global University, Bhubaneswar, Odisha, India*

[2]*Department of Computer Science Engineering, C.V. Raman Global University, Bhubaneswar, Odisha, India*

[3]*C.V. Raman Polytechnic, Bhubaneswar, Odisha, India*

ABSTRACT

Since the development of Internet of Things (IoT) it has given the world a lot of amazing things. IoT is not just limited to the latest technology. It has basically played a vital role in transformation of world. Even though IoT came into hike in the late 1970s but its development has been started a long back. Starting in the late 1960s with the Industries getting into a powerful medium for development. It gave rise to IIoT, abbreviated as industrial IoT. Basically industrial IoT is termed as the extension of IoT. It all started with the industries that were in need of a powerful system so that they can automate their devices to reduce the work load and increase the profit. Combining the IoT devices like sensors, actuators, wireless, and mobile devices with high speed Internet into the industries resulted in an explosion in the entire world market. It turned out as a revolution for the industries. The people had got the key to future development. Today IIoT is used primarily in a wide range of Internet applications for items outside the consumer space and IoT business market, such as the umbrella name for applications and usage cases in many industrial sectors.

Internet of Things: Technological Advances and New Applications. Brojo Kishore Mishra & Amit Vishwasrao Salunkhe (Eds.)
© 2024 Apple Academic Press, Inc. Co-published with CRC Press (Taylor & Francis)

10.1   INTRODUCTION

In this modern era, Internet has completely remolded the way of communication for people, what work they do and how they are working together. This attention has now also started shifting toward machines. System developers have been focusing on interconnecting the sensors, edge nodes, and analytics for building smart systems, transforming operations into significant productivity environments since the past few years. All these systems being connected to each other collectively makes up what we call as Industrial IoT (IIoT). IIoT is referred to as the use of inter-related automated machines, devices, and sensors that are running the industrial applications. Being as a centralized focus, big data and machine learning, the IIoT is enabling the industries and enterprises for increasing the efficiency and reliability of operations, with reducing the reliance on human-to-machine interactions. It also enables new business models or sources of revenue from useful data collected and shared.[1] The mindset of the industries are getting modified by the help of IIoT working everyday. Whether it be enabling the predictive analytics for detecting the corroded pipes in refinery system, accessing the live data production so that it can uncover the additional capacity of a plant, or speeding up the productivity and development of new operations by feeding them and the data backup of services into the designing cycle of the product, Industrial IoT with the software-enabled solutions works with powerful business results. With the integration of machine-to-machine communication with the industrial big data analytics, IIoT has given this industry a lot of benefits such as higher level of efficient work, production and superb performance. As a result, industry-related companies in the production of basic machinery, chemicals, food and beverage, automotive, metals, and many other industries will meet the benefits of flexible operating and financing.[2]

10.2   HISTORY OF IIOT

It all started in 1968 with the discovery of programmable logic controller (PLC). Dick Morley on Jan 1 woke up with a hangover. It was really not a good start of the day until he drafted a memo that led directly to the discovery of PLC. General Motors used it in their industry in the automated transmission of manufacturing division. These PLCs are allowed to effectively control items through a series of production. The invention was taken forward by Theodore G. Paraskevakos who conceptualized Machine-to-Machine devices that combined telephony and computing for the first time in history. With the invention of Ethernets in the 1980s, people started working on making a network of smart devices as a result of which we saw the first ever modified Coke Machine in 1982. In 1986, PLCs were linked to PCs for better performance. Then in 1989 with the first success toward establishing the communication channel between Hypertext Transfer Protocol (HTTP) client and server via Internet by Tim Berners Lee led to the discovery of World Wide Web. In 1997, Wireless M2M technology becomes prevalent in industry. Kevin Ashton (1999) was the first person to describe about IoT, which officially announced the beginning of a new world.

10.3   UNDERSTATING IOT

IoT is termed as the matrix of devices interconnected with each other and performs communication with each other for the purpose of performing certain relevant tasks, without the need for personal or personal interaction with the computer. The IoT world consists of smart devices connected to the Internet embedded with other advanced chipsets, sensors, and communicating hardware that collects and transmits daily data collected from the environment. IoT devices share information collected from these sensors by establishing a connection to an IoT gateway or other device at the edge where the data is transmitted to the cloud for analyzing or localization. In some cases, these systems interact among different related devices and process the information they receive from each other. These IoT devices perform most of the tasks without any manual intervention, even though people are able to communicate with the devices. Nowadays, IoT devices are making use of artificial intelligence and machine learning techniques for better data gathering and processing.[12]

IoT is helping people by making their life and work smarter by gaining complete control over their lives. IoT is not just automating homes with smart devices it also plays an important role in business. IoT is aiding the economy with updates on how the systems of the businesses work in reality, providing in-depth knowledge covering all aspects ranging from the efficiency of machines to supply chain and logistics mechanisms. IoT helps the companies to optimize their work and thus aid in reducing the labor costs in total. Hosting is declining and the level of service is also being improved which makes the production and delivery of goods more expensive and easier and transparent in customer sales. Nowadays, IoT has become one of the most important technologies of the daily life system, and will continue to move at a higher rate as businesses begin to recognize the power of connected devices that will help them compete in a growing environment.[12]

10.4 INDUSTRIAL INTERNET OF THINGS

Industrial IoT is termed as the extensive concept of IoT. IoT is described as the connection between the devices and computer systems aiming for automatic transmission of work from any part of the world with ease without any manual intervention. The data gathered from the devices is processed and all other places come to the cloud and are processed there. IoT is going to automate everything from homes to schools, from small stores to big industries. The enactment of IoT in the industries producing different products is termed as IIoT (or Industrial Internet or Industry 4.0). IIoT will transform the production process by enabling greater data access and access, faster, and more efficient than ever. Companies have now started implementing the IIoT for innovation by facilitating intelligent and connected devices in their factories.[10]

10.5 BENEFITS OF IIoT

1. **Increase in efficiency:**
   The largest advantage that IIoT is giving the manufacturers is the ability to automate the things which in result helps in optimizing the operation efficiency. Automated robots and machines can work accurately and completely, speeding up production that helps manufacturers simplify their operations.

2. **Reduce errors:**
   IIoT helps producers digitize every aspect of their business. Reducing the manual process has helped the manufacturers to lower the risk of manual labor—human error.

3. **Improve safety:**
   Along with the help IIoT does in the manufacturing work, it has also been helping in keeping the systems secure, providing security to the workplace.

4. **Reduce costs:**
   Manufactures after gaining the knowledge of IIoT solutions are getting connected to the latest tools that help them in cost cutting

and generating more revenue. Data mining for performance under-standing, production, marketing, sales, and more can help in profit-able growth of businesses.[5]

10.6   IIoT CHALLENGES

The two major challenges that surround the implementation of IIoT are Interoperability and security. As technology writer Margaret Rouse puts it, what is most troubling around the commercial IoT is the connection in between the systems and systems using various protocols with multiple structures. "The texture is an excellent answer for this as it is a platform and built on open source, in the standard IT technology."

The most important thing a company needs on a daily basis is that their information is protected. The proliferation of emotions and other intelligent, connected things has led to explosions very similar to safety risks. This is sometimes another factor in the rise of Message Queuing Telemetry Transport (MQTT) because it is badly protected in terms of the IIoT agreement.[10]

Companies are earning huge advantages by introducing the IIoT techs in their businesses. IIoT has helped them acquire improved intelligence, highly accurate and making decisions more precisely and enhanced productivity, improved asset management, and much more. But as with anything else these achievements come with some big fall as well. Finally we move on to a more complex system. Thousands of thousands of dollars' worth of devices are made in less than an hour by monitoring and communicating with sensitive or critical devices that help maintain smart grids, nuclear plants, safety controls, and production lines.[6]

10.7   KEY TERMS IN IIoT

1. **Data terms:**
   Nowadays most of the industrial IoT work depends on data because of the huge amount of data produced on daily basis:

   - **Big data**—Huge data set for pattern as well as trend analysis.
   - **Streaming data**—Data generated by users all over the world on daily basis.
   - **Sensor data**—The data collected from different types of devices that produce data from the physical environment. Their results are used as input for other systems for guiding other processes.

- **Time-series data**—It is the representation of continuous change of system, process or behavior in continuous time intervals.

2. **Business process terms:**
   - **Predictive maintenance**—This method is designed for predicting device time. This method is useful in minimizing the maintenance cost.
   - **Operational intelligence**—It helps in real-time works like the analytics of dynamic businesses that is used in the delivery of vision and perception for data.
   - **Overall equipment effectiveness (OEE)**—It basically assesses the efforts done to make a work more productive (properties, time, and material) in relation to its full capability as its operation was planned.
   - **Property rental**—It is defined as the procedure of keeping an eye on all operations related to a singular machine.

3. **Technological terms:** Here the things tend to become little technological so we need to get ourselves trained for these things:
   - **Application Programming Interface (API)**—It is defined as the combination of functions and instructions which enables the software for accessing or interaction with different characteristic or dataset of other services or applications.
   - **Programmable Logic Controller (PLC)**—It is a digital computer designed for industries for monitoring the input state of devices so that they can make decisions on the basis of logics which are previously programmed.
   - **Radio Frequency Identification**—This is a medium of connection that operates on frequency of radiowaves for accelerating the devices.
   - **Supervisory Control and Data Acquisition**—It is a controlling mechanism that digital computers and networked communication devices for monitoring control system and controlling the factory floor equipment.

4. **Security and Standards Terms:** Cloud Security of data becomes critical. So we need to get familiarized with the following terms:
   - **Identity and Access Management**—This manages identity digitally of business activities, their policy and the technology.
   - **MQTT**—Protocol for messaging services being above Transmission Control Protocol/Internet Protocol (TCP/IP). It is developed

only for those tasks which are low code footprint or have controlled amount of network bandwidth.

- **TCP/IP**—Language helped in Internet access.
- **Ethernet IP**—It is a protocol of communicating for the transfer of data over electronics.
- **Hyper Text Transfer Protocol (HTTP)**—This is the world known protocol always used by World Wide Web. HTTP tells us how data is transmitted from the sender to the recipient and also about the formatting, and the different steps performed by the Web Servers and web browsers must bc taking in response to multiple commands executed.[8]

10.8 INDUSTRY 4.0

The fourth generation of economic transformation has been identified as Industry 4.0, although it is affected in less visible areas which are often classified as sectoral applications in their subject, such as smart cities. The first revolution in the industry came with the advent of machinery, steam power, and water power. The revolution was followed by a second phase, which focused on manufacturing and assembly lines using electricity. The third period of history came with electronics and IT. Systems and automation, which led to the fourth year associated with cyber body systems. The term Industry 4.0 embodies the promise of industrial transformation—combining advanced production techniques with the Web of Things to create productive systems that not only connect, but also communicate, analyze, and use knowledge to drive other intelligent actions back into the physical world.[11]

Industry 4.0 provides a sign of change within traditional production. Also called the fourth technological (industrial) revolution, Industry 4.0 focuses on three technologies that drive this change: communication, ingenuity, and dynamic automation. This integration became successful because of the rise of the solutions digitally and advancement in technology, which are often associated with Industry 4.0. It consists of IoT, Big Data (Huge Data), Cloud Services, AM (Additive Manufacturing), Modernized Developed Robots, AR/VR (Augmented Reality/Virtual Reality).

These techs help drive digital transformation through a combination of pre-existing systems and systems using digital systems that are integrated across wholesale and procurement. Implementing Industry 4.0, digital production, and therefore the communication which steps in will open huge business benefits, including higher rate of efficiency, adaptability and production.[7]

10.9   ADVANTAGES OF INDUSTRIAL IOT

Industrial IoT brings many benefits some of which are listed below:

1. Predictability and performance
2. Real-Time Monitoring
3. Asset/Resource Optimization
4. Remote Diagnosis[3]

10.10   THREATS IN IIOT

There is a number of safety problems associated with the lack of IIoT in large areas. Security spaces such as open ports, improper verification attempts, and outmoded systems contributing to exposure to risks. Combination of those threats with the web gives invitation to more new risks.

Businesses are likely to grow in popularity with the potential business impact of getting IT systems down due to cyber attack or system getting infected by malwares. However, the integration of IT and OT provides an introduction to something of a new danger: real-world threats that can affect people.

IIoT systems that are not secure finish up within the disruption of operation and losses in money. The more is the connected environment the more is the risk to security, such as:

*   Vulnerability of software uses in attacking to systems.
*   Devices that can be searched publicly.
*   Harmful activities such as hacking into systems, attacking targeted systems and breach into data files.
*   Interruptions in various operations due to system management.
*   Malfunctioning of systems causing damage to gadgets and body parts or damage to operators or nearby people.
*   OT systems held hostage, as they are corrupted by the IT environment.

One of the best known examples of an OT system disrupted by the IT environment is cyber-attacks in December 2015 that was against the influence grid in Ukraine, where the enemy was competent to infiltrate the infrastructure of IT to pack sensitive devices and disturbed the supply of power for a lot of families.[3]

10.11 FUTURE SCOPE

IIoT is considered to be one of the wheels of the technology hub that drives the fourth industrial revolution. This will be a very critical situation for businesses as they will gain the visibility of working to make quick and effective decisions to improve quality and improve costs and time.

In terms of customer service considerations, IoT has been replacing existing technology or layer replacement with existing layers such as connected cars, home lighting, television and smartphones. On the economic side, however, there are some ideas, developed and developed in the first place, because large enterprises and production units work with legacy machines and data tracking and analysis methods to determine the quality of these machines and infrastructure. Therefore, the implementation of large firms is a real problem.[9]

"Efficiency has been improved by IIoT, but companies can also reap more benefits by seeing it as a tool to achieve growth in unexpected opportunities."

The upcoming future of the companies will be like those who want to become really successful they will be using IIoT for their manufacturing tasks for huge benefits in less time by following some of these listed approaches:

- IIoT will be helping in boosting the revenues by increasing the rate of production.
- Growth in business can be achieved by taking in account the latest hybrid business models.
- Using new Intelligent innovation technology and transforming their staff.[4]

10.12 CONCLUSION

Industrial IoT has the power of entirely transforming the manufacturing. Nowadays global market competition has increased a burden to the manufactures to push their manufacturing operations at the next level which has made them to go for smartly manufacturing of products which are all powered the IIoT. The fact is more data will be built from the mechanical systems that are further connected to understand the critical and critical operational understanding that IIoT is supposed to have. Within the next 10 years, IIoT will reconfigure the state-of-the-art environment where most of the objects work automatically. This will help increase profits and reduce labor costs so that products are available to the public at a lower rate. This development will also open a lot of job opportunities in new fields for people resulting in various new subjects for study and research.

KEYWORDS

- **IoT**
- **IIoT**
- **programmable logic controller**
- **Industry 4.0**
- **Big Data**

REFERENCES

1. Connectivity Software Framework for Smart Machines. RTI, n.d. https://www.rti.com/blog/the-iiot-primer
2. Everything You Need to Know About IIoT. GE Digital. GE.com. Building a world that works. General Electric, n.d. https://www.ge.com/digital/blog/everything-you-need-know-about-industrial-Internet-things
3. Industrial Internet of things (IIoT) in manufacturing-Happiest minds. Industrial Internet of Things (IIoT), n.d. https://www.happiestminds.com/Insights/industrial-iot/
4. Industrial Internet of things (IIoT). Trend Micro. Enterprise Cybersecurity Solutions, n.d. https://www.trendmicro.com/vinfo/us/security/definition/industrial-Internet-of-things-iiot
5. Industrial IoT—The top 5 benefits of industry 4.0. Hitachi Solutions, n.d. https://global.hitachi-solutions.com/blog/industrial-iot-benefits
6. Industrial IoT (IIoT)—Challenges, risks & pitfalls. Tiempo Dev. Tiempo Development, August 8, 2020. https://www.tiempodev.com/blog/industrial-iot-challenges-risks-pitfalls/
7. Industry 4.0: 7 real-world examples of digital manufacturing in action. In AMFG, July 3, 2020. https://amfg.ai/2019/03/28/industry-4-0-7-real-world-examples-of-digital-manu-facturing-in-action/

8. Key industrial IoT terms every manufacturer should know. In *Industry Week,* Aug 27, 2019. https://www.industryweek.com/cloud-computing/article/22028146/key-industrial-iot-terms-every-manufacturer-should-know

9. Soni, S. Future of IoT in the manufacturing industry. *Entrepreneur*, n.d. https://www.entrepreneur.com/article/311647

10. What is IIoT? Inductive Automation, n.d. https://inductiveautomation.com/resources/article/what-is-iiot

11. What is industry 4.0? How does it work? (A beginners guide). Joining Innovation with Expertise—TWI, n.d. https://www.twi-global.com/what-we-do/research-and-technology/technologies/industry-4-0

12. What is IoT (Internet of things) and how does it work? In *IoT Agenda,* Feb 11, 2020. https://Internetofthingsagenda.techtarget.com/definition/Internet-of-Things-IoT

CHAPTER 11

Audio-to-Braille Conversion Device (A.B.C.D): An IoT Application

SUBHAM HATI, TULIKA BISWAS, SUVAM SAHA, SOURABH KR. BANIA, PRAFULL SHYAM, and SRIJAN BHATTACHARYA*

Applied Electronics & Instrumentation Engineering Department, RCC Institute of Information Technology, Kolkata, India

ABSTRACT

Blind people in the society require special attention and care. The Braille alphabet system was developed by Louis Braille in 1829. It helped the blind to read and write with the help of tactile feedback. Each braille cell is a 3×2 matrix where each combination of keys represents a particular alphabet. Learning braille keys can be difficult for the visually impaired and specialized schools may not be accessible to all. Audio to Braille Conversion Device is designed to teach braille key by converting the speech from the user using an android application and send the message to the NodeMcu, which converts each character to its corresponding braille key.

11.1 INTRODUCTION

In India, a visually impaired individual has to live in isolation from the society. Blind schools are not present in every corner of this country, which makes it difficult for the person to learn and read new books and journals. Reading and learning are very important activity for an individual as it helps to learn and grow as a human. Learning Braille is difficult in India because

Internet of Things: Technological Advances and New Applications. Brojo Kishore Mishra & Amit Vishwasrao Salunkhe (Eds.)

technology has not penetrated in all corners of the country and the available learning kits are expensive. Paul Pocatilu et al. reported Cloud Computing with its wide range of usage in the field of E-Learning. With the introduction of e-learning, we have found a lot more fascinating and interactive way of learning, but a sound hardware and software system are required for e-learning systems. There are many institutions that cannot afford this kind of investment. Here comes the facility of cloud computing. It runs on wide range of electronic devices and store data in the cloud that can be accessed anywhere using internet. Overall, this chapter gives a wide overview on the benefits of cloud computing for e-learning solutions.[1] Derrick Kondo et al. introduces us with two computational programming, which was traditionally clusters and computational grid. But recently, two cost-efficient and powerful platforms have emerged, namely cloud and volunteer computing, also known as desktop grid. So, overall the chapter deals with cloud computing and volunteer com puting. It tells about the advantages and disadvantages, the cost of using them in each project and then comparing them with graphical representation on basis of cost-benefits overhead for platform construction, application deployment, compute rates, and completion times. Hybrid approaches where a VC server is hosted on a cloud to lower the start-up and monthly costs are also taken care off. Server bandwidth of cloud is particularly expensive. Hence, the whole chapter is a comparison between volunteer computing and cloud computing.[2] A metrics system has been developed in order to measure the efficiency of cloud computing-based e-learning solutions. We have been introduced to the Pareto Principle, which is explained in the "5th" point. The chapter ends with the example of The Academy of Economic Studies from Bucharest that they use their own e-learning solution based on Moodle have their own data center that can be the future of cloud computing.[3] Ronald Cole et al. starts with the problems faced while designing a letter recognition software. The difficulty in distinction between similar-looking letters makes the job difficult. But then, it focuses fully on the system known as EAR as English Alphabet Recognizer. It discusses thoroughly about its use and accuracy. It had about 96% accuracy on the first 30 speakers. Then, moving on its system overview, pitch tracking and system development were measured. Early works applied dynamic programming to frame-by-frame matching input and reference pattern. But, with the success of EAR system, the Letter detection from phonetic sounds has become a very easy job. But, still some difficulty remained in discriminating some similar phonetic letters like B and V, but that was also improved. The Neural Network Segmentation did a great performance and had an important advantage which was easily retained for different databases like continuous telephone speech.[4]

Braille matrix is a 3×2 matrix where each combination refers to alphabet or character from any script. It helps the blind to read using tactile sensation. SD card can be used to store external information and audio files. ARM7-based LPC2148 can be interfaced with SD and can process audio files. A single channel audio with a sampling rate of 8000 Hz, resolution of 8 bits/sample, and bit rate of 64 kbps is most suitable for audio processing.[5] Six contact pins from each braille matrix forms 64 combinations. Grade 1 Braille is used to represent alphabets, whereas Grade 2 braille is used to represent shorthand of each alphabet. Braille display is based on two major mechanisms: Piezoelectric Bimorph Bender and Relay-Lever System. Miniature ultrasonic linear motor is being developed for braille matrix.[6] Microbubble linear actuator can be used in Braille displays. Maximum displacement of 0.6 mm is required for each pin. A 50–100 mN force is applied during fine touch exploration for reading. Linux Angstorm Operating System is best suited for embedded system applications.[7] Tessaract engine with the help of Python wrapper converts words in an image to text. Solenoids (each 5V rated) are used for Braille matrix. Each segment consists of six solenoids. Plunger-solenoid mechanism is used as a linear actuator. The major disadvantage of using a plunger is the size and doesn't fit the braille display standard.[8] The Refreshable Braille Display System (RBDS) is a reading aid, in which computer text is directly converted to the Braille cells which are interfaced directly through the USB. Each Braille cell consists of eight dots which are driven by piezo actuators, which move according to the information sent. Each cell takes power from USB, which gives 5V which is further converted by an electrical circuit to provide 200 V supply. A back panel is used for connecting more than one cell side-by-side so that it forms a continuous pattern of 2, 4, 6, or 8 blocks. This was all about hardware; the software element consists of C# in which all the information is developed and sent to the hardware via USB.[9] A portable Braille learning kit can be made by using Arduino uno, speaker, memory card module, and eight push buttons, which would be a very low-cost electronic device. We just need a small box (even a soap box can work) cut eight holes in it, and just putting buttons in it will make it just like buzzer-type configuration. After doing all connections of speaker, memory card, and buzzer with Arduino, just burning the files on Arduino will do. This module supports English, but we can add different languages according to our needs.[10] Making an EAP-actuated Braille display that are effective and inexpensive is very important for the visually impaired to take maximum advantage of the emerging technology. Various designs were investigated like IPMC, conducting polymers, ferroelectric EAP, dielectric elastomer EAP, and SMP. Alhough efforts are made to closely package the pins to form it a full-screen display with six or eight pins. The developed displays show advancement from the traditional displays but there are still many challenges like low activation voltage for the field-activated EAPs and low generated force for IPMC. Thus, advancement in developing more effective EAP materials may lead to effective refreshable Braille display.[11] The microchip PIC16F877 was used in the programming of electronic and computer-aided periodic table. The RC6 (transmit) pin of PIC16F877 is connected with RXD (receive) pin of serial port through which data is transmitted to the serial port. And TXD pin of serial port sends the data further to the computer. The periodic table is created on a board, which consists of buttons for particular chemical elements of the correct order. Whenever a button is pressed, the individual hears the name of the element corresponding to the location of the chemical element placed in the table. PIC16F877 is used to program the hardware part and to ensure the proper transmission of data from the buttons to the PC.[12] Cloud computing is an alternative to conventional computing models like cluster computing and grid computing. In cloud computing, a program must be extensively written such that there is proper division of tasks between nodes and inter-connection between a number of notes must be taken care of. This makes programming in clouds more complex. Dynamic scalability, multilatency, reliability, fault tolerance, and debugging are the most crucial challenges faced during cloud computing.[13] Multimedia content and management are important aspects of cloud. Restrictive multimedia access and processing are facilitated to improve security as well as reduce load on the virtual machines (VMs). Private cloud with authenticating protocols provides a controlled architecture. Content providers have more content over cloud data. Controlled cloud means that the Super Cloud is having unrestricted access to the private cloud.[14] Clouds can be both private and public in nature. This new method of computation reduces processing time and required storage space. Image processing and multiscreen projects incorporate cloud computing. Cost is effective on user data to service provider. For multimedia purposes, audio and video optimiza tion is important. Such systems are easily upgradable and can have many storage bases for media. Security protocols and proper encryption of data has to be maintained during storage and sharing of data.[15] In grid computing, a single task is distributed into several same kinds of tasks over a computer network having distributed system. Cloud computing is a totally new class of network technology-based computing where an own private resource is facil itated by the specific service provider. The main function of grid computing is job scheduling using all kinds of computing resources. Cloud computing involves resource pooling through grouping resources on an as-needed basis. Cloud Business Model Framework (CBMF) has three primary layers—infrastructure layer, the platform-as-a-service layer, and the application layer on top.[16] The android operating system has a very vast ecosystem, and a well-develop voice recognition system of its own, which can be used in a project. It is an effective way of cutting the price of development of software. Portability across various platforms is a huge feature of android SDKs.[17] Hidden Markov Method (HMM) uses statistical probability to reconstruct the word transferred from the microphone and then it also checks for the grammatical error to do correction. It is a three-layer method to identify the given input to a satisfactory output. It suits the sequential nature of speech, but it isn't flexible. It works for a small part of audio. "Phone" is interpreted as "pho" and "ne".[18] Neural networks used for speech recognition are very flexible in nature. This system becomes more accurate with training. As the training set increases, the sample input is compared, and the closest output is selected. The difference between the actual output and expected output is fed back to the neural network for increasing the accuracy. Thus, it has a self-learning mechanism based on previous experiences.[19] Recurrent Neural Network (RNN) help to make a powerful model for sequential type of data. This mod el is trained using end-to-end methods. RNN architecture can successfully detect cursive writing. Deep RNN networks with more than three layers and multiple hidden layers are the most accurate models for speech recognition. RNNs map the input to the output using acoustic and phonetic sequences. Weight noise simplifies neural networks by reducing the amount of information required to transmit the parameters.[20]

11.2 BRAILLE SCRIPT

Braille was developed by Louis Braille in 1829 as a tactile writing system for the visually impaired. Each character is constituted of a rectangular block called as cell and small bumps called as raised dots. Braille is multilingual and each language has a particular braille pattern.

English language has three levels of encoding: (1) GRADE I—a letter-to-letter encoding for basic education, (2) GRADE II—consists of additional abbreviations, (3) GRADE III—it is personalized and is mainly used stenography. A complete braille cell involved with six raised dots arranged in two columns, and three dots each column. Each cell represents a letter, number, and sometimes even a word. To read a braille one has to move the hand or hands from left to right for each line. The reading process can involve both hands. Index fingers are generally used for reading purpose. Braille is not a language but a code by which languages such as English, Bengali, Hindi, and many other languages can be written and read. Braille is used worldwide and acts as the primary education method for the blind.

FIGURE 11.1   Braille cell [7].

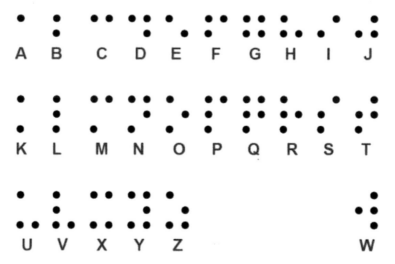

FIGURE 11.2   Braille code for English alphabets [https://en.wikipedia.org/wiki/Braille].

11.3   SCENARIO OF BLINDNESS IN INDIA

The number of visually impaired is very high in India. The statistics and facts are given as follows[21]:

- In India, one out of every 30 people is blind comparing to the world data.
- 12 million people are blind in India.
- In India, 7.4 million (62%) have cataract blindness.
- 19.7 million people are blind for refractive error.
- Every year 3.6 million people become blind.
- Under 16 years, 3.2 million children are blind. 5% of them receive any formal education.
- 80% of blindness is avoidable.
- Incidences of blindness are higher in the rural areas. About 72% of the population of India live in 6.38 lakh villages.

11.4   PROBLEM STATEMENT

To design and implement a Braille script learning kit which is capable of recognizing speech and extracting each alphabet from the word to convert it to its corresponding braille code. Therefore helping in better understanding of the braille script by using practical words and sentences.

The kit should be low cost making it affordable for the regular Indian household. Maintenance and updating the kit should be easy and accessible.

11.5   HARDWARE REQUIREMENTS

- A smartphone operating with Android 4.0 or above
- NodeMcu ESP8266 V3 Wifi Dev. Board
- LEDs

11.6   METHODOLOGY

- ANDROID APPLICATION: The smartphone is connected to the NodeMcu's Wifi access point using the SSID and password given to the user. A simple android application is developed, which uses Google's speech recognition engine to recognize the speech of the user. The voice is converted to text, which is sent to the server side (NodeMcu) from the client side (Android application) using the local IP of the server: http://192.168.4.1/.

RECOGNIZED SPEECH: hello world

NODEMCU RESPONSE: {"data":
{"message":"success","value":"HELLO
WORLD"}}

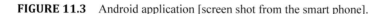

FIGURE 11.3 Android application [screen shot from the smart phone].

- CREATING ACCESS POINT: ESP8266WiFi library is capable of creating a WiFi Access Point using the functions WIFI. Mode() and WiFi.softAP(). This acts as a hotspot for the smartphone to connect.
- RECEIVING THE CLIENT MESSAGE: The NodeMcu receives the client message in the following format: GET /hello%20world HTTP/1.1.
- EXTRACTING TEXT FROM THE MESSAGE: The code is designed to extract the text from the received message and convert it to a character array. Each character is displayed as a braille code using six LEDs corresponding to each raised dot.

- JSON FEEDBACK: For a feedback to the android application from the NodeMcu, a JSON response is sent. JSON response is a payload returned from a web service from a request. The format of the received JSON response is as follows: {"data":{"message":"success","value": "HELLO WORLD"}}.

11.7 BLOCK DIAGRAM

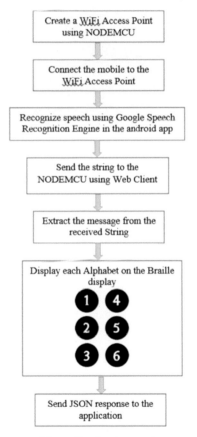

FIGURE 11.4 Block Diagram of the entire development process.

11.8 HARDWARE SETUP

The setup consists of a NodeMcu connected to a 5V-1A charger for power supply and six LEDs representing six raised dots of a braille cell.

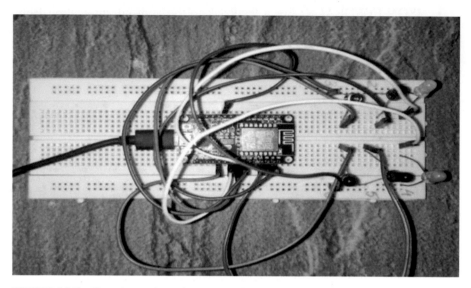

FIGURE 11.5   Experimental Hardware setup for the data transmission.

11.9   RESULTS

The NodeMcu displays messages on the serial monitor when connected to a computer.

FIGURE 11.6   Experimental Output received through serial monitor in computer.

The messages displayed on the serial monitor are as follows:

GET/hello%20world HTTP/1.1

Client disconnected

Cleaned String: HELLO

WORLD Length: 11

Displaying H

Displaying E

Displaying L

Displaying L

Displaying O

Displaying W

Displaying O

Displaying R

Displaying L

Displaying D

The braille pattern is displayed

Each pattern is displayed on the LED segment for 3 s followed by a delay of 1 s where all the LEDs are off.

11.10 FUTURE SCOPE

The design can be improved by adding audio output, which will help in providing additional sensation to the user and helping in learning braille more effectively. The LED segment has to be replaced with micro-actuators for creating an actual refreshable braille display.

11.11 CONCLUSION

Audio to Braille Conversion Device (A.B.C.D.) helps in teaching the braille script to the visually impaired without the necessity of continuous monitoring and expert guidance. This is designed for the common Indian household. The era of Digital India has made mobile phones and an internet connection available to most part of the society. With the help of a basic smartphone and low cost A.B.C.D., the blind can learn Braille in their own house. The android application helps in providing new features and updates based on reviews on a frequent basis.

KEYWORDS

- **braille**
- **speech recognition**
- **learning kit**
- **low-cost**
- **portable**
- **blind**
- **visually impaired**
- **NodeMcu**
- **ESP8266**
- **Wi-Fi**
- **access point**
- **server–client**

REFERENCES

1. Pocatilu, P.; Alceu, F.; Vetrici, M. *Measuring the Efficiency of Cloud Computing for E-learning Systems*; Economic Informatics Department, Academy of Economic Studies.
2. Kondo, D.; Javadi, B.; Malecot, P.; Cappello, F.; Anderson, D. P. *Cost-Benefit Analysis of Cloud Computing versus Desktop Grids* INRIA: France, UC, Berkeley.
3. Pocatilu, P.; Alceu, F.; Vetrici, M. *Using Cloud Computing for E-learning Systems*; Economic Informatics Department, Academy of Economic Studies.
4. Cole, R.; Fanty, M. Spoken Letter Recognition. Department of Computer Science and Engineering, Oregon Graduate Institute of Science and Technology.
5. Jadamali, N.; Jadamali, P.; Shirsat, K.; Basavaradder, A. Electronic Progressive Braille Learning Kit for Blind (Low Cost, All Languages and Multiline Braille Screen). SKSVMA College of Engineering & Technology, Gadag, Karnataka and BVB College of Engineering & Technology, Hubli, Karnataka.
6. Velázquez, R.; Hernández, H.; Preza, E. A Portable Piezoelectric Tactile Terminal for Braille Readers. Mecatrónica y Control de Sistemas, Universidad Panamericana, Aguascalientes, Mexico.
7. Wu, X. Kim, S-H.; Zhu, H.; Ji, C-H.; Allen, M. G. Fellow, IEEE. A Refreshable Braille Cell Based on Pneumatic Microbubble Actuators. *J. Microelectromech. Syst.* **2012,** *21* (4).

8. Gang, H.; Bhave, T. Refreshable Braille Display. Tandon School of Engineering.
9. Eldem, A,; Başçiftçi, F. Electronic and Computer-Assisted Refreshable Braille Display Developed for Visually Impaired Individuals. *World Acad. Sci. Eng Technol. Int. J. Comput. Inform. Eng* **2015**, *9* (1).
10. FarhanF4. Interactive Portable Braille Learning Kit for Blind Children. Instructables.
11. Bar-Cohen, Y. Refreshable Braille Displays Using EAP Actuators. Jet Propulsion Lab, California Institute of Technology, 4800 Oak Grove Drive, Pasadena, CA 91109-8099.
12. Eldem, A.; Başçiftçi, F. The Electronic and Computer-Aided Periodic Table Prepared for the Visually Impaired Individuals. *World Acad. Sci. Eng. Technol. Int. J. Electron. Commun. Eng.* **2013**, *7* (8).
13. Sadashiv, N.; Dilip Kumar, S. M. Cluster, Grid and Cloud Computing: A Detailed Comparison. *The 6th International Conference on Computer Science & Education (ICCSE 2011)*; SuperStar Virgo, Singapore, August 3–5, 2011.
14. Kesavan, S. Controlled Multimedia Cloud Architecture And Advantages. DXC technology.
15. Bindhu Shamily, P.; Durga, S. A Review on Multimedia Cloud Computing, Its Advantages and Challenges. ISSN: 2278 – 1323, *IJARCET* **2012**, *1* (10).
16. Weinhardt, C.; Blau, B.; Borissov, N.; Meinl, T.; Stößer, J. Cloud Computing—A Classification, Business Models, and Research Directions. Universität Karlsruhe (TH) Institute of Information Systems and Management, Englerstr. 14,76131 Karlsruhe, Germany.
17. Raghavendhar Reddy, B.; Mahender, E. Speech to Text Conversion Using Android Platform. Department of Electronics Communication and Engineering Aurora's Technological and Research Institute Parvathapur: Uppal, Hyderabad, India.
18. Chavan, R. S.; Sable, G. S. Department of E&TC, Savitribai Phule Women's Engineering College, Aurangabad, Maharashtra, India. An Overview of Speech Recognition Using HMM. *Int. J. Comput. Sci. Mobile Comput*, ISSN 2320–088X
19. Robinson, A. J.; Almeida, L.; Boite, J. M. A Neural Network Based, Speaker Independent, Large Vocabulary, Continuous Speech Recognition System: The Wernicke Project' ISCA Archcive, 1993.
20. Graves, A.; Mohamed, A-R.; Hinton, G. Speech Recognition with Deep Recurrent Neural Networks. Department of Computer Science, University of Toronto.
21. https://www.anugrahadrishtidaan.org/Blindness-Global-&-Indian-Scenario.htm

CHAPTER 12

Internet of Things: Applied Science and Technologies

DEEPTI MISHRA and BHAIRVEE SINGH

Department of CSE, G.L. Bajaj Institute of Technology and Management, Greater Noida, India

ABSTRACT

Internet of Things (IoT) is the execution of numerous devices based on distinct technologies for transfer of data in real time with security additionally followed by encryption techniques. IoT is grasping its roots in the market very deeply. It has an integration of various technologies and devices functioning at a common platform. Enabling technologies for IoT may belong to distinct domains, such as mechanical science, digital discipline, computing methods, and communication tools to convey data. IoT technology comprises of hardware devices, software, communication protocols, and an assembling platform. Platform acts as a base to operate and execute all the integrated devices simultaneously. Hardware devices included in IoT are wireless systems on chip, prototyping boards, such as Raspberry pi and Arduino. Software such as RIoT OS plays the crucial role in implementation of IoT. Technologies such as radio frequency identification (RFID), ZigBee, Sigfox, Bluetooth, wireless techniques, radio protocols, NB-IoT, and many other offer connectivity solutions for IoT. IPv4, IPv6, UDP, and TCP are a few key components of IoT. On the root level, IoT applies to protocols from networking domain for communication and data transfer. IoT utilizes multiple varieties of technologies during its implementation and

Internet of Things: Technological Advances and New Applications. Brojo Kishore Mishra & Amit Vishwasrao Salunkhe (Eds.)

execution. The current scenario, which is the beginning of IoT, smart sensors directly communicate without any human interference. The next level of this technology will touch every aspect of human life. It will connect different types of physical entities. The chapter focuses on the technologies meant and used for operating IoT. The chapter elaborates the detailed specifications of enabling technologies utilized for IoT. This chapter covers all security and integration related issues in detail. It also explores the relationship of IoT with other emerging technologies and their effect on each other.

12.1   INTRODUCTION

Internet of Things (IoT) is an integration of various physical devices via Internet. Connection of Internet implies the transfer of information among various devices which makes them smart. It is involved in numerous devices in everyday life, which are connected through Internet. All the devices can be managed at the same platform.

IoT covers a wide domain driven by various technologies. It is no doubt a boom to the market. The concept of IoT technology can be foreseen as the largest market holder in future. IoT is designing the foundation of the world as more intelligent and responsive by integrating physical and communicating devices. An emerging technology creating its own influence in all categories around the world.[1]

In the current scenario, IoT is highlighted as eminent technology for developing numerous applications in distinct domains. IoT technology is furnished with the idea of autonomous computing in which various devices function together while reducing human effort.[2]

IoT outbids in such a manner that it transformed the daily routine and usual life. Applications of IoT which impacting daily life are diabetic monitoring control devices, tracking tools, heartbeat monitoring, autonomous systems, and vehicles.[3]

Mainly, IoT technology is comprised of four basic components that can be termed as devices, communication, data processing, and user interface. Devices include sensors and smart sets. Sensors collect data from environment and transfer it to connected smart devices. A small chip attached with sensors via wireless communication can add high level of intelligence to devices that are able to exchange real-time data. The gathered data is transmitted using network techniques, such as Bluetooth or cloud connectivity. Collected data need processing to retrieve useful information and further conveyed it to users through user interfaces.

As more consumers embrace IoT technologies and smart devices become a normal feature of daily lives, it has introduced new areas of security vulnerabilities. While there are many IoT devices available in the market with multiple types of applications, not all of them are adequately secured. The demand is rising, and device producers are grappling to meet the demands for IoT devices. One of the casualties in the face-paced production and delivery cycles is the security aspect. Because of the cut-throat competition and desire to release the product as soon as possible, producers tend to compromise on the security aspects by not focusing heavily on the testing and quality control of the products. So far, IoT device producers have been unable to ensure adequate security from hacking, malware, denial of service attacks, or other system-related security issues. While some cyber-attacks remain localized, others have more global effects, leading to large-scale security threats. This is an area where work is in progress albeit with substantial scope for improvement.

Like security issues, the uses of IoT technologies are also responsible for the practice of invasion of privacy. Privacy problem has been a persistent issue since the Internet revolution and is becoming increasingly rampant as more devices are getting connected to the Internet. It is estimated that there will be more than 60 billion IoT-connected devices by late 2025. With these numbers, the issue of ensuring privacy and minimal invasion is set to become paramount. Even in the present context, the amount of data generated, stored, and transmitted by numerous IoT devices is unprecedented. More so, this data is not limited to a single device or a single brand of producer. With so many producers in the game, the data tend to be shared between many companies, which can lead to privacy invasions at any stage. At the same time, it remains difficult to ensure end-to-end security because even a single poorly secured device within the network can become responsible for a privacy breach. It is equally important to understand that the current legal regulations or privacy laws have not progressed sufficiently when compared to the pace with which IoT technology and its applications are advancing.

IoT devices generate huge amount of data which can be further applied in machine learning techniques as well as artificial intelligence.

12.1.1 HISTORY OF IOT

The term IoT has been coined around 22 years before. However, the interaction of machines has been started around 1980. Wireless telegraphy, interaction of machines, Coca-Cola vending machine, connection of toaster with

Internet in 1990 are some examples that resemble with the concept of IoT. But, IoT term is given by Kevin Aston in 1999 while working in Procter & Gamble. IoT again arose in the frontline around mid-2010 when Google started to gather data using Internet. China also involved IoT in strategies and services. In 2011, marketing and research company Gartner applied the concept of IoT. Then after IoT picked the market very speedily. Over the years, IoT is likely to provide smart home and business solutions which will certainly change the life. It will also open new doors for design industry. But all of this requires a strong Internet, powerful communicating protocols, and smart physical objects. There are various architectural and security related challenges that need attention.

12.1.2   ADVANTAGES OF IOT

As is clear by now, the popularity and varied applications of IoT is a result of the advantages it offers. For businesses or individuals' users, IoT technologies and solutions present many opportunities that were impossible by sticking to the traditional practices.[4,5] This section touches upon some of the advantages that IoT offers for businesses as well as individuals.

Improve monitoring and control—One of the most evident benefits of adopting IoT is the ability to enhance monitoring of events and have greater control over outcomes. For instance, IoT solutions allow businesses or users to monitor developments that they are interested in, especially in real-time. The integration of various portals, platforms, technologies has made it possible to monitor and track a wide array of tasks or area. This minimizes the possibilities of contingencies or errors because imminent problems can be noticed in advances and addressed in a timely and effective manner. It also adds to one's safety and security.[6,7] Overall, the possibility of monitoring things remotely provides people greater bandwidth and time to focus on other priorities and direct efforts toward more fruitful tasks.

Enhance customer experience—IoT has helped businesses substantially improve the customer experience by increasing customer retention and interaction. The usage of artificial intelligence, virtual reality, chatbots, etc., has given businesses new ways to reach out to potential customers, enhance their attention span, improve the frequency and quality of customer interaction, etc. For businesses, these are increasingly important requirements, especially in the current era when the wave of social media and Internet has affected the attention span of customers, increased competition, and made it more difficult to stand out among the crowd. IoT allows businesses to get more creative and embrace solutions that take a detour from the usual ways of attaining customer retention and getting their feedback on the services. The combination of these aspects helps businesses take better decisions and continuously look for ways to better the overall customer experience.

Enhancement in data collection—The usage of IoT solutions and technologies results in producing a copious amount of data. If analyzed effectively and with consideration for what is valuable and what is not, the available data generate new insights for both, businesses, and individual users. The data not only generate a comprehensive picture of the subject at hand but also data-driven decision-making also lead to more optimal solutions and better business practices.[8]

Save energy and time—The most important advantage of IoT is that it saves time and energy for users. IoT technologies have proved to be beneficially in synchronizing operations, avoiding duplication of efforts, automating repetitive tasks, better resource utilization, facilitating operations through timely detection of problem areas. All these benefits have naturally made IoT an indispensable for many business and users.

Resource utilization—Managing resources, whether it is human resource or fixed assets, have always been a challenge. Users are always looking for better ways to improve utilization of resources for better workings, minimizing costs, and assigning the right asset toward the right tasks/ job. Through the various functions of IoT such as resource management techniques and relevant software, it is now easier to understand the patterns of resource efforts and assign resources more effectively. All these things are done in a short span of time, which again saves time and consumes minimal.

12.2   TECHNOLOGIES USED FOR IOT

Technologies use smart devices operated by software for processing and communicate data via Internet. Hardware and software technologies operate collectively in IoT.[9] IoT is comprised of wide range of technologies so that it can offer countless services in various domains.[10,11]

With the combination of cloud services and available software, it is not only easier to store, maintain, and access data but also possible to have informed analysis by infusing IoT with big data. Operating system plays a very crucial role in IoT. Wireless technology is the very first choice to build a system. As shown in Figure 12.1, IoT technology is the combination of various devices and software those function together.

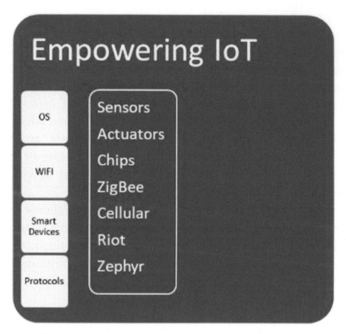

FIGURE 12.1   IoT technology.

12.3   HARDWARE DEVICES

Hardware devices are the key elements for functioning of IoT. The selection of hardware products impact costs, efficiency, experience, and processing. Management of hardware products involves distinct proficiencies' in comparison to the supervision of software.

Hardware devices include in IoT are chips, sensors, actuators, standard devices, controllers, dashboard, routers, bridges, and routing devices. The most used hardware device in IoT is sensors. The hardware devices handle essential tasks such as processing of data, system activation, and security during transmission.

12.3.1   CHIPS

Chips are included in electrical and electronic appliances such as micro-controllers, chips, integrated circuits, etc. It is used in transmission of data at both sender and receiver side connecting through wireless transmission.

IoT chip requires various software for connectivity and linking with other devices. It is because no single kind of chip is like that which can be applied solely in any IoT application.

12.3.2 SENSORS

Sensors are the devices that utilized for data collection. Sensors can be employed in simple manner such as recording temperature and be applied in a complex approach as video feed altogether. Sensors can be used as may be single or multiple in IoT.

Sensors are the key component of IoT technology. Sensors are equipped with different modules such as sensing elements, power management segment, energy segment, and radio frequency elements.

12.3.2.1 MODULES OF SENSORS

Radio frequency module: It is an electronic device which is benefitted for transmission of signals between two devices wirelessly. It communicates through its signal processing, WiFi, Bluetooth, Zigbee, radio transceiver, duplexer, and BAW.

The tiny device transmits the radio signals and in voltage range 3–12 V. Radio frequency technology is becoming popular as it does not need line of sight. RF module is comprised of a 433 MHz transmitter and receiver. The transmitter transmits the data sequentially and that data is received by adjusted receiver. For transmission of data, two microcontrollers are interfaced with transmitter and receiver.

While communicating logic zero transmitter operates on no power with suppressed carrier frequency. Whereas transmitting logic one, it operates with 3 V power supply. It is made up of RF CMOS technology.

Power management segment: IoT devices uses sensors to acquire data from the environment which is applied in decision making whether remotely or locally. Here, sensors play crucial role while gathering data and its transferring as it consumes power to do it. So, sensors should be capable enough to optimize power management.

Sensing elements: It is an observational element of sensors. It observes data from environment in the form of signals or stimulus. It is the fundamental transduction mechanism that converts one form of energy into another. Those sensors that have more than one sensor element are termed as compound sensors.

12.3.2.2 CATEGORIZATION OF SENSORS BASED ON FUNCTIONING

12.3.2.2.1 Active or Passive

Sensors having their own source of light are termed as active sensors. Active sensors need external source of power to operate. In reverse passive sensors measures energy when the sun shines and reflect it back. It detects and responds to some type of input from the physical environment.

12.3.2.2.2 Analog or Digital

The analog sensor measures continuously the variable and detects any proportional value between 100% and 0%. Unlike, digital sensors can only detect two possible outcomes whether it is 100% and 0%.

12.3.2.3 CATEGORIZATION BASED ON TECHNIQUE

Mostly used sensors in IoT are temperature sensor, pressure sensor, optical sensor, IR sensor.

1. **Temperature sensors**—Temperature sensors are analog sensors and take input in the form of temperature from its surrounding environment. It detects, senses, measures, and responds to the changes in the environment. It senses and measures the heat energy in a resource for finding the temperature. These changes are gathered and converted into data. The devices used in sensors usually need to be set on specific temperature at certain levels. Further, the data is transferred to other devices connected in network. The required functioning voltage is 4–30 V.
2. **Pressure sensors**—Pressure sensors are used to sense and measure pressure in gas and liquids and further convert them into electrical signals. These pressure sensor devices are available in different types and sizes. Usually in IoT systems, they are used to observe devices that are pressure driven. A notification is sent to connected devices, if pressure sensor notices any nonconformity from usual pressure range.

The presence of pressure sensor in phone or any wearable device makes user to monitor tracking calculations, altitude, walking, and tracking. Pressure sensors can also be used in monitoring weather. Pressure sensors are gaining popularity in IoT systems due to having feasible size and cost effectiveness.

3. **Optical sensors**—Optical sensors are devices that convert light rays into electric signals. They are utilized to monitor electromagnetic energy and communicate it to connected devices.

    There are many application fields such as vehicle industry, biomedical science, and smartphones. Optical sensors play a crucial role in designing of automated vehicles. In biomedical science, optical sensors are used in monitoring heart rates and breath. Optical sensors are great boom to smartphones, computers, and Xerox machines.

    Photodetector, fiber optics, pyrometer, proximity, and infrared are a few types of optical sensors.

4. **IR sensors**—IR sensors are commonly known as infrared sensors. It is an electronic device used to sense and detect infrared radiation during either receiving or transmitting to detect motion. They can also sense heat emitted by devices. Anything having a temperature above or around 5°C emits heat and produces infrared radiation.

Infrared sensors can also be used in various domains such as healthcare, entertainment, industries, art, and design. They can be used to measure blood pressure and blood flow devices in the heath sector. Infrared sensors are also used for interpreting signals by televisions that are transmitted by remotes. Infrared sensors are also used to detect the differentiation between original and fake art pieces.

12.3.3 ACTUATORS

These devices provide the motion to a data collection system, such as the solenoids, comb drives, etc., to fetch details based on movements.

12.3.4 SMART DEVICES

Standard devices constitute of the generally used devices such as tablets, smartphones, switches, routers, etc. Each of these devices has its own set of settings that allow them to collect data.

12.4 SOFTWARE DEVICES

12.4.1 OPERATING SYSTEM IN IOT

Internet has touched every aspect of human life. It has changed the way we look at the world. Now the whole world can be viewed as a global village. It slowly changed everything which was related to man, like payment mode, shopping, information sharing, education, and analysis. It not only affected our working style but also changed the environment and behavior of people.

The development of powerful microcontrollers and sensors made connectivity easier and a new technology named IoT emerged. IoT connected everything including man and machine. The concept of smart home, smart city, and smart government became possible because of Internet. The concept of IoT started in 1990 and it is growing since then. Its future is unpredictable. IoT connects various objects so that they can communicate with one another without any human intervention. These objects can differ in shape, size, and architecture. Moreover, the data generated by them can be of heterogeneous nature. Here comes the role of operating systems, which hide the differences of various devices and make the connection seamless.

As IoT has huge numbers of nodes and they all are of different characteristics, so OS can be organized in different categories. Firstly, the architecture of OS must be identified. It can be monolithic, microkernel, or layered architecture. The next decision of scheduling policy plays a big concern. Other than these two, there are various other issues to be considered while designing the OS.

Some of the important features are as follows:

1. **Architecture:** The selection of OS mainly depends on the architecture. Broadly the OS can be categorized as monolithic, microkernel, and layered. Monolithic kernel is a single executable handling all kernel functions. In microkernel, the OS handles only extremely specific work like scheduling and memory management. Rest of the work is assigned to user space. It is more flexible and easier to update in comparison to monolithic. The layered architecture is an improvement over monolithic. Here OS is designed in such a way that the lower layer provides services to the upper layer and hides the complexity. The selection of architecture depends on environment and application. MantisOS uses layered architecture, TinyOS uses monolithic, and RIoT is based on microkernel.

2. **Scheduling Criteria:** The scheduling algorithm plays an especially important role in designing of an OS. It impacts on overall system

performance and CPU utilization. There are two OS scheduling algorithms. In preemptive algorithms, processor switches to the higher priority process while in nonpreemptive, every process which is assigned to processor completes its execution. IoT OS uses preemptive as well as nonpreemptive scheduling algorithm. A few of them like Contiki use both algorithms.

3. **Programming Model:** We know that every application is developed by using some programming language. The application is somehow dependent on programming model of OS. So, the selection of programming language is dependent on programming model of OS. It can be event-driven or multithreaded programming model. The example of IoT OS that implement event-driven programming model is TinyOS. RIoT-OS uses multithreaded environment.

4. **Memory Management:** Memory management define how memory is utilized throughout the execution of a process. It deals with the relocation of program, restoring of unused space, and memory protection. Normally the memory management schemes are categorized in static and dynamic. Static allocation is fixed, and nonflexible and dynamic allocations are flexible. IoT OS uses static as well as dynamic schemes. Static allocation is used in Nano-RK and TinyOS, whereas Contiki, RIoT, and MantisOS support dynamic allocation.

5. **File management:** One of the major issues while designing the IoT OS is of file management. As the various objects connected in network do not have a proper file management system, it becomes a challenging task to manage the file system. There are various IoT that provides file system, such as TinyOS, Contiki OS, and LiteOS.

6. **Real-time capabilities:** IoT system needs real-time execution, so it requires that every task execute in a fixed time constraint. Real-time operating systems are broadly categorized in soft and hard real time systems. Whereas soft real-time system requires a task to be completed in a fixed deadline but can accept some delay like online transaction system. Hard real-time systems are very much strict for time and can produce serious consequences if not executed in time. There are several IoT OS that run on RTOS.

The above-mentioned features play an important in designing of OS. IoT has applications in every field. It ranges from education and farming to medical diagnosis. Every field requires a different style of networking, data, and processing. Similarly, the choice of OS is totally dependent of the area of application. One should use an appropriate OS to get maximum performance and smooth communication among devices. No doubt that Contiki and RIoT are the most widely used OS for IoTs application as they fulfil the most of the requirements, but other OSs like TinyOS, Nano-RK, LiteOS, and MantisOS have also shown their importance in different fields.

TABLE 12.1 IoT-enabled Software Technology.

Technology	Features	Remarks	Sources
Edge computing	Deal data in different way. Data processing is performed at collection point rather passing it to other devices. Applied in real-time applications and processing of videos.	Developing	Cisco, EdgeconneX, Clearblade
Cloud computing	It is the accessibility of computer resources specifically data requirements and storage.	Well developed	AWS, Google cloud services, IBM cloud services
IoT foundations	It is multipurpose technique dealing with connected devices and their management.	Well developed	Augury, Ayyeka, Bastille, filament networks
Machine learning	Applied to deal with huge amount of data generated through IoT devices.	Developing	Tachyus, Sentrian, Augury, Veros system
Digital twins	A technology that applies the concept of use of virtual replicas of physical devices.	Developing	Azure, Siemens
Deep learning	Applies the concept of human brain in learning process for processing of data and problem solving.	Developed	TensorFlow, R

12.5 COMMUNICATION TECHNOLOGY

IoT is empowering worldwide due to applying strongly different communication technologies.

12.5.1 LPWANS: LOW POWER WIDE AREA NETWORKS

It is a kind of wireless telecommunication wide area network. With low bit rate, it permits long-range communications. The key characteristics of LPWANS are low bit rate, low cost, long range, and low power. The usual range is 10 km in urban areas. It requires low power consumption and can run for 20 years on batteries. It involves star topology which further reduces complexity of hardware and design.

12.5.2   CELLULAR (3G, 4G, 5G)

Cellular networks are good alternative to LPWANS. Cellular networks provide reliable and secure IoT services. It is the primary technique of connection in today's scenario as user gets voice and data at any location. Cellular network can manage industrial IoT to critical IoT. It is method of connecting sensors or other physical devices with Internet. Arrival of 5G, it is arising very strongly. Cellular IoT is empowered with the capabilities such as low power intake and low cost for managing long-range applications. It requires exceedingly small infrastructure to be installed as towers, base stations, and electricity are already in place. This technology can cover a wide area in kilometers very efficiently.

12.5.3   NFC: NEAR FIELD COMMUNICATION

Data transmission in near-field communication uses electromagnetic radio fields between two devices. Both the devices must be equipped with chips for communication and data transmission. It is essential that both the devices should be extremely near to each other within range of centimeters. Further this makes the transmission error-free and more accurate.

NFC is short-range wireless technology which is incredibly good for transmission and connectivity. It makes tablets, smartphones, wearable devices, payment cards, and laptops smarter than usual. The transfer of data can be conducted very quickly and efficiently. NFC has gripped its roots in the payment industry.

12.5.4   BLUETOOTH AND BLE

Bluetooth plays the crucial role in IoT for data transmission. It is eminently flourishing in IoT for connectivity and data transmission. It is short-range wireless communication that offers rapid and efficient service. Two devices follow the rule of parent–child connection while connecting via Bluetooth. One device plays the role of parent when transmitting the data and other device follows the concept of child at that time when receiving the data. Bluetooth can be connected to seven devices while transmission. It can be considered as a parent can have seven children during transmission via Bluetooth. Bluetooth Beacons are increasing the pace of IoT for indoor. The sole issue with Bluetooth is that it has low bandwidth.

Bluetooth can be classified in two categories, one as Bluetooth classic and another is BLE. Usually, Bluetooth is used in infotainment, speakers, and headphones. BLE is used generally in those devices which consume low power and are equipped with sensors. But Bluetooth devices and BLE devices are not compatible with each other. BLE has been raised as the popular protocol in IoT for connectivity and data transmission.

12.5.5   WIFI

IoT requires diverse connectivity for its various applications. As IoT applications cover the wide range of domains needing efficient connectivity for data transfer.[12] WiFi plays a crucial role in IoT, in terms of efficiency, diversity, device-to-device communication, and rapid transfer of data. WiFi is a wireless transmission protocol for communication and data transfer. It offers short-range connectivity and ease to use.

12.5.6   RFID

RFID is radio frequency identification system. RFID technology transfers the data through radio waves. RFID is an automatic technology used in smart agriculture, data warehouse, retail industry, healthcare, manufacturing, recording metadata, identifying objects, and controlling targets.

12.6   APPLICATIONS OF IOT

The advent of IoT has had a remarkable impact on numerous industries and fields ranging from healthcare to retail and home services. The widespread application of IoT has eased operations in these fields and opened new avenues and introduced new ways of doing the traditional tasks for effectively. Despite this, there is limited cognizance of the real-world application of IoT. The following paragraphs provide a brief snapshot of the application of IoT in key industries or areas of work.

12.6.1   HEALTHCARE INDUSTRY AND HOSPITALS

One of the most prominent areas where IoT has eased operations and interactions in the healthcare industry, especially considering the COVID-19 pandemic.

IoT greatly facilitates the interactions between the doctors, patients, health insurance companies, and hospitals. IoT helps to track the vital and crucial parameters of the patient in real-time. This is made possible using wearable devices such as fitness tracking bands that help monitor the vital parameters of a subject such as heartrate, blood pressure, calorie intakes, patterns of physical activity, etc. The wide range of information is not only available to the patient but can also be transmitted to their doctors or physicians on their smartphones.[5,13] Additionally, relevant software help doctors, hospitals, or care staff to track details of the patient round the clock on their personal devices thereby making it easier to study patient's adherence to the prescribed schedule of medicines, body responses to stipulated treatments, etc.

TABLE 12.2 IoT Enables Communication Technology.

Technology	Features	Remarks	Sources
Cellular network	It connects IoT devices, such as smartphones and computers.	Fully functioning	Cisco, Ericsson
WLAN	It provides users to use Internet while moving from one place to another.	Fully functioning	Cisco,
LPWAN	It is low powered wide area network belongs to class of wireless technology.	Nearly developed	Sigfox, LoRa,
eSIM	Like SIM but have capability to authenticate the identity with the carrier.	Under development	America Movil, Sony, Samsung
TSN	Time-sensitive network offers highly deterministic services in ethernet network is a set of standards.	Under developing	Cisco, Siemens

Even hospitals can track their inventories, medical equipment, patient records with greater ease while minimizing operational errors.[2,3] Without IoT, it has been traditionally challenging for hospitals to manage the vast data of the patients and configure it effectively. Furthermore, the ability to share and access data allows greater transparency between the hospital, patients, and health insurance companies. This adds to one's ability to detect frauds in a timely manner, improve the pace of operational procedures, and smoothen the process of interaction between various stakeholders.[14]

IoT also proved to be helpful in the Covid era. Due to the crucial need of maintaining social distance and limiting one's exposure to the Covid-19 virus, it has become increasingly difficult to access healthcare facilities in the traditional manner. This is where IoT proved to most effective and rewarding. Not only patients were able to consult doctors virtually but could also get their reports, advice while sitting in the comforts of their homes. All this was made possible with the effective infusion of hardware, software, management system, etc.

12.6.2   *RETAIL INDUSTRY*

The retail industry is one of the most complex and demanding industries comprising many departments and various types of operations. The utility of IoT in the retail industry is largely aimed at bettering the experience of its customers, reducing costs, making the supply chains, and logistics more effective, cheaper, and faster. Through IoT technology, retailers can solicit feedback of the customers through various ways. The big data generated can be analyzed to find solutions or new help to improve the retailer's services. IoT is most crucial for supply chains and logistics as it forms one of the main arteries of retail operations.

IoT technology not only helps retailers keep a track of their supplies and consumptions but also make it easy to review other relevant aspects such as expiry, temperatures, perishability, etc. This allows for more effective food quality control and less wastage. In addition, by automating some retail-based operations, retail companies can minimize repetitive tasks, which make it easier to utilize human resource for more advanced operations or for customer-facing roles.

12.6.3   *AGRICULTURE, POULTRY, AND FARMING INDUSTRIES*

The agriculture and farming industries have always evolved with the advancement of technology. This is even true when it comes to IoT technology. IoT is positioned to substantially change the trajectory of agriculture and farming. It has the potential to impact the field starting from understanding the demand of the produce to supplying it. The infusion of IoT and farming is visible in what is known as "smart farming." IoT is likely to be used in numerous ways. Using drones, sensors, and advance machinery, farmers can understand the topography of the farming area and review the relevant parameters such as the soil temperature, soil texture, acidity, etc. This helps in making more informed decisions and judgments. Through various portals and apps, farmers can also keep track of the changing weather conditions, which is crucial in various phases of crop production.

The Internet and many disruptive apps related to the field helped to remove the middle person, which has already made it easier for the farmer to supply their crops to the necessary markets easily. There are a number of multinational companies that have begun pilot projects with IoT technologies to improve the agriculture and farming sectors by providing them real-time image analysis, offering valuable details related to viable sowing periods, seed treatments, accurate weather details; cutting the middlemen in the area of tractor contracting, etc.

Similarly, in poultry, IoT technologies and solutions can be applied starting from basic tasks to complex functioning involving various phases of poultry farming. Applications have been used to monitor hens, their daily feed, nutrition, and meat weight. All these parameters make it easier to detect diseases, overall health, which is essential for poultry owners. Furthermore, it is easier to control the temperature, lighting, and other aspects of the hen's house remotely. All these facilitating factors were not possible through traditional practices of poultry management but are now available at the click of a button. It is IoT technology has transformed all these industries in a span of short time and this trajectory will continue in the coming years.

12.6.4 SMART CITY

As the world toward greater urbanization, the concept of "smart cities" has become an eventuality. It has become the buzzword in many developed and developing countries. The very concept of smart cities embraces the potential of IoT technologies and seeks to utilize them to make more livable and sustainable cities. As noted by Larissa R. Suzuki, in smart cities, "IoT is used to seamlessly interconnect, interact, control and provide insights about the various silos of fragmented systems within cities." In smart cities, IoT can be applied to a range of uses. For instance, IoT can be utilize in smart grids that can help in efficient energy consumption and energy saving. Using technologies to keep track of the building lightings, streetlights, ability to turn them on and off as per requirements, address changes in voltage, energy load across the city, etc., helps in energy conservation and lower costs. Similarly, IoT can be used to better regulate and manage city traffic and public transportations alongside. There have been successful pilot projects where IoT has been used to effectively manage the parking spots in cities so that people do not spend additional amounts of time locating parking spots. These are just some of the applications of IoT. Considering that smart cities entail all areas starting from transports to electricity, education, security, etc., the usage of IoT is limitless and its application in almost any field is going to advance the very idea of a smart cities.

12.6.5   HOME AUTOMATION

Just like the cities have become "smarter," the advent of IoT has made our homes more technologically advanced and smarter to cater to our changing needs. Many companies are involved in the concept of home automation and working toward integrating home appliances, electric controls, lighting systems, home entertainment systems, etc. IoT allows users to control every aspect of the home through their smartphones. It is now possible to switch on or off the air conditioner of one's home from far away, control the lights even when not at home, keep track of one's toddlers while sitting in another room, etc. IoT is also applicable to enhance the overall security of the home. There are many IoT-based security systems that allow one to prevent intrusion, theft, or unwanted access to the home, etc. Furthermore, IoT can also be applied to improve the wiring system of the home, which can be tracked for any faults in the system (in real-time), any loose wire connections, or any potential disasters that can be mitigated through early warning systems.

12.6.6   SUPPLY CHAIN AND LOGISTICS

Regardless of the industry one works in, one of the key aspects includes the supply and delivery of the product to the customers or other businesses in a B2B model. The process of logistics and supply chain is a demanding, time- and manpower-consuming field, and requires unique solution to specific operational challenges or problems. This is where IoT technology plays a crucial role in reducing the time spent in supplying, real-time tracking of driver activities, inventory review, etc. Some of the most prominent applications of IoT technology in supply and logistics include location management system (which tracks the driver and vehicles locations, the status of ongoing deliveries in real-time); tracking inventories, their locations, status; optimization of delivery routes; detecting impending problems before they take place such as spoilage of deliveries, thefts, damage; use of drone-based deliveries. By integrating the various components, IoT solutions allow users to have a comprehensive picture of all parts of the vast supply chain (whether at local level or global level) and notice changes or interruptions in the supply chain.

12.6.7 IOT IN WEARABLE

IoT in wearables is the most ubiquitous trend nowadays. Starting from fitness trackers to smartwatches baby monitoring applications, we see them all around. As covered in the section of healthcare, wearable have made it easier for patients and doctors to easily access data on their phones.[14,15] Wearables are also used for parental control making it easy for parents to monitor the kids' movement in the cribs to making sure that kids are back from school safely, health, and movements of senior citizens.[16] There are also apps for pregnant women to track their pregnancy related developments of the mother and the baby at the same time. Other related things are also recorded such as contractions, changes in vital parameters, movement of the baby not only help track the data but also generate prognosis and reports. Having noted these applications, it must be realized that this area is still relatively underexplored and in the coming years, the world is set to see many new applications when it comes to wearables.[17,18]

12.7 CHALLENGES OF IOT

As IoT has touched every possible area connected with man and its surrounding environment, so the challenges are numerous. Everyday new technologies are emerging and compatibility between them become a serious issue. IoT has opened door for many interesting opportunities but it also laid down various requirements for this. Following are some important and considerable challenges:

1. **Data Integrity:** IoT systems are receiving data from various channels and receivers. There are sensors embedded in devices which continuously send data in big amount. It is exceedingly difficult to identify important and relevant information. Data integrity becomes a big issue if repetitive information is received again and again.
2. **Interoperability:** Lack of a common framework and poor standardization is a big issue when we need to connect various devices. This problem does not allow us to achieve the vision of truly connected devices.
3. **Scalability:** As IoT systems receive data in large volume and in different formats, so the storage of this data becomes a challenge. The system that stores the data must be scalable and should be compatible with latest mining tools.

4. **Designing Issue:** The aim of IoT is to connect the machines without human intervention. Its application can be seen in diverse areas. As more and more systems connect, the designing becomes a prominent issue. It emphasizes on minimum wastage of memory, resources, energy, and processing power. The challenge is to design such systems that are efficient yet focus on less wastage.

5. **Security and Privacy:** The data, which is moving among various devices connected, is vulnerable. This data may be confidential and should be protected from the attacker and unauthorized people. The situation becomes complicated as different devices use different standards and protocols. The security and privacy of data is a major challenge, and a lot of work is going on in this field.

12.8 CONCLUSION

IoT gripping the key role in future technologies and market successfully. IoT utilizes broad range of devices providing its applications in numerous domains. It is the interconnection of different devices via Internet all over the world further offering various services. It involved in day-to-day routine rapidly via connection of smart devices through Internet. The life becomes better and affluent by the use of IoT-enabled technologies and devices.

Still some issues need concerned such as cyber security, hacking, unauthorized users, obscure communication protocols, and security of enormous, to generated data.

Furthermore, even as the application of IoT has gained popularity and tech companies are investing in advancing devices, there are legitimate challenges faced by the industry. Primarily, the industry faces problems due to the constraints of smart objects. To expand, smart objects, which form the backbone of the vision of IoT, tend to be packed with several things, such as microcontrollers, radio transceivers, sensors. These smart objects have limitations when it comes to memory, power, energy efficiencies, computations, especially because all the inserts run simultaneously. Because of such constraints, the performance gets impacted. Another concurrent problem is related to the lack of seamless integration between smart objects and the existing networks, which are not designed to cater to the above-mentioned constraints. Therefore, it is becoming increasingly crucial to design upcoming operations systems, frame ware, network protocol, software in a way that they can compensate for the limitations of the smart objects in order to ensure enhanced IoT tasks and performance. Similarly, the use of IoT in the industry has resulted in challenges when it comes to operations of coexisting devices nearby. Numerous studies have shown that when large-scale devices operate concurrently in crowded industrial, scientific, and medical band, they experience operational interferences. Smart devices have inherent limitations when managing such interferences and these problems get aggravated when new features of IoT technologies are added to the mix.

Having noted the various types of challenges faced by both consumers and industries, it has become incumbent on the producers to resolve the associated problems efficiently and in a timely manner. This is more important because the field of IoT technologies is expanding rapidly and there is a limit window of opportunity to address the insufficiencies and challenges that currently exist.

KEYWORDS

- **IoT Technology**
- **Sensors**
- **Communication**
- **Protocols**

REFERENCES

1. Sobhan Babu, B.; Srikanth, K.; Ramanjaneyulu, T.; Narayana, L. IoT for Healthcare. *Int. J. Sci. Res. (IJSR)* **2014,** *5* (2), 322–326.
2. Baker, S.; Xiang, W.; Atkinson, I. M. Internet of Things for Smart Healthcare: Technologies, Challenges, and Opportunities. *IEEE Access* **2017**. DOI: 10.1109/ACCESS.2017.2775180
3. Bui, N.; Zorzi, M. Health Care Applications: a Solution Based on the Internet of Things. In *Proceedings of the 4th International Symposium on Applied Sciences in Biomedical and Communication Technologies*; ACM, 2011. DOI: 10.1145/2093698.2093829
4. Dziak, D.; Jachimczyk, B.; Kulesza, W. J. IoT-Based Information System for Healthcare Application: Design Methodology Approach. *Appl. Sci.* **2017**. DOI: 10.3390/app7060596
5. Hu, F.; Xie, D.; Shen, S. On the Application of the Internet of Things in the Field of Medical and Health Care. In *IEEE International Conference on Green Computing and Communications and IEEE Internet of Things and IEEE Cyber, Physical and Social Computing*; IEEE, 2013. DOI: 10.1109/GreenCom-iThings-CPSCom.2013.384

6. Jita, H.; Pieterse, V. A Framework to Apply the Internet of Things for Medical Care in a Home Environment. In *Proceedings of the 2018 International Conference on Cloud Computing and Internet of Things*; ACM, 2018; pp 45–54. DOI: 10.1145/3291064.3291065

7. Patrick K.; et al. CYberinfrastructure for COmparative Effectiveness REsearch (CYCORE): Improving Data from Cancer Clinical Trials. *Transl. Behav. Med.* **2011,** 83–88. DOI: 10.1007/s13142-010-0005-z

8. Khalil, N.; Abid, M.; Benhaddou, D.; Gerndt, M. Wireless Sensors Networks for Internet of Things. In *IEEE Ninth International Conference on Intelligent Sensors, Sensor Networks and Information Processing (ISSNIP)*; IEEE, 2014; pp 1–6.

9. Khan, R.; Khan, S. U.; Zaheer, R.; Khan, S. Future Internet: The Internet of Things Architecture, Possible Applications and Key Challenges. In *Proceedings of the 2012 10th International Conference on Frontiers of Information Technology*, 2012; pp 257–260. DOI: 10.1109/FIT.2012.53

10. Ma, X.; Wang, Z.; Zhou, S.; Wen, H.; Zhang, Y. Intelligent Healthcare Systems Assisted by Data Analytics and Mobile Computing. *Wirel. Commun. Mob. Comput.* **2018,** *Article ID 3928080.* DOI: https://doi.org/10.1155/2018/3928080

11. Mishra, P. A.; Roy, B. A Framework for Health-Care Applications Using Internet of Things. In *International Conference on Computing, Communication and Automation (ICCCA)*; IEEE: Greater Noida, India, 2017. DOI: 10.1109/CCAA.2017.8230001

12. Purri, S.; Kashyap, N. Augmenting Health Care System Using Internet of Things. In *8th International Conference on Cloud Computing, Data Science & Engineering (Confluence)*; IEEE: Noida, India, 2018. DOI: 10.1109/CONFLUENCE.2018.8443002

13. Roman, R.; Najera, P.; Lopez, J. Securing the Internet of Things. *Computer* **2011,** *44* (9). DOI: 10.1109/MC.2011.291

14. Sicari, S.; Rizzardi, A.; Grieco, L.; Porisini, A. C. Security, Privacy and Trust in Internet of Things. *Comput. Netw. Int. J. Comput. Telecommun. Netw.* **2015,** *76,* 146–164. DOI: 10.1016/j.comnet.2014.11.008

15. Sethi, P.; Sarangi, S. R. Internet of Things: Architectures, Protocols, and Applications. *J. Electr. Comput. Eng.* **2017,** *Article ID 9324035.* DOI: https://doi.org/10.1155/2017/9324035

16. Sun, W.; Cai, Z.; Li, Y.; Liu, F.; Fang, S.; Wang, G. Security and Privacy in the Medical Internet of Things: A Review. *Secur. Commun. Netw.* **2018.** DOI: https://doi.org/10.1155/2018/5978636

17. Tarouco, L. M.; Bertholdo, L. M.; Granville, L. Z.; Arbiza, L. M. Internet of Things in Healthcare: Interoperatibility and Security Issues. In *IEEE International Conference on Communications*; IEEE, 2012. DOI: 10.1109/ICC.2012.6364830

18. Velasco, C. A.; Mohamad, Y.; Ackermann, P. Architecture of a Web of Things eHealth Framework for the Support of Users with Chronic Diseases. In *Proceedings of the 7th International Conference on Software Development and Technologies for Enhancing Accessibility and Fighting Info-Exclusion*; ACM, 2016; pp 47–53. DOI: 10.1145/3019943.3019951

CHAPTER 13

Health Tracking System Using the Internet of Things

ANSHU YADAV, TANISHA RASTOGI, and DEEPAK KUMAR SHARMA

Department of Information Technology, Indira Gandhi Delhi Technical University for Women, Delhi, India

ABSTRACT

Health has been a major field of concern from the past till today and will remain in future also. In past, mortality rate was higher as compared with present due to lack of proper medication. With the rise in technology and improvement in the quality of education, we are able to control mortality rate to a greater extent. However, in past few years, it has been observed and studied that factors affecting proper health monitoring include lack of time (fast pace), high medication cost, unreachability to remote areas, and so on. Here comes the role of Internet of Things (IoT). IoT is a technology that brings physical objects together for their controlling and monitoring via the Internet. IoT embedded to health tracking system has succeeded at building a bridge between fast pace and health tracking or monitoring. It has made available prior diagnosis to various health problems in pockets of each and every person via smart devices such as a smartwatch, mobile apps, and so on. Various health tracking devices using IoT will be discussed in detail in this chapter.

Each and every object comes in this world with some pros and cons attached to it. IoT also has some cons related to it. These cons are majorly

Internet of Things: Technological Advances and New Applications. Brojo Kishore Mishra & Amit Vishwasrao Salunkhe (Eds.)

listed in terms of security such as security issues related to vulnerable web interface, privacy, authentication, repudiation, and so on. On summing up IoT and health care system, we see that health care system using IoT is much beneficial and advantageous than being disadvantageous (harms due to security and manufacturing cost).

13.1 INTRODUCTION TO IOT

A system that consists of interconnected computing devices, machines that can be either digital or mechanical, human beings or other objects that are served with distinguishing and uncommon attributes and along with that the talent and knowledge to deliver data and information over web without any actual human intervention constitute the Internet of Things popularly known as IoT.[1]

IoT has been used by a large number of industries nowadays to operate and manage the working of its tasks more efficiently and also it helps the company in understanding the needs and demands of customers in a better way, thus providing them with enhanced services.[2] It further improves decision making that ultimately helps in increasing the value and money of the business.

If it is possible to design such computers that are able to know everything and anything about each and every topic without the help of any human, then this would help reduce waste, loss, as well as cost and, we would be able to track and count everything. We would easily know when a particular machine requires replacement, repairmen, or recalling of any part. A part of this job is done by IoT for its users. IoT empowers the devices with such ability that without any human intervention the objects and devices are able to identify as well as understand any situation and take suitable steps to cope with it.

Hence, to sum up we can say that the IoT is such a concept that helps in connecting any device to the Internet or even to already connected devices. It can be assumed to be a giant network of connected objects wherein each object collect and share data along with each other.

Such devices are further connected to a common platform, commonly called the IoT platform, which performs several operations on the data.[3] Firstly, it integrates and combines the incoming data from several devices and objects. Then with the help of analytics, it provides important information to the applications built to address specific requirements.

13.1.1   IOT HARDWARE AND WORKING

IoT ecosystem comprises of many components such as

1. Sensors
2. Devices
3. Embedded processors
4. Communication Hardware

All these components help in the gathering and storage of data that is acquired from the environment. With the help of IoT gateway, the IoT devices share their collected data with each other wherein either the data is examined locally or is sent over the cloud for inspection.

Many times, the IoT devices communicate with each other and work upon the data they get from each other. One of the best qualities that IoT devices display is that they have the ability to perform most of the tasks independently without the requirement of any human mediation.

13.1.2   BENEFITS OF IOT

IoT has brought a number of life-changing applications along with their immense benefits to the human and organizations.[4,5] Some of the benefits are as mentioned below:

1. It helps in monitoring the overall processes going on in the business.
2. IoT has been considered a very good resource for the profit of organizations, due to its ability to improve customer experience that directly helps in the profitability of the company.
3. Since IoT works in such an efficient way, it leads to much less wastage of time and money, thus helps in saving resources.
4. Enhancement of employee productivity has also been a major benefit of IoT.
5. It has the power of integrating and adapting business models that are considered as a major advantage by the organizations.
6. With the help of IoT, employees are able to take better and more accurate business decisions that helps in saving major losses.
7. All in all, it has been observed that inculcatement of IoT in organizations has led to the generation of more revenue and hence resulted in their consistent growth.

With the assistance of IoT, businessmen are able to rethink the ways of approaching their business, markets, and customers since the IoT provides them with appropriate tools to improve their business strategies.

13.2   COMPONENTS OF IOT

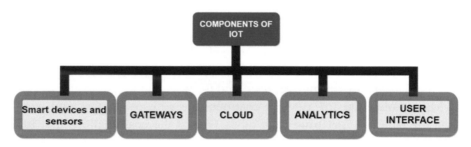

FIGURE 13.1   Components of IoT.

Our devices are becoming intelligent and smarter with the increase of experience and it has been claimed that in upcoming years there will be a lot of visible variations and changes in technologies, precisely IoT.[6] It is defined as a network in which sensors and intelligent devices are interconnected via the Internet to each other.

An unimaginable amount of monitoring and control can be performed by the help of existing sensor nodes provided by the IoT. IoT has perfectly proven its existence and efficiency in every aspect of the industry from small startup companies to giant ventures and corporations. They are able to operate and monitor high-end locomotives and jet engines as well as small home appliances. It also provides extensive monitoring systems that are proved to be enabled by the collection of some cheap and inexpensive constituents such as analytic tools and intelligent sensors. It further helps in providing such devices that not only help in improving the productivity of the owner but also cuts the unnecessary cost.

IoT has proved to not just transform the connectivity among devices and networks but it has also enables people to get the remote access easily and efficiently.[7] But it is to be noted that such a variety of advantages of IoT is achieved with the help of some of the main ecosystem components that IoT works on. The following are some of the main components on which IoT works as shown in Figure 13.1.

13.2.1 INTEGRATING SENSORS TO REAL WORLD DEVICES (DEVICE CONNECTIVITY)

The main components of device connectivity layer (the layer that is responsible for the connection of different distinct devices with each other so as to enable data transfer) are devices and sensors.[8]

These sensors are responsible for the collection of data from the surroundings (i.e., different existing devices) and further transmit this information to the next layer. Also, micro smart sensors are also produced by the help of latest techniques of semiconductor technologies. Some of the common sensors are:

1. Temperature sensors
2. Sensors to check the pressure level
3. Humidity/Moisture level
4. Detectors of the intensity of light
5. Moisture sensors
6. Proximity detection
7. RFID tags

But how are ultimately these devices connected?

The connection of the smart devices and sensors is enabled by the help of low-power nonwired (wireless) networks such as Bluetooth, Wi-Fi, ZigBee, etc. But each of these individual technologies depends on various aspects and thus have their own various pros and cons in terms of efficiency, power generation, energy expenditure, data transfer rate, etc.

IoT has been considered as a boom for low cost and low-power nonwired devices as it provides them with long battery life and a greater amount of efficiency. For achieving energy-efficient data transmission various protocols have been adopted by many companies. One of them is 6LoWPAN- IPv6 that is used over Low Power Wireless Personal Area Networks and has also proven to be very beneficial for them.

13.2.2 GATEWAYS

The connection between the cloud, sensors, intelligent devices, and the controllers is enabled with the help of a physical device (or software program) commonly known as an IoT gateway.[9] All the data passing either to the cloud or away from the cloud has to pass through the established IoT gateway. This can either be a common software program or dedicated hardware. We can also refer to an IoT gateway as a control tier or intelligent gateway.

Data is commonly generated on a daily basis by various sensors in tens of thousands of numbers per second. The gateway is such a device that helps in preprocessing this large amount of data locally before delivering it to the cloud. This preprocessing by the gateway is helpful and recommended as when this data is collected, summarized, and carefully analyzed and evaluated this leads to the reduction in a large amount of data that needs to be sent onto the cloud. If there would have been no gateways and the whole amount of data had to be transferred to the cloud, it would have a major impact on the transmission costs as well as response times.

Also, the IoT gateway is said to provide increased security for the network as well as the data it transfers. IoT gateways have the capability to manage and supervise the information transfer in both directions. So, on one hand, they provide the task of protecting IoT devices from external viruses by providing the required amount of encryption, cryptography, and digital signature techniques, which if not handled can lead to corruption of a large amount of data, and along with that they also protect the data going to cloud from leaks.

IoT gateways are known to perform various important functions such as filtering of data, data processing, providing security, aiding device connectivity, management, and so on.[10]

These days gateways are also becoming an intelligent part of edge device-enabled systems by operating as a platform for application code in which it performs the role of processing the data.

The IoT gateways support and provide the following requirements in order to bridge the gap between IT and OT –

- Trusted Security and connectivity—It ensures that the network is integrated and that too in both the directions.
- Data Bridge—It provides capabilities of bidirectional transfer of information between different types of systems operating using different communication protocols and formats of data.
- Management—It provides with the ability to control and update the access of connected devices to the system as well as policy-based permissions.

Since the use cases of IoT are regularly expanding, thus the demand and popularity of IoT gateways are also getting intensified.

In manufacturing and industrial enterprises, such IoT gateways are required that can confront all the environmental demands and difficulties faced in the real world. If at any point in time, the IoT gateway fails, the whole system fails along with it.

13.2.3 CLOUD

A huge amount of data is gathered and collected from users and devices by the IoT and hence this data has to be managed in a proper and efficient manner. This is where one of the most important components of the IoT, IoT cloud comes into play. IoT cloud provides such tools and techniques that help IoT to manage and store this huge amount of data in real time. Enterprises can easily get access to this data and hence use it for making necessary critical decisions.

IoT cloud is a sophisticated network that provides highly efficient server networks, which are optimally designed to provide fast data processing used in millions of devices and to provide correct analytics on data provided.[11] One of the most crucial factors for IoT cloud is distributed database management system. It combines the various types of devices, sensors, protocols, gateways, etc. present in the environment of the organization. These help enterprises in the development of better tools and technologies for the customers and hence increase the profit of the company.

In future times, IoT devices would become more and more flexible and hence will be able to change the configuration of devices with the help of remote tools and techniques as well as will be able to new applications and services. Further, the security from attackers and invaders would exceed in all the devices. All in all, the main aim is to make IoT devices so self-reliant and self-dependent, that they are able to perform the majority of the tasks performed by humans themselves.

Although at present, it is just the beginning, the future of IoT is emerging at a very fast pace.[12] This is also the reason why such a large amount of investment is being made in specialized IoT devices and servers owing to their increasing popularity and demand in upcoming years.

So, in short, to sum up, we can summarize the benefits and usefulness of cloud for IoT using the following points:

1. Less cost of infrastructure and upfront
2. Decreased cost of computing and storage
3. Availability of highly complexed systems
4. High system capability
5. Increment in the lifespan of sensors and devices

6. Aggregation of huge amounts of data
7. Anything combined with an Internet supply can behave "smartly"

13.2.4 ANALYTICS

The process of transforming analog data received from hundreds of smart devices as well as sensors into such insights, which can be further used for detailed analysis. Analytical solutions are inescapable for the improvement as well as the management of the whole IoT system.

An efficient IoT system is able to provide smart analytical solutions, which serve as a major advantage for the engineers as it helps them in finding out the asymmetry in the data that has been collected and also takes speedy and necessary actions in order to avoid an undesirable scenario.[13] If the data and information are collected accurately at a proper desired time then, the service providers can also prepare for further future steps.

The implementation of tools used in data analytics and the procedures to obtain value from billions of data present and generated via various connected IoT devices is what is called as IoT analytics.

A term in connection to IoT analytics is Industrial IoT. The Industrial IoT helps in collecting and analyzing data gathered from sensors present on smart meters, trucks for delivery, pipelines, equipment, appliances, etc. IoT analytics also serves major benefits for the organizations. These include advantages in health applications, retail apps, or even in data center management and other facilities.

One rather drawback of IoT data is data integration, that is, it is very complex and intricate to integrate IoT data. There are numerous devices present that is not applicable for compatibility with other systems. Hence, the two biggest challenge of IoT development that we are not able to cope up with our data integration and the analytics, which is dependent on it.

Big data is also called as the 3V's model wherein each "V" signify:

1. Volume
2. Variety
3. Velocity

In this, velocity refers to the pace at which the data is processed, variety refers to the large amount and different types of data and devices present, which perform various different functions and last but not the least Volume refers to the humongous amount of data present in billions of numbers.

Hence, the concurrent increase and expansion of all these three factors serve as a major challenge to both IoT analytics as well as big data analytics.

Analytical tools allow the organizations to make good and constructive use of the data present in the following ways[14]:

The volume of data: IoT devices require the usage of a large amount of data. Thus, it becomes the role of the enterprise to manage and work on large amounts of data and also inspect this data for withdrawing relevant information. Data analytic tools can be used for easy and effective analysis of these data sets along with some real-time data provided.

Structure of Data: The data used in applications of IoT may or may not have a variable structure. Also, the data formats present can be of different types. With the assistance and help of data analytics, business executives are able to analyze all the different types and varieties of data with automated tools.

Driving Revenue: With the assistance of IoT analytics in the investments made by the organization, the organizations are able to know about their customers and their preferences and choices in a better way. This would indirectly lead to the enhancement of services as per the demands and expectations of the customer.

Competitive Edge: Use of data analytics in IoT applications provide organizations to offer better services and hence it has proven to increase the amount of competition up to a very large scale.

13.2.5 USER INTERFACE (UI)

Users require a way with the help of which they are able to understand the data collected by IoT. Hence, UI helps the users, that is, the customers to view the data provided by IoT in a better way. In layman language, a UI is a way by which users interact with the computer system. The UI can be anything from software to apps to smartwatches.

UI has various features by which the users interact with the computer. The interaction can be via screens, pages, forms, etc.

User experience is yet another term that is related to the UI.[21] The main between the two is that on one hand, the UI provides a way of interaction in which a user can actually see the things he/she is interacting with, whereas in case of user experience, it provides an overall experience in which the customer has using the product. It includes apps, websites, etc.

Interaction with IoT Solution

Some of the most usual options or ways by which the users can interact with the IoT solution are mentioned below—

1. Auto-generated Notifications: The most common form of interaction is automatic notification or warnings received by the user in case something unusual occurs. The automatic info can be received via short message services, electronic mail, or even phone calls. They are a great source of information that prevents a user from facing any type of loss or mishap.
2. Information Monitoring: There can be a requirement or need and the organization to monitor information in a proactive manner. This could be needed in case the enterprise wants to keep a regular check on some kind of information and hence get warning signs if any unusual activity is realized. Computer, as well as mobile applications, can be used for the same.
3. Remote control over the system: The UI provides yet another advantage to the user, that is, it allows the users to control the IoT system and devices remotely. One such common example of this application is, for example, the user has the ability to turn on and off the buttons of the light of the room, simply with the help of the mob.

13.3   SECURITY THREATS TO IOT

IoT has been recognized as a revolution in the world of IT and business.[15] If IoT can be defined in the simplest ways it can be considered as a day-to-day devices, which have their own computing power and also the ability to send and receive data from and to the Internet.

Devices build on IoT technology play an important role of making our life easier and simpler by managing and helping in tasks that are hard and tiresome for humans to perform. But the exchange of data to the Internet also leads to a lot of issues in protection and security. Following are the security harms to IoT.

13.3.1   *VULNERABLE WEB INTERFACE*

a) This issue highlights those security issues that are concerned with web interfaces embedded into IoT devices. Even though a web interface provides the best possible and easiest technique to a user to interact with complex devices but via this interface, unwanted access can also be gained by attackers that ultimately leads to security issues in the device.

Some of the reasons why our device is vulnerable to such attacks can be due to weak or easily recognizable passwords, weak account settings, private credentials related to accounting exposed in an external network, lack of account lockout, etc.

In order to check for a weak interface, the following methods can be applied -

- We can check that if during the initial product setup the password, as well as the default username, can be changed or not.
- Check that if after three to five failed attempts to log in a user account is locked out.
- By verifying that if we can use methods such as password recovery mechanisms or new user pages in order to identify valid accounts
- An interface can be reviewed for some common issues such as cross-site forgery, SQL injection, etc.

b) But, in order to avoid such issues and attacks, we can make our web interface secure by applying the following techniques:

  i. There should be an option during the initial setup to change the default passwords as well as the default usernames
  ii. We should take into account the robustness of password recovery mechanisms, that is, they should be robust enough and do not provide any kind of information to the attackers regarding the valid account.
  iii. The protection should be such that the private credentials associated with the account are not exposed to external traffic.
  iv. No weak passwords should be allowed to be entered.
  v. The account should get locked after three to five attempts of login.

13.3.2 INADEQUATE AUTHENTICATION/PERMISSION

a) Due to the presence of insufficient mechanisms for authenticating IoT interface and also poor authorization mechanisms in which a user can unethically gain access to higher levels of information, which he/she is not allowed to access.[16] Some of the vulnerabilities related to security that can lead to this can be

1. Passwords being easily detectable, that is, less complex passwords
2. Credentials not being properly protected
3. No Two Factor Authentication is available
4. Password Recovery being insecure
5. Absence of Role-Based Access Control

b) Following are some of the methods that can be adopted in order to protect our devices from such threats and attacks:

I.   Make sure that the passwords required are complex and strong and not simple.
II.   Ensure that access control is present wherever necessary
III. The credentials associated with the account should be protected.
IV.   Usage of Two Factor authentication wherever necessary
V.   Ensuring the security of password mechanisms

13.3.3 *VULNERABLE NETWORK SERVICES*

a) Vulnerable Network Services can lead to weaknesses in the network by allowing the attacker unauthorized access to the private data present of the user as well as to the devices. Some of the security issues that can lead to such attacks are:

1. Services and Networks prone to attack by attackers
2. Overflow in Buffer
3. UDP Services (Exploitable)
4. DOS (Denial of Service)

b) The following methods can be adapted to provide security against these threats:

i.   It is to be ensured that only the necessary ports are available and exposed
ii.   Strict care is to be taken that the services are not affected by buffer overflow
iii   It is to be ensured that fuzzy attacks cannot affect or manipulate our system
iv.   DOS attacks can affect the device of the user as well as other devices or even other users present on the same or other networks. So, it should be noted that our services are not vulnerable to DOS
v.   The ports of the networks should not be exposed to the Internet

13.3.4   *DEFICIENCY OF TRANSPORT ENCRYPTION*

a) The deficiency or lack of transport encryption leads to the exchange of data in an unencrypted format. Encryption helps in providing safety and security to our data from external attackers. Unavailability of encrypted data leads to attack by an attacker on the data and capturing and using this data for their own use. This leads to hindrance in the privacy of the user as well as proves to be harmful to the device itself. The reasons leading to such issues can be:

   i. Presence of Services via the Internet in unencrypted form

   ii Presence of services that are not encrypted and are provided by the mean of Local Network

   iii SSL/TLS being improperly and poorly implemented or being disfigured.

b) Following are some of the methods that can be adopted in order to protect our devices from such threats and attacks:

   1. Making sure that the data that has to be sent over the networks is properly encrypted via various protocols available.

   2. The most suitable protocols are SSL and TLS and hence are recommended for encryption.

   3. In case of absence of SSL or TLS, other encryption techniques can be utilized to keep our data secure.

   4. Keep in mind to use only such encryption standards that are accepted by everyone.

13.3.5   *PRIVACY INVOLVEMENT*

a) Deficiency of relevant security services to the data when there are a large amount of personal and private data available leads to privacy concerns.[17] It is relatively easy to detect and recognize privacy errors by simply reviewing the data that has been collected when the user activates the device. Some other types of automated tools can also be present that can detect the collection of sensitive data.

Following are some of the methods that can be adopted in order to protect our devices from such threats and attacks:

   1. Exposure of unnecessary private and personal information.

   2. Exposure of information in external traffic

b) Following are some of the suggested methods that can be used to protect against this threat—

    i.   Only data that are necessary for the working of the device should be collected

    ii.   It should be tried that no sensitive data is collected, that is, Try to collect only less sensitive data

    iii.   It should be ensured that the data collected is subject to anonymity and de-identified.

    iv.   Ensuring that proper encryption is applied to the data collected.

    v.   The device and its components should be capable enough to keep personal information safe.

    vi.   It should be ensured that only authorized individuals have the right to access any collected private information

    vii.   The users must be provided with an option of "Choice and Notice" if there is a need to collect more data than the desired one.

13.3.6   SUSCEPTIBLE CLOUD INTERFACE

a) This type of security issue deals with problems that emerge due to cloud interface, which is used for interaction with the required IoT device. This typically leads to sending of data in an unencrypted format that indirectly leads to poor authentication and also allows an invader to access the private and personal information and data present. Several vulnerabilities that can lead to this issue are:

    i.   Catalog of the Account

    ii.   No Account layoff

    iii.   Exposure of personal information in external traffic

b) Some of the antidotes that can be adapted to shield against the mentioned above threats are:

Following are some of the methods that can be adopted in order to protect our devices from such threats and attacks:

    i.   During the initial setup of the account, the default passwords, as well as usernames, should be changed.

    ii.   It should be ensured that no one has the capability to enumerate the existing user accounts using functionalities such as a mechanism to reset the passwords etc.

    iii. The account should get locked after four to five failed login attempts.

    iv. It should be ensured that the web interfaces which are cloud-based should not be prone to attacks by XXS, CSRF, or SQL.

    v. The credentials should not be exposed on the Internet at any cost

    vi. If possible two-factor authentication must be used.

13.3.7 VULNERABLE MOBILE INTERFACE

a) Due to the presence of data channels (unencrypted) and weak and slow validation procedure, the attacker and other external entities can easily get the access to the device and hence use the cardinal data of the present IoT device that also uses unsafe mobile applications for better user interaction.

Several vulnerabilities that can lead to this issue are:

1. Catalog of Account
2. No Layoffin Account
3. Leaking of personal information to the external traffic

Following are some of the methods that can be adopted in order to protect our devices from such threats and attacks:

1. During the initial setup, the passwords and usernames must be change.
2. It must be taken care that the accounts of the users should not get enumerated using some specific mechanisms such as reset of passwords etc.
3. The account should automatically get locked after three to five failed attempts of login
4. In case there is a need to connect to wireless networks, the internal information and credentials should not be exposed

13.3.8 POOR SECURITY CONFIGURABILITY

This type of issue is present in case there is no or very little authority given to the users of the device to make changes in the security settings of its device. The insufficiency of security is apparent when there is no option present on the web interface in order to create user permissions or no forcing for the use of strong passwords, etc. This type of negligence further increases the risk of attack to IoT device by giving the attackers unauthorized access to the device. Some of the security susceptibilities that lead to such an issue are-

1. Absence of Grained Permission system
2. Absence of options for secure password
3. Lack of monitoring in security

Mentioned below are some countermeasures that can be used for protection against the above-mentioned threats:

1. Add functionality due to which administrative users can be differentiated from common normal users.
2. The data should be made safe with encryption at transit and rest.
3. The device must be able to force the use of strong passwords
4. The logging of security events must be enabled
5. The users should be informed about the security events from

13.3.9   VULNERABLE SOFTWARE/FIRMWARE

a) If a particular device is not able to get auto-updates, it possesses a high level of security issue for its own. The device should be intelligent enough to get updated whenever it faces security issues. Also, the updates of software can turn out to be harmful and insecure if the updated files and the network connection on which the updation is being carried out are not protected. The updates can turn out to be insecure even when the files involved have hardcore sensitive data such as personal credentials. Once the credentials get leaked to an external network, it leads to huge problems for the people as well as the company.

Some security vulnerabilities that are responsible for this issue are mentioned below-

1. If fetching of data and updates takes place without encryption.
2. The files to be updated are not gone through encryption phase
3. Unverified updates at the time of upload
4. Firmware containing personal credentials is one of the major reasons for this issue.
5. No obvious update functionality present in the device.

Mentioned below are some countermeasures that can be used for protection against the above-mentioned threats:

1. It is to be ensured that the device has the feature to get updated automatically
2. Better encryption methods are used to encrypt the updated file.
3. The transmission of the updated file should take place through an encrypted medium.
4. The updated files should not expose personal data
5. Before allowing the update to get applied and uploaded, it must be ensured that the update is verified as well as signed
6. The security of the update server must be ensured.

13.3.10 INADEQUATE PHYSICAL SECURITY

a) The weakness in physical security can exist if an attacker is able to get access to a device and with the help of which can access the stored private and sensitive information. Weakness can also be present due to the usage of external ports in order to access the devices meant for maintenance. All these can result in invalid access to the data as well as the device.

Some of the susceptibilities that can lead to this issue are:
i. Usage of USB ports to get access to software
ii. Storage Media Removal

Mentioned below are some countermeasures that can be used for protection against the above-mentioned threats:

i. It must be ensured that the data storage medium should not be easily removable
ii. The stored data must be encrypted at rest
iii. Attackers must not be able to use USB or any other external port to access the device without permission
iv. For the product to function correctly, only external and not internal ports such as USB, etc. should be used
v. The product must be able to limit the capabilities of the administration.

IoT devices are a great source to make our lives more comfortable and easier. But, in case the issues related to security are not kept in mind and taken care of, these devices can cause a lot of trouble than what they are worthy of.

13.4   HEALTH TRACKING SYSTEM AND IOT

13.4.1   IMPORTANCE OF HEALTH TRACKING SYSTEM AND MONITORING

With the evolution of time, medical science has advanced in its tools and technologies. This evolution has been one of the major reasons behind the controlled mortality rate over the years. However, with the advancement of medical science, the revolution in the industrial sector and others can also be noticed. This growing industrialization, competitive world, and fast pace have been proved to be some of the significant factors in creating a considerable gap between human and nature. Also, not only this, in today's world human has no time to spare on himself or herself until and unless one of the serious health problems knockdowns to their doors.

The only solution to control some of the major health-hazardous problems such as cardiovascular diseases is prediagnosis. Visiting a hospital all the time for today's person is not possible due to several reasons such as lack of time(fast pace), unreachability (large distance to a recognized and reputed hospital), reluctant nature (do not want to adopt any changes in daily routine), and so on. Somehow, even if we make people aware of these concerned areas there lies another barrier in the success path. This barrier is related to the hospital management system and the cost incurred in prediagnosis tests. In a vast and developing country such as India with a population of about 136 crores (as in 2019),[18] it is not possible to attend each and every patient with proper care and attention. Also, when it comes to priority, serious patients are given more attention and care as compared to those who are there for a routine checkup or prediagnosis.

One of the states changing solutions to this problem is Smart Devices. These smart devices are a result of evolved computer science technology that is capable of gifting us an efficient, portable, and cost-effective instrument in the form of the health tracking system or health monitoring devices. The health tracking system or health monitoring devices have been proved a blessing of god and scientists due to the characteristics mentioned in the figure below (Figure 13.2).[19]

Portable: One of the major problem related to each age group is of handling health tracking devices. Some are giant in size, some are difficult to operate, and some can only be handled by an expert. Because of these reasons, a patient is even bound to stay on the bed in one of the hospitals for proper monitoring after the treatment also. It clearly, demands a technology that is easy to operate, cheaper, small in size, and lightweight or we can say an object or instrument that is portable.

FIGURE 13.2   Characteristics of health tracking system.

Cheaper: While developing a smart device such as health tracking system, one needs to take care of the budget it includes. As developing some of the necessary functionalities are more than enough to save pockets of average-earning human on the planet. Developing a device is only worth if people can afford it and use it for their benefits.

Availability: These devices work 24*7 and hence are more alert than any of the human being to track and report on changes taking place in our body so as to contribute toward detection of any major health issue. Also, they are available on-demand, there is no time and space delay faced by the user.

Simplification: These devices are easy to operate. They behave as a black box, where an individual is only supposed to interact with the UI without knowing the actual working. Moreover, the UI is less or more similar to the one we deal with in our day to day life, that is, smartphones, laptops, and so on.

Multifunctionality: Multifunctionality helps in stabilizing a patient on time by detecting the symptoms prior to any major health issue and is also capable of reporting to a concerned doctor connected to that smart device.

13.4.2   THE NEED FOR IOT

As the name suggests IoT is a technology used to connect a number of real-world objects to the Internet via which they share information and actions are taken accordingly. Before the invasion of the IoT in the health care system, patient's interaction with the physician was limited to the visits, tele, and text communication. However, IoT has brought a revolutionary change in the world of a health-tracking system. Using IoT smart devices one can easily be in touch with their physician for regular monitoring from home only. It has enabled the capability to make patients feel safe and healthy via remote monitoring. Applications based on IoT construct in healthcare proves to be beneficial for physician, hospitals, patient, and insurance companies.[20]

13.4.3   IOT APPLIED TO THE HEALTH TRACKING SYSTEM

IoT AND PATIENT: devices including a fitness band and some other devices based on wireless technology such as heart rate monitoring cuffs, glucometer, blood pressure monitoring cuffs, and so on. provide patients with access to epitomized attention. Other than the mentioned functionalities, tuning can be set in the devices so that they help people in reminding appointments, a regular check on exercise, variations in blood pressure, calorie count and so more.

IoT has been a life-changer for different age groups, especially the elder one. It has enabled continuous tracking of a patient's health. On noticing any kind of abnormal change in the activity of a person, an alert generative mechanism gets activated and performs by sending a notification to the loved ones and caretaker including a family member or a clinical health provider.

IoT AND PHYSICIAN: As mentioned under IoT for the patient, wearables give patients a path to epitomized monitoring. Thus carrying such type of wearables along with some home monitoring equipment, enables physicians with the capability of keeping track of their patients' health in a more effective way. Tracking of patient's compliance along with the treatment arrangements or any other immediate call required for better medical care becomes easy. Also, it enables proactive communication in order to set an effective mean of communication between the professionals of healthcare and patients. Data gathered via IoT-enabled devices to prove to be helpful for physicians in availing the best possible treatment process to their patients and to make the actual outcome as close as possible to the expected one.

IoT AND HOSPITALS: Other than monitoring of patient's health, IoT prove to be useful in the various hospital system. IoT-enabled devices ingrained with sensors are highly utilized in the purpose of apprehending in real-time such as the positioning of medical devices like oxygen pumps, wheelchairs, nebulizers, and so on. The stationing of the medical staff in different places can be carried out in real-time.

The proliferation of diseases is one of the major matter of worry for patients staying in hospitals or visiting for a check-up. IoT-based sanitation auditing devices help patients in getting rid of the infection. IoT devices are also helpful in the management of asset such as environmental monitoring, and pharmacy inventory control, for instance, checking humidity and temperature of the refrigerator and controlling of temperature.

IoT AND HEALTH INSURANCE COMPANIES: There is a wide range of opportunities available for the health insurers based on IoT that is a system of interconnected intelligent devices. Now, insurance companies can make use of data gathered from these smart devices to design their claims, terms, and policies. The data gathered help in fraud claim detection and prospect identification for underwriting. An IoT device is a door to transparency. They serve as a medium for bringing clarity among insurers and customers in the cover, claim handling, pricing, and processes related to the evaluation of risk. With the lightning of rising technology such as IoT, customers will be able to have adequate visibility into the underlying concept forming the basis for every critical decision making and process outcome.

To exploit the benefits of data gathered from the users, insurance companies offer incentives to their customers. They may also reward their customers for using IoT-based devices in order to promote their uses among the customers so that they can have an eye on their routine activities an adherence to precautionary health measures and treatment plans. IoT devices can also help the insurance company invalidating claims based on the data or information gathered via these devices.

Overall, we can conclude that IoT is a key to the door of immense opportunities. Data gathered from all the interconnected devices has the potential to transform healthcare [21-27].

IoT works in four stages as shown below in the diagram (Figure 13.3),

1. DEVICES (Step 1): It includes the interconnected IoT devices via the Internet. This step serves as the medium for raw information used further for decision making.
2. DATA AGGREGATION AND PREPROCESSING (Step 2): Data gathered from the devices is usually in raw form that is an analog

form, which needs to be processed to convert it to a structured form that is digital.

FIGURE 13.3   Stages of working related to IoT.

3. DATA STORAGE (Step 3): After standardization, the data is stored in the database. Most preferred storage is cloud storage that adds to storing data provide security to the data.
4. DATA ANALYSIS (Step 4): Data analytics is carried out at the required level, which helps in focusing in-depth knowledge hidden in the gathered and standardized data.

IoT proves to be useful due to the following characteristics:

1. It reduces monitoring cost and saves time by saving money and time supposed to be spent on each and every visit to the doctor by providing real-time monitoring at home only.
2. It has enabled diagnosis of disease at a fast pace via continuous monitoring and analyzing data gathered in real-time.
3. Improved treatment by using the meaningful information gathered after standardization and analysis and so on.

13.5 HEALTH TRACKING DEVICES

13.5.1 CANCER TREATMENT

The IoT technology can be used for the treatment of cancer by securely integrating the technology of wireless communication for various medical procedures such as monitoring, alerting, chemotherapy treatments, and follow-up. Treatment provided for cancer using IoT technology can be enhanced and made more impactful by attaching WSN that is Wireless Sensor Networks to the patients such that data related to changes taking place inside the body, effects, and allergies due to consumption of recommended drugs by the physician to the concerned patient, complications, any missed medication by the patient, hemoglobin level sensing and monitoring, and so on can be reported to the physician and required changes can be made to the ongoing medication process immediately that is before the arousal of any serious health problem. Using the technology of IoT, a patient can be given care from friends, family, and physician by remotely monitoring the ongoing changes and analyzing the data gathered from all the connected smart devices by making early decisions at right time.[28]

According to a trusted source,[29] in June 2018, data from a random clinical trial of around 357 patients were presented at the ASCO Annual Meeting. The trial was carried out on the basis of usage of Bluetooth-based hand-net and sphygmomanometer, along with an application designed for the purpose of symptom tracking. At the same time updates related to the patient's health were sent to the physician via WSN technology so that necessary changes can be brought to the treatment every weekday.

The smart device used for the trial as mentioned above was named cyber-infrastructure for comparative effectiveness research (CYCORE).

CYCORE—Patients use sensors while in-home or out in the community. The sensors used by the cancer patients used to transmit their data to the Sensor Hub. The Sensor Hub is a small plug-in home computer that is capable of transmitting data to the back-end Cyber Infrastructure (CI). Along with the use of sensors, patients also use a smartphone to answer assessments, which are automatically sent to the CYCORE's Cyber Infrastructure. According to the policies of CYCORE, once the data is uploaded to the Cyber Infrastructure, it is automatically relayed to the authorized physicians or clinical team. The data gathered from all the cancer patients provide an opportunity for the researchers to exploit that data to study various aspects related to cancer and symptoms related to it. As a result, the group of researchers ends up designing some algorithms, filters, and visualizations on the data. In case of any malfunctioning cyber operators manage the user accounts and maintain the Cyber Interface (CI). Interaction between different entities is shown in the Figure 13.4.

On comparing the patients who followed regular weekly visits to the physician without any additional smart monitoring with those who used CYCORE the smart monitoring system it was found that the patients who followed CYCORE experienced symptoms which were less severe related to cancer and its treatment.

After analyzing the whole experts from well-recognized research institutes[29, 30] said that smart technology helps in simplification of treatment for both patients, clinical providers, and loved ones by relying on the principle of early diagnosis enabled by studying data gathered from these smart devices.

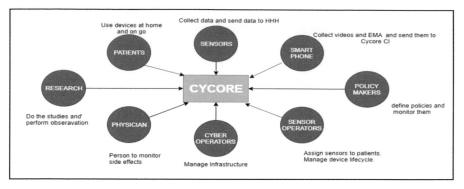

FIGURE 13.4　CYCORE (Cyberinfrastructure for comparative effectiveness research).

13.5.2　SMART CONTINUOUS GLUCOSE MONITORING (CGM)

Understanding the glucose-insulin system and knowledge related to the concentration of glucose in blood proves to be a key point in the examination and cure of diabetes. The adoption of signal processing techniques on information related to the glucose level is not the production of a new era.[31–33] During the gray time, studies were devoted to data gathered from self-monitoring blood glucose method.[34]

From the last 10 years, new scenarios were introduced to the treatment of diabetes. It was started with the invasion of CGM sensors in the health care system, which enabled monitoring of glucose concentration on a continuous basis for several days.[35-42] For a more practical insight into the study of glucose time series, contemplative analysis of CGM is preferred instead of date obtained from self-monitoring blood glucose. In addition to this CGM devices provide recording of ups and downs in level of glucose in real-time.

CGM signals are the fundamental element of the artificial pancreas. Artificial pancreas is a solution specially designed to help patients suffering from type 1 diabetes with the aim of limiting glucose level to the safe ranges. It is carried out by injecting insulin simultaneously using a pump guided by the closed-loop algorithm.[43] Type 1 diabetes is found in about 5 percent of people and is not present in one from birth. It is equally likely in each and every person irrespective of age and gender.[44] Insulin is a hormone involved in the movement of sugar or glucose into the body tissues. This glucose is used by the body cells as fuel. Damage to these cells hinders the process of formation of insulin. As a result, glucose stops moving into the body cells and results in building a heap of it into the blood and body cells starved of glucose. This leads to the problem of high blood sugar that in turn give rise to many other problems.[45]

However, CGM acts as a god gift to such problems. One of the major roles of CGM sensors is to generate alerts whenever the concentration of glucose level is assumed to exceed the normal threshold levels.[46] However, such applications rely on sensors forming the basis for CGM working to behave smartly by using algorithms capable of interpreting glucose levels in real-time.

At the same time there are few challenges faced by CGM as mentioned below:

1. CGM data needs to be calibrated accurately.
2. In order to improve the SNR value, CGM data needs to filter.
3. Some proper and suitable modeling methodologies should be hired for the prediction of future glucose concentrations.
4. Detecting false/missing true events should be minimized significantly.

13.5.3 INSULIN DELIVERY SYSTEM BASED ON CLOSED LOOP ALGORITHM

One of the most engrossing areas in the field of IoT applied health tracking system is an initiative including open-source artificial pancreas system. It is an insulin system based on a closed-loop algorithm (Figure 13.5). Artificial pancreas systems have the capability of taking the technology to the next level by the integration of CGM with a smart algorithm-guided insulin pump, which is responsible for automating the delivery of insulin.[47] Open Artificial Pancreas System differs from CGM in the way used for quantifying the amount of glucose present in a patient's bloodstream.

Automating the insulin delivery system proves to be a life-changing strategy for diabetic patients. OpenAPS works by keeping an eye over blood glucose level and then making necessary adjustments in the amount of insulin delivery in their system automatically such that the blood glucose level remains in a safe range. It helps in preventing cases of extreme highs also known by the name of hyperglycemia that is excessively high glucose and extreme lows also known by the name of hypoglycemia that is excessively low glucose.

The automatic insulin delivery system has ensured safe sleep through the night for diabetic patients without any danger of a drop in their blood sugar level, medically know by the name of night-time hypoglycemia.

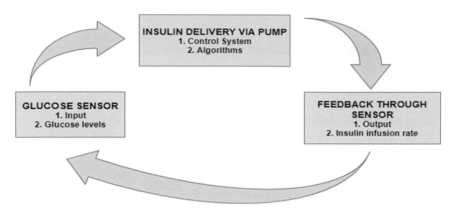

FIGURE 13.5   Closed loop algorith.

13.5.4   *CONNECTED INHALERS*

With the development in the technological field, the way of approaching the long-term conditions is changing. Opportunities to harness these innovations now aim at improving ways of managing and self-managing a condition. In the case of the major health issue found in every age group that is Asthma, technology has been the potential to develop new ways to deal with the persistent challenge around care. Here comes the role of smart health devices that are described as the linking of traditional health devices with smart technologies such as smartphones, which provides an opportunity of self-management to the people to track their inhaler use, avoid triggers and recognize worsening symptoms as in case of Asthma.

One of the commonly used traditional health device available for the medication of Asthma and chronic obstructive pulmonary disease (COPD) includes Inhalers. With each inhalation, the device is designed to deliver a specific dose to the lungs. The assumption made in a very general case is the correct method of using the device as opted by the patients. However, in the real world, situations are not like the assumptions we make in the vicinity. According to some of the trusted studies and researches,[48] it has been noticed that patients often face problems while adopting the correct inhaler technique which in turn implies receival of insufficient medication by the patients. This situation has been observed in both the cases of metered-dose inhalers and dry powder inhalers, leading to degraded control over disease and increment in cost related to healthcare.[48] As a result, healthcare cost associated with a patient with no proper control over health tracking to the one with proper control over health tracking is approximately double. This has been a serious challenge in both the cases of asthma as well as COPD.

According to the results of an in vitro lung deposition study mimicking real-life patient technique and variable inspiratory flow rates, it has been observed that patients make at least one mistake while using inhaler as often as 70–90% of the time, resulting in only 7–4% of the drug being delivered to the lungs.[49] Some of the biggest and most serious errors observed while using an metered-dose inhaler are related to patient inhalation as listed below:

1. Co-ordination between inhalation and triggering the dose release of the inhaler: A short delay can result in only 20% of the medication being actually delivered to the lungs.
2. Breathing problem: Breathing deeply is one of the key points for asthma and COPD patients. However, not breathing deeply enough might cause another problem of 10 percent less medication being actually reaching to the lungs.

Now, the solution to these common errors is already available in the form of a device, which works by measuring patient inhalation airflow. This device has resulted in improved medication, reduced healthcare costs and at the end, improved patient outcomes (Figure 13.6).

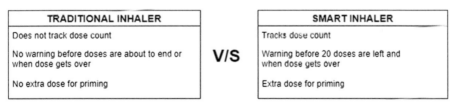

TRADITIONAL INHALER		SMART INHALER
Does not track dose count		Tracks dose count
No warning before doses are about to end or when dose gets over	**V/S**	Warning before 20 doses are left and when dose gets over
No extra dose for priming		Extra dose for priming

FIGURE 13.6 Comparison of traditional inhaler and smart inhaler.

13.5.5 INGESTIBLE SENSORS AND SMART PILLS

It is one of the creations of technology in the field of the healthcare system, which has enabled remote monitoring of a patient by the family and the physician to ensure safe and regular treatment of the patient even from a distance far away. Notifications related to the taking of medicine on time by the patient can be easily popped up to the connected family member and the physician so that treatment can be completed without any missing dosage.[50] The pills included under the system are not the regular ones. They are smart pills (Figure 13.7) consisting of a one-square-millimeter sensor coated in copper and magnesium. The specialty of these pills lies in the fact that both the metals being used in the coating are digestible in nature. The working of the sensor attached to the smart pill start upon swallowing of the pill. As soon as the pill is swallowed electrolytes activate the sensors within the body and start communicating by transmitting a signal to a small, patch placed on the patient's torso and sending the information to the connected family member's smartphone or the physician's smartphone via Bluetooth.

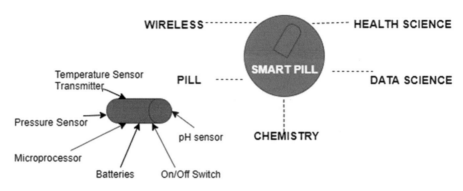

FIGURE 13.7   System design of smart pill.

Such systems like proteus help in controlling the cases where the patient obliterate to follow the recommended medication. Also, in some cases, patients are found following medication in the wrong way. For example, a patient may be mixing two or more medicines or consuming it in a wrong dose that can prove to be fatal. This is a growing concern especially in cases of senior citizens. Ingestible are working to address such issues and toward the improvement of medical health.

Another application of ingestible and smart pills includes an invasive colonoscopy. Mere swallowing of a smart pill has the power of replacing one of the traditional medical technique used for looking inside the large intestine to test any medical issues such as abdominal pain, rectal bleeding, changes in bowel habits, and many more.

It has been achieved by developing a battery-powered camera pill that has the capability of taking the speed up photos of the intestinal tract and then the captured photos are sent to another device placed on the patient's waist followed by the transferring of images to a computer or tablet for the physician use. There might arise a situation where the patient may hesitate on the consumption of a camera-attached pill. However, in reality, it is not the matter of concern as the tablet has been approved by the United States

Food and Drug Administration, which is more than enough to ensure safe consumption of the pill. The device has been named as PillCam COLON by the developing company. The test performed by the noninvasive technology can be used to view the gastrointestinal tract and colon in order to catch polyps so as to figure out the first indicator of colorectal cancer and in this way it helps in promoting the idea of prediagnosis.

Challenges to Ingestible and smart pills:

1. Resistive nature toward consumption of a metallic coated pill or a camera attached pill
2. Harm to the privacy of the patient
3. Possible side-effects, and so on.

However, companies are continuously working toward availing trusted and reliable medical solutions to the patients in the field of ingestible and smart pills. Also, at the same time, some companies are ready to move toward a more strong, challenging but life-changing technology for the patients.

13.5.6   CONNECTED CONTACT LENS

Researchers have introduced a new method of communication between devices that has enabled a number of devices such as contact lenses, brain implants, and small electronic wearables to communicate to the devices of every daily life such as smartphones, watches, and so on.[51] This new method of communication has been named as interscatter communication by the team of researchers.

Interscatter communication processes via carrying out a conversion of signals from Bluetooth into Wi-Fi communication. Moreover, the whole process can be carried out only by using the underlying technology of reflections.

Wireless communication for instilled devices can divert the way we handle some of the attention-seeking diseases such as chronic diseases. However, due to their size and location theses devices lack behind because of the power demands required to deliver the data using conventional wireless transmissions. To overcome the constrained imposed by the traditional method of wireless technology, the team of researchers has developed a method using which devices with power constraint can communicate with each other using standard Wi-Fi technology. Systems supporting such technology are not required to be specialized in some sort of equipment. They completely rely on mobile devices that are generally available with people. Generating Wi-Fi transmission based on mobile devices consumes energy 10,000 times less than conventional methods.

Bluetooth devices use the process of scrambling to randomize data transmission. The team of researchers figured out a method of reverse engineering applied to the process of scrambling so as to send out a signal that is a single tone in nature from Bluetooth devices. However, the challenge lies in the process of backscattering, which is responsible for the creation of an undesirable mirror image that is the copy of the signal. This results in increased bandwidth and interference. To overcome this drawback a technique known as "single sideband backscatter" in order to remove the unwanted outgrowth.

Smart Contact Lenses (Figure 13.8) helps in monitoring many health-related problems. Mainly they can be used to monitor diabetic patients.

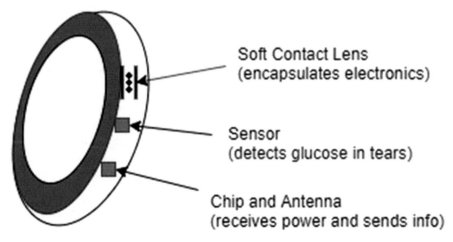

FIGURE 13.8   Smart contact lens.

Applying interscatter communication to contact lenses, engineers developed a smart contact lens embedded with a tiny antenna. Here the smartwatch acted as a source of Bluetooth signal. The antenna attached to the contact lens able to shape Bluetooth signal. Other than this they carried out the functionality of encoding data from the contact lens and then converting it to the Wi-Fi signal. The encoding and conversion were done in such a way that made it readable by any other device. Although the structure for a connected contact lens may appear to be quite complicated the benefits it provides are significant and valuable from the medical point of view. In response, it is capable of sending a notification to the connected family member or the physician for remote and timely monitoring.

13.5.7 APPLE WATCH MONITORING DEPRESSION

Studies on medical health have found depression as one of the major public health issues. Other than being a health issue it has been proved as a major reason behind rising suicidal cases.[52] The diagnosis of depression proves to be a challenging task due to the lack of laboratory tests. As a result, this has made psychiatrists to completely build on the clinical syndrome. Moreover, the absence of pathognomonic signs[53] has imposed the use of clinical syndromes, which are not much reliable. As an attempt toward achieving reliability of diagnosis researchers introduces operational criteria. The operational criteria defined found to be one essentially counting symptoms of depression with little regard for context, coping, personality and stress. Epidemiological[54] studies based on depression make use of trackable instruments, which failed to evaluate conditions related to stress and hence are not capable enough to address short-term adjustments.[55] It is because of flexible concepts of depression and the tough applications of the diagnostic hierarchy and criteria that the people with depression secondary to disease, people who confront below par with depression with the common requirements of life and normal people under severe stress qualifies for the major depression.

Cognitive[56] testing provides an opportunity to detect and understand the patterns of cognitive symptoms found in patients with a major depressive disorder that is MDD. It helps in monitoring people outside the lab in the real world and day-to-day life, which helps in maximizing patients engagement and provide potential treatment.

Ability to collect information or data from real-world helps in developing a project or a device relying not on the assumptions and imaginations made by the researcher. However, it helps in developing a project based on day-to-day statistics related to the concerned field of study and developing a solution capable of resolving problems, which are being faced by the people in the real world. Also, It helps in differentiating the product in the competitive market while also satisfying the demands of patients. A solution being developed in real-world evidence helps in improving health outcomes for patients with reduced medical costs. However, on another hand developing a device outside the boundaries of clinical settings in the real world requiring compliance from patients and a little invasion to their privacy proves to be a challenging task.[57]

How wearable (system architecture is shown in Figure 13.9) can be used to reliably collect data from the real world

Cognition Kit developed by the team cognition is one such platform made for measuring real-world cognitive health, which enables a researcher to work on real-world data and clinical to make better treatment decisions. Features of cognition kit include real-world cognition, no need for laboratory coats, high-frequency measurement, and gold-standard science.[58]

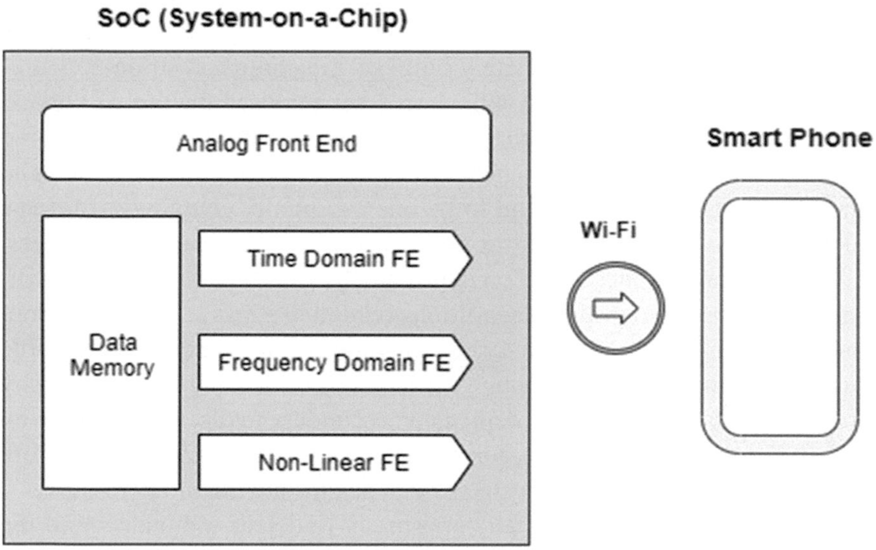

SoC (System-on-a-Chip)

FIGURE 13.9　Wearable depression monitoring system.

1. REAL-WORLD COGNITION: Cognition Kit has been designed to work in real-world rather than within clinic boundaries. Tests carried by cognition kit fit into everyday life and can be carried out during the day-to-day activities such as meetings, walking, or just before the bed.
2. NO REQUIREMENT OF LABORATORY COATS: As mentioned before, the cognition kit works in the real world. Therefore, it eliminates the usage of white laboratory coats and proves to be a time saver and a reliable solution for both researchers and clinicians.
3. HIGH-FREQUENCY MEASUREMENT: Cognition Kit allows measurement of cognition several times a day, which enables it to capture daily fluctuations.
4. GOLD STANDARD SCIENCE: Cognitive tests are validated against CANTAB battery. CANTAB stands for Cambridge Neuropsychological

Test Automated Battery[59] that includes highly sensitive, precise, and objective measures of cognitive functions. CANTAB tests have proved sensitive to the detection of changes in neuropsychological performance. It is said to be built on gold standard science because CANTAB is seen as a gold standard in cognitive testing.

13.5.8 COAGULATION TESTING

Clotting helps to prevent excessive bleeding in case injuries. However, it is to be noticed that clots should not form in the blood moving through vessels. In case, these clots start forming then there are high chances that these blood clots might reach to the heart, lungs, or brain via the bloodstream. As a result, it may cause a heart attack, stroke and hence can prove to be fatal. Coagulation tests are meant to measure the ability of blood to develop a clot, and the time required to clot.

Clotting disorders may prove to be fatal in cases of excessive bleeding or clotting. Various tests available for coagulation includes Complete Blood Count, bleeding time, and so on.[60] These tests act by measuring different proteins and the way they process.

Several conditions that may cause problems related to coagulation are listed below:

1. Liver disease
2. Thrombophilia, case of excessive bleeding
3. Hemophilia, inability to clot in a normal way

Coagulation tests are useful for monitoring people undergoing some medication that may affect clotting ability. Also, it is recommended before surgeries to ensure the necessary precautions.

A device for patients with the functionality enabling the user to test their own blood coagulation parameters is CoaguChek Vantus.[61] The device looks similar to a cellular phone having Bluetooth connectivity that enables it to dump International Normalized Ratio readings recorded by it to the patient's smartphone. Next, to it, these readings are then automatically forwarded to the connected physician and family member. The idea while developing this device was to reduce visits to the clinic and at the same time keeping things simpler and easier to keep track of patients ensuring successful remote monitoring. If the device is set up and used correctly, it can alleviate any other manual tracking of coagulation readings. With advancing medical science there is a race of developing tools and technology that are favorable to both the patients and the physicians. This device proves to be a cost-effective solution on part of users and a reliable mean of continues monitoring in real-world for the physicians helping them to improve methods opted for treatment from time to time.

13.5.9   APPLE'S RESERCH KIT AND PARKINSON'S DISEASE

Parkinson's Diseases

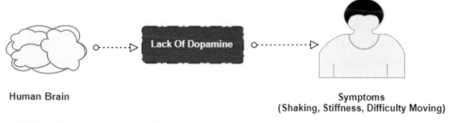

FIGURE 13.10   Parkinson's disease.

It is a progressive nervous system disorder that affects the movement of a person. Symptoms that can be noticed for the diseases start occurring very gradually (Figure 13.10). It can barely noticeable tremor in a hand. Prediagnosis of Parkinson's disease is very difficult as there are many chances that the face of an affected person might show little or no expression. Parkinson's disease gets worse over time.[62] Parkinson's diseases are tough to be cured almost next to impossible. However, attempts are made with the hope of improvement in the symptoms. For the same, doctors may suggest some surgical methods to regulate certain regions of the brain resulting in some improvements in the symptoms.

Some of the common surgical methods for treating Parkinson's disease include Pallidotomy, Thalamotomy and Deep Brain Stimulation.[63] It is to be noticed that these surgical methods have opted only when medicines fail to treat.

Pallidotomy

According to the studies on Parkinson, it has been found that one of the reasons behind Parkinson is the hard-working of a part of the brain called globus pallidus. This behaves like a break and makes the movement of the body tougher. Pallidotomy named is based on globus pallidus. It includes the destruction of globus pallidus to make patients feel better. As a result, it helps in making a patient suffering from Parkinson less rigid, improve body balance and make body movement easy. Also in the case of patients with advanced Parkinson, it helps medicines to work in a better way.

Thalamotomy

According to researchers tremors are due to trouble with the thalamus. Thalamus is known for controlling balance and the one responsible for making one to feel his or her arms and legs. The process carried out as a part of thalamotomy includes the destruction of the things of a part of thalamus in order to block things that are responsible for causing tremors. This treatment is only used to control tremors.

Along with the mentioned pros, there are some cons in the form of serious side effects related to the mentioned treatment. Therefore, doctors use them less frequently for treating Parkinson.

Deep Brain Stimulation

Under these electrodes are implanted in some of the areas of the brain. These electrodes function by generating impulses that acts by restricting other impulses that may cause the disease. A device similar to pacemaker[64] goes under the skin in the chest to control the impulses.

Monitoring Parkinson's Symptom Using Apple Watch

A new application in the form of API has been added to open source Research Kit framework of Apple. The API has been designed to continuously monitor Parkinson's disease symptoms. Continuous monitoring has been achieved based on two of the significant symptoms related to Parkinson's disease that are Tremors and Dyskinesia.[65] As mentioned before Tremors are related to shaking and quivering and Dyskinesia is related to the side-effects of treatments for Parkinson's that is responsible for causing fidgeting and swaying motions in patients.

At the current scenario, a physician asks a patient to undergo physical diagnostics tests to figure out the severity of these symptoms. In some cases, patients are often asked to keep diaries in order to record several symptoms when they are not present in the clinic. This is in reference to provide the physician with a wider view angle toward the symptoms. The motive of designing Movement Disorder API for Apple Watch users is to bring automation and continuous evaluation to the field of Parkinson for better treatment. Using the concept of automation and continuous evaluation, apps are able to present the data for patients and physicians in a graph representation so as to extend the view angle to the reports associated to hourly breakdowns in spite of limiting it to the daily breakdowns. It helps in gathering data related to hourly and minute fluctuations.

13.5.10   ADAMM ASTHMA MONITOR

Asthma is a condition in which airways get narrow and swell and start producing extra mucus. As a result, it creates a problem in breathing. Also, it is characterized by coughing, wheezing and shortness of breath.[66] In some cases, asthma is just minor trouble while in others it is a major problem. In major cases, it becomes a source of interference in daily activities and may also prove to be fatal leading to a life-threatening asthma attack. Asthma is a medical problem that can not be cured of the root. However, one can control its symptoms by following proper medication at the right time. As asthma keeps on spreading with time, therefore it becomes very important to get it diagnosed at right time by the physician a start following the necessary treatment as prescribed by the physician to get control over it.

Automated Device for Asthma Monitoring or Management or ADAMM is a wearable smart device. It is in the form of a monitor with a role of detecting the symptom associated with an asthma attack before its onset. By providing an indication prior to a severe asthma attack, it allows the user to take necessary precautions before the attack get worse. An indication is given to the user before the potential attack in the form of vibrations generated by the smart device ADAMM. Other than creating vibrations it is also capable of sending text messages to the registered or connected physicians to notify them to take necessary actions at the same time.

Other than acting as a life savior it also helps in tracking inhaler activity followed by the user. The device can detect and track the usage of inhaler. In case a patient forgets whether the inhaler has been used or not, the status can be checked as per recorded by the device. Also, it proves to be helpful by keeping a record of changes, feeling, and behaviors being observed in a patient. To bring the capability of differentiating a situation with genuine changes from the one with normal changes, special algorithm technology have been used in the designing of the device.

Features of ADAMM

1. Symptom Detection: Sensors embedded in the wearable play the role of detecting the symptoms by keeping a track of cough rate, heartbeat, respiration patterns, temperature and some other related symptoms of interest.

2. Notifications: In case of deviation from the normal behavior to the abnormal one, alerts are generated in the form of device vibration and notification messages to the connected physician or the family member.

3. Inhaler Detection: It helps in monitoring usage of the inhaler by keeping a track on its status that is being used or not. Also, it helps to control the level of dosage required by the patient at any point in time.

4. Voice Journaling: Whenever the user feels abnormal changes in the body, he or she can immediately press the wearable to record the changes going on. It helps in avoiding the need to write such changes in order to mention it to the physician later on. The record gets stored in the long-term memory in the original form without any middleware changes.

5. Autonomous Rechargeable: Since the wearable does not depend on the smartphone for processing power, therefore there is no necessity over the availability of the smartphone. Also, at night, there is no need to wear the device. It can be placed in a rechargeable cradle on the nightstand with the continuation of monitoring for coughing, the most common night-time symptom.

6. Unique Algorithm Technology: Algorithms are used to recognize the unique behavior to a particular person. It helps in distinguishing a person's normal behavior with the abnormal one. On observing relevant changes notification is sent to the connected loved ones, family, friends, or physician.

13.6 CONCLUSION

13.6.1 HEALTHCARE AND ECONOMY

The quality of service offered by a health care system gets highly influenced by the way it is financially supported. In the market of the health care system, the three major role players are consumers or users, health care providers, and a third party. While going for opting a medical health care service, a consumer seeks to maximize the benefits out of it in terms of health care and self-satisfaction. On the other hand, health care providers seek to maximize their profit in exchange for investments made by them and the services they provide. The third-party includes people associated with insurance companies (private and government). They act as an intermediary between the user or customer and the health care providers exploiting the uncertainties related to the incidences of illness and healthcare cost. Also, to control the risk that comes with the purchasing of a healthcare service the third-party acts as a medium to the healthcare providers for minimizing their cost while having proper control over their budgets.

However, the increasing popularity of IoT based smart health tracking systems is promoting the adoption of remote care as a result of possible remote monitoring and ability to prediagnose a severe disease before worsening. The persistence and continue the growth of IoT in healthcare at a rapid pace has provided healthcare team a significant opportunity to reduce the cost of care.

With the evolving time and technology, as the medical devices such as wearables, electronic health records becomes more interoperable, the evolution of systems-of-systems will gradually enable a fully digitized and connected healthcare endurance. A connected system of healthcare devices will enable patients to access and track their health status and an opportunity to directly send health information to the connected physician or family member. For physicians, it provides an opportunity to remotely monitor their patients and reduce their visits to the hospital and hence reduction in cost a crowd to the hospital with improvised quality of medical treatment and better performance to the patients.

13.6.2 IOT AND HUMAN BEHAVIOR

The way humans interact with each other and with technology influences the world around it to a great extent. IoT has provided humans with the automation of machines whether it is in the industry of healthcare, entertainment or so on. The three major fields in which benefits of IoT to human can be broken down are the availability of more data in real-time, advancement in technology, and more personalization.

1. MORE DATA: Other than gathering data through traditional sources, now the data can be collected in real-time from anywhere at any

point in time. In the field of medical health care when we talk about data gathering from traditional sources then it implies collecting data by examining patients in the clinics via medical tests available for the diagnosis of a particular disease. While advanced technologies such as smart devices based on the principle of the IoT has enabled the gathering of data continuously that is 24×7. The data collected from the devices interconnected to each other via IoT technology provides human with a variety of data available on hand in real-time. Processing such a large data helps researchers to develop interesting tools and technologies with the evolution of time which might prove to be a life savior for many and helps in prediagnosis of a number of diseases which either require continuous monitoring or are treatable only by reducing the effects of their symptoms via prediagnosis.

2. ADVANCEMENT IN TECHNOLOGY: Advancement in technology has made monitoring of patients from their home possible in real-time. It has helped in reducing the cost of medication to a great extent. Patients are not required to visit the hospital on a regular basis. They can be monitored by their physician via smart devices that acts by monitoring the patient continuously and sending notifications to the physician or a connected family member in case of any severe changes or missing dosage. As a result, it helps in treating the patients at the right time via prediagnosis and hence saves the cost required for advance treatment otherwise. On the other hand, it enables people to use the device in the correct way that they might not be doing in some cases such as that of the inhaler.

3. MORE PERSONALIZATION: With the advancement in technology, patients become capable enough to monitor themselves without any external help. Now there is no more need to make a visit to the hospital for each and every diagnosis. Now, it is not required for a patient to keep an assistant or a family member or a friend to help him with the daily stuff that is taking medicines at the mentioned time in the right amount or using devices such as inhaler in a correct way and so on. Devices such as ADAMM has even provided patients with the functionality of monitoring at night without even wearing the device.

13.6.3   BENEFITS OF HEALTH CARE SYSTEM USING IOT

As mentioned in the benefits of the above section of IoT can be listed in short as below,

1. Remote Monitoring: Smart devices available in the form of wearables, ingestible, connected lenses, and so on to enable remote monitoring by collecting data related to patient's behavior and body activity and generating alerts in case of any abnormal behavior. Notification related to it is generated to the smartphone of the patient along with those connected to the device including the physician, family member or a friend.

2. Advanced Tools and Technologies to prediagnosis the disease: Using the smart devices based on IoT one can easily prediagnosis the disease such as asthma, Parkinson and so on which are well known for their inability to get cured of the root. The only treatment possible is to get their symptoms cured and they are also controllable only when diagnosed in early stages.

3. Reduced Cost of Medication: Smart technology highly reduces the cost of medication by reducing the number of visits to the hospitals, reduces the cost to be spent on treatment of diseases after reaching to an advanced stage using the mean of prediagnosis.

4. Automated Working: Automation to the field of health care enables patients to handle complicated objects on their own without facing any trouble as automation helps in the proper handling of such devices with a perk of getting notified on any alerts or for the daily course schedule to be followed.

5. Simplification: Internal processing of such devices is complicated. However, for the users, it provides one of the most simplified interfaces to interact and understand.

6. Authentication and Authorization: All the data collected via these devices in real-time is generally stored on cloud storage where strong security services are provided to it. These security services include authentication and authorization. Authentication and authorization are the terms used to ensure that the data is coming from a trusted and registered party. Other than that on the network level, routing algorithms guiding the transfer of data from one device to another ensures the safety of the data via cryptographic methods.

7. Data Processing: A huge amount of data collected from all the devices provides an ample opportunity for the researchers to study and develop new tools and technologies after performing refining of data using data processing techniques.

13.7 FUTURE ADVANCEMENT OF IOT

In coming years of progression, roots of IoT will penetrate deep into the technology world. It can be visualized via following activities:

1. People will become more addictive to technology: In coming years people would prefer to have connection with their loved ones that is friends and family. For the same, they would be ready to sacrifice their security at the cost of getting close to their relatives. As a result, it will increase the number of IoT devices in the technology hub.
2. People will stay plugged in all the time: According to studies, growing digitization would lead people to stay connected to the Internet all the time in coming future.
3. Increased Internet Participation: As mentioned above, in coming future all the platforms would be digitized. Therefore, ultimately it would lead to increased Internet participation.
4. More IoT, More Risk: With the increase in IoT, chances of risk will increase. However, they can be controlled using advanced technologies.

KEYWORDS

- **authentication**
- **fast pace**
- **Internet of Things**
- **medication cost**
- **mortality**
- **privacy**
- **rate**
- **repudiation**
- **security**
- **smart devices**
- **unreachability**
- **web interface**

REFERENCES

1. Castro, D.; Coral, W.; Cabra, J.; Colorado, J.; Méndez, D.; Trujillo, L. *Survey on IoT Solutions Applied to Healthcare*; Dyna: Medellin, Colombia, 2017, 12 Oct.
2. Applications of IoT in Health Tracking System, 2019. https://econsultancy.com/Internet-of-things-healthcare/
3. Introduction to UIs and UX for IoT, 1st ed.; Leverage (n.d), 82–91. https://www.leverege.com
4. Kamble, A.; Bhutad, S. Survey on Internet of Things (IoT) Security Issues and Solutions. *2nd International Conference on Inventive Systems and Control (ICISC)*; Coimbatore, India, 2018, 19 January.
5. Ramakrishna, C.; Kiran Kumar, G.; Reddy, A. M.; Ravi, P. A Survey on Various IoT Attacks and Its Counter Measures. *International Journal of Engineering Research in Computer Science and Engineering (IJERCSE)*; Hyderabad, India, 2018, 4 April.
6. Hasan, M. 25 Most Common IoT Security Threats in an Increasingly Connected World, 2019, 14 March. https://www.ubuntupit.com/25-most-common-IoT-security-threats-in-an-increasingly-connected-world/
7. Trait, A. Internet of Things Vulnerabilities, 2017, 23 February. https://blog.learningtree.com/10-Internet-of-things-security-vulnerabilities/
8. India Population Live, 2019. https://www.worldometers.info/world-population/
9. Weber, R. H.; Studer, E. *Cybersecurity in the Internet of Things: Legal Aspects*; University of Zurich; Zurich, Switzerland, 2016, pp 1–5.
10. Atzoria, L.; Ierab, A.; Morabito, G. *The Internet of Things: A Survey*; Computer Networks: Cagliari, Italy, 2010, 1 June.
11. Bayani, M.; Karol, L.; Mayra, L. IoT Advantages on E-learning in Smart Cities. *Int. J. Dev. Res.* 2018, Jan.
12. Aleksandrova, M. IoT in Agriculture: Five Technology Uses for Smart Farming and Challenges to Consider, 2018, 10 June. https://dzone.com/articles/IoT-in-agriculture-five-technology-uses-for-smart
13. Wearable Devices and Internet of Things. (n.d). https://www.mouser.in/applications/article-IoT-wearable-devices/
14. Rajiv. What Are the Major Components of Internet of Things? 2018, 10 Jan. https://www.rfpage.com/what-are-the-major-components-of-Internet-of-things/
15. Dayal, P. IoT Ecosystem Components: The Complete Connectivity Layer, 2018, 28 May. https://www.newgenapps.com/blog/IoT-ecosystem-components-the-complete-connectivity-layer
16. How IoT Works, 4 Important Components of IoT, 2018, 1 June. https://data-flair.training/blogs/how-IoT-works/
17. Rouse, M. IoT Gateway, 2018, 21 Apr. https://Internetofthingsagenda.techtarget.com/definition/Internet-of-Things-IoT
18. Haikun, T.; Xinsheng, L. *Research and Application of the IoT Gateway Based on the Real-Time Specification for Java*; Heibe University: Heibe City, China, 2018, Mar.
19. Rouse, M. IoT Cloud, Salesforce IoT Cloud, 2016, Jan. https://searchcustomerexperience.techtarget.com/definition/IoT-Cloud-Salesforce-IoT-Cloud
20. McClelland, C. What Is the Cloud? How Does It Fit Into IoT? 2019, 6 Jan. https://www.IoTforall.com/what-is-the-cloud/

21. Internet of Things Analytics, IoT Analytics. (n.d). https://www.techopedia.com/definition/31460/Internet-of-things-analytics-IoT-analytics

22. Dhakad, P. Internet of Things (IoT) Analytics Guide, 2018, 1 Dec. https://edu.varistor.in/role-of-data-analytics-in-IoT/

23. Yang, D-L., Liu, F.; Liang, Y-D. *A Survey of the Internet of Things, Proc*, 1st ed.; School of Management Science and Engineering, Dalian University of Technology, Dalian, China, 2010; p 358.

24. Onasanya, A.; Elshakankiri, M. IoT Implementation for Cancer Care and Business Analytics/ Cloud Services in Health Care System, 2014, May.

25. 10 Examples of Internet of Things in Healthcare, 2019, 1 Feb. https://econsultancy.com/Internet-of-things-healthcare/

26. CYCORE, 2014, 5 June. http://cycore.ucsd.edu/overview.php

27. O'Meara, N. M.; Sturis, J.; Van Cauter, E.; Polonsky, K. S. Lack of Control by Glucose of Ultradian Insulin Secretory Oscillations in Impaired Glucose Tolerance and in Non-Insulin-Dependent Diabetes Mellitus; *J. Clin. Invest. Chicago, US* **1993**.

28. Simon, C.; Brandenberger, G.; Follenius, M. Ultradian Oscillations of Plasma Glucose, Insulin, and C-Peptide in Man During Continuous Enteral Nutrition. *J. Clin. Endocrinol. Metab.* **1987**.

29. Hollingdal, M.; Juhl, C. B.; Pincus, S. M.; Sturis, J.; Veldhuis, J. D.; Polonsky, K. S.; Pørksen, N.; Schmitz, O. Failure of Physiological Plasma Glucose Excursions to Entrain High-Frequency Pulsatile Insulin Secretion in Type 2 Diabetes; Diabetes: Denmark, 2000.

30. Sparacino, G.; Facchinetti, A.; Cobelli, C. Smart Continuous Glucose Monitoring Sensors: On-Line Signal Processing Issues. *Sensors (Basel)*, 2010, 12 July.

31. Klonoff, D. C. Continuous Glucose Monitoring: Roadmap for 21st Century Diabetes Therapy. *Diab. Care*, **2005**.

32. Skyler, J. S. Continuous Glucose Monitoring: An Overview of Its Development. *Ther: Diab Technol.*, **2009**.

33. Buckingham, B. Clinical Overview of Continuous Glucose Monitoring. *J. Diab. Sci. Technol.*, **2008**.

34. Deiss, D.; Bolinder, J.; Riveline, J.; Battelino, T.; Bosi, E.; Tubiana-Rufi, N.; Kerr, D.; Phillip, M. Improved Glycemic Control in Poorly Controlled Patients with Type 1 Diabetes Using Real-Time Continuous Glucose Monitoring. *Diab. Care*, **2006**.

35. Garg, K.; Zisser, H.; Schwartz, S.; Bailey, T.; Kaplan, R.; Ellis, S.; Jovanovic, L. Improvement in Glycemic Excursions with a Transcutaneous, Real-Time Continuous Glucose Sensor. *Diab. Care*, **2006**.

36. Beck, R. W. The Effect of Continuous Glucose Monitoring in Well Controlled Type 1 Diabetes. *Diab. Care*, **2009**, 8 May.

37. De Block, C.; Vertommen, J.; Manuel-y-Keenoy, B.; Van Gaal, L. Minimally-Invasive and Non-Invasive Continuous Glucose Monitoring Systems: Indications, Advantages, Limitations and Clinical Aspects. *Curr. Diab. Rev.*, **2008**.

38. Nichols, J. H.; Klonoff, D. C. The Need for Performance Standards for Continuous Glucose Monitors. *J. Diabetes Sci. Technol.*, **2007**.

39. Francis, J. D. III.; Lauren, M. H.; Joon, B. L.; Howard, C. Z.; Dassau, E. Closed Loop Artificial Pancreas Systems: Engineering the Algorithms, 2014, May. https://care.diabetesjournals.org/content/37/5/1191

40. Classification and Diagnosis of Diabetes, 2017, 27 Jan. https://care.diabetesjournals. org/content/40/Supplement_1/S11
41. Type 1 Diabetes. (n.d). https://www.webmd.com/diabetes/type-1-diabetes#1
42. Buckingham, B. Hypoglycemia Detection, and Better Yet, Prevention, in Pediatric Patients. *California, US: Diabetes Technol. Ther.*, **2005**.
43. Closed-Loop Artificial Pancreas' Insulin Delivery System Offers Better Glucose Control, Reduced Risk of Hypoglycemia. *Diabetologia*, 2018, 3 Oct. https://www.eurekalert.org/ pub_releases/2018-10/d-cp100118.php
44. Flow Measurement in Smart Inhalers for Connected Drug Delivery. *ON Drug Deliv. Magaz.* **2018**, 10 Dec, 22–25.
45. Biswas, R.; Hanania, N. A.; Sabharwal, A. Factors Determining In Vitro Lung Deposition of Albuterol Aerosol Delivered by Ventolin Metered-Dose Inhaler. *J. Aerosol. Med. Pulm. Drug Deliv*. **2017**, 256–266.
46. How Smart Pills and Ingestible Will Revolutionize Healthcare. (n.d.). https://www. marsdd.com/news/ingestibles-smart-pills-revolutionize-healthcare/
47. Langston, J. Inter-Scatter Communication Enables First-Ever Implanted Devices, Smart Contact Lenses, Credit Cards That 'Talk' Wi-Fi, 2016, 17 Aug. https://www.washington. edu/news/2016/08/17/interscatter-communication-enables-first-ever-implanted-devices-smart-contact-lenses-credit-cards-that-talk-wi-fi/
48. Gooding, M. Apple Watch Used in the Fight Against Depression, 2017, 28 Feb. https://www. cambridge-news.co.uk/business/technology/apple-watch-used-fight-against-12666135
49. Pathognomonic Symptoms, 2018. https://www.webmd.com
50. What Is Epidemiology? (n.d). https://www.bmj.com/about-bmj/resources-readers/publi-cations/epidemiology-uninitiated/1-what-epidemiology
51. Jacob, K. S. Major Depression: A Review of the Concept and the Diagnosis. *Adv. Psychi Treat.*, **2009**, 279–285.
52. Cognitive Science, MIT Department of Brain and Cognitive Science, 2018–2019. http:// catalog.mit.edu/schools/science/brain-cognitive-sciences/
53. Cognition Kit Wearable Technology Demonstrates High Compliance Among Patients with Major Depressive Disorder (MDD), 2017, 28 Nov. https://www.cambridgecognition.com/ news/entry/cognition-kit-wearable-demonstrates-high-compliance-among-MDD-patients
54. Measuring Cognition in Everyday Life, 2018. https://www.cognitionkit.com/
55. CANTAB. (n.d). https://www.cambridgecognition.com/cantab/
56. Pietrangelo, A. Coagulation Tests; Chicago, US, 2017, 5 May. https://www.healthline. com/health/coagulation-tests
57. Roche Unveils Blood Coagulation Checker with Bluetooth Features, 2018, 30 June. https://www.medgadget.com/2018/06/roche-unveils-blood-coagulation-checker-with-bluetooth-features.html
58. Parkinson's Diseases, 2018, 30 June. https://www.mayoclinic.org/diseases-conditions/ parkinsons-disease/symptoms-causes/syc-20376055
59. Lava, N. Surgery for Parkinson's Disease, 2017, 15 July. https://www.webmd.com/ parkinsons-disease/guide/parkinsons-surgical-treatments
60. Pacemaker, 2019, 25 June. https://www.mayoclinic.org/tests-procedures/pacemaker/ about/pac-20384689
61. Kahn, J. Apple's New Reserach Kit API Monitors Parkinson's Disease Symptoms on Apple Watch, 2018, 6 June. https://9to5mac.com/2018/06/06/apple-watch-researchkit-parkinsons-movement-disorder-api/

62. Patients Care and Health Information, Asthma, 2018, 13 September. https://www.mayo-clinic.org/search/search-results?q=Asthma

63. ADAMM Helps You Understand and Monitor Your Asthma More Easily, Health Care Originals, 2017, February. http://healthcareoriginals.com/

64. Chen, G. J.; Feldman, S. R. Economic Aspects of Health Care System. *North Carolina, USA: Dermatol. Clin.*, **2000**, 18 April.

65. The Internet of Things and Healthcare Policy Principles. (n.d). https://www.intel.com/content/dam/www/public/us/en/documents/white-

66. Moores, L.; VP-Strategy, Dstillery. The IoT Impact on Human Behavior. (n.d). https://media-entertainment.cioreview.com/cxoinsight/the-IoT-impact-on-human-behavior-nid-14822-cid-6.html

CHAPTER 14

Smart Antennas in IoT-Based Systems

SHAILESH[1] and GARIMA SRIVASTAVA[2]

[1]*Guru Gobind Singh Indraprastha University, Dwarka, Delhi, India*

[2]*NSUT East Campus, Geeta Colony, New Delhi, Delhi, India*

ABSTRACT

Smart antennas, which are also recognized as multiple input multiple output (MIMO) antennas, are the arrays of an antenna having smart signal processing algorithms for identifying spatial signal signs such as the direction of arrival of signal, which are used for calculating beam forming vectors which track and find beam of antenna on mobile or target. Internet of Things (IoT) applications are likely to provide many routine items using intelligence and connectivity such as wearable, healthcare, smart home equipment, agriculture, smart cities, and industrial applications. Smart antennas can completely enhance the performance of IoT network and for this, they do not require any changes in wireless IoT devices population. Only IoT gateway terminals, which are comparatively limited in population, require improvement. However, eventually everyone gains advantages such as the capacity of data, location services and network resilience, network operators from enhanced coverage, and network users from cheap and low-power required IoT devices. Because of the progression in different IoT-based devices, a few MIMO antennas are presented. In this part, different sorts of MIMO antennas are introduced dependent on the working frequency bands, for example, ultra-wideband (UWB), single-band and multiband. The UWB MIMO antennas are utilized in flexible IoT wireless devices, lower 5G bands and different wireless and IoT devices. The single-band MIMO antenna discovers applications in 4G, 5G, and IoT devices. Multiband MIMO antenna is helpful

Internet of Things: Technological Advances and New Applications. Brojo Kishore Mishra & Amit Vishwasrao Salunkhe (Eds.)

in various wireless communication having frequency bands alluring for the IoT gadgets, 4G/5G for cell phones. The examination hole of UWB MIMO antenna for IoT applications is huge size, high mutual coupling at higher frequencies, and absence of shared ground of antenna elements. Likewise the vast majority of the antenna have a 2 × 2 arrangement. The fundamental examination hole of single and multiband MIMO antenna for IoT applications are nonplanar construction of antenna, poor impedance matching, and low isolation.

14.1 INTRODUCTION

The rising market of the IoT provides numerous sorts of electronic appliances and wireless communication of applications for wide spectrum comprising of vehicles and smart cities, home automation, telemedicine, and industrial applications. Clearly, the better working of these applications is reliant on a trustworthy wireless component.[6] Smart antennas are also called as adaptive array antennas, multiple antennas, and so on. These antennas are used for increasing the efficiency in wireless communication. It is possible with the benefit of the diversity impact at transceiver, that is, source and the destination of wireless communication system. The word diversity impact denotes the reception and transmission of multiple radio signals, which are utilized for decreasing inaccuracy throughout the communication of data and also increasing speed of data between source and destination.[4] The smart antennas can be categorized based on number of outputs and inputs, which are used in devices like multiple input single output (MISO), single input multiple output (SIMO), and multiple input multiple output (MIMO). In SIMO, only single antenna element is used at the transmitter and multiple antenna elements are used at the receiver. In MISO, multiple antenna elements are used at the transmitting side and only single antenna is used at the receiving side. In MIMO, multiple antenna elements are used at both the transmitting and the receiving side. This is the best effective technique among all types of smart antenna. This technique is extended according to IEEE 802.11n standard. This technique obviously supports spatial information processing.[4]

Ultra-wideband (UWB) antennas are continuously grabbing attention because of their favorable benefits such as less consumption of power, cheap, and high throughput. UWB is operated in computer peripherals, wireless personal area networks, imaging, and numerous other applications.[3] UWB

MIMO antenna have been established to additional rise in channel capacity in comparison to fundamental limited band MIMO schemes.[17] To minimize the performance deteriorating effects of multipath fading in indoor UWB communication systems, diversity antenna arrays can be valuable as viable arrangement. However, radiating antenna elements of these arrays should be extremely uncorrelated.[15] Single-band MIMO antenna has just a single working frequency and operates for just a single application, though multi-band MIMO antenna has different working frequencies and has numerous applications at the same time. In this section, MIMO antennas for IoT applications are examined dependent on the range of frequencies, such as UWB, single-band, and multiband antennas.

14.2 BASICS OF SMART ANTENNAS

Smart antenna can remove the problem of multipath fading using the property of antenna diversity. Also, it can rise the capacity of the system with the help of multiple cochannel users in transmission and reception in wireless communication.[16]

Smart antenna contains a base station having array of antenna, which refer to as single-antenna mobile terminal. This single antenna mobile terminal has the following advantages.

1. **Improvement in system reliability and quality**—Since smart antenna can decrease signal variation. That is, peak-to-peak fading and antenna performance depends on multipath fading, there is increase in quality and reliability.[9,18]

2. **Expanded system capacity**—The smart antenna can improve signal to interference ratio, which is responsible to decrease the capacity of system.[2,14]

3. **More battery life of handset**—Smart antenna contains diversity gain (DG) at the base station and allows less power, which is to be transmitted from mobile terminal to base station. This increases the battery life of handset. For instance, transmitted power of handset is <9 dB, if an eight antenna element array base station obtains DG of 9 dB.[16]

4. **Solution to alignment issue**—Smart antenna can solve the alignment issue using adaptive steering of the beams of the receiver or transmitter for maximizing the signal power at all times.[11]

  5. Increment in the range of base station—Because of DG, large range is provided by the smart antenna.[16]

Therefore, there is trade-off between increase range and battery life. On the one side, customer satisfaction increases with long battery life and on the other side, infrastructure installation cost can be decreased with increased range.[16]

Figure 14.1 presents the simple architecture of a smart antenna system. Smart uplink and downlink algorithms process the signal received from antenna array. Smart uplink algorithm determines the uplink weight vector to perform beam forming on the received signals. Smart downlink algorithm provides downlink weight vector for performing the beam forming on the transmitted signals.[16]

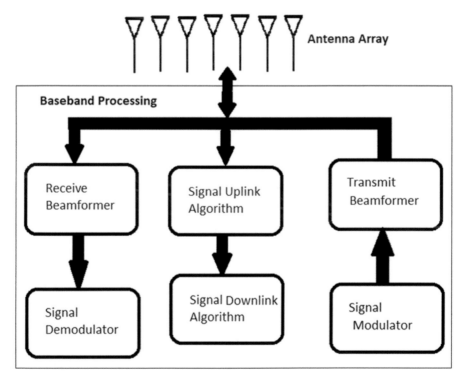

FIGURE 14.1 Space diversity multiple access (SDMA).[16]

MIMO system can able to enhance the communication link with two distinct approaches such as spatial diversity and spatial multiplexing. In spatial diversity, same information is guided across independent fading channel to combat fading, which in turn improves the reliability of transmission link. In spatial multiplexing, each bit of data stream is multiplexed on the different spatial channel. This improves the link capacity and data rate.

14.2.1   PERFORMANCE METRICS OF MIMO ANTENNA

There are different performance metrics of MIMO antenna like envelope correlation coefficient (ECC), DG, channel capacity loss (CCL), mean effective gain (MEG), etc.

ECC

This parameter measures how much the communication channels are isolated or correlated with each other when simultaneously operated. It can be measured by using S-parameters or by using 3D field radiation pattern. In a real-world application, the upper value of ECC is 0.5.[1]

$$\rho_e = \frac{\left|S_{ii}^{*}S_{ij} + S_{ji}^{*}S_{ii}\right|^2}{\left(1-\left(\left|S_{ii}^2\right|+\left|S_{ji}^2\right|\right)\right)\left(1-\left(\left|S_{ii}^2\right|+\left|S_{ji}^2\right|\right)\right)} \tag{14.1}$$

$$\rho_e = \frac{\left|\iint_{4\pi}\left[\overrightarrow{F_i}(\theta,\phi)^{*} \ \overrightarrow{F_j}(\theta,\phi)\right]d\Omega\right|^2}{\iint_{4\pi}\left|\overrightarrow{F_i}(\theta,\phi)\right|^2 d\Omega \iint_{4\pi}\left|F_j(\theta,\phi)\right|^2 d\Omega} \tag{14.2}$$

where $\overrightarrow{F_i}(\theta,\phi)$ and $\overrightarrow{F_j}(\theta,\phi)$ denote the radiation characteristics of the antenna when port-I and port-j is energized, respectively.

DG

DG supplies development in multiantenna devices with respect to single-antenna devices. In practical application, DG value should be close to 10. It is measured by using the following equation:[1]

$$DG = 10\sqrt{1 - ECC} \tag{14.3}$$

MEG

In a predefined wireless environment, MEG measures the antenna performance, where the impact of the environment is considered in the gain performance of the antenna. MEG can be evaluated using S-parameters. For two-element, MIMO antenna system following equations are used.[5]

$$MEG_1 = 0.5\left[1 - |S_{11}|^2 - |S_{12}|^2\right] \tag{14.4}$$

$$MEG_2 = 0.5\left[1 - |S_{22}|^2 - |S_{21}|^2\right] \tag{14.5}$$

The difference between MEGs (MEG_1–MEG_2) should be less than 3 dB for equal power level.

$$MEG_1 - MEG_2 < 3\,dB \tag{14.6}$$

CCL

It provides an insight about the higher limit of the message rate up to which signal can be constantly transmitted over communication channel. For good MIMO performance, CCL should be <0.4 bits/s/Hz. For two-port MIMO antenna, it is given by the following equations.[1]

$$CCL = -\log_2 \det\left(\beta^R\right) \tag{14.7}$$

$$\beta^R = \begin{bmatrix} \beta_{11} & \beta_{12} \\ \beta_{21} & \beta_{22} \end{bmatrix} \tag{14.8}$$

$$\beta_{11} = 1 - \left(|S_{11}|^2 + |S_{12}|^2\right) \tag{14.9}$$

$$\beta_{22} = 1 - \left(|S_{22}|^2 + |S_{21}|^2\right) \tag{14.10}$$

$$\beta_{12} = -\left(S_{11}^* S_{12} + S_{12}^* S_{22}\right) \tag{14.11}$$

$$\beta_{21} = -\left(S_{22}^* S_{21} + S_{12}^* S_{22}\right) \tag{14.12}$$

14.2.2   ISOLATION IMPROVEMENT TECHNIQUES IN MIMO ANTENNA

Isolation improvement is one of biggest challenge. Several isolation enhancement methods are discussed in the MIMO for improving diversity performance. These techniques are as follows.

- ### Generation of orthogonal modes

It is easy to generate orthogonal modes. It does not affect the radiation characteristics, since this method does not require any extra structure.

• **Excitation of degenerated modes**

In this, two different modes are excited at the same resonant frequency. But, it is difficult to excite two different modes at the same frequency.

• **Introduction of defected ground structure (DGS)**

A segment of the ground is etched between the antenna elements to diminish the port coupling. This method influences the radiation attributes in terms of gain and radiation effectiveness.

• **Use of decoupling structure**

This method needs additional matching circuit or antenna elements. This strategy influences the radiation attributes in terms of radiation efficiency and gain.

• **Introducing meta-surface/frequency selective surface/ electromagnetic bandgap (EBG)**

These designs give a bandgap in their frequency response. The bandgap acts as band reject filter and limit the mutual coupling between the antenna elements.

14.3 UWB MIMO ANTENNAS FOR IOT DEVICES

In this segment, three UWB MIMO antennas for IoT devices presented as shown in the Figure 14.2, Figure 14.3 and Figure 14.4. These antennas are clarified as far as various boundaries like design, sort of radiating element, number of elements with direction, kind of feed line, ground surface, dielectric substrate, impedance matching, isolation, radiation characteristics, rejected bands, applications, benefits, and drawbacks in Table 14.1.

The results of the above-mentioned antennas are demonstrated in Table 14.2, which consists of different parameters like year, size, bandwidth, isolation, peak gain, efficiency, DG, ECC, and multiplexing efficiency.

TABLE 14.1 UWB MIMO Antennas for IoT devices.

Ref.	UWB flexible MIMO[6]	UWB F-shaped MIMO Antenna with fractured ground[7]	Flag-shaped UWB MIMO[12]
Structure	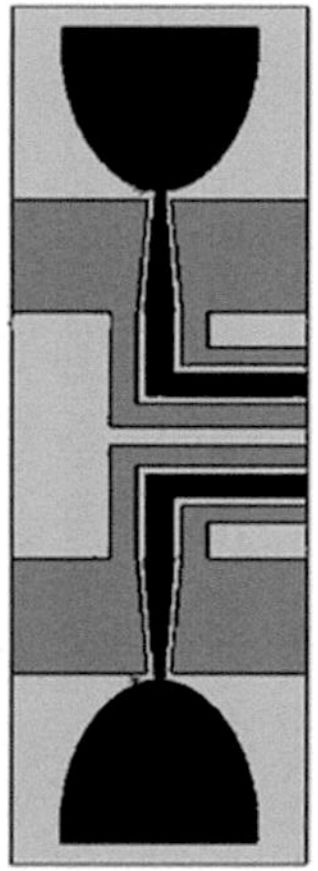 FIGURE 14.2 Flexible UWB MIMO.[6]	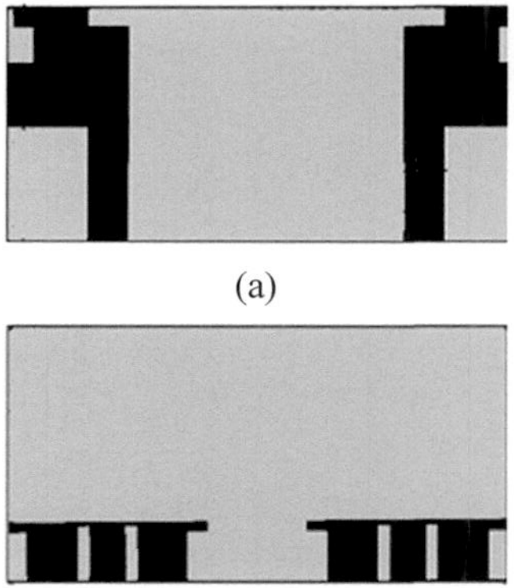 (a) (b) FIGURE 14.3 UWB F-shaped MIMO antenna with fractured ground.[7]	 FIGURE 14.4 UWB flag-shaped MIMO antenna.
Type of radiating patch	Half-elliptical	F-shaped patch is opted because of its wideband properties and improved antenna properties in S, C, and X bands.	Flag-shaped monopole radiator
Number of antenna elements with direction	Two, opposite sides	Two, opposite sides	Two, opposite sides
Feed line	tapered CPW	Microstrip	Microstrip
Ground surface	Extended ground of CPW line	Fractured ground surface is used to achieve desired impedance bandwidth.	Partial ground
Substrate	Kapton Polyimide substrate is used.	Rogers 5880 substrate is used.	0.8 thick FR4 substrate is used.

TABLE 14.1 *(Continued)*

Ref.	UWB flexible MIMO[6]	UWB F-shaped MIMO Antenna with fractured ground[7]	Flag-shaped UWB MIMO[12]
Impedance matching	MIMO antenna can cover the full UWB range by changing the major axis of the ellipse shape radiator. The linear tapering provides a smooth impedance change which leads to a decrease in reflection coefficient.	—	The T-shaped stub in ground enhances isolation and matching.
Isolation	Isolation is obtained by keeping the radiating elements in a back-to-back fashion. This orientation provides less fields contact and provides change in the phases of the intersected surface currents.	Gap of 13.9 mm (half wavelength at upper operating frequency) is maintained between antenna elements for reducing mutual coupling	For improvement of isolation, two split ring resonators are placed on left and right of the feed line. To further increase the isolation, T-shaped stub in the ground is used.
Radiation characteristics	Omnidirectional pattern at 2.5 GHz, and directional pattern at 4.5 GHz and 8 GHz. But, the omni-directional pattern disturbs at high frequency bands	Approximately isotropic pattern in E-and H-plane	Almost isotropic pattern in XY-plane, YZ-plane and ZX-plane
Notched bands	—	—	Two split-ring resonators are used for designing two notch bands C-band, X-band.
Application	Flexible IoT Systems	Lower 5G Bands	Wireless and IoT devices
Advantages	Flexible	• Antenna also operates over IEEE 802.11 a/ac/b/g/n. • Less size	
Disadvantages	• Big size • Without common ground	• Without common ground • More gap between antenna elements	Less isolation at high frequencies

TABLE 14.2   Results of UWB MIMO Antennas for IoT applications.

Ref.	Size (mm²)	Bandwidth (GHz)	Isolation (dB)	Peak gain (dB), efficiency (%)	ECC	DG	MUX eff (dB)
Raad[6]	100 × 22	3.1–13	>23	5.5, 94	≤0.001	>9.98	>−2.2
AL-Saif et al.[7]	13 × 25	2–12	>20	4.8,–	≤0.009	>9.8	–
Sanam et al.[12]	32 × 24	3.1–10.6	>15	4.2, 89	<0.5	≤10	–

14.4   SINGLE AND MULTIBAND MIMO ANTENNAS FOR IOT APPLICATIONS

In this section, recently reported single and multiband MIMO antenna for IoT applications as presented in the Figure 14.5, Figure 14.6, and Figure 14.7. These antennas are explained in terms of different parameters such as structure, operating frequency, height, antenna type, number of elements with orientation, feeding, ground, substrate, impedance matching, isolation, radiation pattern, specific absorption rate (SAR), application, advantages, and disadvantages in Table 14.3.

The results of all the above antennas are displayed in Tables 14.4 and 14.5, which consists of various parameters like year, size, bandwidth, isolation, peak gain, efficiency, DG, ECC, and multiplexing efficiency.

14.5   CONCLUSION

There are three kinds of MIMO antenna for IoT systems like UWB, single-band, and multiband antennas. The UWB foldable MIMO antenna has huge size, and flag-like UWB MIMO antennas have low isolation. The sizes of the single and multiband antennas are practically similar. Detecting and lower LTE band MIMO antenna have less isolation.

KEYWORDS

- **ultra-wideband**
- **multiple input multiple output**
- **isolation**
- **multiband**
- **diversity**

TABLE 14.3 Single and Multiband MIMO Antennas for IoT applications.

Ref.	PIFA MIMO antenna[8]	Sensing and Lower LTE band MIMO antenna[10]	L shape PIFA MIMO antenna[13]
Structure	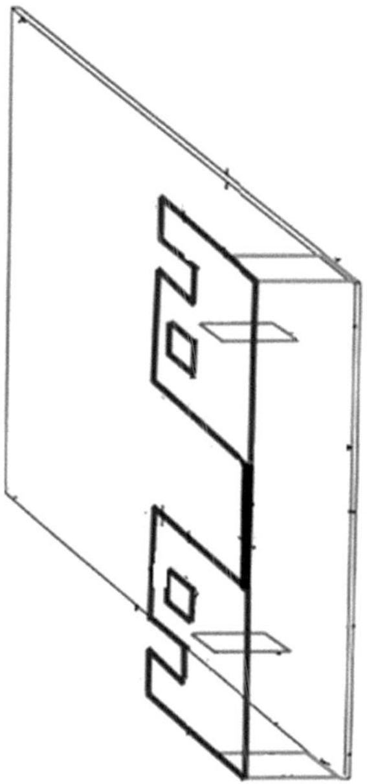 FIGURE 14.5 PIFA MIMO antenna.[8]	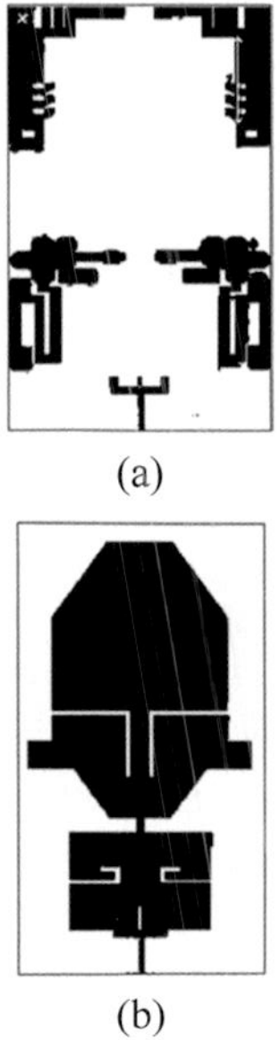 (a) (b) FIGURE 14.6 Sensing and lower LTE band MIMO antenna. (a) Top plane and (b) Bottom plane.[10]	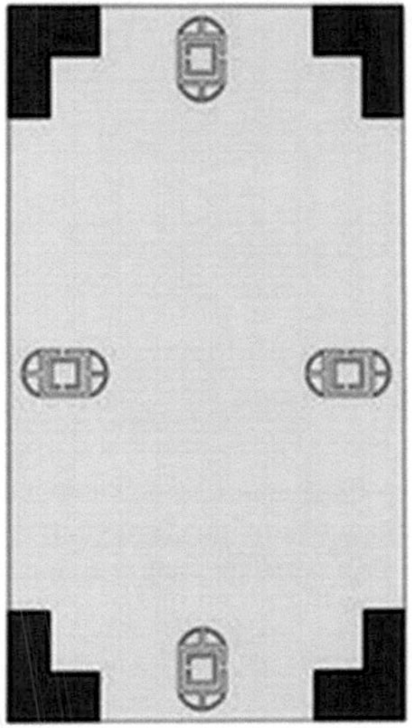 FIGURE 14.7 L-shaped PIFA MIMO antenna.[13]
Operating frequency (GHz)	single-band 2–3.6	Multiband 0.67–1.9, 3–4.6, 0.686–0.813, 0.755–0.971 1.65–1.83, 2–3.66, 3.9–4.1 4.8–5.5, and 5.82–5.93	Multiband 3.5, 12.5, and 17

TABLE 14.3 *(Continued)*

Ref.	PIFA MIMO antenna[8]	Sensing and Lower LTE band MIMO antenna[10]	L shape PIFA MIMO antenna[13]
Height (mm)	3.5	1.6	3.2
Antenna type	Planar Inverted-F Antenna (PIFA) element	**Sensing Antenna (ant 1)** Monopole antenna with coplanar waveguide feeding is used. The monopole antenna is changed to tapered rectangular like patch with a finite ground plane. **Lower LTE band antenna (Ant 2–5)** Meandered reconfigurable antenna is used.	L-shaped PIFA element
Number of elements with orientation	Two antenna elements are oriented like mirror image of each other on same plane.	There are total five antenna elements. Four antennas are located at four corners of the substrate. The fifth antenna at port 1 acts as sensing antenna plus ground surface for the other four antennas.	Four antenna elements are placed at four corners of rectangular substrate using characteristic mode analysis (CMA)
Feeding	The plates of feedings are positioned under the top plane of each PIFA	The sensing antenna has coplanar waveguide feeding.	Edge feeding is used
Substrate	0.51 mm thick Taconic TLC (tm)	FR4 substrate	—
Impedance matching	closed and open-ended rectangular slots are added in the top plate of each PIFA antenna for achieving wide operating bandwidth	To enhance the bandwidth, the proposed topology is stub-loaded.	—
Isolation	A rectangular slot is etched in the center of ground surface to obtain better isolation. Also, small rectangular strip is attached between top plates of two PIFAs for further increase in isolation	—	Complimentary Metamaterial design on the ground surface improves isolation

TABLE 14.3 *(Continued)*

Ref.	PIFA MIMO antenna[8]	Sensing and Lower LTE band MIMO antenna[10]	L shape PIFA MIMO antenna[13]
Radiation pattern	Directional	Sensing antenna #1 shows wide beam width with omnidirectional shape like pattern. Poor linear polarization is indicated by high level of cross polarization.	Directional and omnidirectional radiation pattern in E-plane and H-plane.
SAR	—	—	SAR analysis is done using hand (Talk) mode, two-hand (TH) data mode, and SAM head.
Application	IoT, 4G and 5G	• Cognitive radio in LTE 700 MHz band • Radio frequency identification bands	4G/5G and IoT applications (for mobile devices)
Advantages	• Antenna operates over WLAN band, 4GLTE bands, WiMAX bands, and sub-6 GHz 5G band • −10 dB bandwidth	Less height (planar configuration)	Antenna operates in 4G/5G and at 17 GHz for IoT devices
Drawbacks	• Nonplanar structure	• −6 dB bandwidth • Low isolation	Nonplanar structure

TABLE 14.4   Results of Single and Multiband MIMO Antennas.

Ref.	Size (mm³)	Number of antenna elements	Bandwidth (GHz)	Isolation (dB)	Gain (dB)/ Efficiency (%)
Chattha[8]	50 × 100×3.5	2	2–3.6	>20	–/70–95
Jha et al.[10]	65 × 120 × 1.6	5	Sensing frequency range (0.67–1.9, 3–4.6) and communication frequency range (0.686–0.813, 0.755–0.971 1.65–1.83, 2–3.66, 3.9–4.1, 4.8–5.5, 5.82–5.93)	>10	5.2 (Ant. 4)/–
Kumar and Khanna[13]	55 × 110 × 3.2	4	3.5, 12.5, 17	−21.73, −18, −19	6.34, 7.99, 8.61/80

TABLE 14.5   SAR and Diversity Performance of Single and Multiband MIMO Antennas.

Ref.	ECC	DG	TRAC (dB)	CCL (bps/ Hz)	MEG Ratio	SAR for 1 g of tissue (W/Kg)
Chattha[8]	<0.21	<10.086	–	–	–	–
Jka et al.[10]	<0.5	–	–	–	–	–
Kumar and Khanna[13]	<0.08	>9.95	<−6	<0.4	≈1	<1.6 in both cases

REFERENCES

1. Ibrahim, A.; Abdalla, M. A.; Hu, Z. Compact ACS-Fed CRLH MIMO Antenna for Wireless Applications. *IET Microw. Antennas Propag.* **2018,** *12* (6), 1021–1025.
2. Nagnib, A.; Paulraj, A.; Kailath, T. Capacity Improvement with Base-Station Antenna Arrays in Cellular CDMA. *IEEE Trans. Veh. Technol.* **1994,** *43*, 691–698.
3. Awais, Q.; Tariq Chattha, H.; Jamil, M.; Jin, Y.; Tahir, F. A.; Ur Rehman, M. A Novel Dual Ultrawideband CPW-Fed Printed Antenna for Internet of Things (IoT) Applications. *Wirel. Commun. Mobile Comput.* **2018,** *10*, 1–9.
4. *Circuit Today*, n.d. Retrieved from https://www.circuitstoday.com/smart-antennas
5. Thakur, E.; Jaglan, N.; Gupta, S. D. Design of Compact UWB MIMO Antenna with Enhanced Bandwidth. *Prog. Electromagn. Res. C* **2019,** *97*, 83–94.
6. Raad, H. An UWB Antenna Array for Flexible IoT Wireless Systems. *Prog. Electromagn. Res.* **2018,** *162*, 109–121.
7. AL-Saif, H.; Usman, M.; Chughtai, M. T.; Nasir, J. Compact Ultra-Wide Band MIMO Antenna System for Lower 5G Bands. *Wirel. Commun. Mobile Comput. (Hindawi)* **2018,** 1–6.

8. Chattha, H. T. Compact High Isolation Wideband 4G and 5G Multi-Input Multi-Output Antenna System for Handheld and Internet of Things Applications. *Int. J. RF Microw. Comput. Aided Eng.* **2019,** 1–10.

9. Parsons, J. D.; Henze, M.; Ratliff, P. A.; Withers, M. J. Diversity Techniques for Mobile Radio Reception. *IEEE Trans. Veh. Technol.* **1976,** *25,* 75–84.

10. Jha, K. R.; Bukhari, B.; Singh, C.; Mishra, G.; Sharma, S. K. Compact Planar Multi-Standard MIMO Antenna for IoT Applications. *IEEE Trans. Antennas Propag.* **2018,** *66* (7), 3327–3336.

11. Celik, N.; Iskander, M. F.; Emrick, R.; Franson, S. J.; Holmes, J. Implementation and Experimental Verification of a Smart Antenna System Operating at 60 GHz Band. *IEEE Trans. Antennas Propag.* **2008,** *56* (9), 2790–2800.

12. Sanam, N.; Madhav, B. T. P.; M.; Rao, V.; Nekkanti, V. S. K.; Pulicherla, V. K.; Chintapalli, T.; Yadlavalli, A. P. A Flag-Like MIMO Antenna Design for Wireless and IoT Applications. *Int. J. Recent Technol. Eng.* **2019,** *8* (1), 3023–3029.

13. Kumar, N.; Khanna, R. A Compact Multi-Band Multi-Input Multi-Output Antenna for 4G/5G and IoT Devices Using Theory of Characteristic Modes. *Int. J. RF Microw. Comput. Aided Eng.* **2019,** 1–19.

14. Kohno, R.; Imai, H.; Pasupathy, S. Combination of an Adaptive Antenna Array and a Canceller of Interference for Direct-Sequence Spread. *IEEE J. Select. Areas Commun.* **1990,** *8,* 675–682.

15. Ren, J.; Mi, D.; Yin, Y. Compact Ultrawideband MIMO Antenna with WLAN/UWB Bands Coverage. *Prog. Electromagn. Res. C* **2014,** *50,* 121–129.

16. Jeng, S. -S.; Okamoto, G. T.; Xu, G.; Lin, H. -P.; Vogel, W. J. Experimental Evaluation of Smart Antenna System Performance for Wireless Communications. *IEEE Trans. Antennas Propag.* **1998,** *46* (6), 749–757.

17. Tao, J.; Feng, Q. Compact Ultrawideband MIMO Antenna with Half-Slot Structure. *IEEE Antennas and Wireless Propagation Letters* **2017,** *16,* 792–795.

18. Jakes, W. C. A Comparison of Specific Space Diversity Techniques for Reduction of Fast Fading in UHF Mobile Radio Systems. *IEEE Trans. Veh. Technol.* **1971,** *20,* 81–92.

CHAPTER 15

Necessity of Time Synchronization for IoT-Based Applications

PRIYANKA SINGH[1] and MANJU KHARI[2]

[1]*Department of Computer Science, NSUT, East Campus, New Delhi, India*

[2]*School of Computer and System Sciences, Jawaharlal Nehru University, New Delhi, India*

ABSTRACT

Advanced data and communication innovations and installed frameworks have offered to ascend to another disruptive innovation: the Internet of Things (IoT). In this study, we report the need of time synchronization and communication in IoT devices. We begin by studying the basic concept of IoT, its related technologies, protocols, and standards. The study also observes the basic applications of IoT and the related issues which required precise time synchronization and the high connectivity technologies. Finally, the major issues that occur due to improper time synchronization of clocks embedded in IoT devices are addressed in this chapter. This chapter also demonstrates that most of the IoT-based devices are still lacking in proper synchronization with time.

15.1 INTRODUCTION

Internet of Things (IoT) is an ecosystem of connected physical devices that are web-enabled. IoT imagines a future wherein advanced physical elements

Internet of Things: Technological Advances and New Applications. Brojo Kishore Mishra & Amit Vishwasrao Salunkhe (Eds.)

can be connected by suitable methods of information and communication technologies to empower an entirely different class of utilizations and administrations. The machine-to-machine (M2M) communication emerged the concept of IoT, that is, the communication among machines without human intervention. IoT is a network of sensors and millions of smart devices that connect systems, people, and other applications to share and collect information. M2M offers connectivity that enables IoT. With just a limited degree of programmability and customizability, IoT systems link together highly specialized devices designed for specific purposes. We can use a term called cyber-physical systems for IoT unlike just purely cyber systems. The sensors embedded are also collecting the information from the physical world.

To associate the computerized world from the actual world, IoT is furnished with a plenty of sensors and actuators. The layered design of IoT comprises of three fundamental layers,[1] for example, the Sensing layer which comprises of sensors for gathering data, Network layer where gadgets are associated through various guidelines like IPv6LoWPAN, ZigBee0, RFID, 4G/5G. The application layer of IoT offers types of assistance to clients. The idea of IoT additionally presented various applications that make the actual world more brilliant incorporates keen homes, keen farming, and keen vehicles, shrewd leaving, and so on. Some industry examiners have overviewed it, that as of now, around 8 billion gadgets are associated with the organization and this gauge will increment up to 25 billion by 2020.[2] Over the next few years, more IoT devices will be found embedded in different real-time-based applications. Which create the need for Real-Time synchronization for future smart IoT application? The clocks on IoT gadgets are considerably more significant than we might suspect. An IoT gadget changes its inner check to line up with the checks of different gadgets in an organization for correspondence, shows the significance of constant synchronization between all the IoT gadgets at the focal point of large numbers of the present IoT challenges.

This chapter is organized as follows. Section 15.2 covers the IoT and its layered design. In Section 15.3, Technologies/Protocols/Standards of IoT are discussed. In Section 15.4, Related work is mentioned. IoT and time synchronization challenges are described in Section 15.5. Section 15.6 detailed the conclusion and future research area.

15.2   IOT AND ITS LAYERED DESIGN

The basic concept of IoT and its layered design have been discussed in this section.

15.2.1 INTERNET OF THINGS

The IoT had developed by the year 2013 into a framework utilizing various technologies, running from the Internet to remote technologies and from miniaturized scale electromechanical frameworks (MEMS) to inserted frameworks. The conventional fields of automation which include the remote sensor systems, GPS, control frameworks, automated homes, buildings, and others, all reinforce IoT. The term "Internet of things" abbreviated as IoT was the first time coined by Kevin Ashton in 1999 while making a presentation for Procter & Gamble at MIT. According to Ashton IoT as remarkably recognizable interoperable associated objects with radio frequency ID (RFID) innovation. He concludes up if all gadgets were "labeled," computers could oversee, track, and inventory them. Basically, the IoT can be treated as a superset of connecting devices that are uniquely identifiable by existing near field communication (NFC) techniques. Pretz in 2013[3] has demonstrated that the IoT is a network of connected things, where things are remotely associated by means of sensors.

Sensors, actuators, RFID Tags, cloud servers are the major components of IoT. Sensors/actuators are of two different types of transducers. The transducers convert some physical signals to an electrical impulse. Sensors and actuators are worked in reverse order. sensors collect information and route it to the data centers for taking decisions with a corresponding command sent back to an actuator in response to that sensed input. RFID Tags works through a unique addressing system used to effectively identify and communicate to devices.[4] At cloud servers, all the received data are stored. These components are organized in the design of IoT to enable the interaction of devices and are used by the sensing or hardware layer of IoT presented by layered architecture.

15.2.2 THE LAYERED DESIGN

IoT architecture varies from application to application, based on the area of application which we intend to build. IoT platform majorly uses four main components, such as sensors/actuators, devices, gateway, and cloud, over which architecture is framed. The integration of these components makes the layered design of IoT with sensing, gateway, and middle ware and application layer discussed below.[4]

i) **Sensing Layer** or a hardware layer consists of sensors, actuators, RFID tags, edge processors, etc., such kind of embedded devices for sensing and information collection of the physical world. The smart objects or other physical parameters of the physical environment are identified by the hardware devices of this layer.

ii) **Gateway Layer** data received from the above layers are handled at this layer. It routes the information and also enables communication among cross platforms.

iii) **Middleware Layer** is an interface between the application and the hardware layer. Due to the heterogeneity of 'Things' and lack of standards, it plays a key role and provides communication between applications. It is also responsible for data and device management, semantic examination, data filtering, access control, the discovery of data like object-naming service and electronic product code data administration.

iv) **Application Layer** is the topmost layer that enables the interaction between users and applications. This layer is used to provide a user interface for using IoT smart applications, such as agriculture, road monitoring, pollution monitoring, healthcare, retail, public safety, smart home. With the expanding development of RFID innovation, various applications are advancing which will be under the umbrella of IoT.[5]

The implementation of IoT platforms to make things smart needs several technologies and protocols. The technologies and protocols used by different layers make the IoT devices to communicate with each other. The next section gives a brief overview of IoT layers protocol and technologies used.

15.3   TECHNOLOGIES/STANDARDS/PROTOCOLS OF IOT

This section detailed the data layer or messaging protocols and network-layer protocols which help the IoT to establish communication between billions of IoT devices.

15.3.1   MESSAGING PROTOCOLS OF IOT

Messaging protocols covers data transfer from one device to other systems for an IoT platform. Some devices consist of sensors to transfer data at a regular interval of time. For the data transmission, we can use some data protocols in IoT. The most popular data protocols include the following:

Messaging Queuing Telemetry Transport Protocol (MQTTP): This is the most used transport layer protocol developed by Andy Stanford-Clark of IBM and Arlen Nipper of Arcom in 1999, and is designed for Machine-to-Machine communication. It is a lightweight messaging protocol of IoT for data transmission between users and servers. It requires little bandwidth around a few Mbps and uses a client-server model for different operations like publish and subscribe to the data.

Constrained Application Protocol (CoAP): This was developed as a standard (RFC 7252) based on the REST model. It is designed for IoT systems based on HTTP protocols-based IoT systems used this standard and to join simple, constrained devices to IoT through low bandwidth-constrained networks.

Extensible Message and Queuing Protocol (XMQP): This is based on XML technology for real-time communication, and it is a message-oriented protocol for middleware environment. XMQP is an open standard (RFC6120) that has allowed instant messaging, scalability, and security for IoT.

15.3.2 NETWORK PROTOCOLS OF IOT

LoRaWANP (Low-Power Wide Area Network Protocol) is used for networks of wide area and it is made to connect millions of low-power devices in a huge network such as smart cities. It uses a frequency range of 2–15 km with data rates of 0.3–50 kbps and provides low-cost bidirectional communication.

ZigBee is a low power, low-data rate (250 kbps) wireless protocol based on IEEE 802.15.4 based standard. 'Dotdot' a universal language was created by its Alliance for IoT which allows a smart object to work securely and understand every other object on any network.[6] **RFID** uses a reading device called readers and tag systems called RFID tags which use small radio frequency transponders having distance reading capabilities by using unique programmed information. RFID uses a frequency band of 125 kHz–13.9 MHz with a data rate of 4 Mbps.

Bluetooth uses frequency hopping and ISM band of 2.4 GHz. With a data rate up to 3 Mbps, this technology is significant for IoT applications due to its lower power consumption rate, low latency and lower setup time.

Z-Wave is a wireless communication protocol envisioned by Zensys, it operates on low frequency 868–908 MHz and low data rate of 40 kbps. Z-Wave protocol allows devices to connect and exchange control commands and brings low-cost wireless connectivity to home automation. The standard

IEEE 802.11 through 2.4 GHz UHF and 5 GHz ISM frequencies utilizes by **WiFi** is wireless local area network abbreviated as WLAN. It provides internet access to devices that are within devices range about 66 ft from access point to get internet access by WLAN.

NFC (Near Field Communication) is short-range high-frequency wireless technology based on the standard ISO/IEC 18092:2004, using inductively coupled devices at a center frequency of 125 kHz–13.56 MHz with the data rate up to 424 kbps, and the range is with a few meters, short compared with the wireless sensor networks.

Cellular Technology: It is a form of communication mostly referred to as M2M which allows devices such as mobile phones to send and receive data through a cellular network. Cellular technology uses standards such as GSM/GPRS/3G/4G LTE for reliable high-speed connectivity which is the best fit for the IoT applications. Applications that need high throughput data and require operations over long distances via mobile devices use cellular communication. It is the most viable and interesting technology for users due to its universal compatibility and stable connection with the boom of IoT in the upcoming era based on cellular technology.

5G Technology: It is a trending radio access innovation which retrofits the existing cellular technologies such as 2G/3G/4G with the greater coverage area, higher density of the network, greater accessibility with respect to cells and devices.[7] The vehicular applications of IoT will get a greater benefit from 5G technology for the most reliable low latency vehicular communication. The existing 4G LTE integrates the WiFi and other unlicensed spectra. Now, 5G extends the existing 4G LTE capability by integrating 3G, 4G, Bluetooth, WiFi, and ZigBee technologies. 5G would expect communication between devices covering a wider area to give creative proximity-based services and data access. 5G communication is based on proximity service (ProSe) to provide information by identification of devices and services using location information. ProSe platform used in 5G-enabled IoT applications that provide discovery of ad hoc location like moving cars on roads. With the development of 5G networks, the current IoT systems migrate toward the platforms of advanced communication is the trend toward wireless.[8]

15.4   TIME SYNCHRONIZATION ERRORS AND RELATED APPLICATIONS

The two main components that have to be calculated for synchronizing reference clock of server and the local clock of device are (1) clock offset is a delay of given clock source and (2) clock skew is the time gap between the expected arrival of clock to its actual arrival also referred as jitter, it occurs due to the instability of parameters of system. These drifts in atomic and reference clocks create synchronization errors and make the system unstable. Different clock synchronization protocols such as NTP (Network Time Protocol), SNTP (Simple Network Time Protocol), MQTT, SPoT (Simple Packet exchange protocol) have been developed to compensate for these delays. The variations in configurations, operating conditions make the existing protocols, such as SNTP, MQTT, and MNTP ineffective. To maintain the synchronization of clocks in IoT devices SPoT protocol is used that provides better clock offsets in all different configurations, conditions or platforms and maintain clock accuracy.[11] Still, there is no protocol or methodology found to be most appropriate for the developers that help them to find a good solution for every condition like temperature, configurations, correct offset values or reduced clock skews with wireless networks.[12] This happens due to the limitations of existing protocols and inaccuracy in time traceability from local time servers.

The financial sectors, such as Bank, stock exchange that works on real or dynamic data require highly accurate timekeeping. As the number of devices of IoT family continues to grow within the internet architecture, the necessities of time synchronization become crucial. To provide better synchronization, reference clock should be synchronized with standard time which is more accurate and provides better traceability. To provide transparency and stability in some sectors such as trading and stock exchange, there is a need for implementation of traceable time with the standard clock time.

15.4.1 IOT-BASED APPLICATIONS REQUIRING TIME SYNCHRONIZATION

Time synchronization and stamping are essential for all real-time applications in terms of safety, security, etc. A brief overview of various sectors of IoT where time synchronization is the key issue and makes a colossal difference is as follows.

Strategic Sectors: Precise time measurement and synchronization are essential for various strategic sectors, including ISRO, DRDO, Armed Forces, Indian astronomical observatories. Space application and astronomical research relies on accurate surveillance, accurate targeting, satellite launching, and placing them in right orbits relies mostly on precise time synchronization.

Navigation: Time synchronization of nanosecond accuracies of the onboard satellite clocks with the base receivers and transmitters is essential for pinpointing the position of an object on the earth.

Digital Archiving: It is storing electronic data in an ordered manner; it is important for the efficient operation of a trade or any other sector which has multiple branches. An error in time can cause significant problems and even include legal liability.

National Security: Monitoring of any violence or national calamity (natural and man-made disasters) and immediate action against it requires time synchronization among the security agencies and other related organizations.

Smart Weather Prediction and Disaster Management: It includes dynamic mapping and evolution of any natural disaster, such as a cyclone, flood, tsunami. relies on accurate time synchronization among the associated devices. Smart weather application of IoT giving disaster alert, civil alert, traffic information, early warning on health or weather requires time synchronization of network devices and associated systems.

Smart Transportation: Efficiency of an automatic signaling system, air traffic control and navigation of all transport systems, including road traffic, railways, aviation, etc. depends on accurate time synchronization of the associated devices.

Power Grid Application: A significant amount of electric power can be saved if the grids are time-synchronized, as depending upon the requirement, the power can be re-routed, and grid failures are detected without wasting time. Due to lack of synchronization, there have been several major power failures, and also identifying the causes behind any grid failure took an unnecessary long time, which is avoidable, if precise time dissemination facilities are linked with the grid system.

Electronic Transactions: In all financial transactions they require accurate time stamping for fraud protection and synchronization of all associated network devices to a common reference time. A primary server as a stratum 1 server that receives a UTC time signal directly from an authoritative clock source, for example, atomic clock or GPS signal source. A stratum 2 server gets its time signal from a stratum 1 server, a stratum 3 server from stratum 2 servers, etc.

The next section is divided into two subsections which give the details of existing researches based on real-time applications, and other basic applications of IoT.

15.5 RELATED WORK

The related work has consistently provided information which includes the published work of researchers. This section reviews some existing work in the field of IoT based on real-time and other applications.

15.5.1 REAL-TIME APPLICATIONS OF IOT

In vehicle, smartphone sensors connected with the backend platform over the internet are used for screening of the road conditions and generates alert. Ghose and Biswas[15] bring an Application (App) for road condition monitoring. This energy-efficient App used the agnostic accelerometers for analytics in mobile phones. By using a set of sensors, such as GPS, accelerometers, simulators, and compass in the user's phone provides the alert based on road conditions, such as potholes, bumps, etc. The app consists of a dashboard application and a real-time alert system for the road condition map view. A geospatial database with backend server runs fusion module and periodic clustering which added multiple readings of location based on same feature also find aggregate score using fusion. The location simulator instead of GPS updates the information of the vehicle's position and transmitted it via. WiFi to the backend server for generating alerts if hurdles are identified.

The real-time IoT application scenario discussed in[16] where the lane velocity is independently decided by multiple autonomous vehicles collaborated with roadside units to utilize intersection with minimal environmental impact. The intersection of traffic account for a significant amount of traffic delays and accidents in real-time. The authors proposed a consensus-based 'constant step size gradient descent algorithm' for a near-optimal solution. Simulation of urban mobility (SUMO) mobility simulator is used to embed the microscopic behavior of traffic flows. A secure, reliable, short-range, low latency WAVE (Wireless Access in Vehicular Environment) communication technology is used for the high mobility conditions. The proposed algorithm collects locally available data from the neighbors, and every agent performs averaging and updating step. The next step is to obtain an estimate of current system variables by calculating the weighted average and updates its local objective function. This approach implements an advance traffic intersection management for autonomous vehicles of better performance in terms of traffic delays and safety.

Khanna and Anand[17] present an on-site deployment IoT module for a smart parking system that monitors and signalize the availability state of each single free parking slot. The mobile application used for smart parking is connected to the cloud and provides information on parking spaces on a real-time basis. The system consists of parking sensors, such as passive infrared (PIR) and ultrasonic sensors to sense the parking area space, and the ultrasonic sensors are connected with processor raspberry Pi processor on-chip. The IBM MQTT server hosted on cloud integrates with IoT-based mobile. The concept of automated self-driving cars in heavy traffic jams and another approach of dynamic destination discovered in[18] by using a three-wheeled mobile robot. The idea of a dynamic destination covers the linking of two vehicles in which one vehicle automatically following the destination of another vehicle. Multiple sensors are embedded in the vehicle which helps it to communicate with API (Application Program Interface) of Google Maps. The mobile vehicle gets a route from Google Maps API via GPRS and moves in that direction. To avoid and detect the obstacles ultrasonic sensors have been fixed all around the targeting and following vehicle. The target vehicle identifies its live location coordinates through GPS and sends it to GPRS Arduino, the ninth eform of a message, it is sent to the following vehicle to fetch the target vehicle coordinates after every time span. These two vehicles coordinate through GPRS arduino which connects to Google Maps and compares existing locations.

15.5.2   OTHER APPLICATIONS OF IOT

Using IoT and automation technologies paper[19] includes GPS based remote-controlled robots to perform tasks like weeding, moisture sensing, keeping vigilance, etc. Smart agriculture concept also includes smart irrigation with advanced control and smart decision making based on real-time data. Temperature, humidity maintenance, and theft detection operations in the warehouse are performed by using interfacing sensors like humidity, temperature, light sensors. Motion detectors are used for security which detects the motion and sends an alert signal to users via Raspberry pi. Camera and GPS systems are also connected to the raspberry pi. Robots are controlled using wireless signals sent via ZigBee module to the raspberry pi which forwards them to microcontrollers and finally they give signals to motor drivers to drive a robot.

Kumar and Rajasekaran in their paper[20] focused on patient health status monitoring, such as body temperature, respiration rate, heartbeat and body movement by using different sensors on the Raspberry pi platform. Raspberry pi collects all information from these sensors and sends it to the IoT website. This development reduces the patient's waiting time at hospitals and their money even they can record their health status on mobile phones.

Narrowband IoT (NBIoT) wireless communication technology is used by authors[21] to connect intelligent things for smart hospital applications. Edge computing servers are introduced for latency requirements in the medical process. The real-time drop rate and remaining drug volume during the intravenous infusion is monitored by an infusion monitoring system that uses infrared sensors for terminal monitoring. The existing researches describe the different technologies, ideas, protocols used by researchers for different IoT applications having some limitations. The next section measures some existing research challenges raised in different IoT-based applications.

15.6 IOT AND TIME SYNCHRONIZATION CHALLENGES

IoT is in the beginning process of the digital revolution that is yet to be harnessed and implemented. The real-time applications of IoT have challenges being faced by the citizens is not yet fully harnessed by the IT Industry in India. This section phrases some major challenges of IoT in this perspective.

Interoperability and Compatibility of IoT Devices: Every machine is not equipped with advanced sensors and networking capabilities to effectively communicate and share data. It becomes really difficult to maintain interoperability between different IoT devices.

Security and Authentication Risk: Connecting billions of IoT devices with public networks lead to the data breaching by attackers. It needs an architecture that can identify and authenticate each IoT devices.

Poor Connectivity: The unavailability of the internet everywhere at the same speed makes the communication poor between IoT devices. Still, low speed and low-network coverage communication technologies are used like 3G/4G/WiFi which creates networking and tracking problems. 5G technology is still into its sake to implement in IoT devices for better connectivity.

Data Capturing Capabilities: Real-time data are collected from various sources in a standard format that can be analyzed and automated. The certain anomalies in run time make the incorrect data to record due to lack of time synchronization in applications.

Delays in autonomous vehicle applications: Poor coordination among vehicles running on roads generates delays in vehicular communication which may lead to road accidents and may increase traffic congestion. Delays occur due to the poor connectivity of the internet with no time synchronization between IoT-enabled vehicles.

Instability of clocks: The drifts in time of reference clocks and local clocks found due to inaccuracy in time traceability.

The next section concludes the paper with the scope of future work.

15.7 CONCLUSION

Time synchronization is a key element of the IoT that require many parameters, protocols, techniques that we have discussed in this paper. Also, it needs accurate time traceability and synchronization for the effective and stable communication of IoT devices. In this chapter, the clock synchronization errors with time synchronization-based applications have been discussed. Also, the challenges related to time synchronization occurred in IoT-based applications are presented in this chapter. The future direction of this study is to study new IoT-based applications which contain the clocks with accurate time synchronization with the standard time. This syncing will reduce the rate of uncertainties that occur due to the variations in time. In order to synchronize different sectors over the internet, a new architecture needs to be developed that not only takes care of time sync aspects but also works on the upcoming IP6 architecture where each device interacting over the internet has its unique IP address and favorable in all conditions.

KEYWORDS

- **Internet of Things**
- **time synchronization**
- **clock errors**
- **IoT protocols**

REFERENCES

1. Guoqiang, S.; Yanming, C.; Chao, Z.; Yanxu, Z. Design and Implementation of a Smart IoT Gateway. In *2013 IEEE International Conference on Green Computing and*

Communications and IEEE Internet of Things and IEEE Cyber, Physical and Social Computing; IEEE, Aug, 2013, pp 720–723.

2. *The Emerging Internet of Things*. https://www.cigionline.org/articles/emerging-internet-things, 2016.
3. Pretz, K. *The Next Evolution of the Internet*, cited May, 2013.
4. Al-Sarawi, S.; Anbar, M.; et. al. Internet of Things (IoT) Communication Protocols: Review. In *8th International Conference on Information Technology*, 2017.
5. Govinda, K.; Saravanaguru, R. A. K. Review on IoT Technologies. *Int. J. Appl. Eng. Res.* **2016,** *11* (4). ISSN 0973-4562.
6. Samie, F.; Bauer, L.; Henkel, J. October. IoT technologies for Embedded Computing: A Survey. In *2016 International Conference on Hardware/Software Codesign and System Synthesis (CODES+ ISSS)*; IEEE, 2016; pp 1–10.
7. Xu, L.; Collier, R.; et al. A Survey of Clustering Techniques in WSNs and Consideration of the Challenges of Applying Such to 5G IoT Scenarios. *J. IEEE Internet Things* **2017,** *6* (1).
8. Ali Shah, S. A.; Ahmed, E.; et al. 5G for Vehicular Communications. *IEEE Commun. Mag.* **2018,** *56* (1).
9. http://www.nplindia.in/clockcode/html/how_to_sync.php
10. http://www.nplindia.in/indian-standard-time-metrology-division-d60
11. Mani, S. K.; Durairajan, R.; Barford, P.; Sommers, J. *A System for Clock Synchronization in an Internet of Things*, 2018. Preprint arXiv:1806.02474.
12. Mani, S. K.; Durairajan, R.; Barford, P.; Sommers, J. An Architecture for IoT Clock Synchronization. In *Proceedings of the 8th International Conference on the Internet of Things*, Oct, 2018; pp 1–8.
13. Tirado-Andrés, F.; Rozas, A.; Araujo, A. A Methodology for Choosing Time Synchronization Strategies for Wireless IoT Networks. *Sensors* **2019,** *19* (16), 3476.
14. https://www.geographyandyou.com/indian-standard-time/(magazine)
15. Ghose, A.; Biswas, P. *Road Condition Monitoring and Alert Application Using In-Vehicle Smartphone as Internet-Connected Sensor*, Mar, 2012.
16. Philip, B. V.; Alpcan, T.; Jin, J.; Palaniswami, M. Distributed Real-Time IoT for Autonomous Vehicles. *IEEE Trans. Industr. Inform.* **2018,** *15* (2), 1131–1140.
17. Khanna, A.; Anand, R. IoT Based Smart Parking System. In *International Conference on Internet of Things and Applications (IoTA)*, Jan, 2016.
18. Memon, Q.; Ahmed, M.; et al. *Self-Driving and Driver Relaxing Vehicle*, Nov 2016.
19. Gondchawar, N.; Kawitkar, R. S. IoT Based Smart Agriculture. *Int. J. Adv. Res. Comput. Commun. Eng.* **2016,** *5* (6), 838–842.
20. Kumar, R.; Rajasekaran, M. P. An IoT Based Patient Monitoring System Using Raspberry Pi. In *2016 International Conference on Computing Technologies and Intelligent Data Engineering (ICCTIDE'16)*; IEEE, Jan, 2016; pp 1–4.
21. Zhang, H.; Li, J.; et al. Connecting Intelligent Things in Smart Hospitals Using NB-IoT. *IEEE Internet Things J.* **2018,** *5* (3).

CHAPTER 16

A Review on Applications of Machine Learning in IoT: Challenges and Future Prospects

SUBRATA PAUL[1] and ANIRBAN MITRA[2]

[1]*Department of CSE, Brainware University, Barasat, West Bengal, India*

[2]*Department of CSE, ASET, Amity University, Kolkata, West Bengal, India*

ABSTRACT

The Internet of Things (IoT) applications have grown in exorbitant numbers, generating a large amount of data required for intelligent data processing. However, the varying IoT infrastructures (i.e., cloud, edge, fog) and the limitations of the IoT application layer protocols in transmitting/receiving messages become the barriers in creating intelligent IoT applications. Deep learning and other machine learning (ML) approaches are deployed to many systems related to Internet of Things or IoT. However, it faces challenges that adversaries can take loopholes to hack these systems through tampering history data. Throughout this chapter, the authors shall review on the studies made in the application of ML in IoT. The major issues and challenges faced during the application is focused. In the final part of the chapter, the future prospects are discussed.

16.1 INTRODUCTION

The Internet of Things (IoT) is a novel paradigm that allows, via standard electronic and wireless identification systems, to identify and communicate

Internet of Things: Technological Advances and New Applications. Brojo Kishore Mishra & Amit Vishwasrao Salunkhe (Eds.)

with physical objects. Thus, in order to measure and exchange data between the physical and virtual worlds, IoTs are playing a vital role. In other words, we can define IoTs, as a set of objects with virtual identities, operating in smart spaces while using smart interfaces to connect and communicate in a variety of use cases.[1] A connected device has the ability to pick up data and send it via the internet or other technologies, to be viewed, stored, and analyzed. These devices can be a car, an industrial machine or a smartphone and so on.[2] They become able to interact with their environment through sensors: temperature, speed, humidity, vibration, and others. In addition, IoT consists of a heterogeneous set of networks that allow the communication of these objects. Among them, we note the cellular networks of telecom operators that allow devices equipped with a machine-to-machine (M2M)-based subscriber identity module (SIM) card to trace and send the data.

Artificial intelligence (AI) is a modern science for discovering patterns and making predictions from data based on statistics, data mining, pattern recognition, and predictive analytics.[3] Machine learning, which relates to the AI field, is a process of development, analysis and implementation leading to establish a systematic process. It provides machines' capabilities to find solutions to complicated problems, by exploiting the Big Data. This offers an opportunity to analyze and highlight the correlations that exist between two or more given situations, and to predict their different implications.[3]

Machine learning (ML), especially deep learning, is increasingly popular not only in daily life but also in many science disciplines, including Internet of Things or IoT.[4] For example, computer security in terms of IoT network intrusions' detection, and malware identification relies on automatic approaches stemming from deep learning (DL), but those are only two examples of DL in IoT security. Whereas, DL is effective at average normal cases, such as the well-known example of sorting fish automatically by their inherent features. On the other hand, security is targeted on worst tricky cases.[5] It would be easy to bypass a DL-based IoT analysis filter through malicious tasks in adversarial settings.[6] An example of this is combining malicious samples with benign files, evading several PDF malware classifiers. Therefore, the safe adoption of DL approaches in IoT security settings is an unsolved challenge. Adversarial DL is crucial in life-critical IoT systems,[7] such as roadside sign recognition used by autonomous vehicles. To be specific, small nonobvious manipulations in roadside signs can lead to distinct opposite results in specific DL methods.[8] Accuracy and sensitivity simultaneously are trade-off in several systems.

16.2 LITERATURE REVIEW

Ara and Ara,[9] studied how Zion China technical solution E-Followup which was based mostly on traditional Business Intelligence with data sourced from on-premises and various devices or cloud storage. In this engagement, they wanted a smart, fast, and cost-effective way to continuously feed data from devices to the cloud and had other technical goals. The result provides an insight how they handled massive data volumes efficiently and improved the analysis of data.

In their article,[10] outlined a flexible smart-metering architecture that can provide device monitoring and management in a unified manner over disparate underlying network technologies, such as narrow-band IoT (NB-IoT), LTECat-M1, Zigbee, Wi-Fi, wireless smart ubiquitous network (Wi-SUN), long-range wide area network (LoRaWAN), and Sigfox. The specifics of the underlying physical and link layers are abstracted away by using uniform, lightweight application layer protocols, such as Constrained Application Protocol (CoAP) and Message Queuing Telemetry Transport (MQTT). Then, we describe how this IoT architecture can be used to predict future energy consumption using past measurements and publicly available weather data. More specifically, we use energy measurements taken at 15-min intervals and build a random forest model that slightly outperforms the best autoregressive baseline. We use the test mean absolute error (MAE) and mean absolute percentage error (MAPE) as performance metrics. The significance of forecasting the future power demand lies in that it enables both consumers and grid operators to meet such demand in a more economical, efficient, and environmentally friendly way.

Dey et al.,[11] proposed and describe the real-time, streaming system called Namatad that we developed to infer insights from many sensors typical of Internet of Things (IoT) deployments. We evaluate the effectiveness of this platform by leveraging ML to infer new insights from environmental sensors within buildings. We describe how we built the components of our system leveraging several open source, streaming frameworks. We also describe how we ingest and aggregate from building sensors and sensing platforms, route data streams to appropriate models, and make predictions using ML techniques. Using our system, we have been able to predict the occupancy of rooms within a building on the University of Washington campus over the last 3 months, in real time, at accuracies of up to 95%.

In order to overcome the need to real-time big data stream processing to ensure an effective and scalable solution, Ed-daoudy and Maalmi[12] propose a new architecture for real-time health status prediction and analytics system using big data technologies. The system focuses on applying distributed ML model on streaming health data events ingested to Spark streaming through Kafka topics. Firstly, we transform the standard decision tree (DT) (C4.5) algorithm into a parallel, distributed, scalable, and fast DT using Spark instead of Hadoop Map Reduce which becomes limited for real-time computing. Secondly, this model is applied to streaming data coming from distributed sources of various diseases to predict health status. Based on several input attributes, the system predicts health status, send an alert message to care providers and store the details in a distributed database to perform health data analytics and stream reporting. We measure the performance of Spark DT against traditional ML tools including Weka. Finally, performance evaluation parameters, such as throughput and execution time are calculated to show the effectiveness of the proposed architecture. The experimental results show that the proposed system is able to effectively process and predict real-time and massive amount of medical data enabled by IoT from distributed and various diseases.

Endler et al.,[13] propose a new semantic model for data stream processing and real-time reasoning based on the concepts of Semantic Stream and Fact Stream as a natural extension of complex event processing (CEP) and RDF (graph-based knowledge model). The main advantages of our approach are that (1) it considers time as a key relation between pieces of information; (2) the processing of streams can be implemented using CEP; (3) it is general enough to be applied to any data stream management system (DSMS). Lastly, we will present challenges and prospects on using ML and induction algorithms to learn abstractions and reasoning rules from a continuous data stream.

Priyashman and Ismail[14] have presented a thorough understanding of the influences that affect the performance of the windshield tag and developing a prediction model based on the most influential factor. In addition, two ML algorithms are proposed to achieve the objective of the paper. Linear regression analysis provides a reliable estimation of the RSSI levels of the windshield tag from all the selected location. The second proposed algorithm is based on the logistic regression model which provides an accurate prediction model based on tag readability by the reader. The predicted tag detectability model coupled with the RSSI level estimation model gives a complete overview of the behavior of the RFID tag when deployed on the windshield of the vehicle. This will serve as a guideline for the RFID transportation application which may extensively rely on RFID as a part of the IoT transformation.

Ruta et al.[15] propose a framework for a semantic-enhanced data mining on sensor streams, amenable to resource-constrained pervasive contexts. It merges an ontology-based characterization of data distributions with nonstandard reasoning for a fine-grained event detection by treating the typical classification problem of ML as a resource discovery. Outputs of classification are endowed with machine-understandable descriptions in standard Semantic Web languages, while explanation of match making outcomes motivates confidence on results. A case study on road and traffic analysis has allowed validating the proposal and achieving an assessment with respect to state-of-the-art ML algorithms.

Mahdavinejad et al.[16] assess the various ML methods that deal with the challenges presented by IoT data by considering smart cities as the main use case. The key contribution of this study is the presentation of taxonomy of ML algorithms explaining how different techniques are applied to the data in order to extract higher level information. The potential and challenges of ML for IoT data analytics will also be discussed. A use case of applying a support vector machine (SVM) to Aarhus smart city traffic data is presented for a more detailed exploration.

Shanthamallu et al.,[17] provide a brief survey of the basic concepts and algorithms used for ML and its applications. We begin with a broader definition of ML and then introduce various learning modalities including supervised and unsupervised methods and DL paradigms. In the rest of the paper, we discuss applications of ML algorithms in various fields including pattern recognition, sensor networks, anomaly detection, Internet of Things (IoT), and health monitoring. In the final sections, we present some of the software tools and an extensive bibliography.

Chafii et al.[18] propose a new method for enhancing the NB-IoT coverage based on ML algorithms. Instead of employing a random spectrum access procedure, dynamic spectrum access can reduce the number of required repetitions, increase the coverage, and reduce the energy consumption.

16.3 DIFFERENT ASPECTS OF IOT

16.3.1 CHARACTERISTICS OF IOT NETWORKS

In the following, we discuss some unique characteristics of IoT networks.

Heterogeneity: In an IoT network, a multitude of different devices with different capabilities, characteristics and different communication protocols communicate with each other. More precisely, the devices could use different standards for communication, and different communication paradigms (such as cellular or Ethernet) and variable constraints on the hardware resources. Such heterogeneity on one hand enables cross platform communication among different devices, but on the other hand introduces new challenges to the IoT network.

Massive deployment: It is speculated that the billions of devices connected with each other and through Internet will likely surpass the capabilities of the current Internet. The deployment of IoT on massive scale also brings challenges. Some of these challenges include design of networking and storage architecture for smart devices, efficient data communication protocols, proactive identification and protection of IoT from malicious attacks, standardization of technologies, and devices and application interfaces[19,20] etc.

Interconnectivity: IoT devices are expected to be connected to global information and communication infrastructure and can be accessed from anywhere and anytime. The connectivity depends on the type of service and application provided by the IoT service provider(s). In some cases, the connectivity could be local (such as in case of connected car technology or swarm of sensors), whereas in other cases, it could be global such as in the case of smart home access through mobile infrastructure and critical infrastructure management.

Communication in close proximity: Another salient feature of IoT is the communication in close proximity without involving the central authorities such as base stations. Device-to-Device communication (D2D) leverages the characteristics of point-to-point communication such as Dedicated Short-Range Communication (DSRC) and similar technologies. The architecture of traditional Internet is more inclined toward network-centric communication, whereas decoupling of networks and services enables device-centric as well as content centric communication which enriches the IoT service spectrum.

Ultra-reliable and low latency communication (URLLC): This property of IoT networks is required in critical real-time applications, such as industrial process automation, remote surgery, and intelligent traffic transport system, where the major performance constraints are both delay and reliability.

Low-power and low-cost communication: Massive connectivity of IoT devices requires ultra-low-power and low-cost solutions for efficient network operations.

Self-organization and self-healing characteristics: These are required for urgent and contemporary IoT communication that includes emergency or disaster situations. In such situations, reliance on the network infrastructure is not an option, and therefore, self-organizing networks should be deployed.

Dynamic changes in the network: IoT consists of massive number of devices that need to be managed in an efficient way. These devices will act dynamically, for instance, the sleep/wakeup time of devices will depend on the application, when do these devices use Internet and when do they communicate directly, and so on.

Safety: Safety is considered for both the consumers and devices because the large number of IoT devices connected to Internet may jeopardize the personal data that is shared through these devices. Furthermore, privacy and the security of device itself is also an important factor.

Intelligence: One of the most intriguing characteristics of IoT is the intelligence through which timely and informed decisions are made based on the processed data.

16.3.2 SECURITY CHALLENGES IN IOT DEPLOYMENT

Security and privacy are two of the main factors in the commercial realization of the IoT services and applications. Current Internet is the luring playground for security attacks ranging from simple hacks all the way to corporate level well-coordinated security breaches that have adversely affected different industries, such as healthcare and business. The limitations of the IoT devices and the environment they operate in, pose additional challenges for the security of both applications and the devices. To date, security and privacy issues have been extensively researched in the IoT domain from different perspectives such as communication security, data security, privacy, architectural security, identity management, malware analysis, and so on.[21]

Fernandes et al.,[22] focused on similarities and differences of the security issues in IoT and the traditional IT devices. Furthermore, they also focused on the privacy issues. The main driving factors to argue on the similarities and differences include software, hardware, network, and applications. Based on these classifications, there are fundamental similarities between the security issues in traditional IT domain and the IoT. However, the primary concern of the IoT is the resource constraints that hinder the adoption of already available sophisticated security solutions in IoT networks. Furthermore, solutions to the security and privacy issues in IoT require cross-layer design and optimized algorithms. For instance, due to computational constraints, IoT devices may need new breeds of optimized cryptographic and other algorithms to cope with security and privacy. A holistic security and privacy approach toward IoT will have nominations from the existing security solutions as well as development of new intelligent, robust, evolutionary, and scalable mechanisms to address security challenges in IoT.

16.3.3   MACHINE LEARNING: A SOLUTION TO IOT SECURITY CHALLENGES

ML refers to intelligent methods used to optimize performance criteria using example data or past experience(s) through learning. More precisely, ML algorithms build models of behaviors using mathematical techniques on huge data sets. ML also enables the ability to learn without being explicitly programmed. These models are used as a basis for making future predictions based on the newly input data. ML is interdisciplinary in nature and inherits its roots from many disciplines of science and engineering that include artificial intelligence, optimization theory, information theory, and cognitive science.[23]

ML is utilized when human expertise either do not exist or cannot be used such as navigating a hostile place where humans are unable to use their expertise, for instance robotics, speech recognition. It is also applied in situations where solution to some specific problem changes in time (routing in a computer network or finding malicious code in a software or application). Furthermore, it is used in practical smart systems, for instance, Google uses ML to analyze threats against mobile endpoints and applications running on Android. It is also used for identifying and removing malware from infected handsets. Likewise, Amazon has launched a service Macie that uses ML to sort and classify data stored in its cloud storage service. Although, ML techniques perform well in many areas. However, there is a chance of false-positives and true-negatives. Therefore, ML techniques need guidance and modification to the model if inaccurate prediction is made. On the contrary, in deep learning (DL), a new breed of ML, the model can determine the accuracy of prediction by itself. Due to self-service nature of DL models, it is rendered as more suitable for classification and prediction tasks in innovative IoT applications with contextual and personalized assistance.

Although traditional approaches are widely used for different aspects of IoT (e.g., applications, services, architectures, protocols, data aggregation, resource allocation, clustering, analytics) including security, the massive scale deployment of IoT however, advocates for intelligent, robust, and reliable techniques. To this end, ML and DL are promising techniques for IoT networks due to several reasons, for example, IoT networks produce a sheer amount of data which is required by ML and DL approaches to bring intelligence to the systems. Furthermore, the data generated by the IoT is better utilized with the ML and DL techniques which enable the IoT systems to make informed and intelligent decisions. ML and DL are largely used for security, privacy, attack detection, and malware analysis. DL techniques can also be used in IoT devices to perform complex sensing and recognition tasks to enable the realization of new applications and services considering real-time interactions among humans, smart devices, and physical surroundings.

Some of the security-related real-world applications of ML are as follows:

- Face recognition for forensics: pose, lighting, occlusion (glasses, beard), make-up, hair style, etc.
- Character recognition for security encryption: different handwriting styles.
- Malicious code identification: identifying malicious code in applications and software.
- Distributed denial of service (DDoS) detection: detecting DDoS attacks on infrastructure through behavior analysis.

Using ML and DL techniques in IoT applications on the other hand brings multifaceted challenges. For instance, it is challenging to develop a suitable model to process data from diverse IoT applications. Similarly, labeling input data effectively is also a cumbersome task. Another challenge is using minimum labeled data in the learning process. Other challenges stem from the deployment of these models on resource-constrained IoT devices where it is essential to reduce the processing and storage overhead.[24] Similarly, critical infrastructure and real-time applications cannot withstand the anomalies created because of ML or DL algorithms. In the above context, it is imperative to systematically review the security solutions of IoT that leverage ML and DL techniques.

16.3.4 MACHINE LEARNING TECHNIQUES USED IN IOT SECURITY

In the following, we discuss various ML algorithms focusing on the underlying security and privacy problems in IoT networks. More precisely, we consider authentication, attack detection, and mitigation, DDoS attacks, anomaly and intrusion detection, and malware analysis.

Supervised learning algorithms work with labeled data and are utilized in IoT networks for spectrum sensing, channel estimation, adaptive filtering, security, and localization problems. This category holds two distinct types of techniques: classification and regression. Classification under supervised

ML is used for predication as well as modeling of the available data sets. Regression is used for predicting continuous numeric variables. SVM, Naive Bayes, Random Forest, Decision Tree are few of the widely used classification algorithms. While, Nearest neighbors and logistic regression are to famous regression algorithms. These algorithms are also known as "instance-based," that make predictions for each new observation by searching for the most similar training data.

The family of unsupervised learning algorithms deals with unlabeled data and utilize input data in a heuristic manner. These are used in anomaly, fault, and intrusion detection, cell clustering, and load balancing. Clustering under unsupervised learning category is used for data groupings based on some inherent similarities and dissimilarities. The clustering is unsupervised, and therefore, there are no right or wrong answers. To evaluate the accuracy of the results, data visualization is used. If there is a possible right or wrong answer, then the clusters can be pre-labeled in data sets and in this scenario, classification algorithms are preferred.

RL techniques learn by exploiting various stages and develop the reward and action relationship between agent and the environment. This relationship of action reward is very useful in solving various IoT problems.[25] It does not require extensive training data set; however, the agent is required to have the knowledge of the state transition function.

Most of the IoT applications befit the use of unsupervised learning approaches with very less initial information about the environment. For instance, the zero-day attacks on IoT networks have little or no information to start with. Therefore, the unsupervised learning class of ML can be a promising learning technique in the IoT networks to combat such security attacks.

Supervised ML algorithm, such as SVM, DT, and Naïve Bayes are also used in IoT security. For instance, SVMs are able to model nonlinear decision boundaries. However, it becomes difficult to use with large data sets. Therefore, random forests are usually preferred over SVM. Random forest algorithms are easier to implement and are also adaptive to the size of the available data set. It achieves a higher degree of accuracy and takes less time for prediction. However, it takes longer time to train as compared SVM and NB. NB is suitable for problems such as text classification and spam detection. Logistic regression and Nearest neighbor algorithms are memory-intensive and perform poorly for high-dimensional data. Considering the unsupervised ML algorithms, K-means and hierarchical clustering are two popular clustering algorithms. K-means clustering is most popular because it is a simple and flexible algorithm that forms clusters based on geometric distances between data points. Clusters are grouped around centroids resulting into globular with the same size. However, the number of clusters has to be specified before clustering starts and it is not always possible and efficient to do. Also, if clusters are not globular, it results into poor cluster formation.

RL techniques are computationally simple but require significant time to converge to a steady state. This slow convergence and knowledge of the state transition function or optimal policy are the key challenges in using RL algorithms in dynamic environments of IoT networks. The optimal policy is determined by trial and error and is obtained after many transitions.

DL also relies on strong function approximation, estimation and the learning capabilities thus providing more efficient solutions in various problem areas of IoT domain including security and privacy. Due to their resource constraints, IoT devices may not be able to host or run complex computational algorithms for any type of task, such as communication, analytic and prediction. Therefore, DL-based algorithms show better performance with lower latency and complexity compared with conventional theories and techniques.[26] Additionally, DNNs are good in locating and defining low-dimensional representations from any type (text, image, audio) of high-dimensional data patterns. DRL and its variants are used for authentication and DDoS detection in heterogeneous IoT networks. The major DRL algorithms used for security and privacy include deep deterministic policy gradient, continuous DQN, prioritized experience replay, asynchronous N-step Q learning, deep SARSA, and dueling network DQN.

16.4   LIMITATIONS OF APPLYING MACHINE LEARNING IN IOT NETWORKS

Most of the traditional ML techniques are not inherently efficient and scalable enough to manage IoT data and thus need considerable modifications.[23] In the following, we discuss some of the common limitations of using ML techniques in IoT networks.

1. Constraints on processing power and energy: IoT devices are small and typically have energy constraints with limited processing power. Therefore, direct application of conventional ML techniques is not suitable in such resource-constrained environments.

2. Analytics of heterogeneous data: Wireless data can be generated from different sources including networked information systems, and sensing and communication devices.[27] The data generated in IoT networks is diverse in nature with different types, formats and semantics, thus exhibiting syntactic and semantic heterogeneity. Syntactic heterogeneity refers to diversity in the data types, file formats, encoding schemes, and data models. Semantic heterogeneity refers to differences in the meanings and interpretations of the data. Such heterogeneity leads to problems in terms of efficient and unified generalization, specifically, in the case of big data and various data sets with different attributes. The data require preprocessing and cleaning before fitting to a specific model.

    ML-based networks are developed assuming that the entire data set is available for processing during training phase. However, this may not be true for the IoT data. Also, the prediction ability of an algorithm decreases with the increase in the dimensionality of data.[28]

    Selecting an appropriate ML algorithm for a particular scenario is also a challenging task. IoT application can generate combination of structured (and relational), semi-structured, or unstructured data. If we have labeled data, classification (supervised) algorithms can be used and if the data is unlabeled, clustering (unsupervised) algorithm can be used for grouping and aggregating of the available data. If we have hybrid data, a combination of both types will be required.

    The preceding discussion is, at par, applicable for the security-related functions in the IoT where real-time data are processed for possible attack vectors such as intrusion.

3. Hardware technology and security requirements: IoT applications involve combination of versatile devices and processing units, ranging from high performance cloud servers to ultra-low-power edge devices. These heterogeneous devices demand advanced ML capabilities and stronger security features. Emerging IoT applications, such as autonomous vehicles, wearable devices, and drones require higher performance and security with minimum energy consumption. However, such high performance and energy-efficient multicore microprocessors, special circuit and chip design for ML, and DL neural networks are scarce, and also required to unleash the real potential of ML-enabled security. New paradigm shifts in terms of neuromorphic computing circuit design is required for efficient integration of special ML accelerators and hardware

security processors. Furthermore, energy constraint nature of IoT devices calls for design and development of ultralow-voltage logic and memory circuits and ultra-lightweight encryption engines.

16.5 THE CONVERGENCE OF MACHINE LEARNING AND IOT

The convergence of machine learning and IoT paves the way for a prospective advancement in efficiency, accuracy, productivity, and overall cost-savings for resource-constrained IoT devices. When ML algorithms and IoT work together, we can achieve improved performance for communication and computation, better controllability, and improved decision making. Due to advanced monitoring from thousands to billions of ubiquitous sensing devices and improved communication capabilities, IoT has enormous potential to improve the quality of human life and potential applications for industrial growth (toward Industry 4.0). IoT's potential has significantly improved with the convergence of ML and artificial intelligence. Advanced machine intelligence techniques have made it possible to mine the huge volume of IoT sensory data to have better insights into a range of real-world problems, as well as the ability to make critical operational decisions. Therefore, to solve the real-world complex problems and to meet the computation and communication requirements successfully, IoT and ML must complement a framework for ML and knowledge discovery for IoT each other. In recent years, IoT data analytics has gained significant importance and attention because of the following reasons:

High volume of data generated from distributed IoT devices: According to the mobility report by Ericsson, the forecasting shows that there will be 18 billion connected IoT devices globally by 2022.[29] This number will keep increasing over time due to the wide adoption of IoT devices in a wide range of critical applications. Intelligent data analytics will play an important role to identify and predict the future states of any process or system by mining this huge amount of data efficiently and intelligently.

High variability of data types from heterogeneous data sources: Due to a wide range of applications and requirements, a large variety of IoT devices exist, which include mobile phones, PC/Laptop, tablets to short-range and wide area IoT devices. Due to the heterogeneity of the data, the features, formats, and attributes of the data are different. Also, based on different IoT application domains, the data sources also vary. For example, the IoT devices used for medical applications will be different from a smart home

IoT. Moreover, the quality, processing, and storage of data have also become a challenging task because of its heterogeneity. In Sun et al.,[30] the authors highlight some key questions arising due to heterogeneity of data sources. It includes answers to critical questions, such as how to deal with the sampling procedure of the high-frequency streaming data, noise cancellation and filtering of the data, gathering and merging of the data from heterogeneous data sources, data interpretation and interoperability, reasoning, situation awareness and knowledge creation from the data, gathering and storing data from heterogeneous data sources to meet application's constraints.[30]

Uncertainty in the IoT data streams: Uncertainty is very common in practical data analysis.[31] It may arise in the IoT data stream due to the failure of any IoT device or communication channel during data transfer. Gross errors and missing data are omnipresent in IoT data streams, which require advanced analytics to preprocess the data. Even cyber intrusion could be a valid reason for uncertainty in data. In order to enhance the accuracy during decision making, it is critical to ensure the proper assessment, propagation, and representation of uncertainties and develop models and solutions that can deal with these factors.[30]

Balancing scalability with the efficiency: Most of the IoT data analytics are performed in the cloud. Transferring data from the IoT device to the cloud is expensive (in terms of delay), which may be challenging for time-critical applications especially when the number of IoT devices is high. For example, in a connected vehicle environment, a large pool of cars may be required to make decisions in real-time or near real-time. Here, it is important to balance the speed and accuracy of the analysis when the number of vehicles increases.

16.6   APPLICATIONS OF IOT DATA ANALYTICS

16.6.1   *IOT DATA ANALYTICS FOR SMART VEHICLES*

IoT has enormous potential in the connected vehicle environment, especially for efficient and accurate decision-making using advanced data analytics. Within an Internet of vehicle (IoV) paradigm,[32] a large number of broadcasting messages are frequently generated with very high granularity and volume. Therefore, one of the biggest challenges is storing and intelligent management of the huge amount of data.[33] Another key issue is related to ensuring the security of the data, as any cyber-related anomalies or cyber intrusion attempts will jeopardize the system and may cause fatalities.

Hence, it is important to look for intelligent solutions that can deal with such cyber-related incidents. Moreover, a centralized solution approach may not be feasible as it is more prone to a single point of failure.

16.6.2 IOT DATA ANALYTICS FOR SMART HEALTHCARE

The rapid growth of IoT has benefited different application areas including healthcare.[34] IoT technology along with data analytics can help to achieve more accurate and improved health diagnoses.[35] One critical requirement is to gather data, predict and make decisions in real time. In Firouzi et al.,[35] the authors highlight the importance of the real-time pattern recognition technique deployment for the construction of genomics-based patient models. A dynamic and adaptive computational model with intelligence needs to be developed. These innovative models should be able to capture the data produced by thousands of IoT connected nodes within the smart healthcare paradigm. Advanced analytics and communication within a connected healthcare system can ensure lots of benefits, including improved resiliency, seamless fusion with different technologies, big data processing and analytics, personalized forecasting of patient condition, lifetime monitoring of patient health, ease of use of wearable devices, overall medical health cost reduction, physician oversight with real-time patient data, availability and accessibility of the doctors through advanced communication and efficient healthcare management.[35]

16.6.3 IOT DATA ANALYTICS IN AGRICULTURE

IoT-based frameworks can be adopted to improve the operational efficiency and accuracy by using advanced analytics of the data generated from smart end devices. Several challenges and benefits of IoT and data analytics-enabled smart agriculture frameworks are discussed in Elijah et al.[36] In the recent past, the prospects, opportunities, and feasibility of Wireless Sensor Networks (WSN) in agriculture have been widely studied.[37] The application of WSN in agriculture includes environmental monitoring, precision, agriculture, machine and process control automation, and traceability.[36,38] Recently, the importance of IoT has been highlighted because of its versatility of the adoption of different wired and wireless technologies as well as the capability to integrate with advanced data analysis mechanisms. IoT in agriculture empowers the farmers with advanced and improved automation and decision-making processes.[36] It also enables seamlessly integration among agricultural products, services and knowledge to improve the quality and productivity.[36]

16.6.4   IOT DATA ANALYTICS IN ENERGY SYSTEMS

In recent years, the energy grid has transformed significantly due to the integration of photovoltaics solar cells, electric vehicles, and storage with the low-voltage distribution network. These distributed energy resources need to be effectively coordinated and controlled. One viable solution is to use the capabilities of smart meter. Within an IoT environment, smart meters are interconnected and linked with each other. Advanced analytical decisions are necessary for improving the efficiency and reliability of energy operations. Therefore, in Al-Ali et al.,[39] the authors pointed out that the combination of IoT and Big Data can be used for effective energy management. The authors develop an energy management system that can be used in a smart home. Based on the unique ID address for each IoT object, a System-on-Chip (SoC) module is deployed for data acquisition. A centralized server is used within a Home Area Network, where data is collected, stored and processed. One advantage is that the proposed solution is capable of using off-the-shelf business intelligence tools. The solution architecture can significantly improve the efficiency of high energy consumption applications such as air conditioning. This has been validated in a lab environment. Considering a smart home architecture, IoT and sensor data optimization-based peer-to-peer energy trading architecture is proposed in.[40,41]

16.6.5   DETECTION OF AMBULANCE IN TOLL ROADS: IOT HEALTHCARE APPLICATION

With rapid growth of Indian economy in India, the development of traffic management system makes use of intelligent transportation system which helps in detecting the ambulance in toll road and thus helps to release it as soon as possible from the traffic by RFID (Radio Frequency Identification) process for detecting ambulance which makes electrostatic coupling usage in the portion of radio frequency in electromagnetic spectrum for identifying objects specially.

Depending on different ranges of frequency, RFID tags are of three kinds, namely, low-frequency, high-frequency, and ultrahigh frequency. IR transmitter sender and IR receiver communicate with each other by means of line-of-vision propagation method. There are eight-digit distinct serial numbers in all RFID tag, which are arranged on ambulance. RFID reads the tag serial by means of electromagnetic waves when the ambulance travels through the roads. RFID tags are embedded within the databases which are then matched with the tag which RFD reads from the ambulance.

So, when the ambulance passes through the toll roads, the tag of the ambulance is displayed on the screen. This will reduce the standby for ambulance in toll roads. It has been noted that the accuracy of RFID process is more than camera's view for determining the ambulance on roads. Thus, we can use this process in more advanced way for future enhancement. It can also send message to respective doctors so that he can make ready for the next process to be undertaken before the patient arrives in hospital. Thus, it can also provide for better and fast treatment for the patient.[42]

16.7 OPEN ISSUE AND FUTURE WORKS IN MACHINE LEARNING ALGORITHMS FOR IOT

16.7.1 LIGHTWEIGHT MACHINE LEARNING APPROACHES FOR IOT

The large-scale deployment of IoTs especially in smart cities environment generate large amount of data. The present ML schemes are unable to cope with large amount of dynamic data in real-time environment, hence much data are wasted without information extraction.[43] The large amount of unlabeled data can be mixed with small amount of labeled data for better convergence of ML schemes. In this context, lightweight ML approaches can be developed which are suitable to handle large amount of data generated by IoT devices.[44] The concept of data analytics can be used in this regard where sensor location, type and data can help to develop the lightweight models.[45]

16.7.2 DISTRIBUTED MACHINE LEARNING FOR IOT

The ML applications for IoT have to cope with large amount of data. The real data sets for industrial ML applications can be thousands of GBs.[46] In such a scenario, the ML models which are normally complex and power intensive cannot be run on a single machine. The overall workload can be divided using distribute ML with worker machines, but it also opens certain challenges to be met.[47,48] Bandwidth is one of the crucial issues to be faced by powerful worker machines. The worker machines have to frequent exchange data between them at a high transfer rate but such high bandwidth is usually not available which creates a bottleneck.[49] The machines should also need to synchronize them to perform sequential tasks.[50] In realistic scenario, all worker machines are not exactly of identical processing power which slows down the learning and optimization process.

16.7.3   FEDERATED MACHINE LEARNING FOR IOT

The IoT ML applications have to overcome the traditional centralized learning networks that face an increasing challenge in terms of privacy preservation, communication overheads, and scalability. In such scenario, the ML models which are complex and numerous with heterogeneous gathered data cannot be run in a centralized manner and meet users' QoS.[51] Federated learning networks have been proposed as a promising alternative paradigm to support the training of ML models.[52] In contrast to the centralized data storage and processing in centralized learning, federated learning exploits a number of edge devices to store data and perform training distributively.[53] By the way, the edge devices in federated learning networks can keep training data locally, which preserves privacy and reduces communication overheads. However, since the model training within federated learning networks relies on all the edge devices' contributions, the training process can be disrupted if some of the edge devices upload incorrect or falsified training results.[54]

16.7.4   MACHINE LEARNING AT THE EDGE FOR IOT

The huge amount of connected devices has switched the whole network community in a new era called Internet of Things (IoTs).[55] The concept of IoT has facilitated the community at one end but the delay sensitive and context aware applications have put certain challenges on the performance of lightweight IoT devices.[56] To meet the demand of real-time data computing, edge computing has provided promising solutions by executing the data computing requests of IoT devices by some nearby devices.[57] The conventional ML may become confused with the data generated by edge devices due to the fact that it is more complex to identify the real data from complex and noisy environment.[58] DL can play its role in edge devices for better learning and also for keeping the privacy of data preserved during intermediate data transmission.[59]

16.7.5 PRIVACY AND SECURITY CONCERNS IN MACHINE LEARNING APPROACHES FOR IOT

ML approaches for IoT can be attacked by malicious data which breaches the trust of IoT users.[60] The user data privacy is a fundamental concern of any ML scheme which should be taken care of while classification and ML.[61] The intrusion detection or malicious data detection can be done with the help of ML but they should be light weight to be applicable for IoT based applications.[62]

16.7.6 LOW-LABELED MACHINE LEARNING FOR IOT

For supervised ML schemes, labeled data are required. However, large amount of data generated by IoT devices contains unlabeled data in majority and very less amount of labeled data are found.[63] For effective learning, the labels can be used as sources for unlabeled data.[64] Such schemes need to be developed which are capable of performing learning with low-labeled data.[65]

16.7.7 DATA MUNGING FOR IOT MACHINE LEARNING

The data collected from IoT devices, which are massive, heterogeneous, inconsistent, and riddled with typos, cannot be used as input for sophisticated ML applications.[66] To overcome this issue and get the trends of the data by making it uniform, data gathered from IoTs must go through a cleansing process.[67] The process is also called as data munging, which commonly includes data exploration, transformation, enrichment exploiting metadata, cleaning or scrubbing the data, that is, inputting the missing values, removing the unnecessary or invalid data which are not required for getting the underlying trends of data, and then data validation.[68] This conventional method has several limitations, especially when huge loads of generating data daily from IoT Industry 4.0 and smart cities. For those, the need for accurate and trustworthy analytics in real-time remains crucial, in order to immediately cope with sudden problems, and occurred issues.[69]

16.7.8 INTERACTION WITH HUMANS USING IOT

The human users must be facilitated with the deployment of smart IoT devices. As the size of these smart devices have been reduced tremendously that touch screens cannot be mounted for user input, hence, the sensors should be smart enough for interacting with users utilizing speech recognition and users' special movements.[70,71] Lightweight ML schemes should be developed to provide real-time communication between users and machines.[72,73]

16.7.9 *ADAPTIVE DATA RATE TRANSMISSION FOR IOT*

IoT devices are generally operated with limited energy batteries, hence power consumption is an issue for these devices.[74,75] To conserve energy, low-power consuming protocols to transmit data are famous in IoT. Recently, low-power wide area network (LPWAN) has gain attention of researchers to provide low bit rate communication between IoT devices at a long range.[76] Although high data rate infrastructures are also present for IoT, for example, Wi-Fi, but they consume large power when connected for a long time. However, depending upon the user requirement, the adaptive scheme can be adopted.[77] ML schemes can be used in this regard to learn the data pattern to decide the data rate requirement for IoT devices.[78-80]

16.8 FUTURE RESEARCH CHALLENGES

In this section, we discuss the challenges faced by and future research opportunities in ML and DL techniques for the security of IoT networks.

16.8.1 *CHALLENGES AND LIMITATIONS OF DL AND DRL*

1. DL—one size does not fit all: DL techniques are very much application-specific where a model trained for solving one problem might not be able to perform well for another problem in the similar domain. The models usually need to be retrained with respective data to be used for other similar problems. This might not be a problem for some static networks. However, for the real-time IoT applications, such models will be difficult to use. We believe that more insights are needed for DL techniques to be optimized and used for particular IoT applications.

2. Neural networks are black boxes: Deep neural networks act like a Black box, as we do not know how does any DL model reach a

conclusion by manipulating the input data using the neurons at the intricately interconnected layers. Similarly, in DNN, it is impossible to see how complex is the process of decision-making from one layer is transported to the next. Therefore, it becomes unsuitable for those applications in which interpretability is important.

3. Longer convergence time: In most of the RL algorithms, the longer convergence time of RL algorithms may make them unsuitable for real-time applications. Furthermore, in the case of safety-critical systems, time is important, and the system cannot accommodate delays. Therefore, more research is needed to improve the convergence rate.

4. Butterfly effect of ML and DL: Butterfly effect is a phenomenon where a minute change in the input of a system creates chaos in the output. In this regard, ML and DL are also susceptible to this effect where a slight change in the input data to the learning system will create enormous change in the output which is the learned model. This phenomenon exposes the ML and DL techniques used in IoT to security attacks where the attackers deliberately change the input data to make the system unstable. Such attacks are more dangerous since these attacks do not need an access to the system itself. More investigation is needed in this direction to devise integrity mechanisms for different IoT application domains.

5. Challenges for DL in the edge: IoT will leverage the advantages of edge computing which will increase the IoT applications and services space. However, due to the sheer amount of data generated by IoT devices, it will be hard to implement DL techniques in the edge devices. Furthermore, the time required for training a deep network also plays an important role. Therefore, real-time and time-critical applications might not able to take the advantage of DL in the edge. The stability of DL models is also important where newly available information will affect the already trained model. Therefore, more investigation is needed in this direction.

6. Over-fitting requirements and hyper parameters: Training off-line from the fixed data logs (specified with external behavior policy) and learning from limited samples on the real system greatly affect the credibility of decision-making of DL models.

In essence, the efficacy of an ML model is judged by its ability to perform well on a new dataset and not by its performance on the training data fed to it. Due to the difference in training and test distributions of data sets, ML classifiers usually fail when employed in real-world applications. Typically, ML model is trained on a specific training data set and memorizes the training examples, but does not learn to generalize it for new data sets and for new situations. As a result, errors occur in unseen new dataset and during training dataset, specifically in complicated models with too many parameters as compared with the number of observations.

Almost every ML algorithm has hyper parameters whose value is defined prior to the learning process and these parameters influence the behavior of the learning system. These are selectively or randomly selected and can invoke large change in models performance by even slight change in these parameters. Supervised learning is considered as stable due to fixed data sets, whereas, RL and DRL are not stable at all.[81]

7. Real-time response requirements: Real-time mission critical IoT applications, such as autonomous vehicles, e-health, online banking. perform continuous sensing and information gathering from their surroundings. Therefore, model updates, interferences from surrounding knowledge sources, and predictions are based on live-streaming data. In all of these scenarios, the systems are stochastic and nonstationary, and have strong safety constraints. In contrast, training on a simulated environment has unlimited training data and deterministic system dynamics, and thus does not mimic the real-time behavior. DRL and RL suffer from large and/or unknown delays in the system in calculating rewards and computation due to real-time streaming of data in real-time applications. This phenomenon requires the design of new system architecture that can support flexible, programmable data pipelines (capable of handling variable volume, velocity and variety of real-time data) and algorithms capable of making decisions in real time. Furthermore, real systems do not only have delays in the sensation of the state, the actuators, or the reward feedback, but also experience inference (at the control frequency of the system) in real time.[82]

The existing developed frameworks are capable of dealing with heterogeneous but static data. We need frameworks for dynamic data with stringent latency requirements. These new frameworks must guarantee real-time intelligence and incur extremely small latency.

16.8.2   CHALLENGES RELATED TO IOT DATA

For data-driven ML and DL techniques, there are challenges related to unavailability of appropriate and enough data sets as discussed below.

1. Unavailability of training data sets: Efficient use of ML and DL solutions needs data sets. Authentic data sets from real physical environment are required to analyze and compare the performances of various DL and RL algorithms. The data can contain personal and critical information that would not only identify the users but also their behavior and lifestyle. For instance, the data generated by body area network (BAN) and other healthcare-related applications might compromise the user privacy and the data from smart home might result in exposing personal lifestyle as well as behavior. Therefore, it is important to make sure that the data used by ML and DL techniques do not put the user privacy at stake. To date, many anonymization techniques have been used that anonymize the data before using it for analytics. However, researches have also shown that the anonymization techniques can be hacked and the training models can be compromised by injecting false data. Collection of data while preserving the privacy and anonymity could be challenging. Also, questions such as how to apply ML and DL algorithms to such data and what level of privacy should be preserved by the ML and DL algorithms need to be answered.

   It is, therefore important to investigate data protection and user privacy preservation techniques in ML and DL-based analytics for IoT networks. Note that the data generated via simulations may not fully represent real IoT scenarios. Also, generation of synthetic data for training and testing DL models can be computationally very expensive.

2. Data imbalance: For an IoT system, the collected data sets for ML or DL is very likely to be imbalanced when the attacks are rarely events. These imbalanced data can significantly impact the performance of attack classifiers or IDS methods.

3. Data fusion: Fusion of data from different IoT devices and network elements will need to be done for construction of ML and DL models. However, this can be challenging since data from multiple sources are characterized by different modality and granularity, and also, there could be ambiguity and spuriousness.

16.8.3   ADVERSARIAL MACHINE LEARNING AND IOT

ML is a double-edge sword, where on the one hand, it nourishes the value of the data, but on the other hand, can be used by the attackers for malicious purposes. Such branch of ML is called adversarial machine learning (AML). In AML,the attackers use the features of the ML to attack the system.

For instance, much research has been done by playing with the training parameters and misleading the learning system to learn the opposite of what it is supposed to do. More precisely, DL methods are prone to adversarial enhancements in the input data to launch attacks, such as intrusion, DoS, and so on. In this context, perturbation has been used in object recognition applications where changes into the classifiers cause the system to identify the wrong object. Recently, a one-pixel perturbation was used to fool a DNN.[83] Another sub-class of AML is called generative adversarial network (GAN) which is leveraged by both attackers and the security experts to launch attacks and combat the security issues, respectively.

For instance, GANs have been used for anomaly detection and intrusion detection in IoT networks,[84–88] as well as DoS attack detection.[89] However, on the other hand, GANs as well as some other AML methods such as perturbation have also been used as attack vectors against IoT networks.[90–92] The recent research results show that DL mechanisms could sometime backfire if not safeguarded properly in already-vulnerable IoT networks. It is, therefore, extremely important to investigate the role and effects of AML in the IoT networks and address these challenges.

16.8.4   EFFICIENCY OF SECURITY SOLUTIONS

The degree of sophistication of a security mechanism depends on the capabilities of the device and the system where it is used. The limitations of the IoT devices are a major challenge in applying sophisticated security mechanisms. In the previous section, we discussed the ML- and DL-based security mechanisms. However, the resource constraints create a set-back where a trade-off is needed between the level of security and the capabilities of the IoT devices. Sophisticated security solutions need considerable amount of computing, storage, and communication resources. Furthermore, it is also important to determine where to put the logic of ML and DL techniques in the network. Therefore, in-depth investigation is needed for the efficiency of the security mechanisms that use ML and DL techniques.

In this context, low-cost and highly efficient security mechanisms must be investigated for IoT where they can harness the benefits of the ML and DL as well.

16.8.5   COMPLEX CYBER THREATS

IoT networks use resource-constrained devices ranging from home-appliances to personal gadgets. These devices are usually the easy targets for cyber-attack. As aforementioned, a sheer amount of data are generated by these devices which might be used by ML and DL techniques for different applications. The compromise of these devices will have dire consequences on the outcomes of the applications. It is worth noting that for the applications such as smart home, the consequences of compromise might not be that critical as compared with critical infrastructure and medical applications. These applications will not be able to withstand the results from the ML and DL systems as a result of compromised data. It could even endanger human lives. Therefore, it is essential to make sure the device safety and the health of the data that are input to the ML and DL systems. Furthermore, the compromised devices could also be used as bots by the attackers as launching pads for other attacks. Therefore, for ML and DL systems to work in a safe way, it is essential to focus on the security aspects of the IoT devices and on the health of the generated data. Similarly, the fairly recent cyber-attacks on low power and resource-constrained devices are also alarming for the IoT networks. There is an increased interest in the evolved ML techniques, such as distributed learning and generative adversarial learning-based games. However, in the wake of aforementioned cyber threats and active attacks, the ML and DL models will favor the attackers.

16.8.6   LEGISLATIVE CHALLENGES FOR ML IN IOT SECURITY

The influx of IoT services and applications in various domains has spurred the legislative discussion among the research community and the industry. Some domains of the IoT are still struggling with efficient and acceptable legislative policies. For instance, autonomous car technology is going to benefit from IoT in the customization of user experience. However, there is no clear legislation available for commercialization of the autonomous car technology as well as using the data generated by such technologies for training and analysis. Insurance is another challenge for such technology where it is hard to decide whom to insure. Hussain et al.,[93,94] discussed the policy challenges for autonomous car in detail. These challenges will equally affect the technologies supported by the autonomous car including IoT. Furthermore, the data generated by these technologies will be required for ML mechanism to learn and model different behaviors. However, some data that might be either critical for business or too personal to use (for instance data from healthcare applications and users' data from financial institutions), will be challenging for using with ML-based solutions.

The validation and certification of different components of IoT, for instance, in BAN is also a challenge that is currently keeping the investors at the bay from investing in these technologies and it will equally affect the ML-based solutions. The implementation of General Data Protection Regulation (GDPR)[95,96] and different regulations on the import and export of cryptographic algorithms also pose significant challenges on the IoT security. Furthermore, different legislations on different IoT applications, such as smart home, smart e-health, and so on are shadowed by different regulations in different countries, therefore, one security solution (both traditional and ML-based) might not work for different regions. To date, the USA and European, and some Asian governments are working on legislations that are viable and acceptable to the consumers and service providers (both in services and security). It is believed that the legislative policies will define the course for the success and adaptation of these new technologies among the consumers.

16.9 CONCLUSION

The IoT paradigm has become an integral part of our daily lives. However, IoT devices are constrained in computation and communication resources, which are the bottlenecks in the development of adaptive, intelligent solutions employing ML techniques. Although advances in technologies and platform enhancements pave the way for a future that comprises rapid IoT proliferation, application deployment, and strong analytics of high volume IoT data, we have argued that integrating intelligent solutions from different domains has been proven to be difficult. In this chapter, authors have justified the aspect of ML in IoT. Focus was made in the challenges and the future aspects of its application.

KEYWORDS

- **Internet of Things**
- **deep learning**
- **machine learning**
- **intelligent data processing**

REFERENCES

1. Li, S.; Xu, L. D.; Zhao, S. The Internet of Things: A Survey. *Inf. Syst. Front.* **2015,** *17* (2), 243–259.
2. Lee, I.; Kyoochun, L. The Internet of Things (IoT). Applications, Investments, and Challenges for Enterprises. *Bus. Horiz.* **2015,** *58* (4), 431–440.
3. Michalski, R. S.; Carbonell, J. G.; Mitchell, T. M., Eds. *Machine Learning: An Artificial Intelligence Approach*; Springer Science & Business Media, 2013.
4. Lin, T. *A Data Triage Retrieval System for Cyber Security Operations Center*; Pennsylvania State University Thesis, 2018.
5. Lin, T. A Container—Destructor—Explorer Paradigm to Code Smells Detection. *J. Chinese Comput. Syst.* **2016,** *37* (3).
6. Lin, T.; Fu, X. Flame Detection Based on SIFT Algorithm and One Class Classifier with Undetermined Environment. *Comput. Sci.* **2015,** *42* (6).
7. Lin, T.; Zhong, C.; Yen, J.; Liu, P. Retrieval of Relevant Historical Data Triage Operations in Security Operation Centers. In *From Database to Cyber Security*; Springer: Cham, 2018; pp 227–243.
8. Lin, T. A Novel Image Matching Algorithm Based on Graph Theory. *Comput. Appl. Softw.* **2016,** *33* (12).
9. Ara, A.; Ara, A. Case Study: Integrating IoT, Streaming Analytics and Machine Learning to Improve Intelligent Diabetes Management System. In *2017 International Conference on Energy, Communication, Data Analytics and Soft Computing*, 2017; pp 3179–3182. DOI: 10.1109/ICECDS.2017.8390043.
10. Deligiannis, P.; Koutroubinas, S.; Koronias, G. Predicting Energy Consumption Through Machine Learning Using a Smart-Metering Architecture. *IEEE Potentials* **2019,** *38* (2), 29–34. DOI: 10.1109/MPOT.2018.2852564.
11. Dey, A.; Ling, X.; Syed, A.; Zheng, Y.; Landowski, B.; Anderson, D.; Stuart, K.; Tolentino, M. E. Namatad: Inferring Occupancy from Building Sensors Using Machine Learning. In *2016 IEEE 3rd World Forum on Internet of Things (WF-IoT)*; IEEE, 2016; pp 478–483.
12. Ed-daoudy, A.; Maalmi, K. A New Internet of Things Architecture for Real-Time Prediction of Various Diseases Using Machine Learning on Big Data Environment. *J. Big Data* **2019,** *6* (1), 104.

13. Endler, M.; Briot, J. P.; e Silva, F. S.; de Almeida, V. P.; Haeusler, E. H. Towards Stream-Based Reasoning and Machine Learning for IoT Applications. In *2017 Intelligent Systems Conference (IntelliSys)*; IEEE, 2017; pp 202–209.

14. Priyashman, V.; Ismail, W. Signal Strength and Read Rate Prediction Modeling Using Machine Learning Algorithms for Vehicular Access Control and Identification. *IEEE Sens. J.* **2019**, *19* (4), 1400–1411.

15. Ruta, M.; Scioscia, F.; Loseto, G.; Pinto, A.; Di Sciascio, E. Machine Learning in the Internet of Things: A Semantic-Enhanced Approach. In *Semantic Web*, 2019; pp 1–22.

16. Mahdavinejad, M. S. et al. Machine Learning for Internet of Things Data Analysis: A Survey. *J. Digital Commun. Netw.* **2018**, *1*, 1–56.

17. Shanthamallu, U. S.; Spanias, A.; Tepedelenlioglu, C.; Stanley, M. A Brief Survey of Machine Learning Methods and Their Sensor and IoT Applications. In *IEEE Conference on Information, Intelligence, Systems and Applications*, Mar, 2018.

18. Chafii, M.; Bader, F.; Palicot, J. Enhancing Coverage in Narrow Band-IoT Using Machine Learning. In *IEEE Wireless Communications and Networking Conference*, 2018.

19. Sen, D. B. J. Internet of Things—Applications and Challenges in Technology and Standardization. In *IEEE Transactions in Wireless Personal Communication*, May, 2011.

20. Shanthamallu, U. S.; Spanias, A.; Tepedelenlioglu, C.; Stanley, M. A Brief Survey of Machine Learning Methods and Their Sensor and IoT Applications. In *IEEE Conference on Information, Intelligence, Systems and Applications*, Mar, 2018.

21. Granjal, J.; Monteiro, E.; Silva, J. S. Security for the Internet of Things: A Survey of Existing Protocols and Open Research Issues. *IEEE Commun. Surv. Tutor.* **2015**, *17*, 1294–1312.

22. Fernandes, E.; Rahmati, A.; Eykholt, K.; Prakash, A. Internet of Things Security Research: A Rehash of Old Ideas or New Intellectual Challenges? *IEEE Secur. Priv.* **2017**, *15* (4), 79–84.

23. Qiu, J.; Wu, Q.; Ding, G.; Xu, Y.; Feng, S. A Survey of Machine Learning for Big Data Processing. *EURASIP J. Adv. Signal Process* **2016**.

24. Yao, S. et al. Deep Learning for the Internet of Things. *IEEE J. Comput.* **2018**, *51*, 32–41.

25. Park, T.; Abuzainab, N.; Saad, W. Learning How to Communicate in the Internet of Things: Finite Resources and Heterogeneity. *IEEE Access* **2016**, *4*, 7063–7073.

26. Wang, T.; Wen, C. -K.; Wang, H.; Gao, F.; Jiang, T.; Jin, S. Deep Learning for Wireless Physical Layer: Opportunities and Challenges. *IEEE China Commun.* **2017**, *14*, 92–111.

27. Bogale, T. E.; Wang, X.; Le, L. B. Machine Intelligence Techniques for Next-Generation Context-Aware Wireless Networks. *Arxiv* **2018**, 19, 1–10.

28. L'Heureux, A.; Grolinger, K.; Elyamany, H. F.; Capretz, M. A. M. Machine Learning With Big Data: Challenges and Approaches. *IEEE Access* **2017**, *5*, 7776–7797.

29. Internet of Things Forecast Mobility Report, 2019. https://www.ericsson.com/en/mobility-report/internet-of-things-forecast.

30. Sun, Y.; Song, H.; Jara, A. J.; Bie, R. Internet of Things and Big Data Analytics for Smart and Connected Communities. *IEEE Access* **2016**, *4*, 766–773. DOI: 10.1109/ACCESS.2016.2529723.

31. Anwar, A.; Mahmood, A. N.; Pickering, M. Modeling and Performance Evaluation of Stealthy False Data Injection Attacks on Smart Grid in the Presence of Corrupted Measurements. *J. Comput. Syst. Sci.* **2017**, *83* (1), 58–72. DOI: https://doi.org/10.1016/j.jcss.2016.04.005.

32. Contreras-Castillo, J.; Zeadally, S.; Guerrero-Ibañez, J. A. Internet of Vehicles: Architecture, Protocols, and Security. *IEEE Internet Things J.* **2018,** *5* (5), 3701–3709.
33. Jiang, T.; Fang, H.; Wang, H. Block Chain-Based Internet of Vehicles: Distributed Network Architecture and Performance Analysis. *IEEE Internet Things J.* **2019,** *6* (3), 4640–4649. DOI: 10.1109/JIoT.2018.2874398.
34. Zeadally, S.; Bello, O. Harnessing the Power of Internet of Things Based Connectivity to Improve Healthcare. In *Internet of Things*, 2019; p 100074.
35. Firouzi, F.; Farahani, B.; Ibrahim, M.; Chakrabarty, K. Keynote Paper: From Eda to IoT eHealth: Promises, Challenges, and Solutions. *IEEE Trans. Comput. Aided Des. Integr. Circuits Syst.* **2018,** *37* (12), 2965–2978. DOI: 10.1109/TCAD.2018.2801227.
36. Elijah, O., Rahman, T. A.; Orikumhi, I.; Leow, C. Y.; Hindia, M. N. An Overview of Internet of Things (IoT) and Data Analytics in Agriculture: Benefits and Challenges. *IEEE Internet Things J.* **2018,** *5* (5), 3758–3773. DOI: 10.1109/JIoT.2018.2844296.
37. Merrill, W. Where is the Return on Investment in Wireless Sensor Networks? *IEEE Wirel. Commun.* **2010,** *17* (1), 4–6. DOI: 10.1109/MWC.2010.5416341.
38. Ivanov, S.; Bhargava, K.; Donnelly, W. Precision Farming: Sensor Analytics. *IEEE Intell. Syst.* **2015,** *30* (4), 76–80. DOI: 10.1109/MIS.2015.67.
39. Al-Ali, A. R.; Zualkernan, I. A.; Rashid, M.; Gupta, R.; Alikarar, M. A Smart Home Energy Management System Using IoT and Big Data Analytics Approach. *IEEE Trans. Consum. Electron.* **2017,** *63* (4), 426–434. DOI: 10.1109/TCE.2017.015014.
40. Sebastian, A. J.; Islam, S. N.; Mahmud, A.; Oo, A. M. T. Optimum Local Energy Trading Considering Priorities in a Microgrid. In *2019 IEEE International Conference on Communications, Control, and Computing Technologies for Smart Grids (SmartGridComm)*, 2019.
41. Islam, S. N. A New Pricing Scheme for Intra-Microgrid and Inter Microgrid Local Energy Trading. *Electronics* **2019,** *8* (8).
42. Paul, S.; Das, A. On Issues and Aspects of Medical IoT: A Case Base Analysis. In *Medical Internet of Things: Techniques, Practices, and Applications*; CRC Press: USA, Ref. No.317398; ISBN 9780367331238.
43. Adi, E.; Anwar, A.; Baig, Z.; Zeadally, S. Machine Learning and Data Analytics for the IoT. *Neural Comput. Appl.* **2020,** 1–29.
44. Alam, F.; Mehmood, R.; Katib, I.; Albogami, N. N.; Albeshri, A. Data Fusion and IoT for Smart Ubiquitous Environments: A Survey. *IEEE Access* **2017,** *5,* 9533–9554.
45. Mohammadi, M.; Al-Fuqaha, A.; Sorour, S.; Guizani, M. Deep Learning for IoT Big Data and Streaming Analytics: A Survey. *IEEE Commun. Surv. Tutor.* **2018,** *20* (4), 2923–2960.
46. Yongrui, Q. et al. When Things Matter: A Survey on Data-Centric Internet of Things. *J. Netw. Comput. Appl.* **2016,** *64,* 137–153.
47. Saeid, M. M. et al. Machine Learning for Internet of Things Data Analysis: A Survey. *Digit. Commun. Netw.* **2018,** *4* (3), 161–175.
48. Jithin, J. et al. Machine Learning for Wireless Communications in the Internet of Things: A Comprehensive Survey. *Ad Hoc Netw.* **2019,** *93,* 101913.
49. Jiang, T.; Fang, H.; Wang, H. Block Chain-Based Internet of Vehicles: Distributed Network Architecture and Performance Analysis. *IEEE Internet Things J.* **2018,** *6* (3), 4640–4649.
50. Renjie, G.; Yang, S.; Wu, F. Distributed Machine Learning on Mobile Devices: A Survey, 2019. arXiv preprintarXiv:1909.08329.

51. Nei, K. et al. Ten Challenges in Advancing Machine Learning Technologies Toward 6G. *IEEE Wirel. Commun.* **2020.**

52. Tian, L. et al. Federated Learning: Challenges, Methods, and Future Directions. *IEEE Signal Process. Mag.* **2020,** *37* (3), 50–60.

53. Kulkarni, V.; Kulkarni, M.; Pant, A. Survey of Personalization Techniques for Federated Learning, 2020. arXivpreprint arXiv:2003.08673.

54. Khan, L. U. et al. Dispersed Federated Learning: Vision, Taxonomy, and Future Directions, 2020. arXiv preprint arXiv:2008.05189.

55. Griffiths, F.; Melanie, O. The Fourth Industrial Revolution-Industry 4.0 and IoT [Trends in Future I&M]. *IEEE Instrum. Meas. Mag.* **2018,** *21* (6), 29–43.

56. Vyas, D. A.; Bhatt, D.; Jha, D. IoT: Trends, Challenges and Future Scope. *IJCSC* **2015,** *7* (1), 186–197.

57. Yazici, M. T.; Basurra, S.; Gaber, M. M. Edge Machine Learning: Enabling Smart Internet of Things Applications. *Big Data Cogn. Comput.* **2018,** *2* (3), 26.

58. Jha, D. N. et al. IoT Sim-Edge: A Simulation Framework for Modeling the Behaviour of IoT and Edge Computing Environments, 2019. arXiv preprint arXiv:1910.03026.

59. Li, H.; Ota, K.; Dong, M. Learning IoT in Edge: Deep Learning for the Internet of Things with Edge Computing. *IEEE Netw.* **2018,** *32* (1), 96–101.

60. Chen, J.; Ran, X. Deep Learning with Edge Computing: A Review. *Proc. IEEE* **2019,** 107 (8), 1655–1674.

61. Amiri-Zarandi, M.; Dara, R. A.; Fraser, E. A Survey of Machine Learning-Based Solutions to Protect Privacy in the Internet of Things. *Comput. Secur.* **2020,** 101921.

62. Al-Turjman, F.; Zahmatkesh, H.; Shahroze, R. An Overview of Security and Privacy in Smart Cities IoT Communications. *Trans. Emerg. Telecommun. Technol.* **2019,** e3677.

63. da Costa, K. A. P. et al. Internet of Things: A Survey on Machine Learning-Based Intrusion Detection Approaches. *Comput. Netw.* **2019,** *151*, 147–157.

64. Yao, S. et al. SenseGAN: Enabling Deep Learning for Internet of Things with a Semi-Supervised Framework. *Proc. ACM Interact. Mob. Wearable Ubiquitous Technol.* **2018,** *2* (3), 1–21.

65. Wang, C. et al. SaliencyGAN: Deep Learning Semi Supervised Salient Object Detection in the Fog of IoT. *IEEE Trans. Industr. Inform.* **2019,** *16* (4), 2667–2676.

66. Ge, M.; Bangui, H.; Buhnova, B. Big Data for Internet of Things: A Survey. *Future Gener. Comput. Syst.* **2018,** *87*, 601–614.

67. García, S. et al. Big Data Preprocessing: Methods and Prospects. *Big Data Anal.* **2016,** *1* (1), 9.

68. Milenkovic, M. *Internet of Things: Concepts and System Design;* Springer Nature, 2020.

69. Jena, M. C.; Mishra, S. K.; Moharana, H. S. Application of Industry 4.0 to Enhance Sustainable Manufacturing. *Environ. Prog. Sustain. Energy* **2020,** *39* (1), 13360.

70. Zhuˇ, X.; Ghahramani, Z. Learning from Labeled and Unlabeled Data with Label Propagation, 2002.

71. Moniz, A. B.; Krings, B. -J. Robots Working with Humans or Humans Working with Robots? Searching for Social Dimensions in New Human-Robot Interaction in Industry. *Societies* **2016,** *6* (3), 23.

72. Kim, K. J. Interacting Socially with the Internet of Things (IoT): Effects of Source Attribution and Specialization in Human–IoT Interaction. *J. Comput. Mediat. Commun.* **2016,** *21* (6), 420–435.

73. Monir, S. A Lightweight Attribute-Based Access Control System for IoT. Diss; University of Saskatchewan, 2016.

74. Shirehjini, A. A. N.; Semsar, A. Human Interaction with IoT-Based Smart Environments. *Multimed. Tools Appl.* **2017**, *76* (11), 13343–13365.

75. Muratkar, T. S.; Bhurane, A.; Kothari, A. Battery-Less Internet of Things–A Survey. *Comput. Netw.* **2020**, *180*, 107385.

76. Al-Emran, M.; Malik, S. I.; Al-Kabi, M. N. A Survey of Internet of Things (IoT) in Education: Opportunities and Challenges. In *Toward Social Internet of Things (SIoT): Enabling Technologies, Architectures and Applications*; Springer: Cham, 2020; pp 197–209.

77. Buurman, B. et al. Low-Power Wide-Area Networks: Design Goals, Architecture, Suitability to Use Cases and Research Challenges. *IEEE Access* **2020**, *8*, 17179–17220.

78. Kufakunesu, R.; Hancke, G. P.; Abu-Mahfouz, A. M. A Survey on Adaptive Data Rate Optimization in LoRaWAN: Recent Solutions and Major Challenges. *Sensors* **2020**, *20* (18), 5044.

79. Alagarsamy, G.; Shanthini, J.; Naveen Balaji, G. A Survey on Technologies and Challenges of LPWA for Narrowband IoT. In *Trends in Cloud-based IoT*; Springer: Cham, 2020; pp 73–84.

80. Bukhari, S. H. R.; Rehmani, M. H.; Siraj, S. A Survey of Channel Bonding for Wireless Networks and Guidelines of Channel Bonding for Futuristic Cognitive Radio Sensor Networks. IEEE Commun. Surv. Tutor. 18 (2), 924–948. DOI: 10.1109/COMST.2015.2504408.

81. Dulac-Arnold, G.; Mankowitz, D.; Hester, T. 2019. https://arxiv.org/pdf/1904.12901.pdf

82. Lei, L.; Tan, Y.; Liu, S.; Zheng, K.; Shen, X. S. Deep Reinforcement Learning for Autonomous Internet of Things: Model, Applications and Challenges, 2019. https://arxiv.org/pdf/1907.09059.pdf.

83. Su, J.; Vargas, D. V.; Sakurai, K. One Pixel Attack for Fooling Deep Neural Networks. *CoRR* **2017**, abs/1710.08864.

84. Belenko, V.; Chernenko, V.; Kalinin, M.; Krundyshev, V. Evaluation of Gan Applicability for Intrusion Detection in Self-Organizing Networks of Cyber Physical Systems. In *2018 International Russian Automation Conference (RusAutoCon)*, Sep, 2018; pp 1–7.

85. Ferdowsi, A.; Saad, W. Generative Adversarial Networks for Distributed Intrusion Detection in the Internet of Things. *CoRR* **2019**, abs/1906.00567.

86. Intrator, Y.; Katz, G.; Shabtai, A. MDGAN: Boosting Anomaly Detection Using Multi-Discriminator Generative Adversarial Networks. *CoRR* **2018**, abs/1810.05221.

87. Li, D.; Chen, D.; Shi, L.; Jin, B.; Goh, J.; Ng, S. MAD-GAN: Multivariate Anomaly Detection for Time Series Data with Generative Adversarial Networks. *CoRR* **2019**, abs/1901.04997.

88. Wang, H.; Li, M.; Ma, F.; Huang, S.; Zhang, L. Poster Abstract: Unsupervised Anomaly Detection via Generative Adversarial Networks. In *2019 18th ACM/IEEE International Conference on Information Processing in Sensor Networks (IPSN)*, April, 2019; pp 313–314.

89. Yan, Q.; Wang, M.; Huang, W.; Luo, X.; Yu, F. R. Automatically synthesizing DOS Attack Traces Using Generative Adversarial Networks. *Int. J. Mach. Learn. Cybern.* **2019**.

90. Muñoz-González, L.; Pfitzner, B.; Russo, M.; Carnerero-Cano, J.; Lupu, E. C. Poisoning Attacks with Generative Adversarial Nets. *CoRR* **2019**, abs/1906.07773.

91. Clements, J.; Yang, Y.; Sharma, A. A.; Hu, H.; Lao, Y. Rallying Adversarial Techniques Against Deep Learning for Network Security. *CoRR* **2019,** abs/1903.11688.

92. Yang, W.; Kong, D.; Xie, T.; Gunter, C. A. Malware Detection in Adversarial Settings: Exploiting Feature Evolutions and Confusions in Android Apps. In *Proceedings of the 33rd Annual Computer Security Applications Conference*; ACM: New York, NY, USA, 2017; pp 288–302.

93. Hussain, R.; Zeadally, S. Autonomous Cars: Research Results, Issues and Future Challenges. *IEEE Commun. Surv. Tutor.* **2018a,** 1–1.

94. Hussain, R.; Lee, J.; Zeadally, S. Autonomous Cars: Social and Economic Implications. *IT Prof.* **2018b,** *20*, pp 70–77.

95. Li, C.; Palanisamy, B. Privacy in Internet of Things: From Principles to Technologies. *IEEE Internet Things J.* **2019,** *6*, 488–505.

96. Vojkovic, G. Will the GDPR Slow Down Development of Smart Cities? In *2018 41st International Convention on Information and Communication Technology, Electronics and Microelectronics (MIPRO)*, May, 2018; pp 1295–1297.

CHAPTER 17

A Detailed Review of IoT with Various Applications Using Recent Research Directions

A. VIDHYALAKSHMI[1] and C. PRIYA[2]

[1]Assistant Professor, Department of Computer Science,
AM Jain College, Chennai, Tamil Nadu, India

[2]Associate Professor, Department of Computer Applications,
Dr.M.G.R. Educational and Research Institute, Chennai, Tamil Nadu, India

ABSTRACT

Internet of Things (IoT) is a very unique platform that is getting very popular day by day. The reason for this to happen is the advancement in technology and its ability to get linked to everything. This feature of getting linked has in itself provided multiple opportunities and a vast scope of development. The fact that technology in various fields has evolved through the years is the reason why we observe a rapid change in the shape, size, and capacity of various instruments, components, and the products used in daily life. And, this benefit of simplified technology, when accompanied by a platform like IoT, eases work as well as benefits both the manufacturer and the end user. The IoT gives us an opportunity to construct effective administrations, applications for manufacturing, lifesaving solutions, proper cultivation, and more. Thus, IoT is paving the way for new dimensions of research to be carried out. Various studies and research also signify the need to have more focus on the term IoT. Hence, IoT is also supposed to be the future Internet in the upcoming years. This

Internet of Things: Technological Advances and New Applications. Brojo Kishore Mishra & Amit Vishwasrao Salunkhe (Eds.)
© 2024 Apple Academic Press, Inc. Co-published with CRC Press (Taylor & Francis)

paper presents the recent development of IoT technologies and discusses about ThingSpeak and its connectivity with IoT. The detailed explanation about the origin and existence of IoT has been discussed further in the paper. This paper would help the readers and researcher to understand the IoT and its applicability to the real world.

17.1 INTRODUCTION

Nowadays, around two billion people around the world use the Internet for browsing the Web, sending and receiving emails, accessing multimedia content and services, playing games, using social networking applications, and many other tasks. While more and more people will gain access to such a global information and communication infrastructure, another big leap forward is coming, related to the use of the Internet as a global platform for letting machines and smart objects communicate, dialogue, compute, and coordinate. It is predictable that, within the next decade, the Internet will exist as a seamless fabric of classic networks and networked objects. Content and services will be all around us, always available, paving the way to new applications, enabling new ways of working, new ways of interacting, new ways of entertainment, and new ways of living.

In such a perspective, the conventional concept of the Internet as an infrastructure network reaching out to end-users' terminals will fade, leaving space to a notion of interconnected "smart" objects forming pervasive computing environments.[1] The Internet infrastructure will not disappear. On the contrary, it will retain its vital role as global backbone for worldwide information sharing and diffusion, interconnecting physical objects with computing/communication capabilities across a wide range of services and technologies.

The IoT is an emerging paradigm that enables the communication between electronic devices and sensors through the Internet in order to facilitate our lives. IoT use smart devices and Internet to provide innovative solutions to various challenges and issues related to various business and government and public/private industries across the world.[2] IoT is progressively becoming an important aspect of our life that can be sensed everywhere around us. In whole, IoT is an innovation that puts together extensive variety of smart systems, frameworks, and intelligent devices and sensors (Figure 17.1). Moreover, it takes advantage of quantum and nanotechnology in terms of storage, sensing, and processing speed, which were not conceivable beforehand.[3]

Extensive research studies have been done and are available in terms of scientific articles and press reports both on Internet and in the form of printed materials to illustrate the potential effectiveness and applicability of IoT transformations. It could be utilized as a preparatory work before making novel innovative business plans while considering the security, assurance, and interoperability.

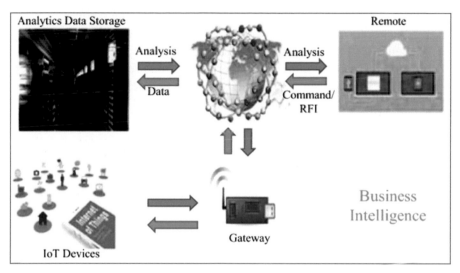

FIGURE 17.1 General architecture of IoT.

17.1.1 BACKGROUND

The principal advantage of IoT consists of its ability to enable communication between an infinite amounts of machines incorporated into a large-scale wireless network.[4] These automated devices and sensors together produce and transmit information in real time, which is useless in the case of incorrect or insufficient filtering and data processing. Moreover, data storage and transmission are the most important and challenging matters in a dynamic IoT network. This section discusses the structure and protocols that have been used in the IoT network.[5] A hybrid IoT architecture consists of the things involved, followed by the insight data processes which end with the action that needs to be done.[6,7] The benefit of it is that it can comprise several subsystem architectures.[8]

- IoT edge devices form the smart IoT actuator since they are able to conduct some processing themselves;
- IoT sensors are connected to the cloud, where they can transmit and receive the data;
- Device provision helps to connect a large number of devices to be registered;
- IoT gateway/framework proves a cloud hub to the IoT devices and provides command, management, and control of the devices;
- Stream processing analyzes complex execution using time windowing ductions, stream aggregation, and external source combing;
- Machine learning allows the algorithms to be predicted and executed using extreme data. It also analyzes and enables predictive maintenance, according to different scenarios;
- Reporting tools help to hold and store the data, while providing the necessary tools for batch processing;
- User management can restrict and permit which users or groups are authorized to perform an action on the device. The process is done by using the capacities of the application of each user.

Generally, IoT systems are designed with two management architectures, including time-based and event-driven architectures. The event-driven architecture consists of sensors transmitting data when activity is sensed, the same as when an alarm is activated once a gate is opened.[9] However, for the time-based architecture, the components of the system transmit data continuously at a specified interval of time.[10] Additionally, it works recurrently after a break to be separately adjusted for each device or setup in a central management system sending queries to endpoint devices and sensors.[11]

17.1.2 BUILDING BLOCKS OF IOT

Let's assume all electronic devices that are currently available are connected to one another through the Internet to form a certain system. And, these small systems rejoin each other to form larger systems. That's IoT for you (IoT-system system). The following are the IoT building blocks:

17.1.2.1 END DEVICES

These are the most essential devices or key things in IoT. These are the active sensing devices or actuators working in collecting the important relevant information and perform the ground-level processing. Examples are, RFID at garment stores, temperature sensors at home, and cameras at the highways.[12]

17.1.2.2 GATEWAYS

It is the local processing node/device. It connects the end devices to the network or an Internet (cloud).[13] It should not only transfer the relevant information collected from the sensors or actuators but also process them to some extent and forward the particular information to the cloud. It also provides the intelligence by sending back the data received from the cloud.

17.1.2.3 CONNECTIVITY

Since IoT is a network-based system; the "connectivity" plays a vital role. The various service providers have given multiple solutions for the connectivity of the end devices to the gateways and then to the cloud. Also, it is a dual/duplex system. Hence, it works in the to-and-fro communication system between applications and hardware.[14] Thus, the connectivity can work both in wireless or wired mechanism. Examples are Bluetooth, Wi-Fi, RFID, GSM, etc.

17.1.2.4 CLOUD-BASED APPLICATION AND STORAGE

The major function of this block is to compute and analyze the data received from the end devices and gateways.

17.1.3 IMPORTANCE OF BIG DATA ANALYTICS IN IOT

An IoT system comprises of a huge number of devices and sensors that communicates with each other. With the extensive growth and expansion of IoT network, the number of these sensors and devices are increasing rapidly. These devices communicate with each other and transfer a massive amount of data over the Internet. This data is very huge and streaming every second and thus qualified to be called as big data. Continuous expansion of IoT-based networks gives rise to complex issue such as management and collection of data, storage, and processing and analytics. IoT big data framework for smart buildings is very useful to deal with several issues of smart buildings such as managing oxygen level, to measure the smoke/hazardous gases and luminosity.[15] Such framework is capable to collect the data from the sensors installed in the buildings and performs data analytics for decision making. Moreover, industrial production can be improved using an IoT-based cyber physical system that is equipped with an information analysis and knowledge acquisition techniques.[16]

Traffic congestion is an important issue with smart cities. The real-time traffic information can be collected through IoT devices and sensors installed in traffic signals and this information can be analyzed in an IoT-based traffic management system. In healthcare analysis, the IoT sensors used with patients generate a lot of information about the health condition of patients every second. This large amount of information needs to be integrated at one database and must be processed in real time to take quick decision with high accuracy and big data technology is the best solution for this job.[17] IoT along with big data analytics can also help to transform the traditional approaches used in manufacturing industries into the modern one. The sensing devices generate information that can be analyzed using big data approaches and may help in various decision-making tasks. Furthermore, use of cloud computing and analytics can benefit the energy development and conservation with reduced cost and customer-satisfaction IoT devices generate a huge amount of streaming data that needs to be stored effectively and needs further analysis for decision making in real time. Deep learning is very effective to deal with such a large information and can provide results with high accuracy.[18] Therefore, IoT, Big data analytics, and Deep learning together are very important to develop a high-tech society.

17.2   TECHNOLOGIES

The IoT was initially inspired by members of the RFID community, who referred to the possibility of discovering information about a tagged object by browsing an Internet address or database entry that corresponds to a particular RFID or Near Field Communication[19] technologies. In the research paper "Research and application on the smart home based on component technologies and Internet of Things," the included key technologies of IoT are RFID, the sensor technology, nano technology, and intelligence-embedded technology. Among them, RFID is the foundation and networking core of the construction of IoT. The IoT enabled users to bring physical objects into the sphere of cyber world. This was made possible by different tagging technologies like NFC, RFID, and 2D barcode, which allowed physical objects to be identified and referred over the Internet.[20] The Internet of Things (IoT), which combines sensor technology and radio frequency technology, is a network that is based on the physical resources of the Internet that are always available. It brings together Internet contents and objects. It is also a new wave of IT industry since the application of computing fields, communication network, and global roaming technology had been applied. It involves in addition to sophisticated technologies of computer and communication network outside, still including many new supporting technologies of IoT, such as collecting Information Technology, Remote Communication Technology, Remote Information Transmission Technology, Sea Measures Information Intelligence Analyzes and Controlling Technology etc.

17.2.1 RADIO FREQUENCY IDENTIFICATION

Radio Frequency Identification (RFID) is a system that transmits the identity of an object or person wirelessly using radio waves in the form of a serial number. First use of RFID device had happened during the Second World War in Britain and it was used for identifying of friend or foe in 1948. Later, RFID technology is founded at auto-ID center in MIT in the year 1999. RFID technology plays an important role in IoT for solving identification issues of objects around us in a cost-effective manner. The technology is classified into three categories based on the method of power supply provision in tags: active RFID, passive RFID, and semi-passive RFID. The main components of RFID are tag, reader, antenna, access controller, software, and server. It is more reliable, efficient, secured, inexpensive, and accurate. RFID has an extensive range of wireless applications such as distribution, tracing, patient monitoring, military apps, etc.[21]

17.2.2 INTERNET PROTOCOL

Internet Protocol (IP) is the primary network protocol used on the Internet, developed in 1970s. IP is the principal communications protocol in the IP suite for relaying datagrams across network boundaries. Two versions of IP are in use: IPv4 and IPv6. Each version defines an IP address differently. Because of its prevalence, the generic term IP address typically still refers to the addresses defined by IPv4. There are five classes of available IP ranges in IPv4: Class A, Class B, Class C, Class D, and Class E, while only A, B, and C are commonly used. The actual protocol provides for 4.3 billion

IPv4 addresses while the IPv6 will significantly augment the availability to 85,000 trillion addresses.[22] IPv6 is the 21st-century IP. This supports around for 2^{128} addresses.

17.2.3   ELECTRONIC PRODUCT CODE

Electronic Product Code (EPC) is a 64-bit or 98-bit code electronically recorded on an RFID tag and intended to design an improvement in the EPC barcode system. EPC code can store information about the type of EPC, unique serial number of product, its specifications, manufacturer information, etc. EPC was developed by auto-ID center in MIT in 1999. EPCglobal Organization (Wikipedia, "EPCglobal," 2010), which is responsible for standardization of EPC technology, created EPCglobal Network (Wikipedia, "EPCglobal Network," 2010) for sharing RFID information. It has four components namely object naming service (ONS), EPC discovery service (EPCDS), EPC information services (EPCIS), and EPC security services (EPCSS).

17.2.4   BARCODE

Barcode is just a different way of encoding numbers and letters by using combination of bars and spaces of varying width. Behind Bars[23] serves its original intent to be descriptive but is not critical. In *The Bar Code* book, Palmer (1995) acknowledges that there are alternative methods of data entry techniques. Quick Response (QR) Codes the trademark for a type of matrix barcode first designed for the automotive industry in Japan. Bar codes are optical machine-readable labels attached to items that record information related to the item. Recently, the QR Code system has become popular outside the automotive industry due to its fast readability and greater storage capacity compared to standard. There are three types of barcodes: alpha-numeric, numeric, and two-dimensional. Barcodes are designed to be machine readable. Usually they are read by laser scanners; they can also be read using a camera.

17.2.5   WIRELESS FIDELITY

Wireless Fidelity (Wi-Fi) is a networking technology that allows computers and other devices to communicate over a wireless signal. Vic Hayes has been named as father of Wi-Fi. The precursor to Wi-Fi was invented in 1991 by

NCR corporation in Nieuwege in the Netherland. The first wireless products were brought on the market under the name WaveLAN with speeds of 1–2 Mbps. Today, there are nearly pervasive Wi-Fi that delivers the high-speed Wireless Local Area Network (WLAN) connectivity to millions of offices, homes, and public locations such as hotels, cafes, and airports. The integration of Wi-Fi into notebooks, handhelds, and Consumer Electronics (CE) devices has accelerated the adoption of Wi-Fi to the point where it is nearly a default in these devices.[24] Technology contains any type of WLAN product support any of the IEEE 802.11 together with dual-band, 802.11a, 802.11b, 802.11g, and 802.11n. Nowadays, entire cities are becoming Wi-Fi corridors through wireless APs.

17.2.6 BLUETOOTH

Bluetooth wireless technology is an inexpensive, short-range radio technology that eliminates the need for proprietary cabling between devices such as notebook PCs, handheld PCs, PDAs, cameras, and printers with an effective range of 10–100 m, and generally communicate at less than 1 Mbps and Bluetooth uses specification of IEEE 802.15.1 standard. At first in 1994 Ericson Mobile Communication company started project named "Bluetooth". It is used for creation of Personal Area Networks (PAN). A set of Bluetooth devices sharing a common channel for communication is called Piconet. This Piconet is capable of connecting 2–8 devices at a time for data sharing, and that data may be text, picture, video and sound. The Bluetooth Special Interest Group comprises more than 1000 companies with Intel, Cisco, HP, Aruba, Intel, Ericson, IBM, Motorola and Toshiba.

17.2.7 ZIGBEE

ZigBee is one of the protocols developed for enhancing the features of wireless sensor networks. ZigBee technology is created by the ZigBee Alliance, which is founded in the year 2001. Characteristics of ZigBee are low cost, low data rate, relatively short transmission range, scalability, reliability, and flexible protocol design. It is a low power wireless network protocol based on the IEEE 802.15.4 standard.[25] ZigBee has range of around 100 m and a bandwidth of 250 kbps and the topologies that it works are star, cluster tree, and mesh. It is widely used in home automation, digital agriculture, industrial controls, medical monitoring, and power systems.

17.2.8   NEAR-FIELD COMMUNICATION

Near-Field Communication (NFC) is a set of short-range wireless technology at 13.56 MHz, typically requiring a distance of 4 cm. NFC technology makes life easier and more convenient for consumers around the world by making it simpler to make transactions, exchange digital content, and connect electronic devices with a touch. It allows intuitive initialization of wireless networks and NFC is complementary to Bluetooth and 802.11 with their long-distance capabilities at a distance circa up to 10 cm. It also works in dirty environment, does not require line of sight, easy, and simple connection method. It was first developed by Philips and Sony companies. Data exchange rate nowadays is approximately 424 kbps. Power consumption during data reading in NFC is under 15 ma.

17.2.9   ACTUATORS

An actuator is something that converts energy into motion, which means actuators drive motions into mechanical systems. It takes hydraulic fluid, electric current, or some other source of power. Actuators can create a linear motion, rotary motion, or oscillatory motion. It covers short distances, typically up to 30 ft., and generally communicates at less than 1 Mbps. Actuators typically are used in manufacturing or industrial applications. There are three types of actuators, namely, (1) electrical: ac and dc motors, stepper motors, and solenoids (2) hydraulic: use hydraulic fluid to actuate motion, and (3) pneumatic: use compressed air to actuate motion. All these three types of actuators are very much in use today. Among these, electric actuators are the most commonly used type. Hydraulic and pneumatic systems allow for increased force and torque from smaller motor.

17.2.10   WIRELESS SENSOR NETWORKS

A wireless sensor networks (WSN) is a wireless network consisting of spatially distributed autonomous devices using sensors to cooperatively monitor physical or environmental conditions, such as temperature, sound, vibration, pressure, motion, or pollutants, at different locations (Wikipedia). Formed by hundreds or thousands of motes that communicate with each other and pass data along from one to another. A wireless sensor network is an important element in IoT paradigm. Sensor nodes may not have global

ID because of the large amount of overhead and large number of sensors. WSN based on IoT has received remarkable attention in many areas, such as military, homeland security, healthcare, precision agriculture monitoring, manufacturing, habitat monitoring, forest fire and flood detection, and so on.[26] Sensors mounted to a patient's body are monitoring the responses to the medication, so that doctors can measure the effects of the medicines.[27]

17.2.11 ARTIFICIAL INTELLIGENCE (AI)

Artificial Intelligence refers to electronic environments that are sensitive and responsive to the presence of people. In an ambient intelligence world, devices work in concert to support people in carrying out their everyday life activities in easy, natural way using information and intelligence that is hidden in the network-connected devices. It is characterized by the following systems of characteristics: (1) embedded: many networked devices are integrated in to the environment, (2) context aware: these devices can recognize you and your situational context, (3) personalized: they can be tailored to your needs, (4) adaptive: they can change in response to you, and (5) anticipatory: they can anticipate your desires without conscious mediation.

17.3 RELATED ON-GOING INITIATIVES

A number of large-scale initiatives on IoT are active in the United States, Europe, Japan, China, Korea, and other countries. In the following subsection, we will briefly report on the most relevant ones. Besides research initiatives, standardization activities are also of key importance in order to ensure a successful widespread adoption of IoT technologies and services.

17.3.1 IOT-RELATED PROJECTS

The growing interest in IoT technologies and applications is well exemplified by the number of research initiatives arising worldwide around such themes. In the United States, the American National Science Foundation (NSF) launched in 2008 a program on cyber-physical systems, aimed at introducing systems that are able to merge computational and physical resources. The program is meant to cover a wide array of application scenarios, ranging from smart electric grid to smart transportation, from smart medical technologies to smart manufacturing. The 2010 report of the President's Council of Advisors on Science and Technology, "Designing a digital future: federally funded research and development in networking and information technology,"[6] encourages further investments in Cyber-Physical System, due to their high-potential impact on a number of critical industrial sectors.

The European Commission has been pushing initiatives related to IoT since 2005,[28] and has recently launched, in the framework of the 7th Framework Programme, an initiative on "Internet-Connected Objects." The focus is on adoption of IoT technologies and services in enterprise environments, with the aim of increasing the competitiveness of European industry through adoption of IoT-enabled solutions[7] (http://www.rfid-in-action.eu/cerp). Activities in such field led to the definition of a strategic research agenda, including a description of European strategies in this sector.[29]

Within the initiatives that have taken place at the European level, four large-scale ones are worth mentioning. The HYDRA project[30] developed a middleware based on a service-oriented architecture, transparent to the underlying communication, supporting distributed as well as centralized architectures, security, and trust models. This project was meant to provide a middleware solution allowing the developers to incorporate heterogeneous physical devices into their applications by offering easy-to-use Web-service interfaces for controlling the physical devices. Support was provided for a number of underlying communication technologies, including Bluetooth, RF, ZigBee, RFID, WiFi, etc. The Hydra middleware included methods for performing effectively device and service discovery, for supporting peer-to-peer interaction models and efficient diagnostics tools. Solutions for distributed security and social trusts were also devised and prototyped.

The RUNES project[31] was meant to create a large-scale, widely distributed, heterogeneous networked-embedded systems that provide a flexible and adaptable ICT tool to leverage environmental data. The main target of RUNES is a fully operational middleware enabling the potential for the introduction of a new class of networked-embedded systems. In RUNES, one of the target challenges was to achieve the required level of self-organization to suit a dynamic environment, while ensuring that proper interfaces were provided to programmers in order to ease the development of applications and services. This was meant to allow for a significant cut in the cost of new application development and a much faster time to market.

The IoT-A project[32] aims at introducing an architectural reference model for the interoperability of IoT, together with a set of mechanisms for its efficient integration into the service layer of the Future Internet. The project is a large-scale one, involving a number of relevant stakeholders and addressing a number of application domains. Particular attention is paid to resolution schemes, whereby innovative approaches are proposed to ensure scalable look-up and discovery of smart objects and associated resources.

The iCORE project[33] aims at empowering the IoT with cognitive technologies and is focused around the concept of virtual objects (VOs), intended as semantically enriched virtual representation of the capabilities/ resources provided by real-world objects fostering their re-usability and supporting their aggregation into more-composite services (composite virtual objects—CVOs). VOs provide a unified representation, thereby hiding any underlying technological heterogeneity and providing a standardized way of accessing objects' capabilities and resources. One key element in the iCORE project is the use of advanced cognitive techniques for managing and composing VOs to improve IoT applications and better match user/ stakeholder requirements. Four use cases are put forward for validation purposes: ambient-assisted living, smart office, smart transportation, and supply chain management.

IoT-centric programs are active also in Japan, under the umbrella of the UNS initiative (ubiquitous networked society, part of the wider "e-Japan" strategy[34]), which focuses on the ubiquitous presence of sensors and RFIDs in order to enable pervasive services, with target applications ranging from smart home environments to supply chain management. While the wide-spread diffusion of research initiatives denotes the vitality of the field and the potential of IoT applications, it brings alongside a risk of fragmentation and of lack of adoption of adequate standards. IoT would require, as the technology gets mature and makes its way into the real world, a careful standardization process, in order to ensure interoperability among devices and applications coming from different countries, building the foundations the real arising of an "Internet" of things.

17.4   ADVANTAGES OF IOT

17.4.1   ACCESS OF DATA

The more information is available, the easier it is to make an appropriate decision. You have access to real-time data and information that is far away from your location. Knowing what you get from the supermarket by going out without checking yourself not only saves time but also remains practical.

This is only possible because a device network gives a person access to all information in the world. This makes it very easy for people to do their work even when they are not physically present.

17.4.2   CONNECTIVITY

On the network of directly connected devices, better communication is possible, making device communication more transparent and reducing inefficiencies. Processes in which machines have to work with each other become more effective and produce better, faster results. The machines in the production or production unit are the perfect examples. Another example is in our home, the computers follow both the quality and durability of things. The knowledge that the product ends before consumption increases safety and quality of life. Moreover, you will never run out of anything when you need it at the last minute.

17.4.3   TIME SAVING

By programming the work, any work whenever needed or required will be completed and doing this will save human valuable time and energy.

17.4.4   EXPENDITURE EFFECTIVE

As mentioned earlier, communication with electronic devices through Internet networks can be easily facilitated. It helps people in their daily work. The transfer of data packets to a connected network saves time and money. The same information that can be transmitted faster can be done less than ever, just by IoT.

17.5   DISADVANTAGES

Though IoT has a large scope in almost all areas of our day-to-day applications, there are some disadvantages that hinders further implementation of the IoT systems at a faster pace. The IoT makes the physical objects in the real environment to be seen in cyber globe and offers the formation of smart systems and applications. Networks of sensors, middleware's, digital communication and computing, protocols, etc., led to the expansion of inter-connected devices.

The advancement in communication, connection, and integration helps to have a lot of choices to choose devices and services. The variety of services and devices that provides similar functions lead to lookup and discovery. The discovery and categorization of similar devices and services cause the system to become more costlier and error prone. Addressing the disadvantages will allow next-generation IoT to recognize and satisfy the information needs.

17.5.1 PRIVACY/SECURITY

Privacy is a big issue with IoT. All information must be encrypted so that you can back up your financial status data. Nowadays, every device is connected worldwide via the Internet This increases the risk of data loss, which can be important. This is a major disadvantage when exchanging information, as confidential information may not be secure and can easily be damaged by third parties.

17.5.2 COMPLEXITY

A diversified network that connects different devices together is what we call IoT. A hole in the system can affect the entire system. It is by far the most complex aspect of IoT that can have a major impact. There are various destruction options in complex systems. For example, you and your family can receive news that the milk is ready and you can all buy the same. This means that you need different quantities. Or, a software error has occurred that allows the printer to order ink multiple times if it only needs one cartridge.

17.5.3 DEPENDENCY

We may not notice it, but we see a large technology transfer and its imple-mentation in daily life. There is no doubt that technology dominates our way of life and reflects human reliability in technology. If there is a malfunction in the system, there is a risk of damaging a connected device. It will affect our daily lives, as we become increasingly dependent on it.

17.5.4   BUSINESS MODEL

In the following, you will find a great impetus to start a business, to invest, and to run a business. Without a good and solid business model for the IoT, we have another bubble. This model should fulfill everything that is required for all types of e-commerce: standing markets, tight markets, and hyper-markets. However, this category is always a victim of regulatory and legal investigation.

17.5.5   SOCIETY

Understanding the IoT from the consumer's point of view is not an easy thing to do because their needs or requirements change over time; they want new features in existing devices as well as new ones. And that happens at a fast pace; before the solution to the previous problem is found, a new problem appears. And solving problems takes time and resources, leaving a bad picture of the IoT as a whole.

17.5.6   REGULATORY STANDARDS

Regulatory standards for the information market are inadequate for information brokers leading to companies that sell data grasped from different sources. Even if the data seems to be the Internet's motto, there is a lack of transparency about who has access to data and how it is used to improve products or services and to sell it to people, announcers, and third parties. Clear guidance on data retention, use, and security, including metadata, is required. The European Union has adopted data and data-sharing regulations.

17.6   MAJOR IOT APPLICATIONS

17.6.1   EMERGING ECONOMY, ENVIRONMENTAL, AND HEALTH-CARE

IoT is completely devoted to provide emerging public and financial benefits and development to the society and people. This includes a wide range of public facilities, that is, economic development, water quality maintenance, well-being, industrialization, etc. Overall, IoT is working hard to accomplish the social, health, and economic goals of United Nations advancement step. Environmental sustainability is another important concern. IoT developers must be concerned about environmental impact of the IoT systems and devices to overcome the negative impact.[35]

Energy consumption by IoT devices is one of the challenges related to environmental impact. Energy consumption is increasing at a high rate due to Internet-enabled services and edge-cutting devices. This area needs research for the development of high-quality materials in order to create new IoT devices with lower energy consumption rate. Also, green technologies can be adopted to create efficient energy efficient devices for future use. It is not only environmental friendly but also advantageous for human health. Researchers and engineers are engaged in developing highly efficient IoT devices to monitor several health issues such as diabetes, obesity, or depression.[36] Several issues related to environment, energy, and healthcare are considered by several studies.

17.6.2   SMART CITY, TRANSPORT, AND VEHICLES

IoT is transforming the traditional civil structure of the society into high-tech structure with the concept of smart city, smart home, and smart vehicles and transport. Rapid improvements are being done with the help of supporting technologies such as machine learning and natural language processing to understand the need and use of technology at home.[37] Various technologies such as cloud server technology and wireless sensor networks must be used with IoT servers to provide an efficient smart city. Another important issue is to think about the environmental aspect of smart city. Therefore, energy-efficient technologies and Green technologies should also be considered for the design and planning of smart city infrastructure.

Further, smart devices, which are being incorporated into newly launched vehicle, are able to detect traffic congestions on the road and thus can suggest an optimum alternate route to the driver. This can help to lower down the congestion in the city. Furthermore, smart devices with optimum cost should be designed to be incorporated in all range vehicles to monitor the activity of engine. IoT is also very effective in maintaining the vehicle's health. Self-driving cars have the potential to communicate with other self-driving vehicles by the means of intelligent sensors. This would make the traffic flow smoother than human-driven cars who used to drive in a stop-and-go manner. This procedure will take time to be implemented all over the world. Till the time, IoT devices can help by sensing traffic congestion ahead and can take appropriate actions. Therefore, a transport manufacturing company should incorporate IoT devices into their manufactured vehicles to provide its advantage to the society.

17.6.3   AGRICULTURE AND INDUSTRY AUTOMATION

The world's growing population is estimated to reach approximate 10 billion by 2050. Agriculture plays an important role in our lives. In order to feed such a massive population, we need to advance the current agriculture approaches. Therefore, there is a need to combine agriculture with technology so that the production can be improved in an efficient way. Greenhouse technology is one of the possible approaches in this direction. It provides a way to control the environmental parameters in order to improve the production. However, manual control of this technology is less effective, need manual efforts and cost, and results in energy loss and less production. With the advancement of IoT, smart devices and sensors makes it easier to control the climate inside the chamber and monitor the process, which results in energy-saving and improved production (Fig. 17.2). Automatization of industries is another advantage of IoT. IoT has been providing game-changing solutions for factory digitalization, inventory management, quality control, logistics, and supply chain optimization and management.

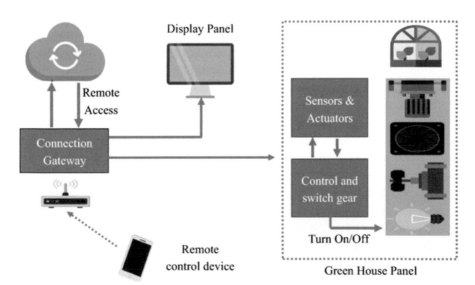

FIGURE 17.2   A working structure of IoT system in agriculture production.

17.7 THINGSPEAK IOT PLATFORM

ThingSpeak is an IoT platform, which allow one to collect, visualize, analyze live data, and react according to it. It is an open source application originally launched in 2010 by ioBridge. It helps one to build IoT systems without the need of setting up extra servers. The data collection is done using REST API or MQTT. The data analysis and visualization is done using MATLAB analytics. There is also option to add various plugins that enable user to display google gauge and other custom visualization and controls in private view. Various actions can be done using apps provided by the platform.

ThingSpeak provides apps that allow us for an easier integration with the web services, social networks, and other APIs. It includes ThingTweet app to tweet alerts and messages, Tweet Control app, which respond to tweet having some trigger words, Time Control App to perform or schedule some specific actions, React app to do some actions when some conditions are met, Talkback app to send command to devices, and ThingHTTP app to interface with various web services and APIs.

The main component of ThingSpeak is its channel, which stores data send from various devices. Each channel can save up to eight fields along with device location, url, etc. The channel can be made public, which can be seen by other users, or private, which need the API key to view the data. The private channel can be shared for some specific users.

17.7.1 CONFIGURE ACCOUNTS AND CHANNELS IN THINGSPEAK

To read and write to a ThingSpeak channel, your application sends requests to the ThingSpeak server by issuing HTTP requests, publishing MQTT messages, or using MATLAB® functions. Each ThingSpeak channel can have up to 8 fields of 255 characters of data, in either numeric or alphanumeric format. A channel also has location information and a status update field. Each channel data entry is stored with a date and timestamp. You can retrieve stored data by time or by entry ID.

Use the ThingSpeak API to process numeric data, which includes time scaling, averaging, median, summing, and rounding. You can create and update a ThingSpeak channel by posting a feed with your API key and data using HTTP POST. The channel feeds support JSON, XML, and CSV formats for integration into applications.

17.7.2   CHANNEL PROPERTIES

- **Channel ID:** Auto-generated ID of your unique channel. Your application uses this ID to read data from the channel. You cannot change its value.
- **Name:** Enter a unique name for the ThingSpeak™ channel.
- **Description:** Enter a description of the ThingSpeak channel.
- **Field#:** Check the box to enable the field, and enter a field name. Each ThingSpeak channel can have up to eight fields.
- **Metadata:** Enter information about channel data, including JSON, XML, or CSV data.
- **Tags:** Enter keywords that identify the channel. Separate tags with commas.
- **URL:** If you have a website that contains information about your ThingSpeak channel, specify the URL.
- **Elevation:** Specify the position of the sensor or thing that collects data in meters. For example, the elevation of the city of London is 35.052.
- **Show Channel Location:** Check this box to enable entering channel location data on this page. The result is a map with a location pinpoint displayed in the channel view. This location is a single entry. Each data point in the channel feed can also include location information, which is different than the channel location information shown here. Even if this box is cleared, you can still read and write latitude and longitude information for the channel and for the feed using the API. For locations close to the poles, a marker is not visible.
  - ○ **Latitude:** Specify the latitude position in decimal degrees. For example, the latitude of the city of London is 51.5072. The value must be between −90 and 90.
  - ○ **Longitude:** Specify the longitude position in decimal degrees. For example, the longitude of the city of London is −0.1275. The value must be between −90 and 90.
- **Show Video:** Check the box to include a video display on your channel view, using the following settings:
  - ○ **YouTube/Vimeo:** Select your video service.
  - ○ **Video URL:** Specify the full URL for your video.
- **Link to GitHub:** If you store your ThingSpeak code on GitHub®, specify the GitHub repository URL to show on your channel view.

- **Show Status:** Check this box to add a window to your channel view for status updates. This window can show executed commands from a TalkBack App that is configured to log commands to this channel. The status can also show information that you send with an API command using the status parameter as described in Write Data.

17.7.3 CHANNEL DATA CONTROL

17.7.3.1 API KEYS

When you read or write data to your channel using the ThingSpeak™ API or MATLAB® code, you need the appropriate read and write permissions. The 16-digit API key allows you to read from a private channel and write to a channel. You do not need an API key to read from a public ThingSpeak channel. Account level API keys are described in User Accounts and Channels.

17.7.3.1.1 Write API Key

Use the Write API key to update a channel. If your Write API key is compromised, you can generate a new key. If you use MATLAB Analysis or MATLAB Visualization, the API info is displayed in the Help pane on the right.

To find your Write API key:

- Click **Channels** > **My Channels.**
- Select the channel to update.
- Select **API Keys** tab.

17.7.3.1.2 Read API Key

The Read API key enables your application to read data from the API. You can generate multiple Read API keys for different applications.

To get a Read API key:

- Click **Channels** > **My Channels.**
- Select the channel to update.
- Select **API Keys** tab.
- Click **Generate New Read API Key.**

17.7.3.2   API ENDPOINTS

HTTP API Address

For nonsecure communication to ThingSpeak using HTTP, use the address:
https://api.thingspeak.com

For secure communication to ThingSpeak using HTTPS, use the address:
https://api.thingspeak.com

MQTT API Address

To communicate with the ThingSpeak MQTT broker at the port 1883, use the address:
mqtt.thingspeak.com

Cross-Domain XML

To post using cross-domain XML, use the address:
https://api.thingspeak.com/crossdomain.xml

17.7.3.3   CHANNEL ACCESS IN MATLAB

To read data from a private channel in MATLAB, use the thingSpeakRead function:
thingSpeakRead(channelID,'ReadKey','Your.Read.API.Key.String');

To write data from MATLAB, use the thingSpeakWrite function:
thingSpeakWrite(channelId,data,'WriteKey','Your.Write.API.Key.String')

17.7.3.4   API RATE LIMITS

A user with a free license can update a ThingSpeak channel every 15 s, and a paid user can update every 1 s. Updating more frequently results in an error. The time between read requests is not limited by ThingSpeak for any users. See "Frequently Asked Questions" and "How to Buy" for the most updated license information. To change settings to meet your application requirements locally, download the source code from GitHub.

17.7.3.5 API CACHING

You can cache data when you transmit it via XML or JSON. Feeds returning more than 100 entries are cached for 5 min. This limit improves application performance. The last call or feeds specifying "results=100" or fewer are not cached, enabling production of live applications.

17.7.4 THINGSPEAK-BASED CLOUD SERVICE

Due to the important merging between ThingSpeak features and MATLAB analytic features, the ThingSpeak-based cloud service is a good candidate for IoT healthcare monitoring systems. The operator can visually access the data stream via ThingSpeak channels with support from an automatic cloud-based diagnosis of the signal conditions by classifying the signals according to the disease datasets.

17.8 CONCLUSION

IoT is one of the main techniques that is used to express the ubiquitous computing approach, but it is still not popular like the cloud computing technology. This work has sought to highlight the IoT concept in general through some sections, namely, an overview about the IoT concept via highlighting its history and its inception. Then, it has reviewed the main idea to design the IoT structure that relies on the integration between three dimensions, which are: information items, independent network, and intelligent applications. This work has also discussed about the popular applications that are offered by IoT and the IoT-cloud paradigm such as healthcare, smart city, smart grid, smart transportations, etc. Based on the aforementioned, it can be considered that the IoT environment is a rich search point and a flourishing area to research in particular in the integration topic with cloud computing, which provides the new sceneries to handle the smart services and applications. IoT uses the ThingSpeak API, which is capable to contribute the services for the purpose of building vast number of IoT applications and helps to implement them on the public platform.

KEYWORDS

- **IoT**
- **technology**
- **ThingSpeak**
- **administrations**
- **end user**
- **manufacturer**
- **feature**

REFERENCES

1. Atzori, L.; Iera, A.; Morabito, G. The Internet of Things: A Survey. *Comput. Netw.* **2010,** *54* (15), 2787–2805.
2. Sfar, A. R.; Zied, C.; Challal, Y. A Systematic and Cognitive Vision for IoT Security: A Case Study of Military Live Simulation and Security Challenges. In *Proceedings of the 2017 International Conference on Smart, Monitored and Controlled Cities (SM2C)*; Sfax: Tunisia, 17–19 Feb, 2017.
3. Gatsis, K.; Pappas, G. J. Wireless Control for the IoT: Power Spectrum and Security Challenges. In *Proceedings of the 2017 IEEE/ACM Second International Conference on Internet-of-Things Design and Implementation (IoTDI)*, Pittsburg, PA, USA, 18–21 April, 2017. INSPEC Accession Number: 16964293.
4. Mekki, K.; Bajic, E.; Chaxel, F.; Meyer, F. A Comparative Study of LPWAN Technologies for Large-Scale IoT Deployment. *ICT Express* **2019,** *5*, 1–7. [CrossRef]
5. Hassan, W.H. Current Research on Internet of Things (IoT) Security: A Survey. *Comput. Netw.* **2019,** *148*, 283–294.
6. Raeespour, A. K.; Patel, A. M. Design and Evaluation of a Virtual Private Network Architecture for Collaborating Specialist Users. *Asia Pac. J. Inf. Technol. Multimed.* **2016,** *5*, 13–50. [CrossRef]
7. Stackowiak, R. Azure IoT Solutions Overview. In *Azure Internet of Things Revealed*; Springer: Berkeley, CA, USA, 2019; pp 29–54.
8. Mojib, G.; Aman, A. H. M.; Khalaf, M.; Hassan, R. Simulation Analysis for QoS in Internet of Things Wireless Network. *3C Tecnol.* **2019,** *2019*, 77–83. [CrossRef]
9. Almeida, R. B.; Junes, V. R. C.; da Silva Machado, R.; da Rosa, D. Y. L.; Donato, L. M.; Yamin, A. C.; Pernas, A. M. A Distributed Event-Driven Architectural Model Based on Situational Awareness Applied on Internet of Things. *Inf. Softw. Technol.* **2019,** *111*, 144–158. [CrossRef]
10. Hu, B.; Guan, Z. H.; Chen, G.; Shen, X. A Distributed Hybrid Event-Time-Driven Scheme for Optimization Over Sensor Networks. *IEEE Trans. Ind. Electron.* **2018,** *66*, 7199–7208. [CrossRef]

11. Windley, P. J. API Access Control with OAuth: Coordinating Interactions with the Internet of Things. *IEEE Consum. Electron. Mag.* **2015**, *4*, 52–58.
12. Gavras, A. K.; Fdida, S.; May, M.; Potts, M. Future Internet Research and Experimentation. *ACM SIGCOMM Comput. Commun. Rev.* **2007**, *37*.
13. Singh, M.; Nandal, P.; Bura, D. Comparative Analysis of Different Load Balancing Algorithm Using Cloud Analyst. In *International Conference on Recent Developments in Science, Engineering and Technology*; Springer: Singapore, 2017; pp 321–329.
14. Fleisch, E. Auto-ID Labs: What is the Internet of Things? An Economic Perspective, 2010.
15. Bashir, M. R.; Gill, A. Q. Towards an IoT Big Data Analytics Framework: Smart Buildings System. In: *IEEE 18th International Conference on High Performance Computing and Communications; IEEE 14th International Conference on Smart City; IEEE 2nd International Conference on Data Science and Systems*, 2016; pp 1325–1332.
16. Lee, C.; Yeung, C.; Cheng, M. Research on IoT Based Cyber Physical System for Industrial Big Data Analytics. In *2015 IEEE International Conference on Industrial Engineering and Engineering Management (IEEM)*; IEEE: New York, 2015; pp 1855–1859.
17. Vuppalapati, C.; Ilapakurti, A.; Kedari, S. The Role of Big Data in Creating Sense EHR, an Integrated Approach to Create Next Generation Mobile Sensor and Wear-Able Data Driven Electronic Health Record (EHR). In *2016 IEEE Second International Conference on Big Data Computing Service and Applications (BigDataService)*; IEEE: New York, 2016; pp 293–296.
18. Mohammadi, M.; Al-Fuqaha, A.; Sorour, S.; Guizani, M. Deep Learning for IoT Big Data and Streaming Analytics: A Survey. *IEEE Commun. Surv. Tutor.* **2018**, *20* (4), 2923–2960.
19. Want, R. An Introduction to RFID Technology. *IEEE Pervasive Comput.* **2006**, *5*, 25–33.
20. Razzak, F. Spamming the Internet of Things: A Possibility and Its Probable Solution. *Procedia Comput. Sci.* **2012**, *10*, 658–665.
21. Moeinfar, D.; Shamsi, H.; Nafar, F. Design and Implementation of a Low-Power Active RFID for Container Tracking @ 2.4 GHz Frequency: Scientific Research, 2012.
22. Bicknell, IPv6 Internet Broken, Verizon Route Prefix Length Policy, 2009. [Citation Time(s):1]
23. Grieco, A.; Occhipinti, E.; Colombini, D. Work Postures and Musculo-Skeletal Disorder in VDT Operators. *Bollettino de Oculistica* **1989**, *Suppl. 7*, 99–111. [Citation Time(s):1]
24. Pahlavan, K.; Krishnamurthy, P.; Hatami, A.; Ylianttila, M.; Makela, J. P.; Pichna, R.; Vallstron, J. Handoff in Hybrid Mobile Data Networks. *Mob. Wirel. Commun. Summit* **2007**, *7*, 43–47. [Citation Time(s):1]
25. Chen, X. -Y.; Jin, Z. -G. Research on Key Technology and Applications for the Internet of Things. *Phys. Procedia* **2012**, *33*, 561–566. http://dx.doi.org/10.1016/j.phpro.2012.05.104. [Citation Time(s):1]
26. Arampatzis, T.; et al. A Survey of Security Issues in Wireless Sensors Networks. In *Intelligent Control. Proceeding of the IEEE International Symposium on, Mediterrean Conference on Control and Automation*, 2005; pp 719–724. [Citation Time(s):1]
27. Chorost, M. The Networked Pill. MIT Technology Review, Mar, 2008. [Citation Time(s):1]
28. Buckley, J. From RFID to the Internet of Things: Pervasive Networked Systems. In *Final Report on the Conference Organised by DG Information Society and Media*; Networks and Communication Technologies Directorate, Mar, 2006.
29. Internet of Things: Strategic Research Agenda, Sept, 2009.
30. Roussos, G.; Kostakos, V. RFID in Pervasive Computing: State-of-the Art and Outlook. *Pervasive Mob. Comput.* **2009**, *5*, 110–131. http:// dx.doi.org/10.1016/j.pmcj.2008.11.004.

31. Akyilidiz, I.; Su, W.; Sankarasubramaniam, Y.; Cayirci, E. Wireless Sensor Network: A Survey. *Comput. Netw.* **2002,** *38* (4), 393–422.
32. Akyildiz, I. F.; Kasimoglu, I. H. Wireless Sensor and Actor Networks: Research Challenges. *Ad Hoc Netw. J.* **2004,** 2, 351–367.
33. Saltzer, J.; Reed, D.; Clark, D. End-to-End Arguments in System Design. *ACM Trans. Comput. Syst.* **1984,** *2,* 277–288.
34. Jacobson, V.; Smetters, D. K.; Thornton, J. D.; Plasee, M. F.; Briggs, N.; Braynard, R. Networking Named Content. In *Proceedings of ACM CoNEXT,* Rome, Italy, 2009; pp 1–12.
35. Colacovic, A.; Hadzialic, M. Internet of Things (IoT): A Review of Enabling Technologies, Challenges and Open Research Issues. *Comput. Netw.* **2018,** *144,* 17–39.
36. Fafoutis, X.; et al. A Residential Maintenance-Free Long-Term Activity Monitoring System for Healthcare Applications. *EURASIP J. Wirel. Commun. Netw.* **2016.**
37. Park, E.; Pobil, A. P.; Kwon, S. J. The Role of Internet of Things (IoT) in Smart Cities: Technology Roadmap-Oriented Approaches. *Sustainability* **2018,** *10,* 1388.

Index

A

ADAMM asthma monitor, 258
    features of, 259
Adversarial machine learning (AML), 322
American National Science Foundation
    (NSF), 341
Application programming interface (API), 180
Applied science and technologies
    advantages, 204–205
    applications, 214
        agriculture, 216–217
        farming industries, 216–217
        healthcare industry, 214–216
        home automation, 218
        poultry, 216–217
        retail industry, 216
        smart city, 217–218
        supply chain, 218
        wearable, 219
    categorization
        active or passive, 208
        analog or digital, 208
    challenges, 219–220
        data integrity, 219
        designing issue, 220
        interoperability, 219
        scalability, 219
        security and privacy, 220
    communication
        Bluetooth and BLE, 213–214
        low power wide area networks
            (LPWANS), 212
        near field communication (NFC), 213
        RFID, 214
        WiFi, 214
    hardware device, 206
        actuators, 209
        chips, 206–207
        sensors, 207
        smart devices, 209
    history, 203–204
    sensors
        categorization, 207–208
        modules, 207–208
        technique, 208–209
    software devices
        operating system, 210–212
    technologies used, 205–206
Artificial intelligence (AI), 300
Audio-to-Braille Conversion Device
    (A.B.C.D)
    block diagram, 195
    Braille script
        cells, 192
        encoding, levels of, 191
        raised dots, 191
    Cloud Business Model Framework
        (CBMF), 191
    English Alphabet Recognizer (EAR), 188
    future scope, 197
    hardware requirements, 193
    hardware setup, 195–196
    Hidden Markov Method (HMM), 191
    India
        visually impaired in, 193
    methodology
        android application, 193
        creating access point, 194
        extracting text from the message, 194
        JSON feedback, 195
        receiving the client message, 194
    microchip PIC16F877, 190
    neural networks, 191
    NodeMcu displays messages, 196
        messages displayed, 197
    problem statement, 193
    Recurrent Neural Network (RNN), 191
    Refreshable Braille Display System
        (RBDS), 189
    SD card, 189
    Super Cloud, 190
    virtual machines (VMs), 190

Automotives
  electric toll collection (ETC), 91
    license plate recognition, 92–94
    vehicle identification, 92
  intelligent transport system (ITS), 88–91
  predictive maintenance, 94–96
    acquire data, 95
    deploy & integration, 96
    identify indicators, 96
    machine learning, 96
    preprocess data, 96
  self-driving, 86–88
  smart parking, 96
    application systems, 97
    cloud storage, 97
    infrared, 97
    RFID tag, 97
    space detection, 98
    ultrasonic sensors, 97

B

Biometric technology
  advantages, 171–172
  availability, 165
  biometrics, 167
  confidentiality, 164
  connected devices, 167–168
  disadvantages, 172
  integrity, 164–165
  in medical sector, 168–170
  safer mining production, 170–171
  security issues, 165
    attacks, 166
    data privacy, 166
    data security, 166
    home invasions, 167
    insufficient testing, 166–167
    lack of updates, 166–167
    specialized concerns, 166
    system vulnerabilities, 166

C

Cancer treatment, 244–245
Cloud Business Model Framework (CBMF), 191
Complex event processing (CEP), 302
Computer numerical control (CNC), 63

Computer-aided design (CAD), 62
Computer-aided manufacturing (CAM), 65
Connected contact lens, 251–253
Connected inhalers, 248–249
Constrained application protocol (CoAP), 289
Cyber Infrastructure (CI), 245
Cyber infrastructure for comparative effectiveness research (CYCORE), 245
Cyber-Physical System, 342

D

Dedicated Short-Range Communication (DSRC), 304
Deep learning (DL), 300
Defected ground structure (DGS), 275
Denial-of-service (DoS), 48
Device-to-Device communication (D2D), 304
Digital transformation technology
  advantage
    greater customization, 72
    improved working environment security, 72
    integration, 72
    upgraded production network, 72
  applications
    ABB, smart robotics, 70–71
    airbus, 71
    Amazon, 71
    caterpillar, 71
    William Boeing, 70
  challenges
    greater customization, 72
    improved working environment security, 72
    manufacturer, 72–74
    upgraded production network, 72
  comparison, 63–64
  computer numerical control (CNC), 63
  computer-aided design (CAD), 62
  computer-aided manufacturing (CAM), 65
  fabrication, 76–77
    CNC operations, 76–77
    digital manufacturing, 75–76
  industrial internet of things (IIoT), 62
  internet of things
    and industry 4.0, 64–66
  monitoring process, 77–78

equipment, 78–80
  production line, 80–81
  supply chain, 81
platform, 67–69
  advantage, 72–75
  applications, 70–72
  challenges, 72–75
  features of IoT, 69–70
  risks, 72–75
risks
  greater customization, 72
  improved working environment
    security, 72
  industrial, 74–75
  upgraded production network, 72
software solutions, 82

E

Electric toll collection (ETC), 91
  license plate recognition, 92–94
  vehicle identification, 92
Electromagnetic bandgap (EBG), 275
Electronic Product Code (EPC), 338
English Alphabet Recognizer (EAR), 188
European Commission, 342
Extensible message and queuing protocol
  (XMQP), 289

F

Food processing, 1
  challenges, 10
    competencies, 12–13
    data, 10–11
    environment, 13–14
    organization, 13
    skills, 12–13
    technology, 11–12
  compelling forces and technology, 2
  competitive market pressure, 9–10
  data and opportunities
    collection & analysis, 9
  early adopters
    advantages of, 9
  IPv6 addressing, 4
  new technology
    compelling forces for, 2–3
  safety, 6–7

sensors
  cost reduction and miniaturization, 3–4
  vertical integration, 4–6
  yields enhancement, 7–8

H

Health tracking system
  ADAMM asthma monitor, 258
    features of, 259
  apple watch monitoring depression, 253
    coagulation testing, 255–256
    Cognition Kit, 254
    deep brain stimulation, 257
    gold standard science, 254–255
    high-frequency measurement, 254
    laboratory coats, 254
    monitoring Parkinson's symptom,
      257–258
    Pallidotomy, 256–257
    Parkinson's disease, 256
    Test Automated Battery, 255
    thalamus, 257
  devices
    cancer treatment, 244–245
    connected contact lens, 251–253
    connected inhalers, 248–249
    Cyber Infrastructure (CI), 245
    cyber infrastructure for comparative
      effectiveness research (CYCORE),
      245
    ingestible sensors and smart pills,
      249–251
    insulin delivery system based on closed
      loop algorithm, 247–248
    smart continuous glucose monitoring
      (CGM), 246–247
  healthcare and economy, 259–260
  IoT
    analytical solutions, 230–231
    availability, 241
    benefits of, 225–226, 261–262
    cheaper, 241
    cloud, 229–230
    data aggregation and preprocessing,
      243–244
    data analysis, 244
    data storage, 244
    device connectivity layer, 227
    devices, 243

gateway, 227–229
hardware and working, 230–231
and health insurance companies, 243–244
and hospitals, 243
human behavior, 260–261
multifunctionality, 241
need for, 242
and patient, 242
and physician, 242
portable, 240–241
simplification, 241
user interface (UI), 231–232
security threats
    inadequate authentication/permission,
        233–234
    inadequate physical security, 239
    poor security configurability, 237–238
    privacy involvement, 235–236
    susceptible cloud interface, 236–237
    transport encryption, 235
    vulnerable mobile interface, 237
    vulnerable network services, 234
    vulnerable software/firmware, 238–239
    vulnerable web interface, 232–233
Hidden Markov Method (HMM), 191
HYDRA project, 342
Hypertext Transfer Protocol (HTTP), 177,
    188

I

iCORE project, 343
Industrial IoT (IIoT)
    advantages of industrial, 182
    benefits of
        improve safety, 178
        increase in efficiency, 178
        reduce costs, 178–179
        reduce errors, 178
    business process terms
        operational intelligence, 180
        overall equipment effectiveness (OEE),
            180
        predictive maintenance, 180
        property rental, 180
    challenges
        Margaret Rouse, 179
        Message Queuing Telemetry Transport
            (MQTT), 179

Coke Machine in 1982, 177
data terms
    big data, 179
    sensor data, 179
    streaming data, 179
    time-series data, 180
future scope, 183
Hypertext Transfer Protocol (HTTP), 177
Industry 4.0, 181–182
Machine-to-Machine devices, 176
programmable logic controller (PLC), 176
security and standards terms
    Ethernet IP, 181
    hyper text transfer protocol (HTTP), 181
    identity and access management, 180
    MQTT, 180–181
    TCP/IP, 181
technological terms
    application programming interface
        (API), 180
    data acquisition, 180
    programmable logic controller (PLC),
        180
    radio frequency identification, 180
    supervisory control, 180
    threats in, 182–183
Intelligent transport system (ITS), 88–91
Internet of Things (IoT)
    advantages of
        access of data, 343–344
        connectivity, 344
        expenditure effective, 344
        time saving, 344
    allied surveys, 116
    application, 111–112
    applications
        agriculture, 348
        emerging economy, 346–347
        environmental, 346–347
        and health-care, 346–347
        and industry automation, 348
        smart city, 347–348
        transport, 347–348
        and vehicles, 347–348
    attack model, 102
        DoS attacker, 102
        jamming, 102
        man-in-the-middle, 103

software attack, 103
spoofing, 102
background, 333–334
big data analytics, 335–336
building blocks
  cloud-based application and storage, 335
  connectivity, 335
  end devices, 334–335
  gateways, 335
challenges
  authentication, 110
  issues, 111
  lightweight cryptosystems, 110–111
  object, 110
  privacy, 110
critical areas
  animal farming, 115
  emergencies, 114–115
  environment, 114
  grids, 114
  home automation, 115–116
  retail, 115
  smart cities, 112–114
disadvantages, 344
  business model, 346
  complexity, 345
  dependency, 345
  privacy/security, 345
  regulatory standards, 346
  society, 346
general architecture, 333
initiatives on
  projects, 341–343
systemic approach, 103–104
  intelligent object, 105
  person, 104
  process, 105
  technological ecosystem, 105
technologies, 336
  actuator, 340
  artificial intelligence (AI), 341
  barcodes, 338
  Bluetooth wireless technology, 339
  Electronic Product Code (EPC), 338
  Internet Protocol (IP), 337–338
  Near-Field Communication (NFC), 340
  Radio Frequency Identification
    (RFID), 337

Wireless Fidelity (Wi-Fi), 338–339
wireless sensor networks (WSN),
  340–341
ZigBee, 339
tension, 106
  authentication, 106–107
  autoimmunity, 109
  identification, 106–107
  privacy, 108
  reliability, 109–110
  responsibility, 108–109
  safety, 109
  trust, 107–108
ThingSpeak
  API caching, 353
  API key and endpoints, 351–352
  API rate limits, 352–353
  channel properties, 350–351
  channels in, 349
  cloud service, 353
  configure accounts, 349
  MATLAB, 352
Internet of vehicles (IoVs)
  architecture, 144–145
  comparative analysis, 147–148
  multi-ant colony (ACO), 150
  open challenges and future directions,
    157–158
  research proposals, 148–149
    anti-theft system, 150–152
    emergency vehicles, 154–155
    monitoring of driver health on road,
      155–157
    real-time vehicle navigation, 149–150
    traffic management, 152–153
  third-generation partnership project
    (3GPP), 143
  5G V2X communication, 145–147
Internet Protocol (IP), 337–338
IoT-A project, 342

L

Leveraging IIoT in reverse logistics
  challenges, 123–124, 136
  cyber-physical system, 127
    big data, 128–129
    wireless sensor network (WSN), 128
  growth, 126

impact on business, 126
implementation of industrial, 129–130
    radio frequency technologies, 132–133
    RL management, 130
    way forward, 135–136
    WSN functionalities, 133–134
need, 124–125
RL management
    monitoring system via WSN, 130–131
works, 126–127
LoRaWANP (Low-Power Wide Area
    Network Protocol), 289
Low power wide area networks (LPWANS),
    212
Low-power wide area network (LPWAN), 318

M

Machine learning (ML), 300
    characteristics of IoT networks
        communication in close proximity, 304
        Dedicated Short-Range
            Communication (DSRC), 304
        Device-to-Device communication
            (D2D), 304
        dynamic changes in the network, 305
        heterogeneity, 303–304
        intelligence, 305
        interconnectivity, 304
        low-power and low-cost
            communication, 304
        massive deployment, 304
        safety, 305
        self-organization and self-healing
            characteristics, 304
        ultra-reliable and low latency
            communication (URLLC), 304
    convergence of
        balancing scalability with, 312
        high volume of data, 311
    data
        adversarial machine learning (AML),
            322
        challenges, 321
        complex cyber threats, 323
        legislative challenges for, 323–324
        security solutions, efficiency of, 322–323
    data analytics
        in agriculture, 313–314

in energy systems, 314
    smart healthcare, 313
    for smart vehicles, 312–313
    tolls, ambulance, detection of, 314–315
    deep learning (DL), 300
    future research challenges
        DL and DRL, 318–320
    limitations of
        hardware technology and, 310
        heterogeneous data, 310
        power and energy, 309
    literature review, 301
        complex event processing (CEP), 302
        decision tree (DT), 302
        RSSI level, 302
        Semantic Web languages, 303
        support vector machine (SVM), 303
    open issues and
        adaptive data rate transmission, 318
        data munging for, 317
        distributed, 315–316
        edge for, 316
        federated, 316
        interaction with humans, 317–318
        lightweight machine learning
            approaches, 315
        low-labeled, 317
        low-power wide area network
            (LPWAN), 318
        privacy and security concerns, 317
    security and privacy, 305
        IOT, solution to, 306–307
        techniques used in, 307–309
Message Queuing Telemetry Transport
    (MQTT), 179
Messaging queuing telemetry transport
    protocol (MQTTP), 289
Multiple input multiple output (MIMO), 270
Multiple input single output (MISO), 270

N

Narrowband IoT (NBIoT) wireless
    communication technology, 295
Near-Field Communication (NFC), 213, 340
NEC iQuarantine, 169–170
Next revolution, 37
    application, 41–45
        wireless architecture, 44

cloud and fog infrastructure, 45–53
  attacks on confidentiality and
    legitimacy, 48
  denial-of-service (DoS), 48
  network availability, 48
  node replication attack, 49
  privacy attacks, 49–53
  privacy-aware security services, 48
  secure data aggregation, 48
  stealthy attack against service integrity,
    48
  storing and retrieving, 46–48
  transport layer attacks, 49
COVID handling, 53–54
environmental monitoring, 39
health applications, 39–40
industrial applications, 40
security, 39
structural monitoring, 40–41
surveillance, 39
wireless architecture
  application, 45
  data link layer, 44
  network layer, 44–45
  physical layer, 44
  transport, 45

O

Overall equipment effectiveness (OEE), 180

P

Post-traumatic stress disorder (PTSD), 27–28
Programmable logic controller (PLC), 176,
  180

R

Radio Frequency Identification (RFID), 337
Recurrent Neural Network (RNN), 191
Refreshable Braille Display System
  (RBDS), 189
RUNES project, 342

S

Sensing mental health, 17
  anxiety disorder
    agoraphobia, 26
    certain medical conditions, 26

    generalized, 26
    panic, 26
    separation, 27
    social, 27
  issues, 19, 24–25
    anxiety disorder, 26–27
    bipolar, 25
    major depressive, 25
    persistent depressive, 25
    postpartum, 26
    post-traumatic stress disorder (PTSD),
      27–28
    specific phobias, 27
    substance-oriented, 27
  prediction, 28–29
  questioners available
    DSM-5, 31
    hospital anxiety, 29
    PHQ-9 scale, 29
    state-trait, 29
  worldwide statistics of cognitive, 19–24
Single input multiple output (SIMO), 270
Smart antennas
  basics of
    alignment issue, 271
    base station, range, 272
    expanded system capacity, 271
    more battery life of handset, 271
    space diversity multiple access
      (SDMA), 272
    system reliability and quality, 271
  MIMO
    CCL, 274
    decoupling structure, 275
    defected ground structure (DGS), 275
    degenerated modes, 275
    DG, 273
    ECC, 273
    electromagnetic bandgap (EBG), 275
    IoT devices, UWB, 275–276
    MEG measures, 273–274
    orthogonal modes, 274
    performance metrics, 273
    single and multiband, 278
  multiple input multiple output (MIMO),
    270
  multiple input single output (MISO), 270
  single input multiple output (SIMO), 270

ultra-wideband (UWB), 270–271
Smart continuous glucose monitoring
  (CGM), 246–247
Space diversity multiple access (SDMA),
  272
Support vector machine (SVM), 303

T

Third-generation partnership project
  (3GPP), 143
Time synchronization
  challenges
    data capturing capabilities, 295
    delays in, 295–296
    instability of clocks, 296
    interoperability and compatibility, 295
    poor connectivity, 295
    security and authentication risk, 295
  errors and applications, 290
    financial sectors, 291
  IoT
    near field communication (NFC)
      techniques, 287
    radio frequency ID (RFID) innovation,
      287
  layered design
    application layer, 288
    gateway layer, 288
    middleware layer, 288
    sensing layer, 287–288
  network protocols
    Bluetooth, 289
    cellular technology, 290
    5G technology, 290
    LoRaWANP (Low-Power Wide Area
      Network Protocol), 289
    NFC (Near Field Communication), 290
    ZigBee, 289
    Z-Wave protocol, 289–290
  related work
    motion detectors, 294
    narrowband IoT (NBIoT) wireless
      communication technology, 295
    real-time applications of, 293–294
  and stamping
    digital archiving, 292

    disaster management, 292
    electronic transactions, 292
    national security, 292
    navigation, 292
    power grid application, 292
    smart transportation, 292
    smart weather prediction, 292
    strategic sectors, 291
  technologies/standards/protocols
    constrained application protocol
      (CoAP), 289
    extensible message and queuing
      protocol (XMQP), 289
    messaging protocols, 288
    messaging queuing telemetry transport
      protocol (MQTTP), 289

U

Ultra-reliable and low latency
  communication (URLLC), 304
Ultra-wideband (UWB), 270–271
User interface (UI), 231–232

V

Virtual machines (VMs), 190
Virtual objects (VOs), 343
Voice recognition, 168
Vulnerable mobile interface, 237
Vulnerable network services, 234
Vulnerable software/firmware, 238–239
Vulnerable web interface, 232–233

W

Wireless architecture
  application, 45
  data link layer, 44
  network layer, 44–45
  physical layer, 44
  transport, 45
Wireless Fidelity (Wi-Fi), 338–339
Wireless sensor networks (WSN), 340–341

Z

ZigBee, 339
Z-Wave protocol, 289–290